G M Meadows

November 2015

Seaforth
WORLD NAVAL REVIEW
2016

Seaforth

WORLD NAVAL REVIEW

2016

Editor
CONRAD WATERS

Frontispiece: The British Royal Navy Type 45 destroyer *Dauntless* pictured entering Portsmouth Harbour after returning from a five months Middle East deployment on 15 May 2015. The future shape of an over-stretched Royal Navy will be determined by a new Strategic Defence & Security Review (SDSR), due to report before the end of 2015. *(Conrad Waters)*

The editor welcomes correspondence and suggestions from readers. Please contact him via Seaforth at **info@seaforthpublishing.com**. All correspondence should be marked **FAO: Conrad Waters**.

Copyright © Seaforth Publishing 2015
Plans © John Jordan 2015

First published in Great Britain in 2015 by
Seaforth Publishing
An imprint of Pen & Sword Books Ltd
47 Church Street, Barnsley
S Yorkshire S70 2AS

www.seaforthpublishing.com
Email info@seaforthpublishing.com

British Library Cataloguing in Publication Data
A CIP data record for this book is available from the British Library

ISBN 978-1-84832-309-4

Typeset and designed by Stephen Dent
Printed by 1010 Printing International Ltd.

CONTENTS

Note on Tables: Tables are provided to give a broad indication of fleet sizes and other key information but should be regarded only as a general guide. For example, many published sources differ significantly on the principal particulars of ships, whilst even governmental information can be subject to contradiction. In general terms, the data contained in these tables is based on official information updated as of June 2015, supplemented by reference to a wide range of secondary and corporate sources, such as shipbuilder websites.

1 OVERVIEW

INTRODUCTION

'Rule one on page one of the Book of War is, "Do not march on Moscow"' stated the distinguished British military commander, Field Marshal Bernard Montgomery, 1st Viscount Montgomery of Alamein, in a debate on the British Army budgetary estimates in the House of Lords in 1962. 'Rule two is, "Do not go fighting with your land armies in China"', he continued. Whilst there is no suggestion that the United States of America and its allies are about to embark on land campaigns against either country, it is clear that the potential threat they pose to global stability is increasingly dominating 'Western' military planning.

In the Pacific, China continues to strengthen its assertive stance towards its territorial claims in neighbouring seas. An increasingly prevalent trend is its strategy of creating a physical presence in disputed waters through a process of land reclamation amongst the coral atolls of the South China Sea. Military installations are then built on the reclaimed territory as part of efforts that many fear will ultimately turn the sea into a Chinese-controlled 'lake'. The United States is attempting to build a diplomatic consensus against these actions whilst continuing to bolster its own forces in the region as part of the 'Pivot to the Pacific'. Maritime surveillance patrols across the disputed waters are being stepped up. Greater profile to these flights was given on 20 May 2015, when a CNN news crew were given access to a patrol over some of the newly-created 'islands' by one of the US Navy's new P-8A Poseidon patrol aircraft to publicise Washington's concerns. However, United States' diplomatic efforts face an uphill struggle, as there is a limit as to how far many of its local partners are willing to go to stand up to a country that is their dominant trading partner.[1]

Meanwhile, Russia's 2014 seizure and annexation of the Crimean peninsula has been followed up by active intervention on the side of pro-Russian separatists in the Donbass region of the Eastern Ukraine. The accidental shooting down of a Malaysian Airlines Boeing 777 jetliner on 17 July 2014 by a 'Buk' (NATO designation SA-11) surface-to-air missile with the loss of all 298 people onboard during the fighting hardened attitudes against Russia's involvement in the United States and Europe. It was quickly alleged that the weapon had been supplied from Russian military stocks to separatist forces, who had mistakenly identified the Malaysian aircraft as a Ukrainian troop transport.[2] A cooling in relations with Russia driven by selective economic sanctions and travel restrictions on business leaders close to Russian Premier Vladimir Putin has been reflected in the mysterious reappearance of unidentified foreign submarines off the shores of Sweden and Finland.

One consequence of these developments has been a renewed, if uneven, willingness amongst many Western European countries to look seriously at defence requirements after two decades or more of

Table 1.0.1: COUNTRIES WITH HIGH NATIONAL DEFENCE EXPENDITURES – 2014

RANK	COUNTRY	TOTAL: US$	SHARE OF GDP: %	CHANGE 2005–14
1 (1)	United States	610bn	3.5%	-0.4%
2 (2)	China	216bn	2.1%	167%
3 (3)	Russian Federation	84.5bn	4.5%	97%
4 (4)	Saudi Arabia	80.8bn	10.4%	112%
5 (5)	France	62.3bn	2.2%	-3.2%
6 (6)	United Kingdom	60.5bn	2.2%	-5.5%
7 (9)	India	50.0bn	2.4%	39%
8 (8)	Germany	46.5bn	1.2%	-0.8%
9 (7)	Japan	45.8bn	1.0%	-3.7%
10 (10)	South Korea	36.7bn	2.6%	34%
11 (12)	Brazil	31.7bn	1.4%	41%
12 (11)	Italy	30.9bn	1.5%	-27%
13 (13)	Australia	25.4bn	1.8%	27%
14 (14)	United Arab Emirates	22.8bn	5.1%	135%
15 (15)	Turkey	22.6bn	2.2%	15%
	World	**1,776bn**	**2.3%**	**21%**

Information from the Stockholm International Peace Research Institute (SIPRI) –
http://www.sipri.org/research/armaments/milex/milex_database
The SIPRI Military Expenditure Database contains data on 172 countries over the period 1988–2014.

Notes:
1 Spending figures are at current prices and market exchange rates.
2 Figures for China, Germany, the Russian Federation and the UAE are estimates.
3 Data on military expenditure as a share of GDP (Gross Domestic Product) relates to GDP estimates from the IMF World Economic Outlook, October 2014.
4 Change is real terms change, i.e. adjusted for local inflation.
5 Figures in brackets reflect rank in 2013, revised for latest information.

stagnant budgets. Perhaps unsurprisingly, those countries with borders closest to Russia are foremost amongst the defence 'hawks'. Whether Russia actually poses a serious long-term threat to Europe's borders has to be open to some conjecture. It is arguable that its finances are not strong enough to support a prolonged period of re-armament given the likely impact of declining energy prices on its commodity-based economy and the extent of ground its moribund defence sector has to regain since the end of the Cold War. Indeed, loss of access to Ukranian factories, which were once an integral part of the Soviet-era military supply chain, is already having an impact on a number of major naval programmes.[3] Also impacted has been the supply of modern technology from the west, most notably the collapse of the deal to acquire *Mistral*-type amphibious assault ships from France. The completed *Vladivostok* and *Sevastopol* remain tied up at the quayside at Saint Nazaire after France bowed to the inevitable and concluded completion of the contract was impossible given the changed political environment.

A big – and as yet unanswered – question is whether increasing tensions will cause the United States to row back from the constraints it has placed on its own military expenditure in the face of these growing challenges to its global dominance. As Table 1.0.1 shows, the impact of the 2011 Budget Control Act means that American defence spending is now well past its peak. The defence budget is nearly 20 per cent lower in real terms than it was at its height in 2010. It has also fallen slightly – when adjusted for inflation – over the past decade. Nevertheless, the United States still accounts for around a third of total world defence spending and its military outlays are almost three times that of China, the second-ranked country in the table. Whilst China's spending has increased more than in any other country over the decade, this is largely a reflection of its economic growth and the share of national wealth devoted to defence has remained largely constant. Another interesting aspect of the table is the large increases in defence spending over the last decade in Saudi Arabia and the United Arab Emirates, driven by considerable regional instability but largely financed by the benefit of high energy prices on their oil and gas sectors. As for Russia, the decline in oil prices that occurred in the second half of 2014 might make their current level of spending unsustainable in the medium term.

The amphibious assault ship *Vladivostok*, one of two constructed in France to Russian order, seen departing Saint Nazaire on trials in 2014. The breakdown in relations between Russia and the West following Russia's intervention in the Ukraine makes it unlikely the two ships will ever enter service with their intended owner. *(Bruno Huriet)*

The Chinese Navy's Type 054A frigate *Yun Cheng* pictured alongside at Portsmouth Naval Base in January 2015, with the Type 071 amphibious transport dock *Changbai Shan* in the background. The ships formed part of China's 18th Escort Task Group deployed to protect shipping in the Gulf of Aden. China's People's Liberation Army Navy is steadily developing 'blue water' capabilities against a backdrop of concern over its assertive stance to maritime disputes closer to home. *(Conrad Waters)*

FLEET REVIEWS

Table 1.0.2, containing the usual estimates of major fleet strengths, has been expanded to cover some of the emergent navies and provide more of a regional perspective. The table clearly demonstrates the unrivalled balance and depth of the US Navy in terms of 'blue water' capabilities. Its dominance in terms of strike carriers, attack submarines and amphibious shipping is particularly marked. The traditional European naval powers have typically been declining in stature as financial constraints have taken their toll, with only France able to offer a full – if thinly spread – balance of forces pending the British Royal Navy's return to the 'carrier club'. The latter's future will be significantly influenced by the 2015 Strategic Defence & Security Review (SDSR). *Seaforth World Naval Review* is fortunate to welcome the return of Richard Beedall to provide an analysis of some of the main decisions that will need to be taken.

The trajectory in Asia is in the opposite direction. Here a number of countries have the potential to create 'blue water' fleets able to influence events on a global basis, with China most evidently taking the lead in this regard. However, the challenges inherent in creating some capabilities – for example, effective strike carrier forces and reliable and silent nuclear submarines – are not to be taken lightly. As such, significant testing and trials of these types is taking place before more substantial numbers are commissioned. Other regional powers such as Australia, Japan and South Korea are also taking tentative steps towards fielding fast jets at sea, with the Australian

The Indonesian 'Parchim I' type corvette *Kri Kerapu* undertaking manoeuvres with the Royal Australian Navy's *Armidale* class patrol boat *Pirie* off the coast of Kupang, Indonesia. Indonesia is a populous country with a numerically large fleet. However, the extent of its constabulary obligations in the vast island archipelago mean that any oceanic 'blue water' naval ambitions need to take second place to ensuring the security of its littoral waters. *(Royal Australian Navy)*

amphibious assault ship *Canberra* and the new Japanese 'helicopter-carrying destroyer' *Izumo* perhaps the most significant ships to have been commissioned in the region over the past twelve months. The inclusion of Indonesia – the world's fourth-largest country by population and one of the top twenty by economic output – in the table illustrates the different force structure required by a country with vast archipelagic waters to police. Mrityunjoy Mazumdar explains the development and current priorities of the *Tentara Nasional Indonesia-Angkatan Laut* in the latest of his series of chapters describing fleets bordering the Indian Ocean.

SIGNIFICANT SHIPS

This year's collection of reviews of significant ships is headlined by a warship type that is at home in both 'blue water' oceanic and 'green water' littoral seas. The *San Antonio* (LPD-17) class amphibious transport docks – designed to deploy globally in support of US Navy and US Marine Corps missions in the littoral – were first conceived some twenty years ago in the immediate aftermath of the Cold War but have had a prolonged and somewhat traumatic birth. As such, it is only now that they are making their mark on navy operations. Scott Truver's chapter explains what went wrong with the original programme, as well as the progress that remedial

Table 1.0.2: MAJOR FLEET STRENGTHS MID 2015

REGION	AMERICAS			EUROPE						ASIA					INDIAN OCEAN	
Country	Brazil	Canada	USA	France	Italy	Spain	Turkey	UK	Russia	Australia	China	Indonesia	Japan	Korea S	India	Pakistan
Aircraft Carrier CVN/CV	1	–	10	1	–	–	–	–	1	–	1	–	–	–	1	–
Support Carrier CVS/CVH	–	–	–	–	2	–	–	–	–	–	–	–	3	–	1	–
Strategic Missile Sub SSBN	–	–	14	4	–	–	–	4	13	–	4	–	–	–	–	–
Attack Submarine SSGN/SSN	–	–	57	6	–	–	–	6	20	–	6	–	–	–	1	–
Patrol Submarine SSK	5	4	–	–	6	3	13	–	20	6	50	2	16	13	13	5
Battleships/Battlecruisers BB/BC	–	–	–	–	–	–	–	–	1	–	–	–	–	–	–	–
Fleet Escort CGN/CG/ DDG/FFG	8	13	87	16	18	11	16	19	25	12	60	6	38	23	23	10
Patrol Escort DD/FFG/FSG/FS	4	–	4	15	6	–	8	–	45	–	35	26	6	19	9	–
Missile Attack Craft PGG/PTG	–	–	–	–	–	–	23	–	35	–	75	20	6	17	12	8
Mine Countermeasures MCMV	6	12	11	14	10	6	20	15	40	6	25	11	28	9	6	3
Major Amp LHD/LPD/LPH/LSD	1	–	30	3	3	3	–	6	–	1	3	5	3	1	1	–

Notes:

1 Figures for Russia and China are approximate.

2 Figures for Indonesian fast attack craft are approximate, with some patrol gunboats being fitted 'for but not with' surface-to-surface missiles.

The LPD-17 type amphibious transport dock *Somerset* (LPD-25), undergoing sea trials in the second half of 2013. The last naval ship likely to be built at the Avondale yard in New Orleans, she is also the latest member of a class that has steadily been overcoming early 'teething troubles' to enter service with the US Navy. *(Huntington Ingalls Industries)*

efforts have made. These have met with such success that the type will be used as the basis of the next US Navy amphibious warship design and has been touted to meet several other potential roles.

Turning more specifically to the littoral, we also examine two classes constructed by Mediterranean neighbours and rivals – Greece and Turkey – which have also experienced a protracted gestation period for a variety of economic and political factors. Greece's *Roussen* class – a modification of former British shipbuilder Vosper Thornycroft's 'Vita' design – is a rare modern example of traditional fast attack craft design and reflects the geographical conditions prevalent in the Aegean. Guy Toremans' chapter provides a full description of a small but extremely powerful warship. Turkey's 'Ada' class corvettes – more commonly referred to under their 'MILGEM' or national warship programme designation – are larger warships which carry a superficial resemblance

The Turkish Navy's new corvette *Büyükada* entered service in the autumn of 2013. The second ship completed under the MILGEM national ship programme, she carries a superficial resemblance to the larger *Freedom* (LCS-1) Littoral Combat Ship variant. She is seen refuelling from the Australian tanker *Success* whilst deployed to the Indian Ocean. *(Royal Australian Navy)*

A landing craft from the British amphibious transport dock *Bulwark* rescuing migrants in the Mediterranean in May 2015. The humanitarian crisis in the Mediterranean is one of the spin-offs from recent instability in the Middle East and North Africa. *(Crown Copyright 2015)*

A Boeing P-8A Poseidon maritime patrol aircraft. Based on the Boeing 737 airliner, the type has already been selected by Australia and India in addition to the United States and is a strong contender for any British requirement to emerge out of SDSR 2015. *(Boeing)*

to the US Navy's *Freedom* (LCS-1) Littoral Combat Ship variant.[4] Devrim Yaylali sets out the background to the project, which is as significant in the impetus it has given to the local defence sector as the additional capability it has brought to an expanding fleet.

A very different type of vessel is represented by the Dutch *Holland* class. This is, perhaps, the most sophisticated warship yet developed for a constabulary policing as opposed to a warfighting mission. A particular feature of the new ships is their Thales integrated mast, which combines all major sensors and communications equipment within a separately fabricated module. The editor explains the rationale behind the class's design and the Royal Netherlands Navy's experience of the ships in operational service.

TECHNOLOGICAL DEVELOPMENTS

As always, *Seaforth World Naval Review* concludes with a review of diverse technological developments. David Hobbs' extended review of naval aviation includes a detailed overview of modern 'high end' maritime patrol aircraft (MPA). The decision to terminate the Nimrod MR4A programme and scrap an airborne maritime patrol capability was possibly the most controversial decision of the last British SDSR in 2010. In view of the vulnerability that this has created to a more active Russian submarine fleet, a revived MPA fleet is considered to be one of the more likely decisions to emerge from the imminent review.[5] The chapter looks at some of the possible alternatives available to the United Kingdom should this speculation prove correct. Although the United States Navy's P-8A Poseidon – converted from the ubiquitous Boeing 737 civilian airliner – looks a clear front runner, the purpose-built Japanese Kawasaki P-1 is an interesting outsider. The Japan Maritime Self Defence Force (JMSDF) has always had a strong anti-submarine emphasis and the new aircraft closely matches British requirements.

Norman Friedman's ongoing series of reviews on different aspects of warship technology turns this year to the 'dark arts' of electronic warfare. Whilst the armament, combat systems and sensors deployed in modern warships are often subject to detailed analysis, it is unusual for their increasingly sophisticated electronic warfare suites to merit much more than a passing mention. However, the effective deployment of electronic support and counter measures has been a key deciding factor in many recent conflicts. The chapter aims to shed some light on this somewhat opaque area, explaining how

these systems could make a decisive difference.

We conclude with a short review on the first new Royal Navy working uniform for almost seventy years, the Royal Navy Personal Clothing System (RNPCS). Tracing its origins to the British Armed Forces' combat experience in Afghanistan, the new uniform aims to combine practicality with a visual boost to the profile of the service its wearers represent. The editor explains how the new outfit was designed and tested, as well as the positive reaction it has received in service.

SUMMARY

Naval news stories over the past twelve months have inevitably been dominated by the ongoing theme of Chinese maritime expansion in Asia, supplemented by the more recent re-emergence of Russia as a potential threat to stability in Europe. However, there have also been a number of secondary themes, some considered at more length in the following chapters of this book. These include the fall-out from the ongoing conflict between Sunni and Shia Muslim spheres of influence in the Middle East, not least the associated humanitarian crisis that has only recently caught the press's attention in the waters of the Mediterranean. A similar, if smaller, crisis is being played out with respect to the Rohingya people of Myanmar in the Andaman Sea.[6] The often linked scourge of piracy has been less in the public eye as of late but combatting it remains a daily danger for many coastguard forces around the world.

ACKNOWLEDGEMENTS

The continued success of *Seaforth World Naval Review* relies much on the ongoing support of publishing editor Rob Gardiner and designer Steve Dent. The latter, particularly displays considerable patience in handling the editor's often pernickety lay-out requests in the short period between the end of June and the book's dispatch to the printers. The willingness of John Jordan to supply his clear, yet detailed, line drawings to illustrate the significant ship chapters is another critical success factor. The high quality work of a team of regular contributors needs little introduction to regular readers, whilst – amongst a growing number of photographers – the help of Moshi Anahory, Derek Fox, Bruno Huriet, Leo van Ginderen, Marc Piché and Arjun Sarup warrants special mention. From industry, Marion Bonnet of DCNS, Esther Benito Lope of Navantia, Craig Taylor of Rolls Royce and Frank van de Wiel of Thales Nederland have done far more than could be expected to be supportive. Last – but by no means least – the willingness of my wife, Susan, to conduct an initial proof read of the edited chapters is a true example of spousal devotion that only twenty-five years of happy marriage could hope to engender!

Comments and criticisms from readers are always appreciated; please direct them for my attention to info@seaforthpublishing.com

Conrad Waters, Editor
30 June 2015

Notes:

1. A good analysis of the challenges China's approach poses to the United States was contained in Charles Clover's and Geoff Dyer's 'US struggles for strategy to contain China's island-building', *The Financial Times* – 7 June 2015 (London: Pearson Plc, 2015).

2. There have been numerous explanations for the destruction of the Malaysian airliner. Whilst there is now almost universal acceptance that a 'Buk' missile was responsible, debate continues as to who supplied and fired the weapon. In June 2015, Almaz-Antey, the current Russian manufacturer of the 'Buk', presented detailed evidence suggesting the missile used was the 9M38-1 variant of the weapon, an older version no longer in production. The implication was that the missile used was more likely to have come from Ukrainian than from Russian sources. However, the balance of evidence still suggests Russian involvement, not least because the bases of many of their past denials have been disproved. For a detailed

account of Almaz-Antey's explanation, see Matthew Bodner's 'Russian Firm: Ukrainians Downed Flight MH17', *Defense News*. 6 June 2015 (Springfield VA: Gannett Government Media, 2015).

3. This problem for the Russian Navy has become more apparent with the passage of time and impacts a number of badly-needed surface warships. For example, see Matthew Bodner again in 'Ukraine Crisis Torpedoes Russia's Naval Expansion', *Moscow Times*, 3 June 2014 (Moscow: OOO United Press, 2015). A more detailed analysis of the situation is also contained in Chapter 2.4.

4. Although there are visual similarities between the 'MILGEM' type and *Freedom* (LCS-1), they incorporate significant differences 'under the skin'. The *Freedom* class are significantly larger ships able to deploy at much faster speeds in support of the US Navy's global presence. The interchangeable mission module concept used for the LCS type is another important distinguishing factor.

5. The ongoing criticism over the lack of a British maritime patrol aircraft capability was recently summed up in Ben Farmer's 'Nimrod cuts "have allowed Russian submarines to spy on Trident"', *The Daily Telegraph*, 30 May 2015 (London: Telegraph Media Group Ltd, 2015).

6. The Rohingya are a Muslim ethnic minority in northern Myanmar denied citizenship by the country's military-controlled government. The current crisis has arisen from the abuse of Rohingya trying to migrate from Myanmar and refugee camps in neighbouring Bangladesh by sea at the hands of people-traffickers, some of whom have abandoned migrants at sea. A good overview of the crisis was provided in 'Rohingya boat people: Myanmar's Shame', *The Economist*, 23 May 2015 (London: Economist Newspapers Ltd, 2015) and currently accessible at http://www.economist.com/news/asia/21651877-poverty-politics-and-despair-are-forcing-thousands-rohingyas-flee-myanmar-authorities

Author:
Conrad Waters

2.1 REGIONAL REVIEW

NORTH AND SOUTH AMERICA

INTRODUCTION

Developments in the Americas continue to be driven by financial considerations. In the United States, the wider debate on defence expenditure remains dominated by the process of sequestration enacted by the 2011 Budget Control Act. This is intended to align government spending more closely with tax revenues by imposing mandatory caps on defence and other public expenditure. The FY2016 Presidential Budget Request, released in February 2015, proposes total defence spending of US$585bn. Of this, US$51bn was allocated to supporting overseas contingency operations (OCO) – essentially the cost of financing wars in the likes of Afghanistan – and US$534m related to the core defence budget. Of this latter amount, US$161bn is earmarked for the US Navy.

The core budget request is over 7 per cent higher than the previous year's amount and c. US$35bn more than that allowed for under sequestration. This has led to a protracted political debate that has become a feature of recent defence spending requests. However, the current international background means that the lawmakers in the US Congress – who have to authorise the budget proposal – are more favourably disposed towards supporting the Pentagon's objectives than hitherto. Attempts to fudge the issue by shifting elements of the core budget into the OCO 'pot' – which is not subject to Budget Control Act restrictions – have encountered opposition. However, it seems some form of compromise will be reached. In 2013, a Bipartisan Budget Act allowed a temporary easing of budget restrictions during FY2014 and FY2015. A similar measure seems the most likely way forward.[1]

Whatever the outcome of this year's financial negotiations, it seems that a consensus on appropriate levels of defence spending is slowly emerging. For example, work by the Congressional Research Service suggests that the gap between the Pentagon's desired level of spending and that allowed by sequestration has steadily narrowed over time.[2] This will undoubtedly help future United States' military planning at a time when global instability is increasing and the re-emergence of a Russian military threat complicates the 'Pivot to the Pacific'. In this environment – even with more stable budgets – a continued emphasis on alliances and partnerships to share the burden is inevitable. This theme was reflected both in the president's 2015 *National Security Strategy* issued in February 2015 and the navy's updated *A Cooperative Strategy for 21st Century Seapower* published the following month.[3] An essential element of greater collaboration with overseas navies is an increasing focus on 'forward presence'. The aim is to have 120 ships 'Where it Matters, When it Matters' by 2020, compared with ninety-seven today.

Turning to Latin America, the financial environment is moving in the opposite direction to the United States as military budgets start to be impacted by a weakening economic outlook. The picture is variable across the region dependent on both financial and political factors and there are exceptions to the overall trend. For example, Mexico is continuing to see military spending rise – and it has already more than doubled in the past ten years – as its armed forces are increasingly used in the war against the drugs cartels. The most significant turnaround has occurred in Brazil. Here, a deteriorating economy has brought ambitious modernisation plans to a halt as procurement has been slashed by as much as 25 per cent. The massive PROSUB (*Programa de Desenvolvimento de Submarinos*) project being carried out to upgrade the submarine flotilla in conjunction with France's DCNS looks certain to be slowed. The equally ambitious but much less advanced PROSUPER (*Programa de Obtenção de Meios de Superfície*) programme to renew the surface fleet may even be shelved in its entirety.

One way to square the financial circle in this environment is to lower procurement costs. This is helping new suppliers break the dominance of United States and, particularly, European industry in the Latin American market. South Korea has been at the head of this movement, donating surplus ships and assisting with the local construction of various vessels in preparation for more lucrative contracts. A more recent entrant is China, which has been linked to the supply of the export P18 variant of its Type 056 corvette to meet a long-standing Argentine requirement for new offshore patrol vessels.[4] The so-called *Malvinas* class would provide greater warfighting capability than the Fassmer OPV80 design that had previously been earmarked for local construction. However, even at a reported unit cost of just US$50m, the price might be too high for a country struggling even to keep its existing ships operational.

The US Navy destroyer *Dewey* (DDG-105) pictured operating with other members of the *Arleigh Burke* class during Exercise 'Valiant Shield' in September 2014. Although this exercise only involved United States forces, there is generally an increased emphasis on collaboration with allied navies to share the burden of a more difficult security environment. *(US Navy)*

Table 2.1.1: FLEET STRENGTHS IN THE AMERICAS – LARGER NAVIES (MID 2015)

COUNTRY	ARGENTINA	BRAZIL	CANADA	CHILE	COLOMBIA	ECUADOR	PERU	USA
Aircraft Carrier (CVN/CV)	–	1	–	–	–	–	–	10
Strategic Missile Submarine (SSBN)	–	–	–	–	–	–	–	14
Attack Submarine (SSN/SSGN)	–	–	–	–	–	–	–	57
Patrol Submarine (SSK)	3	5	4	4	4	2	6	–
Fleet Escort (CG/DDG/FFG)	4	8	13	8	4	2	8	87
Patrol Escort/Corvette (FFG/FSG/FS)	9	4	–	–	1	6	–	4
Missile Armed Attack Craft (PGG/PTG)	2	–	–	3	–	3	6	–
Mine Countermeasures Vessel (MCMV)	–	6	12	–	–	–	–	11
Major Amphibious Units (LHD/LPD/LPH/LSD)	–	1	–	1	–	–	–	30

MAJOR NORTH AMERICAN NAVIES – CANADA

Years of procrastination over the Royal Canadian Navy's recapitalisation programme came home to roost in September 2014 when it was announced that two *Iroquois* class destroyers – *Iroquois* and *Algonquin* – and the fleet's only two replenishment oilers – *Protecteur* and *Preserver* – would be withdrawn from service without immediate replacement. All of the ships were well over forty years old and suffering from either accidental or fatigue-related damage. As such, further repair was either impracticable or uneconomic. Three of the vessels were officially paid off in ceremonies held during May and June 2015 whilst *Preserver* continues to be used as a static refuelling point.[5]

As shown by Table 2.1.2, the withdrawals reduce the number of operational surface vessels to thirteen ships, whilst there is no fleet replenishment capability at all. Two replacement ships – *Queenston* and *Chateauguay* – based on Germany's Type 702 *Berlin* class have been ordered from Seaspan's Vancouver Shipyards. However, work on the first will not commence until late 2016 for a planned 2019 delivery. In June 2015 the Canadian Government rather belatedly announced that it was entering discussions with Chaniter Davie Canada of Quebec for the provision of an interim supply ship capability based on the conversion of a commercial vessel.

The *Queenston* class are being constructed under Canada's National Shipbuilding Procurement Strategy, first announced in 2010. This has split future construction of large ships for the Canadian government between Vancouver Shipyards on the west coast and the Halifax Shipyard of Irving Shipbuilding in the east. The latter has been contracted to build a class of new Arctic patrol vessels first announced as long ago as 2007. It will then progress to constructing a planned fleet of 'up to' fifteen Canadian Surface Combatants that will eventually replace all the remaining surface escorts. The CAD$2.3bn construction award for the Arctic

The Royal Canadian Navy *Iroquois* class destroyer *Algonquin* pictured during her decommissioning ceremony at Esquimalt naval base in June 2015 after completing over forty years of service. Years of procrastination over fleet renewal is starting to have a significant impact on service numbers and capability. *(Royal Canadian Navy)*

offshore patrol ships was announced in January 2015 at the same time as the total budget for the programme was raised from CAD$3.1bn to CAD$3.5bn (c. US$2.8bn). Reports suggest that the fixed price contract only guarantees the delivery of five ships against an original requirement of between six to eight vessels, although Irvine Shipbuilding are strongly incentivised to deliver six.[6] Full production of the ships of the newly-named *Harry DeWolf* class will start in September 2015 for delivery from 2018 onwards. As for the *Queenston* class, there has been considerable comment on the high cost of domestic production compared with similar overseas programmes.

Good news stories over the past year include the long-awaited acceptance in June 2015 of the first six of a planned total of twenty-eight long-awaited CH-148 Cyclone helicopters. They were delivered to an interim standard and under a revised schedule in accordance with an agreement reached with manufacturer Sikorsky in January 2014. Current plans envisage receipt of full-specification, Block-2 variants from 2018 prior to completion of deliveries in 2021. In the meantime, the interim helicopters will largely be used for training, testing and evaluation that will culminate in operational deployments onboard *Halifax* class frigates from 2017. A number of 'at sea' trials have already taken place, notably six

Table 2.1.2: CANADIAN NAVY: PRINCIPAL UNITS AS AT MID 2015

TYPE	CLASS	NUMBER	TONNAGE	DIMENSIONS	PROPULSION	CREW	DATE
Principal Surface Escorts							
Destroyer – DDG	**IROQUOIS**	1	5,100 tons	130m x 15m x 5m	COGOG, 29 knots	280	1972
Frigate – FFG	**HALIFAX**	12	4,800 tons	134m x 16m x 5m	CODOG, 29 knots	225	1992
Submarines							
Submarine – SSK	**VICTORIA** (UPHOLDER)	4	2,500 tons	70m x 8m x 6m	Diesel-electric, 20+ knots	50	1990

months of tests on *Halifax* herself between December 2014 and May 2015.

The *Halifax* Class Modernisation/Frigate Equipment Life Extension (HCM/FELEX) programme also seems to be progressing satisfactorily. In November 2015, it was confirmed that work on the first four ships to be upgraded had been completed. These have been given an enhanced command and control capability to replace that lost with the withdrawal of the *Iroquois* class. Current indications are that the programme will be completed within its CAD$4.2bn budget by 2018.

Underneath the waves, the navy was finally able to declare its flotilla of *Victoria* (former British Royal Navy *Upholder*) class submarines fully operational as of December 2014. At this time, three of the four boats were at sea and ready for operations. The fourth – *Corner Brook* – was undergoing an extended docking work period (EDWP) in line with the class's planned operating cycle. The achievement of the planned force posture – some fourteen years after the first boat was commissioned into Canadian service – reflects the success of the *Victoria* in-Service Support Contract (VISSC) put in place with Babcock Canada. Growing confidence in the class is reflected in reports of plans for a major life-extension programme that would allow the submarines to remain in service until the mid-2030s.[7]

MAJOR NORTH AMERICAN NAVIES – UNITED STATES

Calculations of US Navy 'battle force' strength have returned to previous methodology following Congressional action to reverse the revised counting guidance issued on 7 March 2014.[8] This had allowed some forward-deployed patrol vessels and support ships to be included within the total, increasing overall force strength by a net ten ships. Fleet strength of c. 270 ships as at mid-2015 – based on the re-established methodology – is at a post-war low. However, this trend will reverse throughout the rest of FY2015 and beyond as the pace of withdrawals slows and is exceeded by new commissionings.

The latest annual long-range plan to Congress on naval construction demonstrates continued consistency in the US Navy's planned future fleet. This is currently based on a force structure assessment (FSA) completed in 2012 and subject to an interim update in 2014.[9] The latter has increased the targeted medium-term combatant level from 306 ships to 308 ships. This takes account of the

A Sikorsky CH-148 Cyclone helicopter pictured onboard the Royal Canadian Navy frigate *Halifax* in 2015. Canada is now starting to take delivery of the type after years of delays. *(Royal Canadian Navy)*

procurement of a twelfth LPD-17 class amphibious transport dock pushed through by law-makers in spite of navy reluctance and plans for a third Afloat Forward Staging Base (AFSB). The authorisation of an eleventh Joint High Speed Vessel (JHSV) does not appear to be in the plan. As indicated by Table 2.1.3, growth in fleet size towards this target over the next five years will largely be achieved by higher numbers of surface combatants. This reflects the impact or recommencement of destroyer production and the arrival of large numbers of Littoral Combat Ships to compensate for previous withdrawals of

Table 2.1.3: US NAVY BATTLE-FORCE DEVELOPMENT (FY2015 TO FY2020)

SHIP TYPE	MID 2015	30.09. 2015	30.09. 2016	30.09. 2017	30.09. 2018	30.09. 2019	30.09. 2020
Aircraft Carrier (CVN)	10	10	11	11	11	11	11
Strategic Submarine (SSBN)	14	14	14	14	14	14	14
Attack Submarine (SSGN/SSN)	57	58	57	54	56	54	55
Fleet Escort: Cruiser (CG)	22	22	22	22	22	22	20
Fleet Escort: Destroyer (DDG)	62	62	65	68	69	72	75
Fleet Escort: Frigate (FFG)	3	0	0	0	0	0	0
Patrol Escort: Littoral Combat Ship (LCS)	4	8	11	15	19	23	24
Mine-countermeasures Vessel (MCMV)	11	11	11	11	11	10	9
Amphibious Vessel (LHA/LHD/LPD/LSD)	30	30	31	32	33	33	33
Other – Logistics & Support Ships	59	58	60	57	59	61	63
TOTAL	272	273	282	284	294	300	304

Note:
Forward data is derived from the *Report to Congress on the Annual Long-Range Plan for Construction of Naval Vessels – June 2014* and *Report to Congress on the Annual Long-Range Plan for Construction of Naval Vessels – March 2015*, including their appendices on planned ship decommissionings. The numbers shown for 30.09.2015 reflect delays to delivering *Zumwalt* (DDG-1000); in addition, it seems unlikely a further four Littoral Combat Ships will have been commissioned by then.

FFG-7 type frigates. Surface fleet availability will also be bolstered by continued Congressional reluctance to alloy *Ticonderoga* (CG-47) class cruisers to be paid off into reserve prior to their planned modernisation.

Whilst there are longer-term concerns over the US Navy's ability to fund its force ambitions, shipbuilding continues to be afforded a relatively high priority. The FY2016 budget request encompasses a total of nine ships within a five-year shipbuilding plan of forty-eight vessels. This compares with the total of forty-four vessels included in the previous FY2015 plan. As shown in Table 2.1.4, construction includes steady procurement of two nuclear-powered attack submarines and two destroyers each year. The second of the FY2016 destroyers will be the first of the proposed Flight III DDFG-51 variant, whilst construction of the modified frigate-type Littoral Combat Ships will commence from FY2019. Details of these and other developments are provided under ship-specific categories, below.

Table 2.1.4: USN FY2016 FIVE YEAR SHIPBUILDING PLAN (FY2016–FY2020)

SHIP TYPE	FY2015: ACTUAL	FY2016: REQUEST	FY2017: PLAN	FY2018: PLAN	FY2019: PLAN	FY2020: PLAN
Aircraft Carrier (CVN-78)	Nil (Nil)	Nil (Nil)	Nil (Nil)	1 (1)	Nil (Nil)	Nil (Nil)
Attack Submarine (SSN-774)	2 (2)	2 (2)	2 (2)	2 (2)	2 (2)	2 (2)
Destroyer (DDG-51)	2 (2)	2 (2)	2 (2)	2 (2)	2 (2)	2 (2)
Littoral Combat Ship (LCS-1/2)	3 (3)	3 (3)	3 (3)	3 (3)	2 (2)	3 (3)
Amphibious Assault Ship (LHA-6)	Nil (Nil)	Nil (Nil)	1 (1)	Nil (Nil)	Nil (Nil)	Nil (Nil)
Amphibious Transport Ship (LPD-17)	Nil (Nil)	1 (Nil)	Nil (Nil)	Nil (Nil)	Nil (Nil)	Nil (Nil)
Amphibious Ship (LX-R)	Nil (Nil)	Nil (Nil)	Nil (Nil)	Nil (Nil)	Nil (Nil)	1 (1)
Joint High Speed Vessel (JHSV-1)	1 (Nil)	Nil (Nil)	Nil (Nil)	Nil (Nil)	Nil (Nil)	Nil (Nil)
Mobile Landing Platform (MLP-1)	Nil (Nil)	Nil (Nil)	1 (1)	Nil (Nil)	Nil (Nil)	Nil (Nil)
Replenishment Oiler (TAO(X))	Nil (Nil)	1 (1)	Nil (Nil)	1 (1)	1 (1)	1 (2)
Fleet Tug (TATS)	Nil (Nil)	Nil (Nil)	1 (2)	1 (1)	2 (1)	1 (1)
Total	8 (7)	9 (8)	10 (11)	10 (10)	9 (8)	10 (11)

Notes:

1 Figures in brackets relate to previous FY2015 Budget Request and Shipbuilding Plan.

2 Figures relate to Ship Battle Forces – other ships are not included.

3 The FY2014 and FY2017 MLP mobile landing platform ships will be built as afloat forward staging base (AFSB) variants.

Aircraft Carriers: Strong Congressional support for maintaining the mandated eleven-strong carrier force has halted plans to withdraw the aircraft carrier *George Washington* (CVN-73) half-way through her planned fifty-year life to save money on her scheduled refuelling and complex overhaul (RCOH). Provision for fully funding this expensive midlife refit – amounting to around US$4bn in total – is included in the FY2016 budget.[10] The longer-term future of the carrier force is ensured by construction of the new *Gerald R Ford* (CVN-78) class, with the first of class being scheduled for delivery in the next twelve months. In June 2015, Huntington Ingalls Industries (HHI) received contracts amounting to c. US$4.3bn to complete design and construction work on the second ship, *John F Kennedy* (CVN-79), on which work first started in December 2010. Efforts to stabilise programme costs – which increased significantly during the project's early life – appear to be meeting with success. Indeed, measures to improve construction efficiency and control equipment specifications saw some fall in estimated costs for CVN-79 and the third ship, *Enterprise* (CVN-80), in the FY2016 estimates.

The last year has seen continuation of a massive effort to 'clear-out' former Cold War-era carriers for scrapping. *Saratoga* (CV-60), *Ranger* (CV-61) and *Constellation* (CV-64) have all joined *Forrestal* (CV-59) at the scrapyards in Brownsville, Texas during the last twelve months, with *Independence* (CV-62) also scheduled to make her final voyage shortly.

Surface Combatants: The last twelve months have seen work continue on integrating the first *Zumwalt* (DDG-1000) class destroyer's complex integrated electric propulsion and other systems. In March 2015 it emerged that the first two of the three ships

The US Navy is undertaking a wholesale 'clear out' of decommissioned aircraft carriers. This view shows the former *Ranger* (CV-61) at the start of her lengthy final voyage for disposal at the scrapyards of Brownsville in Texas. *(US Navy)*

of the class would be delayed by about a year because of difficulties completing this task. Lack of sufficient electricians at General Dynamics Bath Iron Works was blamed as a major factor. There has been speculation that production of the class, previously cut to three on cost grounds, might be extended given the additional capabilities they bring. However, the heavy capital investment still associated with the ships would be a prohibitive factor given the tight financial environment.

The skills shortage impacting *Zumwalt* delivery dates is also likely to impact the renewed construction of *Arleigh Burke* (DDG-51) class destroyers, which restarted in 2013. Current production is focused on the previous Flight IIA variant. This will switch to the revised Flight III design starting with the as-yet unnamed DDG-124, which should be ordered under the FY2016 programme. The revised design is built around the new Raytheon AN/SPY-6(V) Air and Missile Defence Radar (AMDR), which replaces the AN/SPY-1 system associated with the Aegis weapons system. The fact that AN/SPY-6 is a scalable design means that it has been possible to design it to fit the existing DDG-51 superstructure with minimal modification.[11] However, the new active radar has greater electrical power and cooling needs than the legacy system and this has resulted in significant changes to the electrical generation and distribution plant. Meanwhile, the restart of *Burke* production achieved a major milestone on 28 March 2015 with the launch of the first of the new batch of destroyers, *John Finn* (DDG-113), by HII.

Turning to smaller surface combatants (SSCs), a decision has now been made to continue production of Littoral Combat Ships – albeit in an upgraded configuration – after a review of alternative designs brought about by concerns over their warfighting capabilities. The upgrades – set to include surface-to-surface missiles, improved air-defence capabilities and an advanced electronic warfare system – will be incorporated into the final twenty ships of a planned 52-ship SSC programme during build. It is also planned to retrofit existing Littoral Combat Ships with these enhanced capabilities in due course; with both the new and upgraded ships being reclassified as frigates. Meanwhile production continues of both the existing *Freedom* (LCS-1) and *Independence* (LCS-2) variants. Orders announced on 1 April 2015, encompassing full funding for three ships and advanced procurement of items for a fourth ship, completes the twenty-ship 'bulk buy' agreed for

The lead US Navy *Zumwalt* (DDG-1000) class destroyer seen fitting out at Bath Iron Works in the autumn of 2014. The workload associated with commissioning her advanced integrated electric propulsion plant means that her delivery has been delayed. *(General Dynamics Bath Iron Works)*

Renewed construction of *Arleigh Burke* class destroyers is now well advanced, with the first of the new ships – *John Finn* (DDG-113) – launched by HII in March 2015. Construction will shift to the modified Flight III variant with effect from the second ship proposed in the US Navy's FY2016 construction programme. *(Huntington Ingalls Industries)*

The final *Tarawa* class amphibious assault ship, *Peleliu* (LHA-5) pictured at sea in August 2014 during a final deployment to the Western Pacific. She was decommissioned at a ceremony at San Diego on 31 March 2015. *(US Navy)*

The second Flight III *Virginia* class submarine *John Warner* (SSN-785) is accompanied by a dolphin during sea trials from HII's Newport News facility in May 2015. *(Huntington Ingalls Industries)*

LCS-5 through to LCS-24. Five of these ships had been launched as of mid-2015. They should start to enter service during the next twelve months to join the existing pair of prototypes of each design variant that are currently in service. They are desperately needed to replace the fast-disappearing FFG-7 type frigates, only three of which remain in service. *Kauffman* (FFG-59) is likely to hold the distinction of being the last of the class in US Navy service, with decommissioning scheduled for 21 September 2015.

Amphibious Shipping: The amphibious fleet said farewell to one of its longest-serving classes with the decommissioning of the last remaining *Tarawa* (LHA-1) type amphibious assault ship, *Peleliu* (LHA-5), on 31 March 2015 after nearly thirty-five years of service. The amphibious transport dock *Denver* (LPD-9) was withdrawn the previous August after an even longer career spanning almost forty-six years. Her sister *Ponce* (AFSB(I)-15) remains in operation to trial the Afloat Forward Staging Base concept prior to entry into service of the first purpose-built vessel, *Lewis B Puller* (AFSB-1), which was delivered in June 2015. Two earlier *Montford Point* (MLP-1) class mobile landing platform variants of the type have previously been handed over and the lead ship spent much of the last year trialling the new concept.[12] The new ships reflect innovative attempts to adapt commercial designs as an alternative to more costly, purpose-built warships; an approach also reflected in elements of the Littoral Combat Ship programme and in the JHSVs. Five of the last mentioned type are now in service following the delivery of *Fall River* (JHSV-4) and *Trenton* (JHSV-5) over the past year. In addition, *Brunswick* (JHSV-6) was launched on 19 May 2015.

Submarines: Serial deliveries of the *Virginia* (SSN-774) class submarines are now transitioning to the Block III variant, which features a redesigned bow with a new sonar and vertical launch system. The first of the new block – and eleventh member of the overall class – *South Dakota* (SSN-784) was commissioned on 25 October 2014. She will shortly be joined in service by *John Warner* (SSN-785), which was delivered at the end of June 2015. Although construction is now progressing at a steady rate of two boats per anum, this will not be sufficient to prevent some reduction in overall submarine force levels as larger numbers of Cold War-era *Los Angeles* (SSN-688) boats start to retire.

Table 2.1.5: UNITED STATES NAVY: PRINCIPAL UNITS AS AT MID 2015

TYPE	CLASS	NUMBER	TONNAGE	DIMENSIONS	PROPULSION	CREW	DATE
Aircraft Carriers							
Aircraft Carrier – CVN	NIMITZ (CVN-68)	10	101,000 tons	340m x 41/78m x 12m	Nuclear, 30+ knots	5,700	1975
Principal Surface Escorts							
Cruiser – CG	TICONDEROGA (CG-47)	22	9,900 tons	173m x 17m x 7m	COGAG, 30+ knots	365	1983
Destroyer – DDG	ARLEIGH BURKE (DDG-51) – Flight II-A	34	9,200 tons	155m x 20m x 7m	COGAG, 30 knots	380	2000
Destroyer – DDG	ARLEIGH BURKE (DDG-51) – Flights I/II	28	8,800 tons	154m x 20m x 7m	COGAG, 30+ knots	340	1991
Frigate – FFG	OLIVER HAZARD PERRY (FFG-7)	3	4,100 tons	143m x 14m x 5m	COGAG, 30 knots	215	1977
Littoral Combat Ship – FS	FREEDOM (LCS-1)	2	3,100 tons	115m x 17m x 4m	CODAG, 45+ knots	<50[1]	2008
Littoral Combat Ship – FS	INDEPENDENCE (LCS-2)	2	2,800 tons	127m x 32m x 5m	CODAG, 45+ knots	<50[1]	2010
Submarines							
Submarine – SSBN	OHIO (SSBN-726)	14	18,800 tons	171m x 13m x 12m	Nuclear, 20+ knots	155	1981
Submarine – SSGN	OHIO (SSGN-726)	4	18,800 tons	171m x 13m x 12m	Nuclear, 20+ knots	160	1981
Submarine – SSN	VIRGINIA (SSN-774)	11	8,000 tons	115m x 10m x 9m	Nuclear, 25+ knots	135	2004
Submarine – SSN	SEAWOLF (SSN-21)	3[2]	9,000 tons	108m x 12m x 11m	Nuclear, 25+ knots	140	1997
Submarine – SSN	LOS ANGELES (SSN-688)	39	7,000 tons	110m x 10m x 9m	Nuclear, 25+ knots	145	1976
Major Amphibious Units							
Amph. Assault Ship – LHD	AMERICA (LHA-6)	1	45,000 tons	257m x 32/42m x 9m	COGAG, 20+ knots	1,050	2014
Amph Assault Ship – LHD	WASP (LHD-1)	8[3]	41,000 tons	253m x 32/42m x 9m	Steam, 20+ knots	1,100	1989
Landing Platform Dock – LPD	SAN ANTONIO (LPD-17)	9	25,000 tons	209m x 32m x 7m	Diesel, 22+ knots	360	2005
Landing Ship Dock – LSD	WHIDBEY ISLAND (LSD-41)	12[4]	16,000 tons	186m x 26m x 6m	Diesel, 20 knots	420	1985

Notes:

1 Plus mission-related crew.   **2** Third of class, SSN-23 is longer and heavier.   **3** LHD-8 has many differences.   **4** Includes four LSD-49 HARPERS FERRY variants.

Meanwhile, design work is ramping up on the replacements for the current *Ohio* (SSBN-726) strategic submarines. The fourteen existing SSBN-726 are approaching the end of service lives that have already been extended from thirty to forty-two years.[13] The first of the 'Ohio Replacements' has to be ready for patrols by 2031 to maintain a fleet of ten operational strategic submarines as the force transitions from the fourteen remaining *Ohio*s to the twelve boats envisaged for the new class. Key design decisions have already been made for the new submarines. They will have a reduced missile load-out of sixteen Trident ballistic missiles compared with the twenty missiles in the existing submarines, utilising a missile compartment that will be shared with the United Kingdom's 'Successor' class. A new reactor core will be developed with a lifespan equivalent to that of the submarine to reduce overall maintenance costs, whilst electric drive propulsion is envisaged. Maximum use is also being made of technology developed for the *Virginia* class boats to try to reduce unit costs of follow-on submarines (i.e. those built after the first-of-class) to around US$5bn per boat.

Operationally, the US Navy is being forced to balance its broad strategic 'Pivot to the Pacific' with the need to commit forces to counter the deteriorating security situation in the Middle East following Islamic State advances in Iraq and elsewhere and to deter Russia's increased assertiveness in Europe. Materials released explaining the navy's element of the 2016 Presidential budget request shows that – in practical terms – the Pacific region is securing by far the largest share of navy resources, accounting for fifty-one of a total of just under a hundred ships on forward deployment as at the end of January 2015. By way of contrast, there were only twelve ships in European waters. This reflects a strategy of bolstering European forces with a small number of 'high-end' capabilities not available to local fleets, most notably those provided by the missile-defence capable *Arleigh Burke* class destroyers based at Rota in Spain. Three of the four destroyers earmarked for this deployment have now arrived at their new home, with *Carney* (DDG-64) scheduled to complete the quartet before the end of 2015. In addition, work on the land-based 'Aegis Ashore' facility at Deveselu in Romania is well underway as

part of the phased approach being adopted to build European anti-ballistic missile defences.

The expansion of the US Marine Corps' Special Purpose Marine Air Ground Task Force (SP-MAGTF) concept referenced in *Seaforth World Naval Review 2015* is progressing in spite of funding constraints. The original SP-MAGTF for Crisis Response in Africa, established in Spain in 2013, has been joined by a similar crisis response force for Central Command in the Persian Gulf. The latter is tasked – *inter alia* – with recovering any aircrew shot down in operations against the Islamic State. A smaller response force for the Southern Command area in Latin America also commenced operations in June 2015. Elsewhere in the Gulf, trials of the prototype laser weapon on *Ponce* (AFSB(I)-15) have proved remarkably successful, demonstrating an ability to operate against targets at far greater ranges than initially envisaged. Trials of an electromagnetic railgun are also scheduled onboard the JHSV *Millinocket* (JHSV-3) during 2016 prior to potential installation on the third of the DDG-1000 class, *Lyndon B Johnson* (DDG-1002).

Turning to the US Coast Guard, planned orders

for the eight *Bertholf* (WMSL-750) national security cutters were completed with the award of a US$500m contract to HII to build *Midgett* (WMSL-757) on 31 March 2015. Five of the class have now been handed over, with *James* (WMSL-754) delivered on 5 June 2015 prior to a planned August commissioning. Deliveries of the smaller fast response cutters of the *Bernard C Webber* (WPC-1101) class are also proceeding apace. The thirteenth vessel, *Richard Dixon* (WPC-1113), was commissioned on 20 June 2015. Another nineteen are under construction or on order. Tenders have also been issued for a further twenty-six vessels to complete construction of the class. A decision will also be taken before the end of 2016 on the preferred design and builder for the intermediate offshore patrol cutter requirement. Consideration is also being given to how best to recapitalise the ice-breaker fleet following the refurbishment of the heavy ice-breaker *Polar Star* (WAGB-10) in 2013.

OTHER NORTH AND CENTRAL AMERICAN NAVIES

In Central America, **Mexico** appears to be stepping up local construction of constabulary assets. This follows an apparent hiatus caused by essential investment in its increased involvement in the internal war

against organised crime.[14] Reports suggest that construction has recently commenced on a third batch of four *Oaxaca* class offshore patrol vessels to supplement the two earlier pairs delivered during 2003 and 2010. These will be equipped with BAE Systems Bofors 57mm guns as opposed to the Oto Melara 76mm mounts found in the earlier ships as their main armament. They may also be fitted with an indigenously-designed sonar, possibly due to a requirement to pick up mini-submersibles used by some of the drugs gangs. Licenced construction of Damen Stan Patrol 4207 inshore patrol vessels is also continuing. At least fourteen of the so-called *Tenochtitlan* class are planned. Modernisation of the small front-line surface force is also becoming pressing as older ships retire. However, it is still not clear whether or not potential transfers of former US Navy FFG-7 type ships will be taken up. The navy has hopes to undertake local construction of frigate-sized ships to a foreign design, further expanding the capabilities of domestic industry.

Damen is also becoming a major supplier to other navies in the Caribbean. The Royal **Bahamas** Defence Force has taken delivery of *Rolly Gray*, the last of four Stan Patrol 4207 vessels being delivered under the 'Sandy Bottom' project. It is expecting the delivery of a landing craft and four smaller Stan

Patrol 3007 ships of the 'Sea Axe' type that comprise the rest of the contract by mid-2016. **Trinidad and Tobago** has also selected Damen for a wholesale coast guard fleet renewal programme, ordering four Stan Patrol 5009 patrol vessels, two Fast Crew Supply 5009 utility vessels and six smaller interceptors.

MAJOR SOUTH AMERICAN NAVIES – BRAZIL

The *Marinha do Brasil* is by far the largest of South America's navies. The current fleet structure is outlined in Table 2.1.6. Its fleet development programme has also been the most ambitious in the region. The long-term 'PEAMB' naval organisation and equipment plan announced at the turn of the decade ultimately envisages a major 'blue water' fleet built around two aircraft carriers, four amphibious assault ships and thirty fleet escorts, as well as conventional and nuclear-powered submarines. Whilst enough money has been provided to make a start on these ambitions, changes in government priorities and a recent deterioration in the country's economy mean that overall progress has been patchy. This situation is made more concerning by the deteriorating condition of the existing fleet, evidenced by ongoing reliability issues impacting the sole carrier *São Paulo* and the decommissioning of surface escorts. The latter has apparently been influenced by the need to cannibalise some ships to keep the rest of the fleet in service. The withdrawal of the Type 22 frigate *Bosisio* and the *Inhaúma* class corvette *Frontin* have both been announced in the last year.[15]

By far the greatest investment committed to date has been made in the vast submarine manufacturing facility and base at Itaguaí, to the south of Rio de Janeiro. This has been built by Brazilian conglomerate Odebrecht in conjunction with France's DCNS under the PROSUB project. The facility has been opened in stages as construction has progressed. The main construction hall was inaugurated by Brazil's President Dilma Rousseff in December 2014. It can support the simultaneous assembly of two submarines from sub-components engineered in the separate manufacturing facility that was opened in 2013, or from elsewhere. As of mid-2015, work was underway on three of a planned initial total of four conventional submarines of France's 'Scorpène' type; a nuclear-powered boat will then follow. Whilst Brazil has recently affirmed the PEAMB plan for fifteen conventional and six nuclear-powered submarines, recent reductions in defence spending

The national security cutter *James* (WMSL-754) was delivered in June 2015 prior to an official commissioning ceremony scheduled for August. Orders for all eight planned ships of this class have now been placed in spite of previous concerns that construction might be curtailed. *(Huntington Ingalls Industries)*

have resulted in a further delay in the lead boat's delivery schedule. Named *Riachuelo*, it seems likely that she will not now be fully operational until around the end of the decade.

The amount of money being consumed by PROSUB has already delayed plans for surface fleet modernisation. These will now be exacerbated by the growing funding crunch. The expensive PROSUPER project for five surface escorts and five offshore patrol vessels is therefore likely to be further postponed. The navy will hope that cheaper plans for four new *Tamandaré* class corvettes armed with British Sea Ceptor missiles and a variant of the Artisan radar system will survive any further economies. There are also plans for an upgraded class of 500-ton patrol vessel to follow-on from the seven *Macaé* class ships being built under licence from France's CMN. The funding crisis has meant that deliveries of these ships are being stretched-out. This has pushed back delivery of the third ship, *Maracanã,* until September 2015.

OTHER SOUTH AMERICAN NAVIES

Amongst the other Latin American countries, **Chile** has the most modern and efficient naval service.[16] However, funding has been less generous in recent years than previously. Consequently, there has been considerable political vacillation over one of the highest priority naval requirements, namely the acquisition of a second dock landing ship to replace the former French *Foudre*, brought into service as *Sargento Aldea* in 2011. *Foudre*'s more modern sister *Siroco* is currently being sold by France but the interest of other countries, including Brazil and

An image of extent of construction of the vast new submarine assembly facility and operating base being built for the Brazilian Navy with the support of France's DCNS at Itaguaí, south of Rio de Janeiro. The assembly hall in the centre of the photograph was inaugurated by Brazilian President Dilma Rousseff in December 2014. The inset, previously published in *Seaforth World Naval Review 2014,* provides an impression of the completed facility. It will be a long time before Brazil's submarine flotilla expands to the ten boats shown in the impression. *(DCNS)*

Portugal, may put the cost of the ship beyond Chile's reach. Authorisation has already been granted for a construction of a fourth *Piloto Pardo* Fassmer OPV-80 type offshore patrol ship at the ASMAR yard at Talcahuano. She will be built to the ice-strengthened design introduced by third of class *Marinero Fuentealba*, which has now been commissioned. ASMAR is also scheduled to build a new icebreaker,

Table 2.1.6: BRAZILIAN NAVY: PRINCIPAL UNITS AS AT MID 2015

TYPE	CLASS	NUMBER	TONNAGE	DIMENSIONS	PROPULSION	CREW	DATE
Aircraft Carriers							
Aircraft Carrier – CV	SÃO PAULO (FOCH)	1	33,500 tons	265m x 32/51m x 9m	Steam, 30 knots	1,700	1963
Principal Surface Escorts							
Frigate – FFG	GREENHALGH (Batch I Type 22)	2	4,700 tons	131m x 15m x 4m	COGOG, 30 knots	270	1979
Frigate – FFG	NITERÓI	6	3,700 tons	129m x 14m x 4m	CODOG, 30 knots	220	1976
Corvette – FSG	INHAÚMA	3	2,100 tons	96m x 11m x 4m	CODOG, 27 knots	120	1989
Corvette – FSG	BARROSO	1	2,400 tons	103m x 11m x 4m	CODOG, 30 knots	145	2008
Submarines							
Submarine – SSK	TIKUNA (Type 209 – modified)	1	1,600 tons	62m x 6m x 6m	Diesel-electric, 22 knots	40	2005
Submarine – SSK	TUPI (Type 209)	4	1,500 tons	61m x 6m x 6m	Diesel-electric, 22+ knots	30	1989
Major Amphibious Units							
Landing Ship Dock – LSD	CEARÁ (LSD-28)	1	12,000 tons	156m x 26m x 6m	Steam, 22 knots	345	1956

for which a budget of US$150m has been allocated. The new ships will provide some compensation for the recent withdrawals of the last two *Tiger* class fast attack craft serving in the north of the country – decommissioned in December 2014 – and of the submarine depot ship *Almirante Meriono,* withdrawn in January 2015.

Argentina, the other member of the 'ABC' club of leading South American naval powers, continues to make noises about fleet modernisation. However, there are few signs of tangible progress beyond the return of the TR-1700-type submarine *San Juan* to the fleet following completion of a lengthy refit between 2007 and 2014. The icebreaker *Almirante Irizar* has been out of service for a comparable length of time but deadlines for the completion of work continue to be missed. Hopes she will be ready to support the annual mission to the Antarctic in 2015/16 seem optimistic, meaning that other capacity will again need to be hired to support the Argentine bases there. Meanwhile, a significant part of the surface fleet remains non-operational due to shortages of spare parts.

The outlook in **Peru** is much more positive, with work well underway on a programme of fleet renewal. Significant attention is also being paid to the development of local construction and upgrade capabilities, both supported by modernisation of the SIMA Shipyard in Callao. This will receive a synchro-lift amongst other new facilities. The yard is currently working on two *Makassar* type amphibious transport docks being built with South Korean support, as well as a number of smaller vessels. Six of the seven remaining *Lupo* type frigates that form the core of the surface fleet are also undergoing – or are scheduled to undergo – various degrees of modernisation. This leaves *Villavisencio* to join her sister *Carvajal* in the coast guard as a patrol ship by 2016. A similar programme of modernisation is scheduled for at least some of the six Type 209 submarines that comprise the underwater flotilla. Overseas acquisitions include the former Dutch replenishment tanker, *Amsterdam* – renamed *Tacna* in Peruvian service – and Seasprite helicopters from New Zealand. There are also hopes of acquiring a second-hand vessel to replace the veteran fleet flagship *Almirante Grau*. A new-build frigate programme is a more distant ambition.

Amongst the other South American fleets, **Colombia** also has an active fleet renewal programme based on an expansion of domestic industrial capabilities. Local construction of Fassmer OPV-80 type

The US Navy amphibious assault ship *America* (LHA-6) pictured operating with Chile's dock landing ship *Sargento Aldea* in August 2014 whilst the former was on its delivery voyage from builders HII to its home port of San Diego, California. It is unclear whether or not the Chilean Navy will be given authority to procure a second major amphibious ship. *(US Navy)*

The Peruvian Navy frigate *Villavisencio* pictured operating off the east coast of the United States in June 2012. Although many of her sisters in Peruvian service are being upgraded, present plans envisage her transfer to the coast guard as a patrol vessel. *(Marc Piché)*

patrol vessels similar to those built in Chile has already seen the delivery of two vessels, with work started on a third. The second of these, *7 de Augusto*, is to deploy as far as the Horn of Africa in support of the European Union-led Operation 'Atalanta' counter-piracy mission. Local build also extends to production of South Korean-designed OPV-46 coastal patrol vessels and an indigenous landing ship design. The much more ambitious *Plataforma*

Estratégica de Superficie (PES) programme envisages local construction of a new class of eight frigates in two batches of four for delivery from 2027 onwards. It is likely that the ships will be built in conjunction with a foreign partner, with European and Korean yards already jockeying for position on the project.

Elsewhere, **Venezuela**'s economic crisis is undoing some of the effort previously devoted to naval modernisation. Repairs of the 'POVZEE' type

oceanic patrol vessel *Warao*, which ran aground off Brazil in 2012, are progressing only slowly through lack of funds. Local construction of the smaller 'BVL' type littoral patrol vessel *Tamanaco* – apparently now renamed *Comandante eterno Hugo Chávez* – has also yet to be completed. Meanwhile **Uruguay** continues to consider various offshore patrol vessel designs. A variant of the Lürssen *Darussalam* design built for Brunei is, apparently, one leading contender.

Notes:

1. Excellent regular analysis on this ever-changing and annually refreshed story is provided by *Defense News*. For example, the strengthening view that some form of compromise to avoid full sequestration of military expenditures for FY2016 is reflected in Aaron Mehta's 'No Sequestration "Pretty Certain," Wok Says', *Defense News*, 22 June 2015 (Springfield VA: Gannett Government Media, 2015).

2. See Amy Belasco, *Defense Spending and the Budget Control Act Limits R44039* (Washington DC: Congressional Research Service, 2015). One of a series of periodically updated reports by the CRS that are not publicly released but posted on the Federation of American Scientists website as a public service, it can be found by searching http://www.fas.org:8080/sgp/crs/. Readers are warned that attempting to understand US budgetary process is not for the faint-hearted.

3. See further *National Security Strategy – February 2015* (Washington DC: The White House, 2015): https://www.whitehouse.gov/sites/default/files/docs/2015_national_security_strategy_2.pdf and *A Cooperative Strategy for 21st Century Seapower – March 2015* (Washington DC: Department of the Navy & United States Coast Guard, 2015): http://www.navy.mil/local/maritime/ 150227-CS21R-Final.pdf

4. Reports of this programme appear to originate from Richard D Fisher Jr.'s 'China, Argentina set for defence collaboration, Malvinas-class OPV deal', *Jane's Defence Weekly*, 1 February 2015 (Coulsdon: IHS Jane's, 2015).

5. Full details of the decommissioning plans were provided by David Pugliese in 'Paying off ceremonies to be held for two destroyers, one replenishment ship – fourth ship to be paid off at a later date', *Ottawa Citizen*, 24 April 2015 (Ottawa: Postmedia Network, 2015).

6. Amongst a number of journalists reporting this news, which was not made at all clear in the subsequent official Government of Canada press release on 23 January, was James Cudmore of *CBC News* in 'Canada's navy to get 5 or 6 Arctic ships, not 8' on 16 January 2015. A copy can

currently be found at: http://www.cbc.ca/news/politics/canada-s-navy-to-get-5-or-6-arctic-ships-not-8-1.2913159

7. The plan was first reported by David Pugliese in 'Canada Plans Major Sub-Life Extension' in *Defense News*, 2 May 2015 (Springfield VA: Gannett Government Media, 2015) and subsequently picked up by a number of Canadian media outlets.

8. The revisions to counting rules, the first since a change in the Reagan-era in 1981, were intended to count ships that were readily deployable overseas and contributed to overseas combat capability. Whilst they were seen by many as a fudge to hide declining fleet numbers – particularly as the new methodology would have included some ships the navy proposed to place in reserve – the new and older counting rules would probably have balanced out over time. A good review of the debate was provided by Megan Eckstein of *USNI News* on 16 March 2015 in 'Battle Over How to Count Navy Ships is Confusing, But Not New', currently accessible at: http://news.usni.org/2015/03/16/battle-over-how-to-count-navy-ships-is-confusing-but-not-new

9. The overall FSA was set out in *Report to Congress: Navy Combatant Vessel Force Structure Requirement – January 2013* (Washington DC: US Navy, 2013). The recent revisions were explained in the yearly *Report to Congress on the Annual Long-Range Plan for Construction of Naval Vessels – March 2015* (Washington DC: US Navy, 2015). Ronald O'Rourke's periodically updated *Navy Force Structure and Shipbuilding Plans: Background and Issues for Congress* (Washington DC: Congressional Research Service) and available on the FAS website provides a good explanation of the various trends and issues arising from these reports.

10. Congress had already allocated some funding towards the RCOH in the approved FY2015 budget and the FY2016 request completes the work. The carrier force's current ten-strong force level has been allowed for by a temporary relaxation of the legislation setting the size of the carrier force (eleven ships are mandated) pending *Gerald R Ford*'s delivery. A full review of current issues relating to the US

Navy's carrier fleet is contained in Ronald O' Rourke's regularly updated *Navy Ford (CVN-78) Class Aircraft Carrier Program: Background and Issues for Congress RS20643* (Washington DC: Congressional Research Service), again hosted on the FAS website.

11. Raytheon describes AMDR as the US Navy's 'first truly scalable radar', being comprised of individual building blocks known as Radar Modular Assemblies (RMAs). Each RMA is a self-contained radar emitter and receiver in a 2ft x 2ft x 2ft box. The RMAs stack together to meet the required array size of any ship. A detailed review of the steps required to fit the new radar into the *Arleigh Burke* design was provided by Richard Scott in 'Beneath the skin', *Jane's Defence Weekly*, 27 May 2015 (Coulsdon: IHS Jane's, 2015), pp.24–8.

12. The overall mobile landing platform programme was described in detail by Scott Truver in 'Montford Point (MPL-1) Class: A "Sea Base" coming to a Theatre near you', *Seaforth World Naval Review 2015* (Barnsley, Seaforth Publishing, 2014), pp.140–55.

13. The *Ohio* class originally comprised eighteen strategic submarines but the oldest four have been converted as guided-missile submarines with a potential load-out of 154 Tomahawk cruise missiles.

14. Inigo Guevara of *Jane's Defence Weekly* has produced two reports highlighting the Mexican Navy's procurement objectives. Detailed programme details were contained in 'Mexico reveals navy shipbuilding details' published in the 24 June 2015 edition, p.5. In addition, a broader review was contained within a briefing on Latin American naval forces entitled 'Open waters' in the 5 November 2014 edition, pp.24–31. Both Coulsdon: IHS Jane's.

15. The Portuguese-language *Poder Naval* website at www.naval.com.br continues to remain an authoritative source of information on Brazilian Navy developments.

16. Readers are directed to the Spanish language websites infodefensa.com and defensa.com for ongoing news of Latin American naval developments.

Author:
Conrad Waters

2.2 REGIONAL REVIEW

ASIA AND THE PACIFIC

INTRODUCTION

It remains difficult to analyse naval developments in Asia and the Pacific with reference to anything other than Chinese actions. There are two obvious reasons for this. One is the ability of China's successful economy to support the progressive modernisation and strengthening of its armed forces, with its capability in the maritime domain an increasing preoccupation. This was a particular emphasis in the country's most recent defence white paper, *China's Military Strategy*, which was published in May 2015.[1] Stating that, 'The traditional mentality that land outweighs sea must be abandoned …', the white paper declares, 'It is necessary for China to develop a modern maritime military force structure … so as to provide strategic support for building itself into a maritime power.' In line with this objective, the People's Liberation Army Navy (PLAN) is steadily shifting from its previous concentration on 'offshore waters defence' to a more balanced structure where blue-water naval capabilities – 'open seas protection' – are accorded equal priority. This balanced approach has already been evident in Chinese naval construction for some time. For example, series production of offshore defence vessels such as the most recent Type 056 corvettes is replicated in the ongoing delivery of larger, ocean-going Type 054A frigates and Type 052C/D series destroyers.

The second reason for China's overwhelming significance in any overview of the regional naval picture is its assertive stance towards disputed maritime boundaries. Whilst such unresolved territorial disagreements remain relatively common in Asian waters, the extent of China's claims in both the East and South China Seas are the source of actual or potential tension with many of its neighbours. The last twelve months have seen China's infamous 'nine dash line' claim in the South China Sea return to prominence. This has primarily been due to its attempts to develop a network of island bases amongst the sea's disputed reefs and shoals through a major land reclamation programme.[2] This unilateral changing of the status quo has resulted in a hardening of attitudes towards China amongst those Association of Southeast Asian Nations (ASEAN) countries not directly involved in the dispute and an intensification of United States' efforts to rebuild its presence in the region. However, in practical terms, it seems little can be done to alter China's de facto realisation of its territorial ambitions.

More broadly, however, China's actions are leading to a progressive redrawing of the East Asian diplomatic map, bringing together countries that have reasons for concern over how far their larger neighbour's ambitions may extend. Whilst most commentary has focused on the steps taken by the United States to strengthen its regional alliances, the steady development of political and military ties at a local level is also significant. Most notably, Japan – locked in its own territorial dispute with China over the Senkaku/Diaoyutai Islands – has been using its overseas aid programme to support the delivery of coast guard patrol vessels to the Philippines and Vietnam on favourable terms.[3] Japan has also recently held its first-ever training exercise with the Philippine Navy and has been reported as considering regular air and sea patrols in the region. Doubtless part of Japan's thinking is a desire to avoid being isolated with respect to its own dispute once China has 'picked off' weaker opponents to its claims.

Regional tensions continue to fuel local naval construction programmes, particularly the acquisition of 'high end' capabilities such as aviation-capable and amphibious shipping, as well as of submarines. This is resulting in a debate in some countries over the extent to which naval projects should be used to create and support a local shipbuilding industry in spite of the potentially higher costs associated with establishing such a sovereign capability. In general, the political decision has tended to favour the industrial – and employment – argument, sometimes in opposition to naval commanders with reservations over the ability of local yards to execute contracts to the required timescales and quality. The argument remains finely balanced in Australia, where problems with delivery of *Hobart* class destroyers and evidence that local-build adds a 30 to 40 per cent premium to programme costs is taking place against the backdrop of local industry facing a 'valley of death' from a gap in orders. Although large submarine and frigate projects are likely to be confirmed in the forthcoming defence white paper, facilities such as BAE System's large Williamstown shipyard in Melbourne are already at the point of closure as work has dried up.[4]

The Philippine Navy's frigate *Ramon Alcaraz*, the former US Coast Guard high endurance cutter *Dallas*, exercising with the JMSDF destroyer *Hatakaze* in September 2014. Fear of China's assertive stance towards maritime boundary claims is leading to greater military co-operation between other countries in the region. *(Royal Australian Navy)*

Table 2.2.1: FLEET STRENGTHS IN ASIA AND THE PACIFIC – LARGER NAVIES (MID 2015)

COUNTRY	AUSTRALIA	CHINA	INDONESIA	JAPAN	S KOREA	SINGAPORE	TAIWAN	THAILAND
Aircraft Carrier (CV)	–	1	–	–	–	–	–	–
Support/Helicopter Carrier (CVS/CVH)	–	–	–	3	–	–	–	1
Strategic Missile Submarine (SSBN)	–	4	–	–	–	–	–	–
Attack Submarine (SSN)	–	6	–	–	–	–	–	–
Patrol Submarine (SSK/SS)	6	50	2	16	13	4	4	–
Fleet Escort (DDG/FFG)	12	60	6	38	23	6	24	8
Patrol Escort/Corvette (FFG/FSG/FS)	–	35	26	6	19	6	1	11
Missile Armed Attack Craft (PGG/PTG)	–	75	20	6	17	–	c.30	6
Mine Countermeasures Vessel (MCMV)	6	25	11	28	9	4	10	6
Major Amphibious Units (LHD/LPD/LSD)	1	3	5	3	1	4	1	1

Notes: Chinese numbers approximate; Some additional Indonesian patrol gunboats are able to ship missiles; Taiwan's submarines are reported to have limited operational availability.

MAJOR REGIONAL POWERS – AUSTRALIA

The Royal Australian Navy is starting to see the benefits of defence decisions taken over a decade ago with the commissioning of the new amphibious assault ship *Canberra* on 28 November 2014. Heralded by the 2000 Defence White Paper and acquired under project JP2048 Phase 4A/B, the new ship is the first of two built to Spain's *Juan Carlos I* design and is the largest front-line warship ever operated by the Royal Australian Navy. The AU$3bn (c. US$2.4bn) programme, under which the ships' hulls were constructed in Spain prior to delivery to BAE Systems in Melbourne for fitting out, has run largely to cost and schedule. Work on sister-ship *Adelaide* is now close to completion and she commenced sea trials in mid-June 2015 prior to a planned 2016 commissioning.

As indicated previously, progress on the SEA 4000 project for three *Hobart* class AWD air-warfare destroyers has been much less straightforward. The lead ship was finally launched from shipbuilder ASC's facility near Adelaide on 23 May 2015 but will not now be delivered until June 2017, some two and a half years behind the original schedule. Delays in constructing the two other ships in the class are comparable, if not greater and the programme is also running around AUS$1.2bn over its c. AUS$58bn (c. US$6.3bn) original budget. The extent of the problems has been such that the former Australian Defence Minister David Johnston memorably stated that he would not trust ASC 'to build a canoe'.[5] New management has been brought into the company to improve performance and a tender is underway to select an industrial partner to help manage the project through to completion.

Meanwhile, the existing fleet is benefitting from the steady delivery of modernised *Anzac* class ships. These are being fitted with the CEAFAR/ CEAMOUNT phased-array combination and

The first of the Royal Australian Navy's new air-warfare destroyers, *Hobart*, pictured under construction at the ASC yard near Adelaide in October 2014. She was launched in the following May but her delivery is running over two and a half years behind the original schedule. There is currently considerable debate in Australia as to how the navy's longer-term construction needs should be addressed. *(AWD Alliance)*

upgraded Saab combat management systems that are also scheduled to equip the new frigates. Half of the class have now received the upgrade following the completion of work on *Warramunga* in the first half of 2015. *Anzac* herself embarked on a 'Northern Trident' deployment to the Mediterranean and Northern Europe; the first time since 2005 that the Royal Australian Navy has travelled so far from home. The frigate was accompanied by her New Zealand sister *Te Kaha* and the replenishment tanker *Success* for part of the voyage, the three ships repre-

senting their countries at a series of commemorations surrounding the centenary of the formation of the Australian and New Zealand Army Corps (ANZAC) and its involvement in the Gallipoli campaign of 1915.

Table 2.2.2 summarises principal Royal Australian Navy fleet units as of mid-2015. Of these ships, the FFG-7 type frigate *Sydney* completed her last voyage on 27 February 2015 and is being used as an alongside training ship until being decommissioned at the end of the year. The fleet also lost one

Table 2.2.2: ROYAL AUSTRALIAN NAVY: PRINCIPAL UNITS AS AT MID 2015

TYPE	CLASS	NUMBER	TONNAGE	DIMENSIONS	PROPULSION	CREW	DATE
Principal Surface Escorts							
Frigate – FFG	**ADELAIDE** (FFG-7)	4	4,200 tons	138m x 14m x 5m	COGAG, 30 knots	210	1980
Frigate – FFG	**ANZAC**	8	3,600 tons	118m x 15m x 4m	CODOG, 28 knots	175	1996
Submarines							
Submarine – SSK	**COLLINS**	6	3,400 tons	78m x 8m x 7m	Diesel-electric, 20 knots	45	1996
Major Amphibious Units							
Amph Assault Ship – LHD	**CANBERRA** (JUAN CARLOS I)	1	27,100 tons	231m x 32m x 7m	IEP, 21 knots	290	2014

The modernisation of the *Anzac* class is proceeding according to plan, with half of the eight Australian ships having completed modernisation. These April 2015 images show *Parramatta* (154) about to undergo the modernisation and *Warramunga* (152) about to be re-launched after her new mast and associated radar equipment had been installed. *Warramunga* also carries the new Royal Australian Navy 'haze grey' colour scheme in place of the greenish-tinted 'storm grey' previously adopted in the 1950s. *(Royal Australian Navy)*

of its *Armidale* class patrol vessels after *Bundaberg* was decommissioned in December 2014 after a major fire whilst under refit. The three remaining *Balikpapan* class landing craft – all well over forty years old – were decommissioned as planned the previous month but have been transferred to Papua New Guinea and the Philippines to continue their careers under other flags.

The forthcoming white paper, scheduled for publication before the end of 2015, will have a significant impact on the future of both the Royal Australian Navy and the local shipbuilding industry. The big decisions that need to be taken relate to replacements for the existing *Collins* class submarines (Project SEA 1000) and *Anzac* class frigates (Project SEA 5000). The former programme originates from 2007 and, at one time, it was planned to start construction in 2016. There has been considerable debate about both the nature of the design to be selected and also the extent of local

The amphibious ships *Tobruk* and *Canberra* anchored in Sydney Harbour in June 2015. The new *Canberra* was commissioned in November 2014 whilst the elderly *Tobruk* is due to decommission at the end of July 2015. *(Royal Australian Navy)*

industrial involvement. The latest stage in a lengthy saga was reached on 20 February 2015 with the release of a ministerial statement about the project's future direction. Companies from France, Germany and Japan will be invited to participate in a competitive evaluation process taking place over a ten-month period to select a partner to take the programme forward. There is no certainty that any of the new boats will be constructed in Australia, with options for design and build locally, overseas or under a hybrid approach all up for consideration. The new submarines will have to provide a range and endurance similar to the existing submarines, as well as improved sensor performance and stealth characteristics. There is a strong preference to use the existing US Navy-based combat system and heavyweight torpedo. Current Australian Prime Minister Tony Abbott has previously been reported

as a strong proponent of the Japanese *Soryu* class in the past and many see them as favourite to win the deal.[6]

There seems to be a greater willingness to continue local production of surface ships in spite of the *Hobart* class's problems but this seems to rely on establishing the feasibility of a continuous build strategy to avoid the issues that inevitably arise from peaks and troughs in construction. A report by the US Rand Corporation released in April 2015 suggests the current 30 to 40 per cent premium for local build could be reduced by, *inter alia*, more predictable and steady production schedules.[7] Suggestions to balance out the current gap in orders include construction of a fourth *Hobart* class destroyer, accelerating the new frigates so as to start build by 2018 and advancing orders for a planned new class of offshore patrol vessels. Orders for two

new replenishment ships are also imminent but it has already been decided it would be uneconomic to build these in Australia.

MAJOR REGIONAL POWERS – CHINA

To some extent, the last year has been a case of 'more of the same' so far as China is concerned. Continued low-level territorial disputes have been largely prosecuted by the white-hulled ships of the State Oceanic Administration controlled coast guard, whilst an ongoing series of international deployments by PLAN warships has steadily enhanced blue-water capabilities. It can be difficult to recall that it was only in December 2008 – less than seven years ago – that the PLAN first embarked on its anti-piracy mission to the Gulf of Aden; an operation that has been maintained on a continuous basis ever since. One notable development occurred in April 2015

Table 2.2.3: PEOPLE'S LIBERATION ARMY NAVY: PRINCIPAL UNITS AS AT MID 2015

TYPE	CLASS	NUMBER	TONNAGE	DIMENSIONS	PROPULSION	CREW	DATE
Aircraft Carriers							
Aircraft Carrier – CV	Project 1143.5/6 **LIAONING** (Kuznetsov)	1	60,000 tons	306m x 35/73m x 10m	Steam, 32 knots	Unknown	2012
Principal Surface Escorts							
Destroyer – DDG	Type 052D **KUNMING** ('Luyang III')	2	7,500 tons	156m x 17m x 6m	CODOG, 28 knots	280	2014
Destroyer – DDG	Type 051C **SHENYANG** ('Luzhou')	2	7,100 tons	155m x 17m x 6m	Steam, 29 knots	Unknown	2006
Destroyer – DDG	Type 052C **LANZHOU** ('Luyang II')	6	7,000 tons	154m x 17m x 6m	CODOG, 28 knots	280	2004
Destroyer – DDG	Type 052B **GUANGZHOU** ('Luyang I')	2	6,500 tons	154m x 17m x 6m	CODOG, 29 knots	280	2004
Destroyer – DDG	Project 956E/EM **HANGZHOU** (Sovremenny)	4	8,000 tons	156m x 17m x 6m	Steam, 32 knots	300	1999
Destroyer – DDG	Type 051B **SHENZHEN** ('Luhai')	1	6,000 tons	154m x 16m x 6m	Steam, 31 knots	250	1998
Destroyer – DDG	Type 052 **HARBIN** ('Luhu')	2	4,800 tons	143m x 15m x 5m	CODOG, 31 knots	260	1994
Plus c. 5 additional obsolescent destroyers of Type 051 **JINAN** ('Luda') class							
Frigate – FFG	Type 054A **XUZHOU** ('Jiangkai II')	19	4,100 tons	132m x 15m x 5m	CODAD, 28 knots	190	2008
Frigate – FFG	Type 054 **MA'ANSHAN** ('Jiangkai I')	2	4,000 tons	132m x 15m x 5m	CODAD, 28 knots	190	2005
Frigate – FFG	Type 053 H2G/H3 **ANQING** ('Jiangwei I/II')	14	2,500 tons	112m x 12m x 5m	CODAD, 27 knots	170	1992
Frigate – FSG	Type 056 **BENGBU** ('Jiangdao')	23+	1,500 tons	89m x 12m x 4m	CODAD, 28 knots	60	2013
Plus c.10 additional obsolescent frigates of Type 053 H/H1/H1G/H2 **XIAMEN** ('Jianghu') classes							
Submarines							
Submarine – SSBN	Type 094 ('Jin')	3+	9,000 tons	133m x 11m x 8m	Nuclear, 20+ knots	Unknown	2008
Submarine – SSBN	Type 092 ('Xia')	1	6,500 tons	120m x 10m x 8m	Nuclear, 22 knots	140	1987
Submarine – SSN	Type 093 ('Shang')	3+	6,000 tons	107m x 11m x 8m	Nuclear, 30 knots	100	2006
Submarine – SSN	Type 091 ('Han')	3	5,500 tons	106m x 10m x 7m	Nuclear, 25 knots	75	1974
Submarine – SSK	Type 039A/039B (Type 041 'Yuan')	12+	2,500 tons	75m x 8m x 5m	AIP, 20+ knots	Unknown	2006
Submarine – SSK	Type 039/039G ('Song')	13	2,300 tons	75m x 8m x 5m	Diesel-electric, 22 knots	60	1999
Submarine – SSK	Project 877 EKM/636 ('Kilo')	12	3,000 tons	73m x 10m x 7m	Diesel-electric, 20 knots	55	1995
Plus c.15 obsolescent patrol submarines of the Type 035 ('Ming' class). A Type 032 'Qing' trials submarine has also been commissioned.							
Major Amphibious Units							
Landing Platform Dock	Type 071 **KULUN SHAN** ('Yuzhao')	3	18,000 tons	210m x 27m x 7m	CODAD, 20 knots	Unknown	2007

when the Type 054A frigate *Linyi*, participating in the deployment, rescued foreign nationals from Yemen's civil war. It was reported that this was the first time China's military had helped other countries evacuate their citizens during an international crisis.[8]

Construction programmes have also followed a relatively steady path, with the growing maturity of the country's naval shipbuilding sector reflected in the continued series production of a number of largely standardised designs. Developments with respect to the major warship categories are summarised below, whilst Table 2.2.3 provides an overview of PLAN fleet strength.[9]

Aircraft Carriers and Amphibious Ships: It is now nearly three years since China's first carrier, *Liaoning*, was commissioned. She continues to take part in an ongoing series of tests and trials – interspersed with lengthy periods of maintenance and repairs – as the PLAN slowly but steadily develops carrier-operating skills. Chinese media have stated that over 100 different scientific tests have been completed during this time. Recent reports also suggest that production variants of the Shenyang J-15 are now starting to be embarked on training deployments, the latest of which commenced in early June 2015.

There have been numerous reports on the construction of a second aircraft carrier, the first built from the keel-up in China, with Guangzhou (Canton) rather than the more likely choice of Dalian now being named as a possible construction site. However, tangible details about the programme are virtually non-existent as Chinese officials try to hide as much as possible from the public eye.

Meanwhile, construction of amphibious shipping has recommenced, with a fourth Type 071 amphibious transport dock, reportedly named *Tanggula Shan*, launched in January 2015. At least two more of the class (to make six in total) are said to be under assembly, whilst fabrication of the smaller Type 072A 'Yuzhao' tank landing ships has also recommenced. These might be needed to help support the increasing number of garrisons in the South China Sea. The same explanation may account for the appearance of a new mobile landing platform similar to the US Navy's *Montford Point* (MLP-1) class. There still appear to be longer-term plans to field a LHD-type amphibious assault ship; a strategy given more credence by reports that research into an indigenous short take-off and vertical landing (STOVL) design is underway.

The Chinese Type 052C destroyer *Haikou* pictured operating in the Indian Ocean during 2014. Construction of this class has now finished with completion of the sixth vessel but deliveries of an improved Type 052D variant are underway. *(Royal Australian Navy)*

Major Surface Combatants: Construction of surface warships continues to follow three main strands, encompassing destroyers, frigates and corvettes. Following the delivery of the sixth and final Type 052C 'Luyang II' type destroyer, *Xi'an*, in the first half of 2015, production in this category is now focused on the improved Type 052D 'Luyang III' type. In contrast to the earlier variant, this is being produced at Dalian as well as the Jiangnan facility at Shanghai, allowing more rapid delivery of a class that is reported to number around twelve units. Of these, the lead ship, *Kunming*, was delivered in March 2014 and at least two others are expected to be commissioned by the end of 2015. In the medium-term, production is likely to shift to the larger, cruiser-sized Type 055, which is also likely to be built in two yards.

The PLAN's satisfaction with the Type 054A 'Jiangkai II' frigates is indicated by ongoing production of the class, which now looks set to extend to a total of at least twenty-four ships. Production has been evenly split between the Huangpu yard in Guangzhou and the Hudong facility in Shanghai, which have delivered nineteen of the class in total to date. The latest ships incorporate some improvements over the earlier ships, including incorporation of variable-depth sonar (VDS) and an upgraded close-in weapons system (CIWS). The PLAN's anti-submarine capabilities are generally regarded as having lagged their proficiency in anti-surface and anti-air warfare so this development may go some way to closing this gap.[10] There have also been reports of a planned switch to a further-enhanced Type 054B design, which could incorporate an acoustically stealthier diesel-electric propulsion system.

The third strand of surface combatant construction is focused on the Type 056 corvette, which is being churned out in rapid order by no fewer than four shipbuilders. Around twenty-three of the class, focused on littoral warfare, have been delivered to date and Western intelligence estimates predict a total class of between thirty and sixty units. Some of these will be of a Type 056A variant equipped with a VDS system similar to that found on the modified Type 054A frigates to supplement the hull-mounted sonar found on all the class. The corvette design is also proving popular in overseas markets, with Bangladesh and Nigeria both having acquired export variants of the type.

Submarines: There continues to be far less visibility surrounding Chinese submarine construction compared with that of surface warships. It appears that three Type 094 'Jin' class strategic missile submarines are currently in service and that they will soon be joined by another pair. These are in the final stages of fitting out at the Huludao yard in the north of the country. Recent US Navy intelligence assessments now indicate that a total of as many of eight of this type may be built. Construction of the Type 093 nuclear-powered attack submarines has also resumed after a considerable gap. US Navy sources suggest that four of an improved Type 093B variant will join the pair of older boats. Of these new submarines, one is already reported to be undergoing sea trials, with a further two launched and now fitting-out. The current generation of Chinese nuclear-powered vessels are believed still to lag the acoustic properties of more recent 'Western' designs. Accordingly, transition to improved Type 095 and

The Type 903A replenishment ship *Chao Hu*, which entered service at the end of 2013. Lack of support ships is a constraint on PLAN deployments and Type 903A vessels are now being built in quantity to fill the gap. *(Conrad Waters)*

have been confirmed. As for nuclear construction, the PLAN seems to be taking time to evaluate the performance of existing submarines before attempting to incorporate improved acoustic performance in the next generation of boats.

Other Warships: The most significant development amongst other warship construction is the accelerated production of the Type 903A variant of the 'Fuchi' class replenishment ships. As of June 2015, no fewer than four of these ships (taking the Type 903/903A class to a total of eight) were in the course of being fitted out at the GSI yard in Guangzhou, reflecting the priority the PLAN is giving to improving its deployment capabilities.

A wide range of other minor and support vessels are in the course of assembly for both the PLAN and coast guard. The latter's most eye-catching programme is for two new oceanic-sized patrol cutters of around 10,000 tons displacement. Armed with a medium-calibre gun and capable of carrying at least two helicopters and several fast interceptors, the new ships are reported as having a range in excess of 10,000 miles to support extended patrols at the edges of China's claimed maritime zones.

Type 096 designs still seems likely once the current generation of boats has been evaluated.

Recent news on conventional submarine programmes has been even more sparse, although previous reports of construction of an improved Type 039C variant of the Type 039A/041 'Yuan'

Table 2.2.4: JAPAN MARITIME SELF-DEFENCE FORCE: PRINCIPAL UNITS AS AT MID 2015

TYPE	CLASS	NUMBER	TONNAGE	DIMENSIONS	PROPULSION	CREW	DATE
Support and Helicopter Carriers							
Helicopter Carrier – DDH	IZUMO (DDH-183)	1	27,000 tons	248m x 38m x 7m	COGAG, 30 knots	470	2015
Helicopter Carrier – DDH	HYUGA (DDH-181)	2	19,000 tons	197m x 33m x 7m	COGAG, 30 knots	340	2009
Principal Surface Escorts							
Helicopter Destroyer – DDH	SHIRANE (DDH-143)	1	7,500 tons	159m x 18m x 5m	Steam, 32 knots	350	1980
Destroyer – DDG	ATAGO (DDG-177)	2	10,000 tons	165m x 21m x 6m	COGAG, 30 knots	300	2007
Destroyer – DDG	KONGOU (DDG-173)	4	9,500 tons	161m x 21m x 6m	COGAG, 30 knots	300	1993
Destroyer – DDG	HATAKAZE (DDG-171)	2	6,300 tons	150m x 16m x 5m	COGAG, 30 knots	260	1986
Destroyer – DD	AKIZUKI (DD-115)	4	6,800 tons	151m x 18m x 5m	COGAG, 30 Knots	200	2012
Destroyer – DDG	TAKANAMI (DD-110)	5	5,300 tons	151m x 17m x 5m	COGAG, 30 knots	175	2003
Destroyer – DDG	MURASAME (DD-101)	9	5,200 tons	151m x 17m x 5m	COGAG, 30 knots	165	1996
Destroyer – DDG	ASAGIRI (DD-151)	8	4,300 tons	137m x 15m x 5m	COGAG, 30 knots	220	1988
Destroyer – DDG	HATSUYUKI (DD-122)	3 (3)	3,800 tons	130m x 14m x 4m	COGOG, 30 knots	200	1982
Frigate – FFG	ABUKUMA (DE-229)	6	2,500 tons	109m x 13m x 4m	CODOG, 27 knots	120	1989
Submarines							
Submarine – SSK	SORYU (SS-501)	6	4,200 tons	84m x 9m x 8m	AIP, 20 knots+	65	2009
Submarine – SSK	OYASHIO (SS-590)	10 (1)	4,000 tons	82m x 9m x 8m	Diesel-electric, 20 knots+	70	1998
Submarine – SSK	HARUSHIO (SS-583)	0 (1)	3,300 tons	77m x 10m x 8m	Diesel-electric, 20 knots+	75	1990
Major Amphibious Units							
Landing Platform Dock – LPD	OSUMI (LST-4001)	3	14,000 tons	178m x 26m x 6m	Diesel, 22 knots	135	1998

Note: Figures in brackets refer to trials or training ships.

MAJOR REGIONAL POWERS – JAPAN

Japan's armed forces are continuing to evolve as the country steadily loosens the constraints imposed on its military posture by the pacifist Article 9 of the Japanese Constitution. A significant – and controversial – revision to the previous constitutional understanding occurred in July 2014 when the current administration led by Prime Minister Shinzo Abe approved a re-interpretation of the article to allow the right of collective self-defence, i.e. the right to assist a friendly country under attack. The move was welcomed by the United States – the most likely beneficiary of the change – but drew criticism elsewhere, including from China and South Korea.[11]

The Japan Maritime Self Defence Force (JMSDF) is steadily acquiring enhanced capabilities that, arguably, better reflect the greater flexibility they will be allowed. The most significant development over the past year was the commissioning of the new 'helicopter-carrying destroyer' *Izumo* (DDH-183) on 25 March 2015. The first of two ships, she is a much enlarged version of the previous *Hyuga* (DDH-181) class and has replaced the 35-year-old *Shirane* (DDH-143). Her large, through-length flight deck is capable of operating five large helicopters simultaneously and she has better facilities for handling amphibious missions. There has been much speculation about her potential ability to operate the STOVL 'B' variant of the F-35 Lightning II Joint Strike Fighter. However, her increased aviation capabilities have been achieved at the expense of reducing some other capabilities. For example, the SeaRAM close-in weapons system (CIWS) replaces the more capable Mk 41 vertical-launch system and ESSM/ASROC missiles found on *Hyuga*, whilst her sonar system has also been simplified.

March also saw the delivery of the *Soryu* class submarine, *Kokuryu,* the sixth of the class to enter service. However, there has not yet been any tangible evidence of progress towards increasing the size of the submarine flotilla's existing sixteen boats (plus

Two images of the new JMSDF 'helicopter-carrying destroyer' *Izumo*, which entered service in March 2015. The carrier-like vessel is the largest front-line warship operated by Japan since the end of the Second World War and is capable of supporting anti-submarine and amphibious missions. There has been speculation she might operate F-35B Joint Strike Fighters in due course. *(JMSDF)*

Table 2.2.5: RECENT JMSDF WARSHIP PROCUREMENT

FINANCIAL YEAR	2006	2007	2008	2009	2010	2011	2012	2013	2014	2015
Helicopter Destroyer (DDH)	1	0	0	0	1	0	1	0	0	0
Aegis Destroyer (DDG)	0	0	0	0	0	0	0	0	0	1[1]
Destroyer (DD)	0	1	1	2	0	0	0	1	1	0
Submarine (SSK)	1	1	1	0	1	1	1	1	1	1
Minesweeper (MCMV)	1	0	1	1	0	1	0	1	1	0
Auxiliary Ships	0	1	0	1	0	0	0	0	1	0
Total	3	3	3	4	2	2	2	3	4	2
Cost: Yen M	169,500	144,800	135,700	189,100	166,700	72,000	170,200	141,500	193,000	232,300

Note

1: Includes equipment for a second destroyer

two training vessels) towards the planned force of twenty-two submarines.

The FY2015 defence budget reflects the priorities contained in the *National Security Strategy* and *National Defense Program Guidelines* for FY2014 and beyond approved at the end of 2013.[12] A small but significant increase in overall defence spending is helping to fund a number of naval programmes. Most notably, these include resumed construction of Aegis-equipped destroyers, the acquisition of an eleventh *Soryu* class submarine and a bulk buy of Kawasaki P-1 maritime patrol aircraft. Further money is allocated for the life-extension of existing ships. Other purchases, including an initial buy of V-22 Osprey tilt-rotors for the Japan Ground Self Defence Force (JGSDF) – intended to help protect the remote southern islands in the event of Chinese attack – also have implications for the maritime force structure. The budget provided some interesting insights into future planned programmes. For example, money is allocated towards overseas studies of LHD-type, multi-purpose amphibious ships and to domestic research into a new 'compact-hulled' destroyer with an associated 'downsized' multi-function radar system.

MAJOR REGIONAL POWERS – SOUTH KOREA

The Republic of Korea Navy is coming to rival the JMSDF in regional terms, although the ongoing and very real threat posed by the inherently unstable North Korea means that its priorities are a little different. More specifically, there is a degree of tension between its ambitions to become a global 'blue-water' maritime power and the need to continue to invest in units focused on littoral warfare to guard against the threat of incursion from

its neighbour. The latter requirement has been taking priority since the loss of the corvette *Cheonan* to a suspected North Korean torpedo in 2010. North Korea's nuclear programme has also focused attention on the threat close to home, reflected in the statement in the country's 2014 defence white paper that, 'The threat to security on the Korean peninsula has never been greater.'[13]

So far as the navy is concerned, the two most important surface ship programmes relating to the littoral continue to be for FFX *Incheon* class patrol frigates and PKX *Yoon Youngha* class fast attack craft. Delivery of the latter type – optimised for anti-surface warfare – is the more advanced. Seventeen out of a planned total of eighteen units

had been commissioned as of mid-2015. The last ship was damaged during a storm in late 2013 whilst under construction by STX and is still some way from completion.

The *Incheon* frigates class have a more general-purpose configuration, albeit with strong anti-submarine credentials that include a hull-mounted sonar, anti-submarine torpedo tubes and an embarked helicopter. Their 127mm main gun reflects their potential use in a shore bombardment role. Three out of a total of six Batch I ships have already been delivered, whilst work is already well underway on long-lead items for the first of eight Batch II vessels to be built by DSME. These will incorporate a vertical-launch system for anti-air and anti-submarine missiles, as well as a more efficient propulsion arrangement. The latter includes the replacement of two GE units by a single Rolls-Royce MT30 gas turbine but not, apparently, the full integrated electric propulsion that was previously reported. Approval for a Batch III, which is likely to encompass further improvements and will cost around US$3bn for six ships, has recently been given. The class are slowly replacing the 1980s-generation *Ulsan* and *Pohang* class escorts. *Ulsan* herself was the first of the former class (along with two more of the *Pohang* type) to be withdrawn from service when she decommissioned on 30 December 2014.

Republic of Korea Navy's PKX-type fast attack craft *Han Munsik* pictured during live-fire exercises in the middle of 2014. Seventeen out of a total class of eighteen ships have been delivered as part of a broader programme of improving South Korea's littoral warfare capabilities. *(Republic of Korea Navy)*

Table 2.2.6: REPUBLIC OF KOREA NAVY: PRINCIPAL UNITS AS AT MID 2015

TYPE	CLASS	NUMBER	TONNAGE	DIMENSIONS	PROPULSION	CREW	DATE
Principal Surface Escorts							
Destroyer – DDG	KDX-III **SEJONGDAEWANG-HAM**	3	10,000 tons	166m x 21m x 6m	COGAG, 30 knots	300	2008
Destroyer – DDG	KDX-II **CHUNGMUGONG YI SUN-SHIN**	6	5,500 tons	150m x 17m x 5m	CODOG, 30 knots	200	2003
Destroyer – DDG	KDX-I **GWANGGAETO-DAEWANG**	3	3,900 tons	135m x 14m x 4m	CODOG, 30 knots	170	1998
Frigate – FFG	FFX **INCHEON**	3	3,000 tons	114m x 14m x 4m	CODOG, 30 knots	140	2013
Frigate – FFG	**ULSAN**	8	2,300 tons	102m x 12m x 4m	CODOG, 35 knots	150	1981
Corvette – FSG	**POHANG**	19	1,200 tons	88m x 10m x 3m	CODOG, 32 knots	95	1984
Submarines							
Submarine – SSK	KSS-2 **SON WON-IL** (Type 214)	4	1,800 tons	65m x 6m x 6m	AIP, 20+ knots	30	2007
Submarine – SSK	KSS-1 **CHANG BOGO** (Type 209)	9	1,300 tons	56m x 6m x 6m	Diesel-electric, 22 knots	35	1993
Major Amphibious Units							
Amph Assault Ship – LHD	LPX **DOKDO**	1	18,900 tons	200m x 32m x 7m	Diesel, 22 knots	425	2007

Submarine production is also being accorded a relatively high priority. The second batch of locally-produced Type 214 air-independent propulsion (AIP) submarines is now starting to enter service, with *Kim Jwa-Jin* being commissioned at the end of 2014. Two of the remaining submarines from this six-boat batch have also now been launched and work is progressing on the other three units.

The focus on the littoral over the past few years has meant that funding for the 'blue water' fleet has been relatively scarce but the situation is starting to change. Notably, Hanjin Heavy Industries announced in early January that it had signed a long-awaited contract for a second *Dokdo* class amphibious assault ship on 23 December 2014. The value of the contract was reported at KRW417.5bn (c. US$375m) and the new ship, expected to be named *Marado*, should be delivered around the end of the decade. In the meantime, the first large tank landing ship of the *Cheon Wang Bong* class has now been commissioned, with the order for a second unit of a planned four-ship class confirmed at the end of 2013. The new ships have a full load displacement in excess of 7,000 tons and can deploy around 300 troops by landing craft and from a helicopter deck located at the aft of the ship.

The next planned project for larger surface escorts is for an additional three Aegis-equipped destroyers. The US Defense Security Co-operation Agency approved the potential sale of three Aegis systems and associated equipment for these ships at a total cost of US$1.9bn in June 2015, suggesting a formal construction order is imminent. It seems likely that these ships will be built to the existing KDX-III design but detailed improvements may be considered.

Korea is steadily modernising its amphibious forces, recently placing an order for a second *Dokdo* type amphibious assault ship. The first large tank landing ship of the *Cheon Wang Bong* class, seen at launch in September 2013, has also now been commissioned. *(Republic of Korea Navy)*

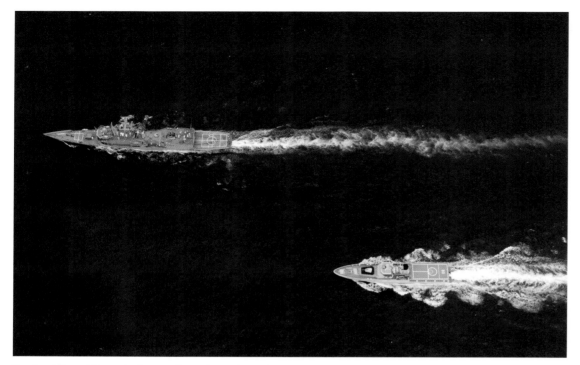

The Royal Brunei Navy missile-armed patrol vessel *Darulamam* pictured operating with the now-retired US Navy FFG-7 class frigate *Rodney M Davis* (FFG-60) in November 2014. Four of these large offshore patrol vessels – along with four coastal patrol ships – now comprise the core of Brunei's fleet. *(US Navy)*

A computer-generated image of the DCNS 'Gowind 2500' design selected for the Royal Malaysian Navy's 'Kedah 2' littoral combat ship programme. Displacing 3,000 tons and equipped with a powerful range of armament, these ships are effectively light frigates. *(DCNS)*

OTHER REGIONAL FLEETS

Brunei: The fourth *Darussalam* class offshore patrol vessel *Daruttaqwa* arrived in Brunei in the second half of 2014, completing the rebuilding of the fleet around a core of four large and four smaller patrol vessels. Two of the larger ships attended the US Navy-led RIMPAC 2014 exercise off Hawaii in mid-2014, successfully testing their Exocet missiles in a sinking exercise against a decommissioned landing craft.

Indonesia: A full review of recent developments in the Indonesian Navy is contained in Chapter 2.2A.

Malaysia: The Royal Malaysian Navy saw the official construction of its new 'Kedah 2' class frigates commence at Boustead Naval Shipyard in June 2015. The six new 'littoral combat ships' are based on the DCNS 'Gowind' 2500 design and are expected to be delivered from 2019 onwards. Displacing over 3,000 tons in full load condition and with a length of 111m, the new ships reportedly feature a diverse suite of equipment. This includes DCNS' SETIS combat system, Thales Nederland sensors, MBDA surface-to-air missiles, the Norwegian Kongsberg surface-to-surface missile system and a BAE Systems 57mm gun. The integration of this equipment may not necessarily be straightforward and it will be interesting to see whether the planned delivery date for the first of class is met. The new ships are significantly larger and more capable than the original 'Kedah 1' class corvettes built to the German MEKO-100. As such, they will essentially supplement the two *Lekiu* class frigates and two 'Scorpène' type submarines that currently form the core of the fleet's capabilities.

The navy is currently stretched in meeting a range of constabulary missions over a large exclusive economic zone. Whilst, therefore, new corvettes, helicopters and other equipment have been requested for incorporation in the next (2016–20) five-year Malaysia Plan, more focus appears to be placed on strengthening separate coast guard operations. Local build of BAE Systems' 'River' class offshore patrol vessels has been pitched as one potential contender for an enlarged constabulary force.[14]

New Zealand: The Royal New Zealand Navy spent much of 2014 finalising equipment choices for the mid-life upgrades of its two frigates. The updates will allow the current ships to serve until around

2030, when replacement ships are scheduled to enter service. In the meantime, the expected tender to replace the existing replenishment tanker *Endeavour* has now closed. A decision is expected before the end of 2015, with BMT/Daewoo and Rolls-Royce/Hyundai design/construction proposals believed to be amongst those on the table.

North Korea: The little-discussed Korean's People's Army Naval Force presents a largely asymmetrical threat to its southern neighbour, encompassing very large numbers of patrol submarines, small amphibious ships and coastal fast attack craft but little in the way of major surface combatants. Split into two fleet commands in the East and West Seas, its major tasks include coastal defence, co-operation with land forces and the prosecution of infiltration missions. A major extension to these potential roles was heralded in May 2015 with the announcement of a test firing of a submarine-launched ballistic missile. Whist many commentators have expressed doubt how far the new system's development may have progressed and, indeed, what precisely the images of the test that were released actually represented, they certainly represent a concerning development. If North Korea could deploy a submarine-launched nuclear missile, they would certainly take the threat posed by its nuclear weapons programme to a new level.

The Philippines: The extent of the challenge faced by the Philippine Navy in modernising its obsolete fleet into a more credible and cohesive force is, perhaps, reflected in the fact no fewer than nine of its fourteen largest surface combatants date back to the Second World War. Equally, not one of its warships has yet to be missile-armed. Significant efforts are being made to bring about the necessary upgrades in line with the 2012 'Philippine Fleet Desired Force Mix' that targets a balanced force of frigates, corvettes, patrol ships, amphibious and support units and, perhaps overly-ambitiously, submarines. However, progress is inevitably slow given the vast amount of equipment that needs to be upgraded. It is notable that many of the 'new' ships being obtained are second-hand veterans that would be considered life-expired by any major fleet.

The picture is, perhaps, brightest so far as the amphibious fleet is concerned. This is a key strategic priority given the extent of the Philippine archipelago, which comprises more than 7,000 separate

The Royal Australian Navy's *Anzac* (top) and *Success* (middle), along with the Royal New Zealand Navy's *Te Kaha* (bottom), pictured in the Mediterranean during their voyage to participate in the ANZAC centenary celebrations in April 2015. The Australian and New Zealand frigates are sister-ships but different approaches to mid-life upgrades is leading to significant differences in appearance. *(Royal Australian Navy)*

The Philippine Navy patrol frigates *Ramon Alcaraz* (foreground) and *Gregorio del Pilar* (behind) exercising with the US Navy destroyer *John S McCain* (DDG-56) in June 2014. The navy would like to acquire more of these ships as they decommission from the US Coast Guard if money can be found. *(US Navy)*

islands. Construction is now underway on two *Makassar* type amphibious transport docks ordered from the Indonesian yard of PT PAL in one of the navy's few new-build projects. The contract will fulfil half the requirement for four SSV strategic sea vessels set out in the 2012 force mix plan. Two former *Balikpapan* class heavy landing ships have also been donated by the Royal Australian Navy to join the mix of both new and older landing vessels of largely US origin that are already in service.

There has been less news with regard to the much-needed upgrade of the front-line surface force, which received a major boost with the transfer of two former US Coast Guard high endurance cutters of the *Hamilton* (WHEC-715) class during 2011–13. It is expected that more of the class will be acquired as they are withdrawn from United States' service and a tender has also been floated for two new-build vessels. The commissioning of a new replenishment tanker, *Lake Caliraya* – the navy's first – in May 2015 will increase the potential range of these and other existing patrol assets. Recently acquired Agusta Westland AW109E Power utility helicopters – for which armament packages have recently been purchased – are also now starting to be embarked on deployments of helicopter-capable vessels. However, the winner of a tender for anti-submarine helicopters has yet to be announced.

Singapore: The commissioning of the pair former of Swedish *Archer* class submarines in 2011 and 2013 has allowed the withdrawal of two of the older *Challenger* class boats. *Challenger* (the former *Sjöbjörnen*) and *Centurion* (the former *Sjöormen*) were both decommissioned on 11 March 2015, the lead boat's name being given to a new submarine training centre that was inaugurated on the same day. The remaining pair of *Challenger* class submarines will be replaced by the two new Type 218SG submarines currently under construction at Thyssen Krupp Marine Systems' HDW yard in Kiel. The new 70m-long AIP-equipped submarines will have eight torpedo tubes and displace around 2,000 tons.

Above the waves, the major surface construction programme is for eight new large, 80m patrol vessels to replace the eleven remaining, smaller 55m *Fearless* class units commissioned in the 1990s.[15] The new ships will be known as the *Independence* class. The keel of the lead ship was laid during a ceremony at builders ST Engineering (Marine) in September 2014 and launch is expected during the latter half of

2015 prior to a first quarter 2016 delivery. All eight of the class are expected to be in service by 2020. The new design has a displacement of 1,200 tons and incorporates a large flight deck as well as a 76mm gun and lighter weapons. A modular mission approach similar to that employed on the US Navy's Littoral Combat Ship will allow operation by a core crew of just thirty. They will be supplemented by up to an additional thirty personnel dependent on a ship's specific tasking.[16]

Taiwan: The pace of modernisation in Taiwan's Republic of China Navy continues to be dwarfed by the rapid transformation in the capabilities of the neighbouring PLAN. Although discussions continue on an indigenous submarine programme following the repeated failure of attempts to source technology from abroad, there is little evidence of tangible progress.

The surface fleet welcomed the arrival of the prototype *Tuo Chiang* (*Tuo River*) missile corvette, which was delivered at the end of December 2014 prior to formal commissioning the following March. A new fast combat support ship was commissioned on the same day. The new corvette is expected to be the first of a class of twelve 500-ton catamaran vessels that will be optimised for anti-surface warfare with a full load-out of sixteen surface-to-surface missiles. However, it is not clear whether work has yet started on the rest of the class.

Drawdown of the navy's eight former US Navy *Knox* (FF-1052) class frigates has commenced with the decommissioning of *Chi Yang* (the former *Robert E Peary*) and *Hai Yang* (the former *Barbey*) in May 2015.[17] Two former US Navy *Perry* (FFG-7) class frigates will arrive to replace them from 2016 but the navy is still debating whether to fund acquisition of a second pair that have also been offered for transfer.

Thailand: The Royal Thai Navy's current acquisition priority is a renewed attempt to create a submarine flotilla. Previous plans, most recently the proposed purchase of second-hand German Type 206A boats, have all foundered over doubts about the value of this very expensive capability given Thailand's largely shallow offshore waters. There has also been much criticism of the current plan. However, the navy seems determined to pursue its objectives, having already established a headquarters and training facility to prepare for the new boats. It appears that two or three submarines will be sought if approval is given, with yards from China, Europe, Russia and South Korea all vying for the order.

The main surface programme is the purchase of frigates from Korea's DSME, the first of which should be delivered by 2018. There has been no further news on additional orders for 'River' type OPVs of the *Krabi* type in spite of the success of the first locally-built ship in service.

The Republic of Singapore Navy frigate *Formidable* exercising with her Malaysian counterpart *Kasturi* in May 2014. With the creation of a modern frigate force completed some years ago, Singapore is now concentrating on the modernisation of underwater and littoral forces. *(Royal Australian Navy)*

Vietnam: Next to the Philippines, Vietnam is probably most impacted by China's expansionary stance in the South China Sea. Unlike the Philippine Navy, however, the Vietnam People's Navy is receiving sufficient funding to build a credible naval force. The last year has seen continued delivery of Russian-built Project 636 'Kilo' class submarines. Three out of the six boats are now in service and the fourth was in the course of delivery by heavy-lift ship as of mid-June 2015. Reportedly armed with both anti-shipping and land-attack variants of the Klub-S version

of the Russian 3M-54 (NATO SS-N-27B) anti-surface missile, the submarines could combine with Vietnam's powerful coastal batteries and surface ships to make life difficult for Chinese forces operating as far away as Hainan Island, or even beyond.

Surface construction is also progressing, with Vietnam reportedly in discussion with Russia to add a further pair of Project 1161.1E 'Gepard 3.9' type frigates to the two that were delivered in 2011 and the additional pair that are currently fitting out. The additional ships may replace plans for the local

construction of Damen 'Sigma' type corvettes, which do not – as yet – seem to have been formally contracted. Local production of Russian-designed Project 1241.8 'Molniya' fast attack corvettes is proceeding, with the third and fourth out of a planned total of six delivered in April 2015. Constabulary forces are also being strengthened, with the coast guard in the course of acquiring vessels from Japan and the United States. Purchases of maritime patrol aircraft also remain under consideration.

Notes:

1. See *China's Military Strategy* (Beijing: Ministry of National Defence, PRC, 2015). A copy can be accessed at: http://eng.mod.gov.cn/Database/WhitePapers/

2. A particularly comprehensive report can be found in James Hardy's 'Footprints in the sand', *Jane's Defence Weekly* – 15 February 2015 (Coulsdon: IHS Jane's, 2014), pp.22–9.

3. Japan's latest deal, which involves provision of a c. US$150m loan on favourable terms to allow the Philippines to acquire ten patrol vessels from Japanese industry, was signed by the two premiers on 4 June 2015 and has been widely reported. See Toko Sekiguchi's 'Japan to Provide Patrol Vessels to Philippines', *The Wall Street Journal* – 4 June 2015 (New York: Dow Jones & Company Inc., 2015).

4. On 16 June 2015, BAE Systems announced, in spite of earlier indications to the contrary, that it would not submit a bid for the new 'Pacific' patrol boat programme – previously seen as a lifeline for beleaguered local industry – because the Australian government wold not award the contract until 2017 and there was no work to sustain the shipyard in the interim. See Nick Toscano's 'Hundreds of jobs under threat in Melbourne's shipbuilding industry', *The Age* – 16 June 2015 (Melbourne: Fairfax Media, 2015).

5. Mr Johnston's remarks were widely criticised and he was subsequently forced to row back on them as a 'rhetorical flourish', as reported by Tom Shepherd in *The Advertiser* – 26 November 2014 (Adelaide: News Corporation 2015). Johnston was subsequently replaced in a cabinet reshuffle the following month.

6. It seems, however, that not everybody shares the Prime Minister's enthusiasm for the Japanese design. For example, see Tom Richardson's 'Defence hoses down PM's *Soryu* sub hype' on the *Indaily* news website (Adelaide: Solstice Media. 2015) at http://indaily.com.au/news/2015/05/25/defence-hoses-down-pms-soryu-sub-hype/

7. See the RAND report produced by a team headed by John Birkler and John F. Schank entitled, *Australia's Naval Shipbuilding Enterprise: Preparing for the 21st Century* (Santa Monica, CA: RAND Corporation, 2015). A copy of this lengthy report, which includes extensive comparisons with costs and timescales relating to European and American shipbuilding programmes, can currently be found at: http://www.rand.org/content/dam/rand/pubs/research_reports/RR1000/RR1093/RAND_RR1093.pdf

8. China's humanitarian activities were widely reported, for example by the BBC at: http://www.bbc.co.uk/news/world-middle-east-32173811

9. As always, accurate information on the PLAN is difficult to obtain and the table needs to be regarded with particular caution. Much of the information provided in this section is derived from web based sources. The *China Air and Naval Power* blog at http://china-pla.blogspot.co.uk/ and the *China Defense Blog* at http://china-defense.blogspot.co.uk/ remain particularly useful. The US Navy's Office of Naval Intelligence has also recently (in April 2015) published an updated assessment of Chinese naval capabilities *The PLA Navy: New Capabilities and Missions for the 21st Century* (Washington DC: Office of Naval Intelligence, 2015) which provides useful analytical material. It can currently be accessed via: http://www.oni.navy.mil/Intelligence_Community/china.html

10. More details on China's recent installation of variable depth sonar on frigates and corvettes can be found in Andrew Tate's 'China adds towed sonars to Type 054As', *Jane's Defence Weekly* – 3 September 2014 (Coulsdon: IHS Jane's, 2014), p.18.

11. Article 9 of the Japanese Constitution prohibits the country's recourse to war as a means of settling disputes and prohibits the maintenance of land, sea and air forces, although the latter has long been interpreted as allowing a purely defensive military. Reports suggest the more recent Japanese cabinet re-interpretation of the article will require

changes to a number of laws but not to the Constitution itself, which would require a larger majority. There has been considerable criticism of this sleight of hand, for example Craig Martin's '"Reinterpreting" Article 9 endangers Japan's rule of law', *The Japan Times* – 27 June 2014 (Tokyo: The Japan Times Ltd, 2014).

12. English translations of both these documents are located on the President of Japan and His Cabinet's website at http://japan.kantei.go.jp/96_abe/documents/2013/index.html. The *Defense Programs and Budget of Japan: Overview of FY2015 Budget* (Tokyo: Ministry of Defence, Japan, 2015) can be found at: http://www.mod.go.jp/e/d_budget/index.html

13. South Korea's lengthy *2014 Defense White Paper* (Seoul: Ministry of National Defense, Republic of Korea, 2015) lacks much of the detail of its shorter Japanese counterpart. A copy can be found at: http://www.mnd.go.kr/user/mnd_eng/upload/pblictn/PBLICTNEBOOK_201506161152304650.pdf

14. This potential sale was revealed by Ridzwan Rahmat and Dzirhan Mahadzir in 'BAE Systems showcases River-class OPV as an option for Malaysia's MMEA', *Jane's Navy International* – May 2015 (Coulsdon: IHS Jane's, 2015).

15. *Courageous*, the other member of an original twelve-ship class, was decommissioned after suffering severe damage in a collision in 2003.

16. Further details of the new ships can currently be found on the Republic of Singapore Navy's website at: http://www.mindef.gov.sg/navy/careers/our-assets/littoral-mission-vessel.html

17. The decommissionings were reported in *The China Post* (Taipei: The China Post Group, 2015) on 2 May 2015 under the headline, 'Taiwan retires two *Knox*-class frigates ahead of *Perry*-class additions'.

2.2A Fleet Review

Author:
Mrityunjoy Mazumdar

INDONESIA Lofty Ambitions tempered by Economic Realities

Indonesia – the world's largest archipelagic nation with a population of around 270 million and Asia Pacific's fifth largest economy – occupies a key geo-strategic location by dint of its location. Along with Singapore and Malaysia, the country straddles an important maritime choke-point at Malacca Straits on a sea route through which a large volume of trade flows from the Indian Ocean into the Pacific Ocean and South China Sea. Other lesser-known choke-points lie in Indonesian territorial waters at Lombok, Sunda and Makassar Straits.[1]

The Indonesian archipelago comprises around 17,500 islands in five large groups with a coastline of between 54,000km and 81,000km long (estimates vary). Indonesia claims an exclusive economic zone (EEZ) of around six million square kilometres, an archipelagic sea of three million square kilometres and a territorial sea of a third of a million square kilometres according to the Indonesian Navy, known as the *Tentara Nasional Indonesia Angkatan Laut* (TNIAL). Crucially, Indonesia's EEZ is replete with rich fish stocks as well as large oil and gas deposits, particularly in the Natuna Islands and the so called Ambalat block.

Indonesia has land borders with three countries – Malaysia, Papua New Guinea (PNG) and Timor Leste. It also has sea borders with seven additional countries – India, Thailand, Singapore, Vietnam, the Philippines, Palau and Australia. The country is an important player in the Association of South East Asian Nations (ASEAN) regional grouping. Jakarta's foreign policy has largely been variations on the 'non-aligned' foreign policy doctrine of *bebas aktif* (independent and active). This is consistent with its historical status as a founding member of the Non-Aligned Movement in 1961. Jakarta sees itself as a neutral party – an honest broker – in a region which is rife with contentious territorial disputes. However, a more assertive foreign policy is likely to emerge under the new President Mr Joko 'Jokowi' Widodo who assumed office from his predecessor Susilo Bambang Yudhoyuno, a former four-star general, in late 2014.

MARITIME SECURITY THREATS: A DOMINANT CONCERN

Absent serious land-based or internal security threats, Indonesia's security challenges are largely maritime in nature. Given Indonesia's geo-strategic location, disruption of the seaborne trade flows through the major Indonesian archipelagic sea lanes (or ALKI as the Indonesians refer to them) would have serious economic and geopolitical consequences. Ensuring freedom of navigation and the security of maritime trade through these vital but piracy prone Sea Lanes of Communication (SLOCs) is therefore a core task for the Indonesian Navy, and for an assortment of other Indonesian maritime security agencies. Indonesia's newly-announced coast guard or 'Maritime Security Board' (*Bakamla*) is an attempt to fix an otherwise dysfunctional maritime security apparatus that has hitherto been operating under the aegis of the *Bakorkamla* (Maritime Security Coordinating Board). This had tried, with limited success, to co-ordinate the activities of around a dozen disparate

The Indonesian Navy's missile-armed attack craft *Hiu*. The navy is largely focused on ensuring maritime security in the face of piracy, poaching, people trafficking and similar threats, maintaining a large force of mainly small ships to try to police the vast waters within its responsibility effectively. *(Royal Australian Navy)*

agencies. The net result of this state of affairs is that, by default, the TNIAL has been forced to pick up the slack in maritime security operations, thereby becoming the dominant player in ensuring Indonesia's maritime security.

Fears of international intervention in securing these SLOCS, particularly in the Malacca Straits, has prompted the creation of multinational initiatives with neighbouring countries. These include the Malacca Straits Sea Patrol (MSSP), Eye in the Sky (EiS) patrols and several other bilateral initiatives. Despite this, lingering regional suspicions about acceding control of territorial waters to neighbours hinder the effectiveness of these efforts, with the net result that piracy is actually on the rise in South East Asian (SEA) waters. This is particularly the case in Indonesia, which has registered the highest number of attacks in recent years.

Besides piracy, the major maritime security challenges include fish poaching, illegal logging, illegal emigration and human trafficking (including inflows of boat people from Bangladesh and of Rohingya from Myanmar, as well as outflows to Australia) and, to a lesser extent, drug trafficking. Fish poaching, in particular, is a huge economic problem. Another serious issue is the rising influence of Islamic State and associated extremist groups – posing a regional problem not only for Indonesia but also for Malaysia and the Philippines. Most of these issues have been difficult to tackle effectively given the geography of the country.

Insofar as threats from state actors are concerned, Indonesia does have lingering territorial disputes, particularly with Malaysia in the oil-rich Ambalat Block in the Celebes (Sulawesi) Sea. Malaysia is often cited as a source of a potential limited military conflict, yet there is a significant level of security co-operation with Malaysia too.

A bigger problem could potentially come from China's unilaterally declared nine-dashed line territorial claims in the South China Sea (SCS), which overlaps Indonesia's claimed EEZ in the resource-rich Natuna Islands. China's use of fishing fleets protected by large 'fisheries research vessels' and armed, white-hulled offshore patrol vessels of China's '*Weiquan*' or 'rights protection' fleet operating in waters falling within the nine-dashed line is becoming prevalent. Since 2010, there have been a number of incidents involving Chinese and Indonesian maritime security forces resulting in serious and potentially escalatory confrontations

Australian and Indonesian warships exercising together in the summer of 2013. In spite of concerns about compromising the sovereignty of its territorial waters, the nature of the Indonesian archipelago (there are borders with ten countries) means that maritime co-operation with neighbours is essential. *(Royal Australian Navy)*

within the overlap off Natuna. The most recent of these incidents, in March 2013, involved the use of the threat of force by a Chinese fisheries patrol vessel to compel a small Indonesian government patrol boat to release the crew of a Chinese fishing vessel it had arrested for illegal fishing. Indonesia does not publicly discuss these incidents; possibly out of concerns on the effect this might have on its image as a neutral party regarding the SCS claimants. At the same time, there is a growing realisation in Jakarta that the Natunas could become a potential flashpoint sooner rather than later. Recently, on 28 April 2015, the Indonesian naval chief Admiral Ade Supandi remarked 'Indonesia is facing strategic issues in the region which has the potential to become one of the conflicts that affect global security.'

Clearly these maritime threats cannot be effectively dealt with by Indonesia's historically land based territorial defensive posture. It requires the navy and, hopefully, the coastguard (*Bakamla*) to play a leading role, supported by the air force (*TNI Angkatan Udara*) and the army (*TNI Angkatan Darat*). Recognising this, and drawing upon Indonesia's historical reputation as a maritime power, President Widodo is focused on making Indonesia a major maritime power in the Indo-Pacific region. His vision – enunciated in the *poros maritim dunia* doctrine – is for Indonesia to become a global maritime nexus (or fulcrum) – a maritime bridge between the two oceanic regions of the Indian Ocean and the Pacific Ocean.[2] Three of the five pillars of this doctrine, viz. (i) the build-up of maritime defence power; (ii) establishing sovereignty over sea-based food resources; and (iii) using maritime diplomacy to end sources of conflict at sea directly involve the Indonesian Navy and Indonesia's maritime security agencies.[3] The doctrine could therefore well result in increased focus on the navy's requirements in due course.

HISTORY: THE INDONESIAN NAVY'S EVOLUTION

The Indonesian Navy's origins go back to the nationalist *Badan Keamanan Rakyat Laut* (*BKR Laut*) – the naval branch of the People's Security Agency – which was founded on 10 September 1945 following the Indonesian proclamation of independence from the Netherlands on 7 August of that year. Manned by a core of nationalists possessing naval experience with the Royal Netherlands Navy or with the Japanese during the period they had occupied the country in the Second World War, this force operated an assortment of wooden vessels, landing craft and merchant ships. The BKR first morphed into the *Tentara Keamanan Rakyat* (*TKR*) *Laut* – the naval branch of the People's Security Army – and then into the *Angkatan Laut Republik Indonesia* (*ALRI*) – the Navy of Republic of Indonesia. The navy retained the ALRI name until 1970, when it became the current *Tentara Nasional Indonesia Angktan Laut* (*TNIAL*) – Indonesian National Armed Forces Navy.

In 1949, the United Nations formally recognised Indonesia as an independent country. Sukarno – decidedly anti-imperialist and neo-Marxist in outlook – was the new country's founding president. The navy began a gradual process of expansion, equipping itself with former Dutch ships and acquisitions from elsewhere, whilst engaging in operations against separatist movements.

However, the western half of the island of New Guinea (Irian Jaya) – now known as West Papua – remained in Dutch hands. The Dutch wanted independence for this region under their 'guidance', much to the chagrin of the Indonesians who claimed it for themselves. By the late 1950s, having failed to achieve his aims by diplomacy, President Sukarno opted to annex Irian Jaya using military pressure in what came to be known as the *Konfrontasi* (Confrontation). At this juncture, he turned for military assistance to the Soviet Union, which was only too glad to oblige, hoping to gain a strategic foothold in the region. From 1958, large quantities of sophisticated weapons started flowing in from the Soviets and Warsaw Pact countries including a flotilla of twelve Project 613 'Whiskey' class submarines (plus two for use for spares). In all, over 150 ships were to be transferred by the Soviets and their allies by the mid-1960s, most notably a *Sverdlov* class cruiser, around fifteen destroyers and frigates, and twelve Project 183R 'Komar' missile-

armed fast attack craft. There was also a substantial naval air arm. At the same time, the 'Western' powers kept supplying military equipment – possibly to dissuade Sukarno from gravitating totally into the Soviet orbit.

In August 1960, Indonesia formally severed diplomatic ties with the Netherlands. Subsequently, on 19 December 1961, Operation 'Trikora' was launched with the aim of annexing Netherlands New Guinea by the end of 1962. A programme of troop infiltrations had limited success due to effective Dutch use of signals intelligence but by the summer of 1962 Indonesia was ready to mount a major air-sea assault on the territory under Operation 'Jaya Wijaya'. However, with limited tangible international support, the Dutch had already decided to cut a deal with Indonesia. With the signing of a settlement – the New York Treaty – on 15 August 1962, the air-sea assault was called off. Western New Guinea was subsequently annexed by Indonesia on 1 May 1963.

Shortly after Operation 'Trikora', Indonesia engaged in another confrontation, this time with the British Commonwealth, over the creation of a united Malaysia. Again fought out largely by means of a campaign of limited infiltrations, Indonesia's numerically powerful fleet had little role to play. Commencing in 1963, the Indonesian-Malaysia Confrontation declined in intensity from 1965 onwards with the weakening of Sukarno's influence following a coup attempt blamed on the Communist Party of Indonesia and the subsequent rise of the pro-Western Suharto. The subsequent breach with the Soviet Union badly impacted the operational readiness of the largely Russian-built fleet, which had always been regarded by many as a 'paper tiger' of doubtful effectiveness.[4]

By the 1970s, the remaining vessels of Soviet origin were being cannibalised for spares to maintain a few operational platforms. Throughout the decade, the United States transferred considerable numbers of elderly platforms to maintain force levels. Operationally, the navy was involved in the invasion of East Timor in 1975. This involved amphibious forces and naval gunfire support.

The 1980s saw the acquisition of more modern platforms and combat systems to arrest declining capabilities. Major acquisitions included new-build *Fatahillah* class missile corvettes and used *Van Speijk* class guided-missile frigates from the Netherlands, German Type 209 submarines, fast attack craft from

The Indonesian 'Sigma' type corvette *Frans Kaisiepo* operating with Bangladesh's Chinese-built 'Jianghu II' type frigate *Osman*, as part of the sea component of the UNIFIL stabilisation mission of Lebanon. Indonesia's new president envisages the navy taking an increased role in maritime diplomacy. *(Indonesian Navy)*

South Korea, and Nomad Searchmaster maritime patrol aircraft from Australia. The last of the 'Whiskey' class boats – *Pasopati* – served alongside newly-acquired German submarines until its decommissioning on 25 January 1990. It was subsequently moved ashore to become a museum in Surabaya.

The early 1990s saw another major development when thirty-nine former German Democratic Republic *Volksmarine* ships were acquired in 1992. This package reportedly cost only US$12.7m, although subsequent ship refitting costs in Germany added up to an estimated US$320m to the bill. In spite of initial fleet integration issues, the ships provided a major boost to fleet strength and have given sterling service. Thirty-seven of these ships remain in service and are expected to do so for many more years.

CURRENT INDONESIAN DEFENCE STRATEGY

Initiated in 2005 and signed into law by former President Yudhoyuno in 2009, the ongoing Indonesian armed forces modernisation programme – known as the Minimum Essential Forces (MEF) programme – aims to arrest the previous decline in Indonesia's ageing armed forces to achieve a level of parity with other regional armed forces. The MEF is being implemented in three, five year-long phases lasting from 2010 until 2024. Phase 1 ran from 2010–2014; Phase 2 from 2015–2019 is ongoing; while Phase 3 lasts from 2020–2024. Broadly speaking, the MEF, along with a policy of enhancing the existing 'strategic industries' that form Indonesia's military industrial base, represent the two pillars' of Indonesia's national strategic plan or *Rencana Strategis* (*Renstra*) for defence. A second strategic plan lasting until 2029 exists but this goes beyond the MEF requirement to look into idealised force levels.

Funding the MEF envisages a progressive increase in the defence budget to 1.5 per cent of the country's gross domestic product (GDP) or annual economic output. During the previous presidency, spending jumped from around IDR22 trillion (US$1.7bn) in 2005 to IDR83 trillion (US$6.4bn) in 2014, still representing only 0.8 per cent of GDP. The 2015 presidential budget request has been set at IDR 97 trillion (US$7.2bn) and a further IDR 5 trillion has been requested by the ministry of defence. Of the base budget, around IRD14 trillion (US$1.1bn) is allocated to the navy and this is likely to be supple-

The 'bulk buy' acquisition of thirty-nine former German Democratic Republic warships in 1992 went a long way to boosting a run-down Indonesian Navy. This image shows the 'Parchim I' type anti-submarine corvette *Wiratno*. (*Royal Australian Navy*)

mented to c. IRD20 trillion (US$1.5bn). The 1.5 per cent of GDP defence budget target remains a medium term commitment.

So far as the TNIAL is concerned, its MEF requirements are influenced by its current doctrinal thinking, known as *Eka Sasana Jaya* or 'Unified Guidance to Victory at Sea'. The doctrine establishes naval defence (sea control and power projection), maritime security operations and naval diplomacy as the navy's core tasks. Naval defence is implemented through the Archipelagic Sea Defence Strategy (*Strategi Pertahanan Laut Nusantara*, SPLN). This is based on deterrence, layered defence and sea control of the three main strategic waterways. More specifically:

- **Deterrence** is driven by naval presence and force modernisation, backed by defence diplomacy.
- **Layered Defence** is focused on an anti-access/area-denial (A2AD) strategy, using surface escorts with long-range surface-to-surface missiles in an outer layer; smaller missile-armed surface craft and submarines in the next layer and the use of amphibious, land and guerrilla forces should fighting extend to Indonesian territory. Extensive use of mining would also deter a hostile fleet from penetrating into Indonesia's archipelagic waters.
- **Sea Control** is more focused towards sea denial given TNIAL's currently limited warfighting capabilities, as well as towards interdiction and peacetime maritime security operations.

The naval MEF is described by the TNIAL as a 'capabilities-based force' designed to tackle multiple threats. When the MEF was being formulated in 2005, this translated into a force of 274 ships with a 'green water' or littoral emphasis. Within this total were 122 'fighting ships'; ten submarines, sixteen frigates, forty large missile-armed escorts, twenty-six missile-armed fast attack craft, twelve torpedo-equipped patrol boats and eighteen mine-hunters. These would be supplemented by sixty-six patrol vessels and eighty-six support vessels, the latter emphasising amphibious types. A naval air arm of 137 aircraft and a force of no fewer than 60,000 marines completed the plan. Whilst details have subsequently changed, these numbers illustrate the scope and magnitude of the intended MEF programme

More recently, there has been something of a change of emphasis, influenced by the writings of former naval chief Admiral Marsetio, who has argued that Indonesia should develop a 'world class navy' capable both of defending sovereign waters and acting as an instrument of Indonesia's foreign policy.[5] However, the ambition is a notoriously amorphous concept say those who are familiar with the situation. It means many things to many people, including the strategic thinkers within the navy.

As might be expected, new President Widodo will review the existing strategic defence programme, doubtless guided by his 'maritime nexus' doctrine. Current Defence Minister Ryacudu has suggested there will be an emphasis on increasing combatant ship force levels and improving maritime domain awareness (MDA) with greater surveillance capability.

CURRENT TNIAL ORGANISATION

The TNIAL is the largest navy in South East Asia. As of December 2014, its strength was 65,190 uniformed personnel and 8,105 civilians (around 70 per cent of its sanctioned strength). The navy also includes a sizeable marine corps – *Korps Marinir* (*Kormar*) – numbering at least 23,000 personnel in 2012 and possibly closer to 30,000.

Afloat assets comprise around 160 commissioned naval ships bearing the *Kapal Republik Indonesia* (*KRI*) prefix, supported by another dozen or so naval auxiliaries such as tugs and yard craft. The average age of the fleet of commissioned ships is over twenty-five years, with over half of the warships being over thirty years old. In addition, there are some 375 non-commissioned patrol boats and patrol craft. The naval air arm (*Puspenerbal*) operates around eighty aircraft, including over twenty helicopters. The marines possess some 500 armoured fighting vehicles plus towed and self-propelled artillery.

The naval headquarters in Jakarta is headed by the Chief of Naval staff – a four-star admiral, currently Admiral Ade Supandi. He is assisted by the Deputy Chief of Staff – currently Vice Admiral Widodo. They are assisted by several assistant chiefs heading up staff branches and directorates. The Navy has four main operational commands (KOTAMA).

■ The Fleet Command – *Komando Armada* (*Koarmada*) – with two fleets: the Eastern Fleet (*Koarmatim*) headquartered in Surabaya; and the Western Fleet (*Koarmabar*) headquartered in Jakarta. The Eastern Fleet (*Koarmatim*) is the larger of the two, with over eighty warships.
■ The Military Sealift Command (*Kolinlamil*) headquartered in Tanjug Priok, North Jakarta.
■ The Marine Corps (*Kormar*).
■ The Development (Training) and Education Command (*Kobangdikal*).

In addition to these commands, major operational entities (branches) are naval aviation (*Puspenerbal*), the Special Forces group known as *Komando Pasukan Katak* (*Kopaska*), and the Naval Police (*Puspomal*).

Fleet Command Organisation: Geographically, the two Fleet Commands cover eleven numbered naval regions centred around a main naval base (*Lantamal*). These *Lantamals* are numbered sequentially from west to east starting with *Lantamal* I in Belawan, *Lantamal* II in Padang, *Lantamal* III in Jakarta, *Lantamal* IV in Tanjung Pinang, *Lantamal* V Surabaya, *Lantamal* VI Makasar, *Lantamal* VII Kupang, *Lantamal* VIII Menado, *Lantamal* IX Ambon, *Lantamal* X Jayapura and *Lantamal* XI Merauke.

Currently *Lantamal* I–IV are under *Kormabar* (Western Fleet) while *Lantamal* V–XI are under *Koarmatim* (Eastern Fleet). *Lantamal* V in Surabaya is the HQ of the biggest naval region administering Indonesia's largest naval base along with eight smaller bases, the main naval aviation centre at Juanda and a dockyard in Surabaya.

Each *Lantamal* typically administers the main base (*Lanal* Class A) along with two or more smaller bases (classed as *Lanal* Class B or Class C) and numerous naval observations posts (*Posal*) which are also classed as Type A or B or C. Some *Lantamals* have naval dockyards (*Fasharkan*) and airfields (*Lanudal*). In all, there are eleven Class A naval bases with Ujung (Surabaya) and Tanjung Priok (North Jakarta) being the largest of these; forty or more Class B and C naval bases; nine naval dockyards, and at least nine airfields.

Fleet Commanders (*Pankoarmada*) are assisted by a chief of staff (*Kas Koarmada*) and the commanders of the Naval Combat Group (*Danguspurla*), Maritime Security Group (*Danguskamla*) and the main naval bases (*Danlantamals*). The Naval Combat Force Group – *Guspurla* – comprises both large escorts and missile boats while the Maritime

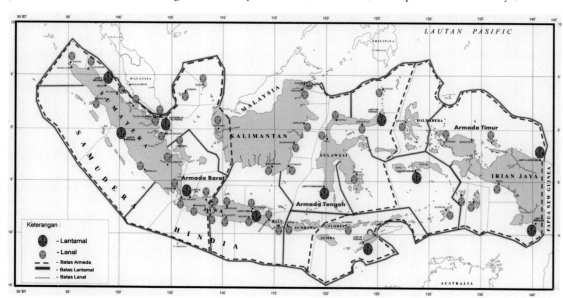

A map of Indonesia showing the overall naval regional command structure. There are currently eleven regions, each centred on a major naval base or *Lantamal*. A number of smaller bases or *Lanal* are located in each region. The eleven regions are currently split between Eastern and Western Fleets but a new third fleet – the Central Fleet Command – is planned. The dotted line shows the proposed demarcation of the three fleets. *(Indonesian Navy)*

Security Force Group – *Guskamla* – is comprised of smaller patrol craft.

Central Fleet Command – The Third Fleet: The current fleet organisation is on the verge of a major change. The navy is awaiting a presidential decree that would formalise the creation of a third fleet – the Central Fleet Command or *Komando Armada Tengah* (*Koarmateng*) – along with a Fleet Command Centre (*Kommando Armada Pusat*). This change, planned since c. 2005, is in line with the establishment of three Regional Joint (Forces) Defence Commands (*Kogabwilhan*) comprised of army, air force, navy and marine formations.

The number of *Lantamals* will also increase from eleven to fourteen under the new structure. *Lanal* Sorong has been designated as *Lantamal* XII, whilst *Lanal* Tarakan in North Kalimantan and the Class B *Lanal* at Pontianak in West Kalimantan will both be upgraded to *Lantamals* in due course.

Under the new structure the Western Fleet (*Koarmabar*) HQ will remain in Jakarta, Central Fleet HQ will be in Makassar, the Eastern Fleet (*Koarmatim*) HQ will move from Surabaya to Sorong while the new Fleet Command Centre will be in Surabaya.

EQUIPMENT – SHIPS

The TNIAL classifies commissioned naval ships (KRI) into those belonging to the Striking Force (*Kekuatan Pemukul*), the Patrol Force (*Kekuatan Patroli*) and the Supporting Force (*Kekuatan Pendukung*). The latter is comprised of amphibious warfare ships, mine warfare ships and auxiliaries.

Pennant or hull numbers follow a three-digit numbering system. Typically, the second digit

Table 2.2A.1: INDONESIAN NAVY – PRINCIPAL UNITS AS AT MID 2015

TYPE	CLASS	NO.	YEAR	TONNAGE	DIMENSIONS	SPEED	PRINCIPAL ARMAMENT
Submarines (2)							
Submarine – SSK	Type 209 (1300)	2	1981	1,400 tons	60m x 6m x 5m	22 knots	8 x 533mm torpedo tubes
A further three submarines of South Korea's *Chang Bogo* variant of the Type 209 are under construction or on order.							
Fleet Escorts (6)							
Frigate – FFG(H)	VAN SPEIJK (LEANDER)	6	1967	2,900 tons	113m x 13m x 4m	20 knots	8 x SSM (see text), 2 x twin Simbad SAM, 1 x 76mm, 6 x TT, 1 x hel.
A further two Dutch DSNS-designed 'Sigma' 10514 type frigates are under construction, with final assembly taking place at PT PAL in Surabaya. At least two more may be ordered.							
Patrol Escorts (26)							
Frigate – FFT	DEWANTARA	1	1981	2,100 tons	97m x 11m x 5m	26 knots	4 x Exocet SSM, 1 x 57mm, 2 x TT, 1 x A/S launcher, hel. platform
Corvette – FSG	DIPONEGORO ('Sigma' 9113)	4	2007	1,700 tons	91m x 13m x 4m	28 knots	4 x Exocet SSM, 2 x quad Tetral SAM, 1x 76mm, 6 x TT, hel. platform
Corvette – FSG	BUNG TOMO	3	2002	1,900 tons	90m x 13m x 4m	30 knots	8 x Exocet SSM, 16 x Seawolf SAM, 1 x 76mm, 6 x TT, hel. platform
Corvette – FSG	FATAHILLAH	3	1979	1,400 tons	84m x 11m x 3m	30 knots	4 x Exocet SSM, 1 x 120mm, 6 x TT, 1 x A/S launcher
Corvette – FS	'Parchim I' (Project 1331)	15	1981	1,000 tons	75m x 10m x 4m	20 knots	1 x twin 57mm, 4 x TT, 2 x A/S launchers
The *Bung Tomo* class are the former Brunei *Nakhoda Ragam* class, ordered from the UK's BAE Systems but never delivered. They were commissioned with the Indonesian Navy in 2014. No Seawolf missiles have been delivered for the SAM vertical-launch system installed. One of the sixteen 'Parchim I' vessels originally acquired is no longer in service following a serious fire.							
Missile-Armed Attack Craft (c. 20)							
FAC – PTG	KCR-60	c.3	2014	500 tons	60m x 8m x 3m	30 knots	4 x C-705 SSM, 1 x 57mm
FAC – PTG	KCR-40	c.8	2011	250 tons	44m x 8m x 2m	30 knots	2/4 x C-705 SSM, 1 x CIWS
FAC – PTG	TODAK (PB57)	4	2000	450 tons	58m x 8m x 3m	30 knots	2 x C-802 SSM, 1 x 57mm
FAC – PTFG	MANDAU	4	1979	300 tons	50m x 7m x 2m	40 knots	4 x Exocet SSM, 1 x 57mm
Some of these vessels are fitted 'for but not with' their missile systems. Conversely, some of the larger patrol vessels such as the *Singa/Pandrong* PB57 type could be missile armed. Further KCR type vessels are being constructed, including a KCR-63 missile-armed trimaran built of composite construction.							
Major Amphibious Units (5)							
Amphibious – LPD	MAKASSAR	5	2003	11,500 tons	122m x 22m x 5m	15 knots	2 x helicopters; 2 x small landing craft/hovercraft
The dimensions of the amphibious transport docks vary slightly and one is operated as a hospital ship. They are supplemented by ten large tank landing ships; twelve medium tank landing ships of the Project 108 'Frosch' type and at least seven troop transports converted from ferries. New tank landing ships are under construction to replace older types being withdrawn.							

Notes:

1. The numerical heart of the fleet comprises around fifty commissioned patrol ships, ranging in size from the c.450-ton PB57 types to the c.100-ton PC-40 and PC-36 types. The latter two, locally constructed designs account for nearly half the commissioned patrol fleet. Ongoing local patrol ship construction includes a slightly larger PC-43 design similar to the KCR-40 missile-armed attack craft. There are numerous smaller non-commissioned patrol vessels, normally found at the smaller local naval bases.

2. The navy's minehunting capability is focused on two Dutch-built 'Tripartite' class minehunters – *Pulau Rengat* and *Pulau Rupat* – complemented by nine elderly *Pulau Rote* ('Kondor II') class minesweepers, which are employed mostly as patrol and survey vessels. Two new specialist-built hydrographic vessels constructed in France will supplement existing tonnage.

3. Other vessels include seven ships capable of providing replenishment-at-sea capabilities, two sail training ships, as well as general support ships and tugs.

4. Year relates to year lead ship of the class was completed.

Two images of the Indonesian Dutch-built *Van Speijk* (*Leander*) class frigate *Oswald Siahaan* test firing a Russian P-800 'Yakhont' surface-to-surface missile. At least two more ships of the six-strong class have been equipped with the more compact Chinese C-802 type. *(Indonesian Navy)*

denotes a class of vessel within the main group and the third digit denotes a ship within that class, although there are exceptions. Escort ships have hull numbers beginning with 3, while it is 4 for submarines, 5 for amphibious ships, 6 for attack craft, 7 for mine warfare ships, 8 for patrol boats and 9 for all auxiliary ships.

Submarines: Of the 160 or so commissioned ships, there are currently only two submarines, both Type 209/1300 boats built by Germany's HDW and commissioned in 1981. *Cakra* underwent a mid-life upgrade performed by South Korea's DSME during 2004–5 and was followed by *Nanggala* in 2010–12. The upgrades included the provision of a Kongsberg MSI-90U combat management system and a new sonar system. Ten years on, *Cakra* needs another major refit to repair extensive corrosion damage.

Surface Escorts: The largest surface combatants are six elderly Dutch-built *Van Speijk/Ahmad Yani* class guided-missile frigates based on the British Royal Navy's 1960s *Leander* class design. All have been re-

powered with diesel engines in place of their steam turbine power plants. Three have also received combat management system upgrades manufactured locally by PT Len, as well as new datalinks and radar. Of these, *Oswald Siahaan* has been equipped with four cells for vertically-launched Russian-made P-800 'Yakhont' (NATO SS-N-26) missiles whilst *Yos Sudarso* and *Abdul Halim Perdanakusuma* have four Chinese C-802 surface-to-surface missile systems. Several have received MBDA 'Simbad' surface-to-air missile launchers in replacement for the obsolete Sea Cat. As for the submarines, these ships' advanced age raises questions about their operational availability. The Yugoslavian-built training frigate *Ki Hajar Dewantara* acquired in 1981 also has a secondary combat role.

The frigates are supplemented by ten missile-armed corvettes. The oldest are three Dutch-built *Fatahillah* class units delivered during 1979–80, the first of which is undergoing a mid-life upgrade valued at £32m (c. US$45m) under a contract with Britain's Ultra Electronics. Enhancements include a new combat management system and a Terma

Scanter 9100 radar. Marine engineering aspects of the work package are being handled by Ultra's partner Nobiskrug and its local sub-contractor in Indonesia. Plans call for a second ship to undergo a similar upgrade.

The four 'Sigma 9113' *Diponegoro* class corvettes, also built in the Netherlands, are the most modern surface escorts in service. Commissioned between 2007 and 2009, they form the core of the surface fleet. They were joined in 2014 by three *Bung Tomo* class vessels originally built by BAE Systems on the Clyde under an order placed by Brunei in 1995 but laid up for several years after that country failed to accept them. These ten-year-old, 'new' ships are likely to face some initial integration issues with the rest of the fleet since several of their systems are new to the TNIAL.

Sixteen Project 1331 'Parchim' type corvettes, known locally as the *Kapitan Patimura* class, were acquired under the 1990s deal with Germany.[6] Armed with RBU anti-submarine rocket mortars and torpedoes, the 'Parchims' are the workhorses of the fleet escort units and will continue to be the fleet's primary anti-submarine platforms for many more years. All have received upgrades to their propulsion system and are likely to receive an improved combat management system and the Chinese Type 730 close-in weapons system in due course.

Missile-Armed Attack Craft: The larger warships are supported by approximately twenty missile-armed attack craft known as *Kapal Cepat Rudal* (KCR). Only around half have operational missile systems, with the others steadily being fitted out with the necessary fire-control systems.

The force currently comprises four *Mandau* class vessels delivered from South Korea in 1979–80 and four more recent, locally-built PB-57 *Todak* class ships derived from the earlier *Singa* class PB-57 derivative designed by Germany's Lürssen. These are supplemented by growing numbers of KCR-60 and KCR-40 types being constructed under ongoing local construction programmes, with three of the former and around eight of the latter commissioned to date. A third programme for KCR-63 *Klewang* class fully composite missile-armed trimarans suffered a serious setback when the nearly-completed lead vessel was destroyed by an electrical fire on 28 September 2012, less than a month after its launch. Builder PT Lundin (North Sea Boats) and designer LOMO Ocean Design Yachts, in co-operation with combat systems supplier Saab, are, however, continuing the innovative project using materials with better fire resistance. The redesigned ship is under construction for entry into service by 2017 as part of a planned initial batch of four.

Patrol Forces: The bulk of the fleet comprises patrol forces. There are around fifty commissioned patrol ships of various origins and sizes, including Project 89.2 'Kondor II' class minesweepers that are primarily used in a patrol role. Further patrol ships are under construction.

The commissioned patrol vessels are supplemented by non-commissioned (*Kapal Angatan Laut*) KAL patrol boats and smaller *Kapal Patroli Keamanan Laut* (*Patkamla*) patrol craft that form the workhorses of the patrol force and are to be found at

An image of the prototype KCR-63 missile-armed trimaran, *Klewang*, after its launch by PT Lundin in August 2012. The vessel was destroyed as a result of an electrical fire a month later but a replacement (with better fire resistance) is under construction. *(Agus Suparto/North Sea Boats)*

The second KCR-40 missile-armed attack craft, *Kujang*, pictured at the LIMA defence exhibition in March 2015. These relatively cheap and unsophisticated ships, armed with the Chinese C-702 surface-to-surface missile, are being built in numbers as part of the Indonesian Navy's layered anti-access/area denial strategy. *(Mrityunjoy Mazumdar)*

the smaller naval bases. The KAL craft tend to be between 16m and 31m in length, whilst the patrol craft are 12m long or smaller. Ongoing construction is focused on 28m patrol boats with water-jet propulsion and smaller combat boats.

Other smaller vessels include at least six 50-knot Vitesse Mk II fast interceptors built of composite materials by PT Rizki Abadi and PT Royal Advanced Fibre for the Special Forces. They also use a number of PT Lundin-built X38 catamaran combat boats, as well as its X2K rigid inflatables.

Amphibious Forces: A large force of amphibious ships provides a vital capability in fulfilling various transport and logistic support requirements, as well as providing humanitarian assistance and disaster relief.

The most important units are five LPD-type amphibious transport docks, including one – *Dr. Soeharso* (ex *Tanjung Dalpele*) – configured as a hospital ship in service. Three of the ships were acquired directly from South Korea's Daesun

Shipbuilding from 2003 through to 2007. The other two were built locally in Surabaya by PT PAL to a modified design and commissioned in 2009 and 2011. With a full-load displacement of over 11,000 tons, these ships can carry twenty-one tanks (or a combination of thirteen tanks and twenty trucks), around 500 troops, two small landing craft or hovercraft in the dock well, and two medium-sized helicopters in the hangar, while simultaneously operating up to three smaller-sized helicopters from the large flight deck. A further two of the class are being built by PT PAL for the Philippines.

Other amphibious shipping includes ten large tank landing ships (LSTs) of largely South Korean or US Navy origin, supplemented by twelve surviving medium-sized vessels of the 'Frosch 1' and 'Frosch II' types that formed part of the bulk purchase from Germany. The largest and newest LST is the locally-built *Teluk Bintuni* which was built by PT Daya Radar Utama shipyard in Banten and delivered in June 2015 after engine issues following a September 2014 inauguration delayed her commissioning. The

ship has a military lift of about 2,000 tons, including ten Leopard main battle tanks, and c. 360 troops in addition to the 120-strong crew. It also has a hangar for a medium helicopter. A pair of slightly smaller ships is under construction by the state owned PT Dok Kodja Bahari (PT DKB) shipbuilding group. Further construction is planned to replace older ships that are being paid off.

There are also a number of smaller landing craft and hovercraft, mostly carried by the amphibious transport docks. A number of converted passenger ships and ferries serve as troop transports.

Auxiliaries: There are seven ships capable of providing replenishment-at-sea capabilities. The most recent, *Tarakan*, was built by PT DKB and commissioned in September 2014. She joined two other large but elderly ships, three old coastal tankers and the command ship *Multatuli*, which also performs limited replenishment duties. A further ship is under construction.

Hydrographic service and mine-countermeasures: The naval hydrographic service received a boost in 2015 with the induction of the first of two multi-purpose research vessels built by France's OCEA. The 60m, 560-ton *Rigel* is built entirely of aluminium to OCEA's OSV-190 SC-WB design. Onboard equipment includes a Kongsberg Hugin 1000 autonomous underwater vehicle with integral side-scan sonar and ECA's H800 remotely operated vehicle. Besides survey work, these vessels can also be used for mine-hunting and patrolling. The second OCEA built ship, *Spica*, is slated for completion in late 2015. The new ships join the former British Hecla survey ship *Dewa Kembar* (ex-*Hydra*) and some smaller ships. Three 'Kondor' class minesweepers out of a total of nine are also primarily devoted to the survey role. With the others focused on constabulary duties, this leaves two Dutch-built 'Tripartite' minehunters as the main mine-countermeasures assets. Reports suggest they are scheduled for replacement in due course.

Other vessels include the sail training ships *Dewaruci* and *Arung Samudera* and a number of tugs.

NAVAL AIR ARM

The Indonesian Naval Air Arm (*Puspenerbal*) was formally established on 17 June 1956, initially operating rebuilt Dutch aircraft and British-built Fairey

A number of Indonesian shipyards are involved in building a host of smaller ships, amongst the most advanced being North Sea Boats (PT Lundin) in East Java. This image shows one of the company's X38 catamaran boats in company with two of its X2K RHIBs. The company is also involved in developing the larger KCR-63 composite catamaran.
(*Agus Suparto / North Sea Boats*)

Gannets with *Skuadron* 100. Currently, the naval air arm is organised into two air wings – Wing *Udara* 1 at Juanda (near Surabaya) and Wing *Udara* 2 at Tanjung Pinang. Over 80 per cent of aircraft are attached to Wing 1. Four squadrons – 200, 400, 600 and 800 – operate around eighty aircraft, with squadron detachments in both air wings. Numbers of operational aircraft may be significantly less than holdings and current force levels fall far short of requirements.

- *Skuadron* 200 (RON 200) is the training unit operating out of Juanda with a secondary base at Ahmed Yani airport at Semarang some 165 miles to the west. The unit operates a variety of training aircraft, typically training twenty to thirty pilots every year.
- *Skuadron* 400 (RON 400) operates helicopters. Holdings are thought to include six to ten BO 105CBs, seven to twelve Bell 412 SP, HP and EP variants and a single AS 565 Panther.
- *Skuadron* 600 (RON 600) operates around a dozen or so NC 212 utility and transport aircraft.
- *Skuadron* 800 (RON 800) has a maritime patrol role with around ten operational Nomad N-22/24 aircraft, three NC 212-200 maritime patrol aircraft and three newly-delivered CN 235-220 maritime patrol aircraft.

Juanda (Surabaya) is the main training base and home of the Naval Flight Centre. Other naval air stations are at Tanjung Pinang, Jakarta, Sabang, Matak in Natuna Island, Semarang, Kupang, Manado, Aru Island (Dobo) and Biak.

Plans calls for a third wing at Sorong, upgrading Tanjung Pinang air station to Class A standard and developing Class B air stations at Bengkulu, Ambon and Tual by 2019. Steps have also been taken to remedy operational gaps in airborne anti-submarine capabilities with a 2014 order for eleven Airbus AS 565 MBe Panther helicopters, which will be operated by a reactivated *Skuadron* 100. Deliveries are slated for completion by 2017. Further acquisitions planned under MEF2 include helicopters configured for anti-surface warfare and more transportation and maritime patrol assets.

MARINE CORPS

The *Korps Marinir* is currently organised into two light divisions known as PASMAR I and PASMAR II; an independent infantry brigade; one inde-

pendent composite infantry battalion, eleven base defence battalions and a secretive Special Forces team with a counter-terrorist role known as Detachment *Jala Mangkara* (*Denjaka*) based in Cilandak.

As noted earlier, plans call for the expansion of the Indonesian Marine Corps to 60,000 personnel and three divisions – one for each fleet command. With the creation of the joint force area commands close to becoming reality, moves are already afoot to establish PASMAR III in Sorong, West Papua with an initial 8,000 marines.

LOCAL CONSTRUCTION CAPABILITIES AND FUTURE PLANS

Indonesia's naval shipbuilding industry has the capability of designing and building relatively complex patrol craft, although build standards need improvement in some cases. Construction of more sophisticated warships began with the building under licence of several variants of Lürssen's PB-57 design by PT PAL in Surabaya in the late 1980s. Building

on this experience, PT PAL developed the in-house designed KCR-60 series attack craft that have been in series production since 2012. The yard has now progressed a stage further, embarking on the construction of corvettes to Damen's 'Sigma' 10514 design under the PKR programme. At the same time, it is also executing an ambitious project to license-build the South Korean *Chang Bogo* variant of the German Type 209 submarine.

PT PAL has also previously undertaken licensed construction of large amphibious transport docks using designs and material packages from South Korea's Daesun. It has gone on to export two ships of a modified design to the Philippine Navy and is talking to Myanmar about a possible sale.

PT PAL was originally slated to build several tank landing ships but resource limitations arising from the corvette and submarine programmes led to these contracts being switched to other shipyards. A number of yards are also engaged in the series production of a range of patrol and attack craft

Future construction is therefore focused on local

Local Indonesian shipyards have steadily been developing capabilities to build warships, although it is only now that local construction of more sophisticated types such as frigates and submarines is being commenced. The image shows the amphibious transport dock *Banda Aceh*, which was completed by the most significant warship builder, PT PAL at Surabaya, to a South Korean design between 2007 and 2011. *(US Navy)*

yards, with the corvette and submarine programmes being the most significant. Two Sigma 10514 corvettes have been ordered to date under the PKR project at a reported cost of US$220m each. Planned delivery dates are December 2016 and October 2017. Uniquely, these ships are being constructed using hull modules built both in Indonesia by PAL as well as those built by Damen overseas. PAL is responsible for building four of the six ship modules for the first ship and all modules except the mast/bridge/operations block for the second ship. Two more of these ships have been budgeted under MEF Phase 2.

The submarine programme is being pursued in conjunction with South Korea's DSME and involves three boats. Two will be built in Korea but current plans envisage the third being assembled by PT PAL, which would need to invest over US$100m in new infrastructure to support the project. Work share issues delayed the project's implementation but the first boat should be delivered in 2017. The overall cost of the programme has been reported as US$1.1bn.

A host of other projects are focused on tank landing ships, attack craft of the KCR-63, KCR-60 and KCR-40 types, as well as numerous patrol boats and craft. A 110m sail training ship, *Dewaruci II*, has been ordered from Astilleros Freire in Spain.

A full list of planned MEF 2 and MEF 3 acquisitions has not yet been released but some details have emerged. Very broadly, plans call for the acquisition of around seventy–eighty ships and thirty–forty aircraft in each phase. Priorities seem to include ongoing construction of missile-armed fast attack craft, of patrol and amphibious vessels, as well as of more corvettes. Submarine construction is likely to continue towards a long-term goal of around ten boats. Larger surface combatants could be sought in the longer term.

CONCLUSIONS

Operationally, the overstretched TNIAL continues to face significant challenges. However, the MEF is gradually paying dividends. Broadly speaking, the service has been underfunded and overstretched over the years, leading to a situation where it needs to deal with ageing equipment and block obsolescence of platforms.

The KCR-60 missile armed attack craft design is one of many ongoing construction programmes. It was developed by PT PAL of Surabaya, which previously built slightly smaller Lürssen-designed PB-57 type vessels under licence. This image shows third of class, *Halasan*. *(Mrityunjoy Mazumdar)*

Serious capability gaps also exist in areas such as maritime domain awareness, command and control and surveillance, and network centricity. As of early 2015, only a dozen or so combatants were known to have Link Y or PT Len built datalinks, although this is set to change. There is no airborne anti-submarine capability, maritime patrol aircraft assets are minimal, while UAV capabilities are at a nascent stage. There is also a shortage of shipborne tactical transport helicopters.

On a more basic level, the navy has been unable to deploy sufficient ships for patrol missions on a sustained basis because of a lack of fuel, spares and munitions. In January 2015, *The Jakarta Post* reported that more than half the fleet is not combat ready due to a lack of munitions, adding that only around sixty ships were available for sea patrol, with fifty on standby and the rest undergoing maintenance.[7] With so few available assets, the navy has had to rely on intelligence inputs to direct operations to problem-prone areas, like the Natunas.

Whilst problems exist, many crucial shortcomings and capability gaps have been addressed under MEF 1, which has achieved significant gains. Since 2010, the acquisition of state-of-the-art warships in various categories has provided a significant force accretion. In addition, there will be a further boost once ships and submarines under construction begin entering service from 2016 onwards. Maritime surveillance capabilities are also being improved and the gap in shipborne anti-submarine helicopters will be plugged with the arrival of the new Panther Mbe

A dramatic image of the Indonesian 'Sigma' type corvette *Frans Kaisiepo* turning at speed. Two larger 'Sigma' 10514 corvettes / light frigates have been ordered for local assembly by PT PAL at Surabaya. *(Royal Australian Navy)*

helicopters. Command and control issues are also being addressed with the retrofitting of combat management systems and data links to the most important vessels.

On an operational level, another welcome development directly affecting the TIANL's ability to execute its constabulary role effectively is a steady increase in its fuel allocation since 2012. In that year, the navy only obtained 13 per cent of its minimum requirement (5.6m kilolitres) but this had increased to 41 per cent by 2015. Consequently, it is now able to fulfil around 60 per cent of its maritime security obligations. Significant qualitative and quantitative improvements in combat and operational effectiveness are therefore being achieved, although block obsolescence issues will loom large in another decade or so.

Looking further forward, the goals of the MEF and – even more so – the visions of the TNIAL becoming a 'world class navy' are very ambitious and expensive. It remains to be seen how much of Mr Widodo's maritime nexus rhetoric translates into military spending over time, given other pressing economic and social issues. Indeed, funding realities might suggest that the TNIAL will be lucky to maintain existing force levels. At best, it can strive towards becoming a 'green water' navy.

A bigger question remains regarding Indonesia's

The 'Sigma' type corvette *Sultan Iskandar Muda* pictured in Sydney Harbour in October 2013 at the time of the international fleet review held to celebrate the Royal Australian Navy's centenary. In spite of lofty ambitions to become a 'world class navy', the TNIAL's development is likely to remain constrained by financial considerations. *(Royal Australian Navy)*

broader security strategy: how will Mr Widodo's maritime nexus vision and a strong maritime Indonesia play out in the face of ongoing regional developments? Going forward, can Indonesia – with a revamped navy and coast guard – stand up to an increasingly assertive China in the defence of its economic and maritime interests yet still maintain its neutrality and sustain friendly trade relations with China at the same time? These are difficult strategic decisions that Indonesia faces. Adroitness and determination – supported by credible naval deterrence – will be required.

Notes:

1. For further reading on the Indonesian Navy, readers are directed to:

– James Goldrick and Jack McCaffrie, *Navies of South-East Asia: A Comparative Study* (*Cass Series: Naval Policy and History*) (Oxford: Routledge, 2012).
– Geoffrey Till and Jane Chan (eds), *Naval Modernisation in South-East Asia: Nature, Causes and Consequences: A Comparative Study* (*Cass Series: Naval Policy and History*) (Oxford: Routledge, 2013).
– Scott Bentley, 'Indonesia's 'Global Maritime Nexus': Looming Challenges at Sea for Jokowi's Administration' in *The Strategist*, the official blog of the Australian Strategic Policy Institute (ASPI) on 24 September 2014 at ,http://www.aspistrategist.org.au/indonesias-global-maritime-nexus-looming-challenges-at-sea-for-jokowis-administration/

There are several websites and blogs that have analytical pieces on current developments. A sample includes The Diplomat, the Center for Strategic and International Studies (CSIS), the Rajaratnam School of International Studies (RSIS), and the Australian Strategic Policy Institute (APSI).

Articles typically contain links to other websites. Particularly interested readers are encouraged to visit the Indonesian Navy's websites at tnial.mil.id, the Defence ministry website at www.dmc.kemhan.go.id, the naval air website at www.puspenerbal.mil.id and the Marine Corps website at www.marinir.mil.id. All these sites are in Indonesian and need translation.

The author would like to thank Scott Bentley, a PhD student and maritime security expert at APSI, who provided valuable insights into Indonesia's maritime security structure.

2. The doctrine is driven by a combination of national security and domestic economic concerns. See Adelle Neary's 'Jokowi Spells Out Vision for Indonesia's "Global Maritime Nexus"', *Southeast Asia from Scott Circle*, Volume V, Issue 24 – 26 November 2014 (Washington DC: Center for Strategic & International Studies, 2014), pp.1–4.

3. For further details of the new doctrine, see Rendi A Witular's 'Jokowi launches maritime doctrine to the world', *The Jakarta Post* – 13 November 2014 (Jakarta: PT. Niskala Media Tenggara, 2014) currently accessible at http://www.

thejakartapost.com/news/2014/11/13/jokowi-launches-maritime-doctrine-world.html

4. For example, in mid-1962, only five of the 'Whiskey' class submarines were considered to be operational according to Dutch signals intelligence assessments.

5. The release of two books by Admiral Marsetio publicising the 'world class navy' concept was also reported on in *The Jakarta Post* (op. cit.) on 12 June 2014. See Novan Iman Santosa's, 'Indonesia should change its views on the sea: Experts' currently accessible at: http://www.thejakartapost.com/news/2014/06/12/indonesia-should-change-its-views-sea-experts.html

6. Of these, one – *Memet Sastrawiria* – suffered a fire in August 2008 and the ship was subsequently decommissioned.

7. See Bagus B T Saragiih's 'Obsolete gear clips war against poachers' in *The Jakarta Post* (op. cit.) on 25 January 2015.

2.3 REGIONAL REVIEW

THE INDIAN OCEAN AND AFRICA

Author:
Conrad Waters

INTRODUCTION

The most notable recent development in the diverse Indian Ocean and African region is the increasingly evident arms race in the Middle East.[1] Major drivers of a splurge in armaments spending include a proxy war for influence being fought out between Saudi Arabia and Iran, respectively the main proponents of the Sunni and Shia branches of the Islamic faith, and the threat to all established regimes posed by the radicalised Sunni adherents of the Islamic State. Other factors include the loss or weakening of a number of unpleasant but stabilising regional strongmen following the Arab Spring. Underlying much of the tension is an evident reluctance on the part of the United States to repeat the costly experience of its invasion of Iraq. Its priority is now to avoid – with the exception of trainers and, perhaps, Special Forces – the burden of 'boots on the ground'.[2] The Sunni Arab monarchies, long reliant on American support, are concerned that the Obama Administration's desire to reduce its military footprint in the region will result in an unfavourable deal on Iran's nuclear programme that could leave it with greater freedom to meddle elsewhere. This is a view shared by many in Israel, perhaps the United States' most important local ally.

The nature of both the perceived threat and the topography in the Middle East means that the bulk of the higher expenditure has been spent on land and air forces. However, sufficient crumbs have fallen into the lap of regional fleets to support a wide range of programmes. Those in the Persian Gulf, where the potential threat of Iranian disruption to trade passing through the Straits of Hormuz has long been a concern, are, perhaps, most advanced. Although the overall situation in this important waterway appears to be generally calmer, Iran's seizure of a Maersk Line container ship registered in the Marshall Islands in April 2015 over an unsettled legal dispute highlights the potential danger. Elsewhere, the need to protect offshore economic resources from the possibility of both state and terrorist attack seems to be a significant influence. For example, Israel's procurement of corvettes from Germany appears to have been motivated by a desire to improve the protection afforded to the country's developing offshore gas industry.[3]

Sub-Saharan African navies are also benefitting from an increased flow of spending, although this is occurring on a much smaller scale. To an extent, this also reflects an increased willingness to invest in constabulary vessels to counter the scourges of piracy and terrorism and protect economic assets. Co-ordinated action in the Indian Ocean – including much greater stability in mainland Somalia – has dramatically reduced instances of piracy in the Indian Ocean. However, the situation in West Africa, a hotspot for attacks, remains volatile.[4] A host of naval programmes is underway to deliver ships ranging from small patrol craft to sophisticated, corvette-sized vessels, with yards in France and China seemingly the chief beneficiaries.

Turning to the Indian Ocean, the arrival of the new political administration in India headed by the nationalistic Narendra Modi has given a kick-start to a previously sluggish procurement process. New frigate and submarine programmes are amongst a number of long-stalled acquisitions that are finally moving ahead. Although an apparently healthy rise of more than 10 per cent in the core defence budget is expected to be counterbalanced by the impact of inflation and exchange-rate factors, steps are being taken to increase efficiency, for example through greater private-sector involvement in new contracts.

The latter is vitally needed in the naval sector given the inability of state-owned facilities to deliver on time or on budget. A recent report by India's Standing Committee on Defence revealed that the cost of the new aircraft carrier *Vikrant* had increased from INR32.6bn (c.US$500m) to INR193.4bn (c.US$3bn) over the project's life. Delivery, now scheduled for the end of 2018, is eight years late. Significant, if somewhat smaller, cost and time over-runs had also been incurred in constructing other ships. Given this background of underperformance, it is, perhaps, surprising that a decision has been taken to place all future warship orders with domestic yards.[5] In particular, the possibility of incorporating the latest design and construction techniques through co-production of prototypes at 'best of class' overseas builders will be lost. Whilst increased use of privately-owned facilities should facilitate better performance, it seems unlikely that this will – on its own – produce the necessary results.

Table 2.3.1 provides an overview of the most significant regional navies as of mid-2015.

Israel's fifth *Dolphin* class submarine, *Rahav*, pictured undergoing maintenance at Kiel in June 2015 in preparation for her delivery voyage to Haifa. Instability in the Middle East is fuelling a wave of naval procurement. *(Leo van Ginderen)*

Table 2.3.1: FLEET STRENGTHS IN THE INDIAN OCEAN, AFRICA AND THE MIDDLE EAST – LARGER NAVIES (MID 2015)

COUNTRY	ALGERIA	EGYPT	INDIA	IRAN	ISRAEL	PAKISTAN	SAUDI ARABIA	SOUTH AFRICA
Support/Helicopter Carrier (CVS/CVH)	–	–	2	–	–	–	–	–
Attack Submarine (SSN/SSGN)	–	–	1	–	–	–	–	–
Patrol Submarine (SSK/SS)	4	4	13	3	5	5	–	3
Fleet Escort (DDG/FFG)	–	7	23	–	–	10	7	4
Patrol Escort/Corvette (FFG/FSG/FS)	6	4	9	7	3	–	4	–
Missile Armed Attack Craft (PGG/PTG)	12	c.30	12	24	8	8	9	3
Mine Countermeasures Vessel (MCMV)	–	c.14	6	–	–	3	7	4
Major Amphibious (LPD)	1	–	1	–	–	–	–	–

Notes:
1 Egyptian fast attack craft and mine countermeasures numbers approximate.
2 Iranian fleet numbers exclude large numbers of indigenously-built midget and coastal submarines.
3 The South African attack craft and mine-countermeasures vessels serve in patrol vessel roles.

INDIAN OCEAN NAVIES

Bangladesh: The Bangladesh Navy is continuing its steady progress towards becoming a modern, three-dimensional fleet in line with the Forces Goal 2030 established in 2009. Much of its success has been due to a developing relationship with China, which provided two second-hand Type 053H2 'Jianghu III' frigates in 2014 to replace vintage British Royal Navy frigates and is helping the development of a local warship-building industry. The delivery of two *Durjoy* class missile-armed fast attack craft by Wuchang Shipyard in 2013 has been followed by the start of local assembly of the type at Bangladesh's Khulna Shipyard. Wuchang subsequently launched two export variants of the PLAN's Type 056 corvette design – *Shadhinota* and *Prottoy* – for Bangladesh towards the end of 2014. It seems that the plan is also to build this larger type at Khulna in due course.

Completion of the Bangladesh Navy's three-dimensional force objective will also require acquisition of submarines, a requirement that has been under consideration for some time. It has been reported that construction of a new submarine base is now underway near Cox's Bazar in the far southeast of the country prior to the delivery of two second-hand Type 035 'Ming' class boats from China by 2016. Whilst unsuitable for front-line service, they will doubtless provide useful experience in developing underwater operating skills until more modern boats are acquired. The possibility of more modern Chinese units gaining access to the Bangladesh base – and similar facilities in Pakistan – has already resulted in an outbreak of submarine hysteria in parts of the Indian media.[6]

Although China is its most significant supplier of naval ships, Bangladesh appears to be hedging its bets by obtaining some equipment from other sources. A former US Coast Guard *Hamilton* (WHEC-715) class high endurance cutter was commissioned at *Somudra Joy* in December 2013 and a second was transferred in May 2015. The former *Rush* (WHEC-723), she will be renamed *Somudra Avijan* in Bangladesh Navy service.

India: By far the most significant regional naval power, India has achieved some tangible steps towards achieving its fleet modernisation programme over the past twelve months. The long-awaited lead ships of two important classes of surface ship have been delivered, whilst the first of a new class of patrol submarines was launched by Mazagon Dock Ltd. Unfortunately, the pace of new deliveries is barely keeping pace with the disposal of older ships. Recourse to purchases from Russia has previously helped alleviate the policy. However, the exclusive 'build in India' policy – as well as the difficulties Russian yards now face in obtaining gas turbines from the Ukraine – now excludes this possibility.

Difficulties also persist with recruitment. The navy's current uniformed manpower is in the region of 70,000 personnel but, according to the Ministry of Defence, this is around 20 per cent below the required level. There is a shortage of civilian staff of roughly the same magnitude. Recent figures suggest that there has been some progress in closing the gap. However, as of 31 January 2015, the navy was still some 1,322 officers and 11,257 sailors below headcount. Terms of service are being improved to attract more recruits but this will inevitably impact funding available for modernisation.

Aircraft Carriers: The newly-refurbished former Russian aircraft carrier *Vikramaditya* has been very active since being declared fully operational in May 2014, taking part in both national and international exercises. A short refit is now underway to provide a close-in weapons system (CIWS) capability, previously criticised as a major deficiency. Meanwhile, progress continues with fitting out the first indigenous carrier, *Vikrant*. She has now completed a final docking period during which her island structure was installed and work completed on propulsion and rudder equipment located below the waterline. In spite of this, planned commissioning at the end of 2018 looks optimistic given previous delays in fitting out locally-built ships. The Indian Navy had hoped to run on the existing *Viraat* (the former British Royal Navy *Hermes*) until the new carrier entered service to maintain a two-carrier fleet structure. However, it has now been decided that the age of the 65-year-old ship precludes further life extensions and she will be decommissioned early in 2016.

Major Surface Combatants: The lead Project 15A destroyer *Kolkata* was finally commissioned on 16 August 2014, nearly eleven years after she was laid down in September 2003. The ship was delivered without the Barak 8 surface-to-air missiles that are intended to be her primary area-defence weapons. These have yet to conclude final testing but should become operational after final weapons trials on the destroyer, which are anticipated before the end of 2015. By this time, the other two Project 15A ships – *Kochi* and *Chennai* – should also be in service. Total programme cost is now estimated at

India's new indigenous aircraft carrier, *Vikrant*, completed her final docking period at the Cochin shipyard on 10 June 2015. All systems below the waterline have been completed and her island structure installed. *(Indian Navy)*

A series of images of the Indian Navy's lead Project 15A destroyer, *Kolkata*, taken during sea trials towards the end of 2013. The dominant feature are the four fixed arrays for the EL/M-2248 MF-STAR active phased array produced by Israel Aerospace Industries Ltd's Elta subsidiary, located high on the forward mast. A multi-function radar capable of identifying potential threats out to around 150 nautical miles, it is supported by a long-range Thales LW-08 search array on the rear mast. Four octuple clusters for Barak 8 surface-to-air missiles are located in separate positions forwards and atop the hangar; the former being positioned immediately aft sixteen strike-length launch cells for BrahMos anti-surface missiles. Also apparent are a 76mm Oto Melara Super Rapid gun forward, two RBU-6000 anti-submarine rocket launchers immediately in front of the bridge and a cluster of AK-630 CIWS around the after mast. *(Indian Navy)*

Table 2.3.2: INDIAN NAVY: PRINCIPAL UNITS AS AT MID 2015

TYPE	CLASS	NUMBER	TONNAGE	DIMENSIONS	PROPULSION	CREW	DATE
Aircraft Carriers							
Aircraft Carrier (CV)	Project 1143.4 **VIKRAMADITYA** (KIEV)	1	45,000 tons	283m x 31/60m x 10m	Steam, 30 knots	1,600	1987
Aircraft Carrier (CV)	**VIRAAT** (HERMES)	1	29,000 tons	227m x 27/49m x 9m	Steam, 28 knots	1,350	1959
Principal Surface Escorts							
Destroyer – DDG	Project 15A **KOLKATA**	1	7,400 tons	163m x 17m x 7m	COGAG, 30+knots	330	2014
Destroyer – DDG	Project 15 **DELHI**	3	6,700 tons	163m x 17m x 7m	COGAG, 32 knots	350	1997
Destroyer – DDG	Project 61 ME **RAJPUT** ('Kashin')	5	5,000 tons	147m x 16m x 5m	COGAG, 35 knots	320	1980
Frigate – FFG	Project 17 **SHIVALIK**	3	6,200 tons	143m x 17m x 5m	CODOG, 30 knots	265	2010
Frigate – FFG	Project 1135.6 **TALWAR**	6	4,000 tons	125m x 15m x 5m	COGAG, 30 knots	180	2003
Frigate – FFG	Project 16A **BRAHMAPUTRA**	3	4,000 tons	127m x 15m x 5m	Steam, 30 knots	350	2000
Frigate – FFG	Project 16 **GODAVARI**	2	3,850 tons	127m x 15m x 5m	Steam, 30 knots	315	1983
Corvette – FSG	Project 28 **KAMORTA**	1	3,400 tons	109m x 13m x 4m	Diesel, 25 knots	195	2014
Corvette – FSG	Project 25A **KORA**	4	1,400 tons	91m x 11m x 5m	Diesel, 25 knots	125	1998
Corvette – FSG	Project 25 **KHUKRI**	4	1,400 tons	91m x 11m x 5m	Diesel, 25 knots	110	1989
Submarines							
Submarine – SSN	Project 971 **CHAKRA** ('Akula II')	1	9,500+ tons	110m x 14m x 10m	Nuclear, 30+ knots	100	2012
Submarine – SSK	Project 877 EKM **SINDHUGHOSH** ('Kilo')	9	3,000 tons	73m x 10m x 7m	Diesel-electric, 17 knots	55	1986
Submarine – SSK	**SHISHUMAR** (Type 209)	4	1,900 tons	64m x 7m x 6m	Diesel-electric, 22 knots	40	1986
Major Amphibious Units							
Landing Platform Dock – LPD	**JALASHWA** (AUSTIN)	1	17,000 tons	173m x 26/30m x 7m	Steam, 21 knots	405	1971

The long-delayed Project 28 anti-submarine corvette, *Kamorta*, pictured undertaking a maiden appearance at the LIMA defence exhibition in May 2015. *(Mrityunjoy Mazumdar)*

INR116.6bn (US$1.8bn) or c. US$600m per ship.

The class will be followed by a further four destroyers of the improved Project 15B type. The first of these, *Visakhapatnam*, was launched by Mazagon Dock in Mumbai on 20 April 2015. The new ships have the same hull, propulsion package and main MF-STAR active phased-array radar of the earlier class but incorporate a number of detailed improvements to data and weapons systems, as well as to stealth. When added to the three original Project 15 type, their completion will provide a total of ten Project 15 series vessels.

2015 also saw contracts being awarded for construction of seven Project 17A frigates, which will be built both by Mazagon Dock and Garden Reach Shipbuilders & Engineers (GRSE) of Kolkata. Deliveries are scheduled from around 2023. Few details of their final design have emerged and it is not certain to what extent they will be based on the three previous Project 17 frigates of the *Shivalik* class. In the meantime, construction of smaller vessels is concentrated on the quartet of Project 28 *Kamorta* class corvettes, which are also late and over budget. The first of these was commissioned on 23 August 2014 and the remainder are expected to follow at approximately yearly intervals.

Left: A major event in the renewal of India's submarine force took place in April 2015 when the lead Project 75 'Scorpène' type submarine *Kalvari* was floated out by Mazagon Dock in Mumbai. It is hoped to have six of these French-designed submarines in service by 2020 but this appears to be an ambitious target. *(Indian Navy)*

Above: India completed its first naval construction order for an overseas customer when the new offshore patrol vessel *Barracuda* was handed over to the National Coast Guard of Mauritius. The 74m-long vessel is lightly armed but will give Mauritius an extended patrol capability that has been missing since the previous patrol vessel, *Vigilant*, was laid up. This picture shows the new ship at her home port. *(Arjun Sarup)*

The arrival of new ships is allowing withdrawal of some of the navy's older frigates, with the steam-turbine powered Project 16 *Godavari* class – a stretched version of the *Leander* design – being the next class slated for withdrawal.

Submarines: A major milepost in the overdue renewal of India's submarine fleet was reached on 6 April 2015 when Mazagon Dock floated out the first of six Project 75 boats being constructed to the French DCNS 'Scorpène' design. Named *Kalvari*, the new submarine is expected to commission before the end of 2016 and be followed by her five sister boats by 2020; another optimistic expectation. Displacing nearly 2,000 tons in submerged condition, the new submarines are armed with six torpedo tubes for torpedoes and SM-39 Exocet anti-ship missiles. Discussions are now underway to select both a design and shipyards for the follow-on Project 75I class after formal approval for the new programme was given by the Indian Defence Acquisition Council in October 2014. As for Australia, there is considerable interest in the Japanese *Soryu* design but European and Russian types will also be considered.

The new strategic missile submarine, *Arihant*, is currently embarked on an extensive programme of sea acceptance trials following an initial voyage in December 2014. Subject to satisfactory progress, it is likely that she will be inducted into the fleet towards the end of 2016. At least one improved variant, *Aridhaman*, is under construction at the secretive Ship Building Centre (SBC) at Visakhapatnam and plans for an eventual force of five boats have been reported. It appears that the SBC will also be involved in a domestic nuclear-powered attack submarine programme in due course following a government decision to target a long term fleet structure encompassing eighteen patrol submarines and six larger attack types.

The existing submarine flotilla is centred on the remaining nine Russian-built 'Kilo' class boats delivered between 1986 and 2000.[7] Many of these have been undergoing extensive upgrades to keep them in service and it has been decided to extend this work to the rest of the class. To date, most of these refits have been carried out in Russia but, in spite of previous scepticism over the ability of local industry to complete her refit, the Hindustan Shipyard returned *Sindhukriti* to sea for trials on 23 May 2015. There has been speculation in the local media that Russian experts sent to supervise the upgrade

purposely extended the scope of the work to ensure any further submarine upgrades were carried out in their own yard.[8]

Other Warships: Construction of front-line warships is being supplemented by a large number of ongoing programmes covering secondary types. The initial batch of four *Saryu* offshore patrol vessels has been completed with the September 2014 delivery of *Sumitra* by Goa Shipyard, which is now focused on completing orders for the Indian Coast Guard. The yard has also been allocated a contract for twelve new mine-countermeasures vessels, which are desperately needed to replace the fast-disappearing *Pondicherry* type. Other projects at a less-advanced stage of development encompass amphibious assault ships, fleet replenishment vessels and new classes of coastal anti-submarine and anti-surface corvettes.

Mauritius: A notable event took place on 20 December 2014 when India handed over the first warship it had specifically built for export at GRSE in Kolkata. The new *Barracuda* is a 74m-long offshore patrol vessel ordered by the National Coast Guard of Mauritius. Replacing the decommissioned *Vigilant*, it is reportedly based on the *Kora* class corvette design but is only armed with light weapons and a platform to support helicopter operations. India's Goa Shipyard is also currently building two smaller, 50m fast attack craft for coast guard use.

Myanmar: Although a maritime boundary dispute with Bangladesh was settled in 2012, naval developments in Myanmar have undoubtedly been influenced by its neighbour's modernisation and expansion programme. The country has long had a capacity to build a range of smaller craft at Naval Dockyard Yangon (Rangoon). This capability has steadily expanded to the construction of corvettes and, most recently, frigates. The last-mentioned programme commenced around 2003 and has resulted in the assembly of a series of *Aung Zeya* class ships to a progressively enhanced design. Two out of a planned total of up to eight frigates are already in

service. They complement two second-hand Type 053H1 'Jianghu II' frigates delivered in 2012 and numbers of corvettes and missile-armed attack craft. Although China has been the most important supplier of equipment historically, Russian and – increasingly – Indian technology is also being sought.

Bangladesh's imminent acquisition of submarines is likely to be resulting in consideration of the merits of obtaining a similar capability. However, no firm details have emerged. There have also been reports of discussions with Indonesia about the potential purchase of *Makassar* type amphibious transport docks.[8]

Pakistan: A summary of current Pakistan Navy fleet strength is provided in Table 3.2.3. Although discussions over a number of programmes, largely in conjunction with China, are underway, there have

been few tangible developments over the past year. The most significant project in the pipeline related to the potential acquisition of Chinese submarines. These will most likely be an export version of the Type 039A/Type 041 'Yuan' class. Chinese support is also evident in the ongoing local construction of *Azmat* class fast attack craft at Karachi Shipyard & Engineering Works. A third ship, reportedly the first of a second pair, was laid down in April 2015.

The ongoing vulnerability of the Pakistan Navy to terrorist attack – it lost two newly-delivered P-3C Orion maritime patrol aircraft in a raid on its airbase at Mehran in May 2011 – was reinforced in September 2014 when news emerged of an audacious attempt to seize the frigate *Zulfiqar*. Al-Qaeda affiliates and rogue navy officers were only prevented from capturing the ship and using it in an attack on US Navy vessels after a prolonged firefight in which ten terrorists were killed.[10]

AFRICAN NAVIES

The flow of naval orders emanating from Sub-Saharan Africa is dominated by constabulary assets. Amongst the most important programmes is **South Africa**'s Project Biro, for which long-awaited requests for proposals (RFPs) were issued in December 2014.[11] The two separate RFPs encompass three 85m-long offshore patrol vessels, equipped with a flight deck and hangar facilities, and a further three, smaller 60m-long inshore patrol vessels. A separate tender is underway under Project Hotel to replace the elderly survey ship *Protea*. It is intended to base the newly-acquired ships at a re-opened facility at Salisbury Island in Durban, thereby reinforcing the naval presence on South Africa's eastern coast. In the meantime, the lead Type 209 submarine *Manthatisi* has returned to operational service after a seven-year gap following a refit and overhaul at Simon's Town dockyard. Her return will allow the second of South

The Pakistan Navy's F-22P *Zulfiqar* class frigate *Saif* pictured on exercises with the Royal Australian Navy in August 2014. The lead ship of the class was subject to an audacious but ultimately unsuccessful seizure attempt by 'Al Qaeda' terrorists the following month. *(Royal Australian Navy)*

Table 2.3.3: PAKISTAN NAVY: PRINCIPAL UNITS AS AT MID 2015

TYPE	CLASS	NUMBER	TONNAGE	DIMENSIONS	PROPULSION	CREW	DATE
Principal Surface Escorts							
Frigate – FFG	ZULFIQAR (F22P)	4	3,000 tons	118m x 13m x 5m	CODAD, 29 knots	185	2009
Frigate – FFG	ALAMGIR (FFG-7)	1	4,100 tons	138m x 14m x 5m	COGAG, 30 knots	215	1977
Frigate – FFG	TARIQ (Type 21)	5	3,600 tons	117m x 13m x 5m	COGOG, 32 knots	180	1974
Submarines							
Submarine – SSK	HAMZA (AGOSTA 90B/AIP)	1	2,100 tons	76m x 7m x 6m	AIP, 20 knots	40	2008
Submarine – SSK	KHALID (AGOSTA 90B)	2	1,800 tons	68m x 7m x 6m	Diesel-electric, 20 knots	40	1999
Submarine – SSK	HASHMAT (AGOSTA)	2	1,800 tons	68m x 7m x 6m	Diesel-electric, 20 knots	55	1979

Africa's three submarines, *Charlotte Maxeke*, to enter the refit cycle. In similar fashion, the lead ship of the four MEKO A-200 'Valour' class frigates, *Amatola*, has just completed a fifteen-month refit at Southern African Shipyards in Durban prior to re-joining the fleet in July 2015.

Elsewhere in Sub-Saharan Africa, **Nigeria** is undertaking considerable naval investment to protect its offshore economy from piracy, illegal fishing and potential terrorist threats. Its approach to naval recapitalisation carries a striking resemblance to that adopted by Bangladesh, with transfers of second-hand former US Coast Guard cutters supplementing orders for newly-built Chinese corvettes. The first of the latter, a P-18N export variant of the Type 056 design, is called *Century* and was commissioned in February 2015. A second vessel, *Unity*, is currently being assembled by the Wuchang Shipyard prior to final outfitting at a new Chinese-developed shipyard at Port Harcourt. The navy has also acquired the former Irish offshore patrol vessel *Emer*, which apparently spent some time being impounded after its new business owner brought her into Nigerian waters illegally. Named *Prosperity*, she will be used as a training ship in Nigerian Navy service. Elsewhere in the Gulf of Guinea, **Equatorial Guinea** has built up an impressive local naval force with Ukrainian assistance.[12] Neighbouring **Gabon**'s much smaller fleet is supplementing its existing fleet of P400 patrol vessels with a refurbished French Navy example and is acquiring a newly-built vessel from the KERSHIP alliance between DCNS and Piriou.

The most ambitious naval expansion programmes are, however, taking place along Africa's Mediterranean coast. A major driver of this trend appears to be **Algeria**, which has been using energy sector revenues to purchase a wide range of advanced naval equipment that appears disproportionate to its immediate security needs. The most ambitious acquisition has been the amphibious transport dock, *Kalaat Béni Abbès*, which is a variant of the Italian Navy's *San Giorgio* design. Reportedly built at a cost of c.€400m (US$450m), she incorporates a powerful air-defence capability in the form of an EMPAR radar and associated Aster missiles. Delivered by Italy's Fincantieri in September 2014, she arrived in Algeria in March 2015 after an extensive training and work up period. Other naval construction currently underway encompasses a broad range of suppliers that might complicate

A picture of the new Nigerian P-18N corvette *Century*, taken during a stopover in Mauritius during her delivery voyage from the inland Wuchang Shipyard on China's Yangtze River. An export variant of China's P-26 corvette, she is longer than the Chinese ships and incorporates a helicopter hangar but a much reduced armament. A second member of the class is under construction. *(Arjun Sarup)*

The South African Navy's Type 209 submarine *Charlotte Maxeke* pictured on training exercises with the British Royal Navy frigate *Portland* in the first half of 2014. She will shortly enter refit now that completion of work on the first South African member of the class, *Manthatisi*, allows her to take her place in the maintenance cycle. *(Crown Copyright 2014)*

A picture of Algeria's new compact amphibious transport dock, *Kalaat Béni Abbès*, at Fincantieri's Muggiano Shipyard in April 2014. Combining amphibious lift capabilities with a sophisticated air-defence system controlled by an EMPAR phased array, she is the most significant ship in a large Algerian naval construction programme. *(Conrad Waters)*

An image of last-minute preparatory work being undertaken on the former French FREMM-type frigate *Normandie* the day before her transfer to Egypt on 23 June 2015 as *Tahya Misr*. Egypt has also recently taken delivery of four sophisticated 'Ambassador IV' fast attack craft from the United Sates and has ongoing programmes for the construction of German submarines and French 'Gowind' corvettes. *(Bruno Huriet)*

future maintenance requirements. It includes an additional two Russian-built 'Kilo' class submarines, two MEKO A-200 frigates subcontracted to German Naval Yards Kiel by Germany's ThyssenKrupp Marine Systems (TKMS), and three large Chinese C-28A type corvettes incorporating Dutch sensors and combat systems. The former ships are similar to South Africa's *Amatola* class and there are options for two more. The recent fall in the oil price makes the exercise of these options, as well as one for a second amphibious transport dock, seem increasingly unlikely.

Perhaps spurred on by developments to its west, **Egypt** is also spending heavily. Purchases of Type 209 submarines from Germany and co-production of 'Gowind 2500' corvettes with France's DCNS have recently been supplemented by acquisition in 'sail-away condition' of the newly-completed French FREMM frigate, *Normandie*. Transferred on 23 June 2015 following signature of a contract in February, she will take the name *Tahya Misr* in Egyptian service. The deal includes the provision of through-life support for an initial period of five years. There will also be ongoing training from embarked DCNS technicians for a period of fifteen months, reflecting the real challenges involved in bringing such a complex, automated ship into full operational service.

MIDDLE EASTERN NAVIES

Along the coast from Egypt, **Israel** is also investing heavily in naval technology, with its purchases from German yards being assisted by generous subsidies from the German government. There are major ongoing programmes involving the acquisition of submarines and missile-armed corvettes, of which the former is more advanced. *Tanin,* the first of a second batch of three *Dolphin*-type submarines arrived at the navy's main Haifa naval base in September 2014 and her sister, *Rahav*, is also expected imminently. The sixth boat remains under construction. With a length of 69m and a submerged displacement of 2,400 tons, the new submarines are considerably larger than the three earlier *Dolphin* types (57m long and displacement of 1,700 tons) and are fitted with air-independent

The Royal Navy of Oman is starting to take delivery of four *Al-Seeb* class patrol vessels from Singapore's ST Marine in another major export success for the Singapore yard. *(ST Marine)*.

propulsion (AIP). An interesting feature of the second batch is their heavy armament of no fewer than ten torpedo tubes, four of which are of an enlarged 650mm diameter. This has served to fuel speculation that the submarines are intended to be capable of operating in a nuclear strike role.[13]

The submarines will ultimately be joined by four new corvettes ordered from TKMS in April 2015 under a deal reportedly valued at €430m (c. US$500m). Over a quarter of this will be funded by the German government. Although few details of the contract have emerged, it is understood that much of the new ships' equipment will be sourced from Israeli manufacturers. As TKMS no longer owns its own surface shipyards, actual construction will follow the same arrangement as for the Algerian frigates and be outsourced to German Naval Yards Kiel.

Turning to the Gulf, both the **United Arab Emirates** and **Oman** have important naval programmes coming to fruition. The former is seeing the local construction of its French CMN-designed *Baynunah* start to draw to a close. All six ships are now in the water following the launch of the sixth, *Al Hili*, in February 2014 and the fourth, *Mazyed*, was formally handed over by local yard ADSB in May 2015. Meanwhile, the Royal Navy of Oman has taken preliminary delivery of its first *Al-Seeb* patrol vessel from Singapore's ST Marine and expects to have all four ships in service before the end of 2016. A heavily-modified variant of Singapore's *Fearless* class, the new ships displace a little over 1,000 tons and are equipped with 76mm and 30mm Oto Melara guns, as well as a Thales combat system and sensors. There is also a platform for operation of a medium-sized helicopter, although no hangar. Having previously accepted all three *Al Shamikh* class corvettes from BAE Systems, Oman also awaits two high-speed transport vessels similar to but smaller than the US Navy's *Spearhead* (JHSV-1) design that are currently under construction by Austal in Australia.

On the other side of the Gulf, **Iran** continues to make progress with indigenous programmes which are steadily progressing to larger and more ambitious construction projects encompassing both frigates and medium-sized submarines. Its navy has been active in the Gulf of Aden, monitoring the naval blockade of Yemen imposed by the Saudi Arabian coalition that has intervened on the side of pro-government forces in Yemen's civil war. Iran stands accused of supporting the Houthi rebels that have all but toppled the established government but there is evidence to suggest that claims of support to its co-religionists have been exacerbated. The naval dimension to **Saudi Arabia**'s involvement may spur that country's long-anticipated fleet modernisation programme, on which there is little tangible news. An intriguing US Department of Defense contract notification released in December 2014 reporting the sale of Mk 41 vertical launch systems to Saudi Arabia has fuelled rumours of the potential sale of *Arleigh Burke* (DDG-51) class destroyers or Aegis-equipped variants of the Littoral Combat Ship. However, further developments have yet to be reported.

Notes:

1. The flow of arms deals, headed by French exports of Rafale jets, has been covered by many media sources. Of these, Peter Beaumont's article, 'The $18bn arms race helping to fuel Middle East conflict' in *The Guardian* - 23 April 2015 (London: Guardian News & Media Ltd, 2015) contains a thorough if not entirely dispassionate analysis of the current regional situation. A longer term analysis of regional military spending is provided by Sam Perlo-Freeman, Aude Fleurant, Pieter D. Wezeman and Siemon T. Wezeman in *SIPRI Fact Sheet: Trends in World Military Expenditure, 2014* (Solna, Sweden: Stockholm International Peace Research Institute, 2015).

2. It is far beyond *Seaforth World Naval Review*'s scope to attempt to provide a detailed analysis of either the complex background to current conflicts in the Middle East or the current United States' approach to the region. A good 'starter' to understanding both these issues is provided in 'America and the Middle East: A dangerous modesty', *The Economist* – 6 June 2015 (London: The Economist Newspaper Ltd, 2015).

3. This explanation was provided by a number of sources, including Herb Keinon's 'Germany to sell four warships to Israel', *The Jerusalem Post* – 25 December 2014 (Jerusalem: JPost Inc., 2014).

4. The International Maritime Bureau (IMB), part of International Chamber of Commerce's Commercial Crime Arm, reported zero instances of piracy off Somalia in the first quarter of 2015. By contrast, there were eleven reported attacks off West Africa over the same timescale, including one death and five kidnappings. The IMB has previously stated that many additional attacks go unreported.

5. The Indian Ministry of Defence directive was reported by Vivek Raghuvanshi in 'India to Limit Ship Buys to Domestic Yards', *Defense News* – 2 May 2015 (Springfield VA: Gannett Government Media, 2015).

6. An example is Sandeep Unnithan's 'China's submarine noose around India' published in the *India Today* magazine and news website on 15 December 2014 (Noida, Uttar Pradesh: Living Media, 2014). A copy can currently be found at: http://indiatoday.intoday.in/story/china-submarine-noose-using-undersea-vessels-to-project-power-in-india/1/405191.html

7. The tenth member of the class, *Sindhurakshak*, was destroyed in an explosion and fire in Mumbai harbour in August 2013. Reports in the Indian press have suggested that failure to follow standard procedures and associated human error on the part of overworked sailors were the most likely cause of the submarine's loss.

8. See Ajai Shulka's 'Russia delayed sub refit to weaken shipyard?', *Business Standard* – 2 September 2014 (New Delhi: Business Standard Private Ltd, 2014).

9. These discussions were first reported by Jon Grevatt under the headline 'Myanmar Navy and Indonesia's PT PAL in LPD Talks', *Jane's Defence Weekly* – 30 July 2014 (Coulsdon: IHS Jane's, 2014), p.17.

10. The story was reported by Syed Shoaib Hasan, Saeed Shah and Siobhan Gorman in 'Al Qaeda Militants tried to seize Pakistan Navy Frigate', *The Wall Street Journal* – 16 September 2014 (New York: Dow Jones & Co, 2014).

11. Much valuable information on ongoing developments with respect to the South African and other African navies can be found on the naval portal of the *defenceWeb* news site, which can be found at: *http://www.defenceweb.co.za/*

12. A detailed report on the considerable investment in the Equatorial Guinean Navy was contained on Jeremy Binnie's 'The rise of the Equatorial Guinean Navy', *Jane's Defence Weekly* – 3 September 2014 (Coulsdon: IHS Jane's, 2014), pp.24–7.

13. Considerable information on Israel's new batch of submarines, including an excellent series of photographs, was published in an article by Christopher P. Cavas in *Defense News' Intercepts* blog on 14 August 2014. The post can be accessed at: http://intercepts.defensenews.com/2014/08/israels-deadliest-submarines-are-nearly-ready/

Author:
Conrad Waters

2.4 REGIONAL REVIEW

EUROPE AND RUSSIA

INTRODUCTION

European navies are currently adapting to two simultaneous challenges calling for the use of very different maritime skills. In the Mediterranean, a slow-burning humanitarian crisis involving mass migration away from ongoing conflicts in several Middle Eastern and North African countries has finally ignited into front-page news across the continent after the sinking of several boatloads of refugees with heavy loss of human life. The immediate origins of the crisis lay in Italy's decision to terminate its own search and rescue mission in the narrow seas between Sicily and North Africa, Operation 'Mare Nostrum', in October 2014. Its government had faced significant political criticism over the heavy expense of maintaining the operation in the absence of other European Union (EU) countries to provide more substantial support.[1] A replacement border security operation was implemented under the auspices of the EU's Frontex organisation – Operation 'Triton' – but was greatly reduced in both cost and scope. The inevitable result was a huge increase in the number of migrants drowned whilst attempting the crossing. More than a thousand people lost their lives in shipwrecks off the Libyan coast in April 2015 alone.

The huge human cost of these events forced the EU's politicians to act. At an emergency summit on 23 April 2015, it was effectively agreed to increase funding for Operation 'Triton' to around the same level as for 'Mare Nostrum'. A number of countries also pledged naval vessels to support search and rescue operations. The decision was taken against a backdrop of considerable ambivalence between a wish to safeguard human life and a desire to avoid increasing the flood of humanity lapping at Europe's shores. Certainly, many had previously argued against planned search and rescue operations, arguing they had created the unintended consequence of encouraging more migrants to make the crossing and thereby caused more deaths.[2] There has therefore been considerable scepticism about the apparent change of course. For example, Amnesty International stated that the European response was a 'face-saving not a life-saving operation'.

One potential way of resolving the quandary is to take more proactive action against the people-traffickers who facilitate – and not infrequently abuse – the flow of migrants. Consequently, the EU has launched a new naval operation – EU Naval Force Mediterranean (EUNAVFOR Med) – headquartered in Rome to identify the criminal networks that are behind the smuggling activities. This is intended to lead to further action to destroy the networks, for example through the seizure or sinking of their boats. The operation will rely heavily on the cooperation of North African countries to execute its mandate. It is by no means sure this will be forthcoming.[3]

Meanwhile, further to the north, European navies have been involved in search and surveillance missions of a very different kind following reports of activity by unidentified foreign submarines close to a number of countries' shores. Swedish vessels were involved in a week-long hunt for an underwater target in October 2014 in the waters of the Stockholm archipelago, with some reports suggesting several submarines were involved. Similar search activity was initiated by Finland in April 2015. On this occasion low-impact depth charges were used to warn off a potential intruder that had been identified within territorial waters close to Helsinki. The pattern fits with other reports relating to Russian submarines attempting to gain intelligence on British strategic submarine movements in and out of the Faslane naval base from deployments off the west coast of Scotland, as well as with increased Russian testing of NATO air-defence capabilities.

It is difficult to assess what impact this activity – and the underlying deterioration in relations with Russia – will have on European fleet structures. The fact that some of the seemingly irresistible downward pressure on defence budgets that was previously a fact of life for many European armed forces has now been removed will certainly protect some planned capabilities. This is reflected, for example, in the long-awaited final approval for Sweden's A-26 class submarine. Equally, there may be second thoughts in some defence ministries about the extent of the switch away from spending on home defence that was previously another fact of post-Cold War life. As such, some of the emphasis on warships suitable for lengthy deployments on constabulary missions such as the German F-125 class frigates might reduce. It has already become apparent that the German Navy's next surface combatants – the MKS-180 – will have a much greater emphasis on high-intensity warfare.

The Irish Naval Service's flagship *Eithne*, shown in the course of rescuing migrants from the waters of the Mediterranean in June 2015, Ireland being one of a number of countries that have sent vessels to mitigate a major humanitarian crisis that has left thousands dead. There remains considerable disagreement over the best way to tackle the flood of migrants attempting to enter the EU's borders. *(Irish Defence Forces)*

TABLE 2.4.1: FLEET STRENGTHS IN WESTERN EUROPE – LARGER NAVIES (MID 2015)

COUNTRY	FRANCE	GERMANY	GREECE	ITALY	NETHERLANDS	SPAIN	TURKEY	UK
Aircraft Carrier (CVN)	1	–	–	–	–	–	–	–
Support/Helicopter Carrier (CVS/CVH)	–	–	–	2	–	–	–	–
Strategic Missile Submarine (SSBN)	4	–	–	–	–	–	–	4
Attack Submarine (SSN)	6	–	–	–	–	–	–	6
Patrol Submarine (SSK)	–	5	9[2]	6	4	3	13	–
Fleet Escort (DDG/FFG)	16	10	13	18[2]	6	11	16	19
Patrol Escort/Corvette (FFG/FSG/FS)	15	5	–	6	–	–	8	–
Missile Armed Attack Craft (PGG/PTG)	–	6	17	–	–	–	23	–
Mine Countermeasures Vessel (MCMV)	14	15[1]	4	10	6	6	20	15
Major Amphibious (LHD/LPD/LPH/LSD)	3	–	–	3	2	3	–	6

Notes:

1 Two further units used as support vessels.

2 Headline figures overstate the actual position, as old ships will be withdrawn once new units are fully operational.

MAJOR REGIONAL POWERS – FRANCE

France has decided to reverse many of the reductions to its defence establishment envisaged in the 2013 White Paper and associated 2014–19 Military Planning Law in view of the deteriorating European security situation. However, the main beneficiary of this changed approach has been the army and the impact on the *Marine Nationale* is largely peripheral. As such, the previous plan for a fleet based on a single aircraft carrier, three amphibious assault ships, fifteen front-line escorts and a submarine flotilla of four nuclear-powered strategic submarines and six attack submarines remains intact. In line with this structure, France's fourth and oldest major amphibious unit, the dock landing ship *Siroco*, returned from her last deployment in April 2015 prior to decommissioning and sale. A summary of major remaining fleet units is provided in Table 2.4.2.

The sale of the second French FREMM frigate, *Normandie*, to Egypt has led to a degree of reshuffling of the front-line surface force. The crew previously assigned to working up *Normandie* have now transferred to the third of class, *Provence*, which was delivered on 12 June 2015. Construction of the remaining French FREMMs will be accelerated to compensate for *Normandie*'s transfer and two of the existing *Georges Leygues* class will be kept in service for longer whilst this takes effect. Meanwhile, the lead ship, *Aquitaine*, has been continuing an exten-

France's sale of its second FREMM frigate *Normandie* to Egypt has resulted in a rejigging of the construction and delivery programme for the remainder of the class. One change has been the transfer of *Normandie*'s crew to *Provence*, the third of the class, before her delivery in June 2015. This image shows her departing Lorient, where she had been built, on her delivery voyage. *(DCNS)*

sive series of post-delivery trials. As part of these, she completed initial firing trials of both Exocet MM40 surface-to-surface missile and Naval Cruise Missiles during May 2015.

In the medium term, it has been confirmed that construction of French FREMMs will be curtailed at just eight ships, comprising six anti-submarine and two air-defence variants. Attention will then turn to

TABLE 2.4.2: FRENCH NAVY: PRINCIPAL UNITS AS AT MID 2015

TYPE	CLASS	NUMBER	TONNAGE	DIMENSIONS	PROPULSION	CREW	DATE
Aircraft Carriers							
Aircraft Carrier – CVN	CHARLES DE GAULLE	1	42,000 tons	262m x 33/64m x 9m	Nuclear, 27 knots	1,950	2001
Principal Surface Escorts							
Frigate – FFG	AQUITAINE (FREMM)	2	6,000 tons	142m x 20m x 5m	CODLOG, 27 knots	110	2012
Frigate – FFG	FORBIN ('Horizon')	2	7,000 tons	153m x 20m x 5m	CODOG, 29+ knots	195	2008
Frigate – FFG	CASSARD (FAA-70)	2	5,000 tons	139m x 15m x 5m	CODAD, 30 knots	250	1988
Frigate – FFG	GEORGES LEYGUES (FASM-70)	5	4,800 tons	139m x 15m x 5m	CODOG, 30 knots	240	1979
Frigate – FFG	LA FAYETTE	5	3,600 tons	125m x 15m x 5m	CODAD, 25 knots	150	1996
Frigate – FSG	FLORÉAL	6	3,000 tons	94m x 14m x 4m	CODAD, 20 knots	90	1992
Frigate – FS[1]	D'ESTIENNE D'ORVES (A-69)	9	1,300 tons	80m x 10m x 3m	Diesel, 24 knots	90	1976
Submarines							
Submarine – SSBN	LE TRIOMPHANT	4	14,400 tons	138m x 13m x 11m	Nuclear, 25 knots	110	1997
Submarine – SSN	RUBIS	6	2,700 tons	74m x 8m x 6m	Nuclear, 25+ knots	70	1983
Major Amphibious Units							
Amph Assault Ship – LHD	MISTRAL	3	21,500 tons	199m x 32m x 6m	Diesel-electric, 19 knots	160	2006

Note:

1 Now officially reclassified as offshore patrol vessels.

building a new *frégate de taille intermédiaire* (FTI), which will start to replace the existing five ships of the *La Fayette* class on a one-for-one basis from 2023. This represents an acceleration of previous plans to ensure continuity of production. The new ships are expected to be in the 4,000-ton range and be more suitable for export than the sophisticated and expensive FREMMS. The two 'Horizon' class air-defence destroyers will make up the balance of the fifteen-strong escort force.

Replacement of the second-line force of patrol and support vessels appears to be progressing on a more piecemeal basis. Confirmation that the option for a fourth B2M *bâtiment multi-mission* of the *D'Entrecasteaux* class would be exercised was one positive piece of naval news to emerge from the recent defence revisions. The lead ship was laid down in April 2014 and should be launched during the summer of 2015. In addition, plans for four BSAH (*bâtiments de soutien et d'assistance hauturiers*) have also been confirmed, whilst two *patrouilleurs légers Guyanais* have already been ordered to provide a constabulary presence in the shallow waters off French Guiana. There is, however, no firm plan for replacing the remaining elderly A-69 corvettes and newer *Floréal* class light frigates. *Nivôse* of the latter class was seriously damaged by a fire that broke out in her engine room on 30 September 2014.

The submarine force has welcomed the return of the strategic missile submarine *Le Triomphant* on completion of a refit to allow her to deploy the new M51 submarine-launched ballistic missile. Three of France's four strategic submarines now have this capability and the fourth, Le *Téméraire* will now also enter the refit programme to undertake the necessary modifications. Progress is also being made with the 'Barracuda' nuclear attack submarine programme, with an order for *De Grasse* – the fourth of six boats – placed in July 2014. Work on the first, *Suffren*, is now well advanced and she is expected to be launched during 2016.[4]

MAJOR REGIONAL POWERS – ITALY

In spite of significant financial pressures on the core defence budget, Italy is making good progress in addressing the problem of block obsolescence that impacts much of its existing fleet. As is apparent from Table 2.4.3, much of the existing fleet dates from the 1980s and will have to be replaced over the next ten years. This is reflected in Table 2.4.4, which sets out the *Marina Militare*'s plans for decommissioning existing warships over the next decade. The navy has persuaded parliament to provide exceptional funding to deal with this potential crisis, with a budget of €5.4bn (US$6.2bn) approved at the end of 2014 to support new construction. The addi-

tional money will support a programme comprising six new frigate-sized multi-role patrol vessels (with options for four more), a new fleet replenishment vessel, a LHD-type amphibious assault ship and two high-speed vessels designed to support Special Forces operations.

The navy has moved quickly to take advantage of the additional funding, appointing Europe's Organisation for Joint Armament Cooperation (OCCAR) to manage the acquisition of the new logistics support and patrol vessels in May 2015. OCCAR has subsequently signed a development and construction contract for one ship of each type with a consortium encompassing shipbuilder Fincantieri and defence conglomerate Finmeccanica. The deal is set in the context of a wider agreement that encompasses further orders for the remaining five patrol ships and the provision of ten years of service and support at a total cost of €3.5bn (c. US$4bn). Delivery of the logistics ship is scheduled for 2019, with the first of the patrol ships following in 2021. The programmes for the amphibious assault ship and the high-speed vessels will be subject to separate contracts, which will be handled nationally.[5]

Details of the new PPA (*Pattugliatore Polivalente d'Altura*) multi-role patrol ships – which appear to be frigates in all but name – are steadily emerging.

Table 2.4.3: ITALIAN NAVY: PRINCIPAL UNITS AS AT MID 2015

TYPE	CLASS	NUMBER	TONNAGE	DIMENSIONS	PROPULSION	CREW	DATE
Aircraft Carriers							
Aircraft Carrier – CV	CAVOUR	1	27,100 tons	244m x 30/39m x 9m	COGAG, 29 knots	800	2008
Aircraft Carrier – CVS	GIUSEPPE GARIBALDI[1]	1	13,900 tons	180m x 23/31m x 7m	COGAG, 30 knots	825	1985
Principal Surface Escorts							
Frigate – FFG	CARLO BERGAMINI (FREMM)[2]	4	6,500 tons	144m x 20m x 5m	CODLOG, 27 knots	145	2013
Frigate – FFG	ANDREA DORIA ('Horizon')	2	7,100 tons	153m x 20m x 5m	CODOG, 29+ knots	190	2007
Destroyer – DDG	DE LA PENNE	2	5,400 tons	148m x 16m x 5m	CODOG, 31 knots	375	1993
Frigate – FFG	MAESTRALE	8	3,100 tons	123m x 13m x 4m	CODOG, 30+ knots	225	1982
Frigate – FFG	ARTIGLIERE	2	2,500 tons	114m x 12m x 4m	CODOG, 35 knots	185	1994
Frigate – FS	MINERVA	6	1,300 tons	87m x 11m x 3m	Diesel, 25 knots	120	1987
Submarines							
Submarine – SSK	TODARO (Type 212A)	2	1,800 tons	56m x 7m x 6m	AIP, 20+ knots	30	2006
Submarine – SSK	PELOSI	4	1,700 tons	64m x 7m x 6m	Diesel-electric, 20 knots	50	1988
Major Amphibious Units							
Landing Platform Dock – LPD	SAN GIORGIO	3	8,000 tons	133m x 21m x 5m	Diesel, 20 knots	165	1987

Note:

1 Now operates largely as a LPH.

2 Class includes BERGAMINI (GP) and FASAN (ASW) variants.

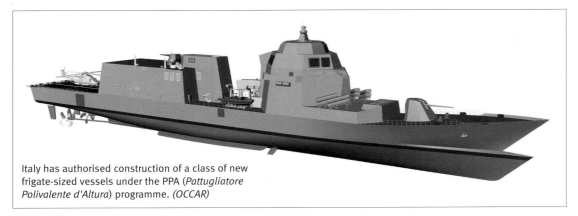

Italy has authorised construction of a class of new frigate-sized vessels under the PPA (*Pattugliatore Polivalente d'Altura*) programme. *(OCCAR)*

With a length of c. 130m and a displacement of 4,500 tons, they will feature combined gas, diesel and diesel-electric propulsion options and be capable of a high maximum speed in excess of 30 knots. The can be configured in 'light' or 'full' configurations, the latter encompassing a full weapons and sensor suite that will encompass advanced phased-array radar and surface-to-air missiles. Whilst five of the six ships will initially be delivered in light configuration, it will be possible to upgrade them at a later date.

Continuity of work at Italian yards before the new programme gets fully underway has been assured by the exercise of a €764m (c. US$875m) option for Italy's two final FREMM type frigates, announced in April 2015. Completion of the pair, to be built in general-purpose configuration, takes production to ten units, fulfilling the original requirement. By

contrast, France's *Marine Nationale* will only see eight of an initial planned class of eighteen completed. Four of the Italian ships are now in service after the delivery of *Carabiniere* on 28 April 2015. The keel of the eighth was laid two months previously. Progress has also been made with submarine assembly with the launch of the third Italian Type 212A boat, *Pietro Venuti*, at Fincantieri's Muggiano yard on 9 October 2014.

The two Italian marines held in India over the deaths of Indian fishermen shot in mistake for pirates when they approached the tanker *Enrica Lexie* remains unresolved, more than three years since the men were first arrested.[6]

MAJOR REGIONAL POWERS – SPAIN

In December 2014, the *Armada Española* saw work start on the two additional *Meteoro* class BAM (*buque de acción maritima*) offshore patrol ships ordered from Navantia in the middle of the year at a unit cost of €166.7m (c.US$200m). Apart from upgrades made to take account of new maritime pollution (MARPOL) regulations and to deal with obsolescence issues, they are identical to the four ships of the first batch authorised in 2006. Construction has been split between Navantia's facilities at Ferrol and in the Bay of Cadiz to maintain employment at both sites until work on the new F-110 frigate programme commences. Deliveries are currently scheduled for July 2018 and January 2019.

The F-110 project now appears to be making progress after a somewhat projected gestation period. A preferred design has been selected from three concepts offering various capability/cost trade-offs and work is now underway on more detailed design work prior to a final decision on construction. The new ships are intended to provide a survivable, multi-mission capability across a range of threat scenarios. There is a particular emphasis on reducing crew size and on other means of lowering through-life costs. Five ships are planned to replace the six current FFG-7 type frigates of the *Santa María* class and it is hoped that the first ship will be ready by 2022.

Meanwhile, redesign work on the troubled S-80 submarine programme has been completed with the technical assistance of the US Navy and General Dynamics Electric Boat. Extra rings are being manufactured to extend the submarines and restore buoyancy after the initial design proved to be overweight. It is hoped that *Narciso Monturiol*, the first boat to

TABLE 2.4.4: ITALIAN NAVY: WARSHIP DECOMMISSIONING PLAN (2015–25)

YEAR	FRIGATES (FFG)	LIGHT FRIGATES/ CORVETTES (FS)	PATROL VESSELS (OPV)	MINEHUNTERS (MCMV)	AMPHIB. (LPH/LPD)	OTHER
2015	Granatiere	Minerva[1], Sibilla[1]	–	Lerici[1], Sapri[1]	–	–
2016	Aviere, Maestrale	Danaide, Fenice, Sfinge, Urania	–	–	–	–
2017	Espero	Chimera, Driade	–	–	–	–
2018	Bersagliere	–	–	Vieste	–	Longobardo (sub), Stromboli (oiler)
2019	Aliseo	–	–	Milazzo, Numana	San Giorgio	Gazzana (sub)
2020	Euro, Grecale	–	–	Gaeta, Viareggio, Rimini	San Marco	Anteo (rescue), Vesuvio (oiler)
2021	–	–	–	Chioggia, Termoli	–	Magnaghi (survey), Pelosi (sub)
2022	Zeffiro	–	Spica, Vega	Alghero, Crotone	Garibaldi, San Giusto	Prini (sub)
2023	Scirocco	–	Borsini, Cassiopea, Fulgosi, Libra	–	–	Galatea (survey)
2024	De la Penne, Libeccio	–	Foscari, Orione	–	–	Aretusa (survey)
2025	–	–	Bettica, Sirio	–	–	Etna (oiler)
Totals	12	8	10	12	4	11

Notes:
1 These ships are already in reserve.

Table 2.4.5: SPANISH NAVY: PRINCIPAL UNITS AS AT MID 2015

TYPE	CLASS	NUMBER	TONNAGE	DIMENSIONS	PROPULSION	CREW	DATE
Principal Surface Escorts							
Frigate – FFG	ÁLVARO DE BAZÁN (F-100)	5	6,300 tons	147m x 19m x 5m	CODOG, 28 knots	200	2002
Frigate – FFG	SANTA MARIA (FFG-7)	6	4,100 tons	138m x 14m x 5m	COGAG, 30 knots	225	1986
Submarines							
Submarine – SSK	GALERNA (S-70/AGOSTA)	3	1,800 tons	68m x 7m x 6m	Diesel-electric, 21 knots	60	1983
Major Amphibious Units							
Amph Assault Ship – LHD	JUAN CARLOS I	1	27,100 tons	231m x 32m x 7m	IEP, 21 knots	245	2010
Landing Platform Dock – LPD	GALICIA	2	13,000 tons	160m x 25m x 6m	Diesel, 20 knots	185	1998

be completed under the revised programme, will be ready for launch before the end of 2017.

Table 2.4.5 provides a summary of current Spanish fleet strength. A number of second-line units laid up since the financial crisis are now being formally decommissioned, notably the former corvette *Diana* in May 2015. Converted to a mine warfare command ship at the turn of the millennium, she had not sailed since 2012 due to budget cuts.

MAJOR REGIONAL POWERS – UNITED KINGDOM

A review of current British Royal Navy programmes in the run up to the current Strategic Defence & Security Review (SDSR) 2015 is contained in Chapter 2.4A. Table 2.4.6 gives an indication of current fleet strength. The Royal Navy has probably reached a low-point in its recent history so far as size is concerned. The decommissioning of the final *Invincible* class carrier, *Illustrious*, on 28 August 2014 leaves the fleet focused on a core of four strategic and six attack submarines, nineteen surface escorts and two active amphibious ships (a third is held in reserve); a situation that is unlikely to change significantly until the first new carrier, *Queen Elizabeth*, is delivered in 2017. Manning levels are also a major problem. A shortage of trained engineers is leading to 'innovative measures' to alleviate the issue, including a re-recruitment drive to attract sailors previously made redundant and the temporary loan of crew from the US Coast Guard to fill the gap.[7]

Operationally, however, the navy remains extremely busy. The need to deploy ships to help deal with the refugee crisis in the Mediterranean and bolster increased NATO exercises in the Baltic is adding to the strain of standing commitments ranging from the South Atlantic to the Persian Gulf. Again, innovation is the order of the day, including the first ever use of a 'River' class offshore patrol

A 2015 computerised image of the Spanish Navy's proposed F-110 type frigate. Anticipated to displace around 6,000 tons, the general-purpose design appears to be based on the previous F-100 class hull form. Armament includes a 127mm gun, two eight-cell VLS modules and a number of remotely-operated weapons stations. The most prominent feature is the integrated mast. Other features include a large hangar and flight deck, as well as what appear to be enclosed boat stations and multi-mission bays amidships and aft. Current plans envisage five of the ships entering service from around 2022. *(Navantia)*

vessel, *Severn*, for the Atlantic Patrol (North) deployment during the winter of 2014/15. This may herald the more regular use of the new Batch II 'River' class vessels in the Caribbean when they start to enter service from 2017 onwards.

Another indication of the pressures facing the fleet was provided by reports that the submarine *Talent* was temporarily patched up to continue a deployment after her conning tower suffered 'ice damage' in late 2014. The damage had initially been spotted in March 2015 when the submarine was

photographed making a daylight return to Devonport. However, pictures have now come to light of the submarine making a previously unreported arrival under the cloak of dusk in early December 2014, suggesting temporary repairs were effected before she resumed her patrol.[8] Meanwhile, a new chapter in the 110-year history of the so-called 'Silent Service' occurred in mid-2014 when the first three female submariners completed their qualifications after training on the strategic missile submarine *Vigilant*.

The Royal Navy's forces are being stretched ever thinner by increasing commitments and reducing resources. This ship shows fleet flagship *Ocean*, the only remaining 'flat top', operating in the Baltic with the US Navy amphibious transport dock *San Antonio* (LPD-17) and smaller ships during BALTOPS 2015. *(Crown Copyright 2015)*

Table 2.4.6: BRITISH ROYAL NAVY: PRINCIPAL UNITS AS AT MID 2015

TYPE	CLASS	NUMBER	TONNAGE	DIMENSIONS	PROPULSION	CREW	DATE
Principal Surface Escorts							
Destroyer – DDG	**DARING** (Type 45)	6	7,400 tons	152m x 21m x 5m	IEP, 30 knots	190	2008
Frigate – FFG	**NORFOLK** (Type 23)	13	4,900 tons	133m x 16m x 5m	CODLAG, 30 knots	185	1990
Submarines							
Submarine – SSBN	**VANGUARD**	4	16,000 tons	150m x 13m x 12m	Nuclear, 25+ knots	135	1993
Submarine – SSN	**ASTUTE**	2	7,800 tons	93m x 11m x 10m	Nuclear, 30+ knots	100	2010
Submarine – SSN	**TRAFALGAR**	4	5,200 tons	85m x 10m x 10m	Nuclear, 30+ knots	130	1983
Major Amphibious Units							
Helicopter Carrier – LPH	**OCEAN**	1	22,500 tons	203m x 35m x 7m	Diesel, 18 knots	490	1998
Landing Platform Dock – LPD	**ALBION**	2	18,500 tons	176m x 29m x 7m	IEP, 18 knots	325	2003
Landing Ship Dock – LSD (A)	**LARGS BAY**	3	16,200 tons	176m x 26m x 6m	Diesel-electric, 18 knots	60	2006

MID-SIZED REGIONAL FLEETS

Germany: The German Navy is seeing the continued rundown of its fleet of F-122 *Bremen* class frigates. Only three of the original eight ships are now in service following the decommissioning of *Niedersachsen* on 26 June 2015. It is taking longer than first anticipated to complete the quartet of 7,000-ton F-125 stabilisation frigates that will replace them, although it is still hoped to deliver the first – *Baden Württemberg* – during 2017. The second ship, *Nordrhein Westfalen*, was christened on 9 April 2015, whilst a keel-laying ceremony for the fourth, *Rheinland-Pfalz*, took place on the previous 29 January. Contrary to previous reports, final assembly of all four ships will take place at Blohm & Voss in Hamburg, to where the forward sections completed by Lürssen – ThyssenKrupp Marine System's (TKMS's) partner in the ARGE125 consortium – are being transported.

The next major surface project is for the MKS-180 (*Mehrzweckkampfschiff* 180) multi-role combat ship. This has steadily metamorphosed from a corvette-sized design to an 8,000-ton behemoth that will be the largest front-line warship class constructed in Germany since the Second World War. In contrast to the F-125, it is intended that the class will be fully capable of participating in high-intensity operations. A contract for four ships, plus another two options, is expected to be placed in 2017 and the first of class should be in service by 2023.

Elsewhere in the surface fleet, the retirement of Type 143A *Gepard* class fast attack craft is also continuing. Only six are left in service following the decommissioning of *Gepard* herself and *Ozelot* in December 2014. These remaining units have been largely withdrawn from UNIFIL stabilisation operations off Lebanon and are expected to leave service during 2016. The outlook is more positive beneath the waves, with the two enlarged Type 212A submarines now ready to join their four older sisters after commissioning problems have been resolved. *U35* was commissioned on 23 March 2015 and *U36* should also be delivered before the end of the year.

Greece: The last year has seen the Hellenic Navy achieve some recovery from the economic woes that have afflicted it in recent years. Most notably, long-stalled construction and modernisation programmes have started to crank back into life after a number of

The German Navy is looking to follow construction of its F-125 class frigates with four MKS-180 type vessels. These have steadily grown from corvettes to 8,000-ton ships the size of a Second World War cruiser. This early conceptual drawing from Germany's MTG naval consultancy shows some similarities with the F-125 class, albeit with weaponry and other systems suitable for higher-intensity warfare. (MTG)

A period of greater stability in Greece – even if potentially short-lived – has allowed agreements to be struck that have unblocked long-stalled modernisation and construction contracts. This image, taken in October 2014, shows the re-delivery of the modernised Type 209 *Okeanos*, which has had an AIP system installed. *(Hellenic Navy)*

The Royal Netherlands Navy's joint support ship *Karel Doorman* pictured in Canadian waters in May 2015. The largest ship ever to serve in the Dutch Navy, she is designed to support both logistical and amphibious requirements. In addition to significant storage and capacity for vehicles and supplies, she is able embark six medium-sized helicopters and operate both personnel and utility landing craft. The Thales I-Mast is the same as that found on the *Holland* class OPVs. *(Marc Piché)*

long-running contractual disputes were resolved. This has allowed the navy to put back into service *Okeanos* – the only one of Greece's four Type 209/1200 submarines to have completed a planned class-wide AIP upgrade – and to take delivery of *Pipinos*, the first of three Type 214 boats assembled in Greece. The other two Type 214 submarines sub-contracted to Hellenic Shipyard are likely to be delivered before the end of 2016. They will combine with the German-built *Papanikolis* to create a four-strong flotilla of this type. This should allow the remaining elderly Type 209/100 submarines to be withdrawn from service. A start has also been made on completing the three *Roussen* fast attack craft yet to be delivered, with sea trials of the fifth of class, *Ritsos*, now underway. Medium-term plans include modernisation of the four MEKO-200 *Hydra* class frigates and more limited overhauls of a number of other platforms. Whether these plans survive the renewed turmoil surrounding Greece's place in the Eurozone remains to be seen.

The Netherlands: The Royal Netherlands Navy is already getting full value out of the new joint support ship *Karel Doorman*, which was deployed to West African waters to help support efforts to counter the Ebola epidemic in November 2014 before she was formally commissioned. The ceremony subsequently took place in April 2015. Her arrival has allowed the disposal of the replenishment ship *Amsterdam*, which was decommissioned on 4 December 2014 and sold to Peru. Meanwhile, the *Holland* class OPV programme has been brought to a successful close with the installation of *Friesland*'s integrated mast in August 2014.

Having achieved the desired fleet structure, the navy's next construction plans envisage the like-for-like replacement of existing vessels. Two major requirements fall due over the next decade or so, viz. the renewal of the existing flotilla of four *Walrus* class submarines and the acquisition of two new frigates as the remaining pair of 'M' class vessels reach the end of their operational lives. The former programme is the more advanced, with local ship-building group Damen collaborating with Sweden's Saab to establish whether the latter's A-26 programme can help meet the Dutch requirement. Whilst there is economic and industrial logic behind the partnership, it may prove difficult to match Sweden's need for a small submarine able to survive in the confined waters of the Baltic with the

Netherlands' preference for a larger type fully capable of 'blue water' operations. A final decision on the way ahead is scheduled for 2018.

The project for replacement frigates is likely to be taken forward in conjunction with Belgium, which also operates two 'M' class ships. Preliminary project definition work is likely to focus on a multi-purpose design with strong credentials in the area of anti-submarine warfare. It seems unlikely that the Netherlands will be able to fund the new ships at the same time as buying new submarines and the two programmes are therefore likely to run consecutively.

Turkey: The last twelve months have seen the Turkish Navy move ahead with important projects. Most significantly, the selection of the local SEDEF shipyard to construct a variant of the Spanish Navy's *Juan Carlos I* design in collaboration with Navantia for the country's amphibious assault ship requirement was confirmed with the award of formal contracts in May 2015. This should be followed by the start of fabrication work early next year prior to launch late in 2018 and delivery in 2021. It seems that the new ship will be a closer copy of the 27,000-ton *Juan Carlos I* than was previously thought, opening up the possibility of the F-35B STOVL variant of the Lightning II Joint Strike Fighter being acquired to expand Turkey's maritime aviation capabilities. In the meantime, work on two smaller tank landing ships is also well underway.

Recent press reports also suggest that construction might soon commence on the Turkish Type 214 submarine project. A deal for the local construction of six of the AIP-equipped submarines was signed as long ago as 2009 but detailed discussions on implementing the agreement have proved difficult. Although the most modern pair of the six Type 209/1200 *Atilay* class submarines have recently completed modernisation, it seems unlikely that the older members of the class can be kept in service much longer and force levels are likely to fall as a result. Indeed, *Saldiray*, the second member of the class to be completed, was decommissioned on 14 November 2014.[9]

Surface vessel construction is focused on the indigenous 'Milgem' ('Ada') class corvette design, more fully described in Chapter 3.3. The award of construction orders has been slowed by political manoeuvrings, which could have a knock-on effect on programmes such as the TF-2000 air-defence frigate and therefore impact overall surface fleet

2015 marked the centenary of the First World War Gallipoli landings and the Turkish Armed Forces held a number of events to commemorate the anniversary. This image shows the German-built MEKO 200 frigate *Turgutreis* with ships that included representatives from Australia, France, New Zealand and the United Kingdom during rehearsals for a commemorative event in the Dardanelles Straits in May 2015. Replacement of Turkey's older MEKO 200 class ships may be delayed by political interference with indigenous naval construction programmes. *(Royal Australian Navy)*

availability further down the line. Plans had been under consideration to acquire additional former US Navy FFG-7 class frigates as the last American ships were withdrawn from service but this option no longer appears available as a result of concerns in the US Congress over Turkey's stance on relations with Cyprus and Israel.

OTHER REGIONAL FLEETS

Black Sea and Mediterranean: Events in the **Ukraine** have badly impacted the navy, which has lost many of its major operating bases, ships and sailors following Russia's seizure of the Crimea. The Project 1135 'Krivak' class frigate *Hetman Sahaydachniy* – fortuitously deployed away from the Black Sea at the time – remains very active and there are plans to import new patrol ships from the United States but it seems likely to be a long time before a balanced fleet is recreated. Elsewhere in the Black Sea, both **Bulgaria** and **Romania** are more focused on the modernisation of existing equipment rather than new acquisitions, particularly as the changed security situation is also resulting in increased demands

from their air and land forces. Of these enhancements, the revival of Romania's previous plans to undertake a phased upgrade of its two former Royal Navy Type 22 frigates looks most advanced.

Turning to the Mediterranean, both **Croatia** and **Montenegro** have plans to modernise some of their patrol assets and the former has also been looking at the potential acquisition of decommissioned German Type 333 *Kulmbach* class minehunters. More tangibly, a c.US$60m contract for five new 42m coastal patrol vessels for the navy's coast guard division was signed with local Croatian builder Brodosplit in December 2014. The new ships will be delivered from 2016 and carry a Turkish-produced Aselsan automated 30mm gun as their main armament.[10] Elsewhere, **Malta** has been badly impacted by the Middle East's refuge crisis and has received assistance from other countries. Notably, Ireland has donated its decommissioned offshore patrol vessel *Aoife* to reinforce the country's maritime squadron.

Atlantic and North Sea: There are some signs that greater stability in **Portugal** is starting to benefit the

Marinha Portuguesa, which was in the early stages of a plan to modernise its patrol forces when the financial crisis struck. It has been decided to restart production of *Viana do Castelo* type offshore patrol vessels at the former ENVC facility, which is now under new ownership as the West Sea Viana Shipyard. An initial pair of vessels ordered under the eight-ship NPO2000 project were commissioned in 2011 and 2013 and approval has now been given to conclude negotiations on a second pair.[11] The class is intended to replace the remaining 1970s-era corvettes which are now being used in secondary roles. There are now five of these elderly ships in service following the decommissioning of *João Coutinho* in September 2014. ENVC was also formerly scheduled to construct a new class of coastal patrol vessels to replace the *Cacine* class but a deal has now been agreed to acquire four former Royal Danish Navy Stanflex 300 ships to carry out this role. Portugal is also one of a number of countries reportedly interested in buying the decommissioned French dock landing ship *Siroco* to meet a longstanding amphibious lift requirement.

Further to the north, **Ireland** has decommissioned the former offshore patrol vessel *Aoife* but has yet to take delivery of her replacement, *James Joyce*. The new ship has been delayed remedying defects found on initial sea trials but is due to depart Babcock's Appledore yard for Ireland in July 2015. A third member of the class is now under construction, whilst decisions on potential further naval investment will be taken in a white paper due to be published in the second half of 2015. The naval service has been one of a number of navies helping alleviate the humanitarian crisis in the Mediterranean, where the flagship *Eithne* has already rescued more than 2,000 refugees since being deployed to the region on 16 May 2015.

Belgium has also been taking delivery of new ships with the arrival of the coastal patrol vessels *Castor* and *Pollux* from France's Socarenam. Known as 'ready duty ships', they will carry out constabulary duties protecting Belgian economic interests in the North Sea.

Scandinavia and the Baltic: Amidst a renewal of Cold War style 'mystery' submarine incursions, it is – perhaps – not surprising that much procurement activity in Scandinavia and the Baltic is focused on strengthening underwater forces. In March 2015, **Sweden** gave the long-awaited go-ahead for the new A-26 submarine programme, with negotiations now underway with Saab's Kockums subsidiary for two new boats at a maximum budget of SEK8.2bn (c. US$1bn). The new submarines will feature an improved version of the Stirling AIP system, a permanent magnet motor and x-shaped stern planes. Delivery of the first submarine is expected around 2023. The order comes against the background of a new 2016–20 Defence Bill that will increase spending by SEK10.2bn (US$1.2bn) over a five-year period and leave 2020 spending of SEK50bn (US$6bn) p.a. around 5 per cent higher than previously planned. The increased budget ensures that two of the existing A-19 *Gotland* class submarines will be modernised to ensure a core underwater flotilla of four boats. Money will also be spent on upgrading the two *Gävle* class corvettes' anti-submarine capabilities so they can continue to serve alongside the new *Visby* class as part of a seven-strong escort force. The *Stockholm* class will be withdrawn from front-line service and reconfigured as patrol ships. However, the increased funding does not stretch to all naval requirements. Previous plans for a new logistical support capability have been scrapped in favour of running-on existing ships whilst no provision is made for installing a much needed anti-air capability in the *Visby*s.[12]

Having completed the induction of its *Fridtjof Nansen* class frigates and *Skjold* class corvettes, **Norway** is also turning its attention to submarine procurement. The existing *Ula* class submarines were commissioned between 1989 and 1992 and need to be phased out during the 2020s if a costly life-extension programme is to be avoided. The Norwegian Ministry of Defence announced in December 2014 that a two-year project definition

The Portuguese Navy's offshore patrol vessel *Figueira da Foz* docked at the West Sea Viana Shipyard in northern Portugal in October 2014. The newly re-opened shipyard looks set to receive an order for a further two members of the class. *(West Sea Viana Shipyard)*

Whilst Finland's Squadron 2020 concept involves orders for 'blue water' capable ships, current deliveries are focused on U-700 class landing ships. Twelve of the 20m craft, which feature Rolls-Royce waterjet propulsion and a remote weapon system incorporating a heavy machine gun or a grenade launcher, have been ordered. They can transport as many as twenty-five troops around the coast at speeds of over 40 knots. *(Rolls-Royce)*

phase would be commenced, leading to formal proposals on a replacement capability by the end of 2016. Saab and TKMS are likely to be key contenders for any eventual order.

A further regional submarine programme is been driven by **Poland**, which aims to commission three new boats to replace its existing underwater flotilla during 2022–3. It has emerged that a key function of the new class will be to act as platforms for cruise missiles, with the United States' Tomahawk and France's Naval Cruise Missile being seen as potential weapons to provide this capability. Selection of the latter would give DCNS' 'Scorpène' type an edge in the contest, albeit Poland might prefer a submarine optimised for Baltic conditions. A tender process is expected to commence before the end of 2015 to reach a decision that is becoming increasingly urgent given that the majority of Poland's existing submarines are already life-expired.

Elsewhere in the Baltic, **Finland** is shortly expected to take delivery of its third *Katanpää* mine countermeasures vessel and is looking to develop its Squadron 2020 concept. This envisages the construction of a new class of 'blue water' capable surface combatants to replace the existing minelayers and the four *Rauma* class attack craft. At least four new ships are envisaged. In the interim, the existing *Hamina* class fast attack craft will be upgraded to extend their service lives into the 2030s. Coastal forces are also being strengthened, with deliveries of the new U-700 type high-speed landing craft expected to commence before the end of 2015.

RUSSIA

Russia's 2014 seizure of the Crimea from Ukraine and intervention to assist pro-Russian separatists in the east of the country have significantly shifted the political and military environment in Europe. These actions have allowed Russia to achieve its short-term objectives of securing the Sevastopol headquarters of the Black Sea Fleet, protecting ethnic Russians and maintaining its sphere of influence in Europe's east. They have also undoubtedly served to make NATO sit up and take note of Russia's capabilities, another key objective for a Putin administration that has harboured something of an obsession to restore respect for Russia's world status. This 'respect' has been bolstered by a dramatic ramp-up in defence expenditure as the country attempts to modernise its armed forces under the 2011–20 State Armaments Plan.

However, this is only half the story. Sanctions imposed on Russia by the United States and allied countries following events in the Ukraine have materially impacted the country's economy. Even more significantly, a commodity boom that had fuelled Russian growth has come to an abrupt end with the collapse in the price of oil. As such, there is simply insufficient money to finance the previously planned growth in defence spending.[13] This will most likely continue to grow over time – but at a slower pace than previously planned. Equally, whilst it is clear that modernisation will continue to be accorded a high priority, access to the Western technology needed to recover lost ground is no longer assured. With access to key Ukrainian components also impacted, the outlook for future naval modernisation looks uncertain – particularly for the surface fleet – as reflected in the review of individual programmes below. The extent of the problem is highlighted further when the age of many of the ships listed in Table 2.4.7 is taken into account.[14]

Submarines: The modernisation of Russia's submarine forces, particularly its strategic missile submarines, remains of paramount concern to the Russian military. The protracted programme to bring the new Project 955/955A 'Borey' type submarines and the associated RSM-56 'Bulava' (NATO: SS-NX-30) ballistic missiles into service is making progress after completion of three consecutive successful trials of the previously unreliable weapon between September and November 2014. All three of the Project 955 variant are now in service with the commissioning of *Vladimir Monomakh* in December 2014. It would seem that the current plan is to transfer her, as well as *Aleksandr Nevsky* (the second member of the class), to the Pacific during 2015/16 to replace the handful of life-expired Project 667BDR 'Delta III' submarines that remain operational. Three out of a planned total of five Project 955A boats are also now under construction after the fifth and sixth units were laid down in June and December 2014. The acceleration of construction at the Sevmash plant in Severodvinsk, Northern Russia suggests growing confidence in the programme's stability.

Sevmash is also stepping up construction of nuclear-powered attack submarines of the improved Project 855M 'Yasen II' type, with four boats currently under construction. The turmoil in the collapse of the former Soviet Union meant that it took twenty years to complete the sole Project 855 variant, *Severodvisnk*, but much improved progress with the 'Boreys' suggest that deliveries should be well underway by the end of the decade. The new submarines are desperately needed to replace the remaining elderly Project 971 'Akula' and Project 949A 'Oscar II' class units that form the core of the current fleet, some of which are receiving life-extension upgrades. One of the latter, *Orel*, suffered a serious fire whilst docked at the Zvezdochka yard in April 2015 in the latest of a series of similar accidents to impact Russian submarines in recent years.

Turning to conventional submarines, two of the six improved Project 636.3 'Kilo' class – ordered when the extent of problems with the replacement Project 677 'Lada' type became apparent – have now been delivered. A third, *Stary Oskol*, will be handed over in July 2015 and the others before the end of 2016. Once they have completed trials and work-up, the current plan is to incorporate them in a reinforced Black Sea Fleet. Meanwhile, it appears that work on the Project 677 type has re-started; with local media reports suggesting recommencement of work on a third boat at St. Petersburg's Admiralty Shipyards in March 2015.

Aircraft Carriers and Amphibious Ships: The likely non-delivery of the French-built *Mistral*s is forcing a rethink of amphibious capabilities. In particular, there is increased focus on indigenous construction of the Project 1171.1 *Ivan Gren* type landing ships at the Yantar shipyard in the Kaliningrad enclave. In common with many post-Cold War Russian projects, the first of class has suffered from a protracted build-time but is expected to be delivered by the end of 2015. A formal keel-laying ceremony for the second ship of the class, *Petr Morgunov*, was held on 11 June 2015 and as many as five may ultimately be built. The 6,000-ton ships are able to transport more than 300 troops and their armour over distances in excess of 3,000 nautical miles. However, they have a much more limited helicopter-operating capability than the French types.

The veteran aircraft carrier *Admiral Kuznetsov* continues to soldier on, punctuating regular Mediterranean deployments with significant periods under refit. There has been much discussion of ordering new ships for entry into service towards the end of the next decade and a new Project 23000E *Shtorm* super-carrier of around 100,000 tons displacement was revealed by the Krylovsky State

Research Centre in mid-2015. There seems to be little prospect of such a programme becoming a reality given the real problems Russia is facing in fielding smaller surface ships.

Surface Vessels: Russia's protracted efforts to bring new classes of surface warship have been badly impacted by the cessation of deliveries of gas turbines and diesel engines from, respectively, Ukraine and Germany at a time when new ships are finally starting to be delivered.

The first Project 2235.0 frigate, *Admiral Gorshkov*, commenced long-delayed sea trials in November 2014, reportedly after replacement of one of its Ukrainian gas turbines following a fire that occurred during harbour testing. Another three of a planned class of up to twenty ships are under construction. Of these, *Admiral Kasatanov*, was launched in December 2014 but has surrendered one of its turbines to its sister to make good her repair. Accordingly, until a new production line can be established at a Russian manufacturer, the

France's decision not to honour its contract with Russia for the supply of *Mistral* type amphibious assault ships due to events in the Ukraine has left the fleet increasingly reliant on Soviet-era ships. This image shows the 1970s-built Project 775 landing ship *Alexander Otravosky* passing through the Bosporus on the regular supply run to and from the beleaguered Assad regime in Syria. *(Devrim Yaylali)*

programme looks set to make little headway.

A similar bottleneck is impacting production of Project 1135.6 *Admiral Grigovorich* class frigates

based on the *Talwar* class previously completed for India. Reports suggest that deliveries of turbines for only three of the six ships had been completed before relations with the Ukraine broke down, thereby leaving the last three ships in limbo. The lead frigate began sea trials in April 2015 and the second ship, *Admiral Essen*, started harbour testing during the following month.

The smaller Project 2038.0 light frigates use Russian engines but the redesigned and improved Project 2038.5 variant is reliant on imports from the German MTU subsidiary of the United Kingdom's Rolls-Royce. Work on two of the latter type is already underway but a major redesign may be necessary to incorporate a different propulsion plant. In the meantime, builder Severnaya Verf in St Petersburg has recommenced work on the earlier type, laying down two new ships to add to the four it has already completed in February 2015. The Far Eastern Komsomolsk yard is also close to completing the first of two of the Project 2038.0 type it also has on order and which was started as

TABLE 2.4.7: RUSSIAN NAVY: SELECTED PRINCIPAL UNITS AS AT MID 2015

TYPE	CLASS	NUMBER[1]	TONNAGE	DIMENSIONS	PROPULSION	CREW	DATE
Aircraft carriers							
Aircraft Carrier – CV	Project 1143.5 **KUZNETSOV**	1	60,000 tons	306m x 35/73m x 10m	Steam, 32 knots	2,600	1991
Principal Surface Escorts							
Battlecruiser – BCGN	Project 1144.2 **KIROV**	1 (1)	25,000 tons	252m x 29m x 9m	CONAS, 32 knots	740	1980
Cruiser – CG	Project 1164 **MOSKVA** ('Slava')	3	12,500 tons	186m x 21m x 8m	COGAG, 32 knots	530	1982
Destroyer – DDG	Project 956/956A **SOVREMENNY**	c.5	8,000 tons	156m x 17m x 6m	Steam, 32 knots	300	1980
Destroyer – DDG	Project 1155.1 **CHABANENKO** ('Udaloy II')	1	9,000 tons	163m x 19m x 6m	COGAG, 29 knots	250	1999
Destroyer – DDG	Project 1155 **UDALOY**	c.8	8,400 tons	163m x 19m x 6m	COGAG, 30 knots	300	1980
Frigate – FFG	Project 1154 **NEUSTRASHIMY**	2	4,400 tons	139m x 16m x 6m	COGAG, 30 knots	210	1993
Frigate – FFG	Project 1135 **BDITELNNY** ('Krivak I/II')	c.2	3,700 tons	123m x 14m x 5m	COGAG, 32 knots	180	1970
Frigate – FFG	Project 2038.0 **STEREGUSHCHY**	4	2,200 tons	105m x 11m x 4m	CODAD, 27 knots[2]	100	2008
Frigate – FFG	Project 1161.1 **TATARSTAN** ('Gepard')	2	2,000 tons	102m x 13m x 4m	CODOG, 27 knots	100	2002
Submarines							
Submarine – SSBN	Project 955 **YURY DOLGORUKY** ('Borey')	3	17,000+ tons	170m x 13m x 10m	Nuclear, 25+ knots	110	2010
Submarine – SSBN	Project 941 **DONSKOY** ('Typhoon')	1	33,000 tons	173m x 23m x 12m	Nuclear, 26 knots	150	1981
Submarine – SSBN	Project 677BDRM **VERKHOTURYE** ('Delta IV')	6	18,000 tons	167m x 12m x 9m	Nuclear, 24 knots	130	1985
Submarine – SSBN	Project 677BDR **ZVEZDA** ('Delta III')	3	12,000 tons	160m x 12m x 9m	Nuclear, 24 knots	130	1976
Submarine – SSGN	Project 855 **SEVERODVINSK** ('Yasen')	1	12,500 tons	120m x 14m x 9m	Nuclear, 30+ knots	90	2013
Submarine – SSGN	Project 949A ('Oscar II')	c.5	17,500 tons	154m x 8m x 9m	Nuclear, 30+ knots	100	1986
Submarine – SSN	Project 971 ('Akula I/II')	c.10	9,500 tons	110m x 14m x 10m	Nuclear, 30+ knots	60	1986
Submarine – SSK	Project 677 **ST PETERSBURG** ('Lada')	1	2,700 tons	72m x 7m x 7m	Diesel-electric, 21 knots	40	2010
Submarine – SSK	Project 877/636 ('Kilo')	c.20	3,000 tons	73m x 10m x 7m	Diesel-electric, 20 knots	55	1981

Notes:

1 Table only includes main types and focuses on operational units: bracketed figures are ships being refurbished or in maintained reserve.   **2** Some sources state CODOG propulsion.

Right: The lead Project 2235.0 frigate *Admiral Gorshkov* seen departing for preliminary sea trials in November 2014. Displacing 4,500 tons in standard condition, the 135m long ship has a large crew of c. 200 sailors and features CODAG propulsion. The cessation of supplies of gas turbines from the Ukraine will delay completion of follow-on members of the class. *(reflex Yu)*

long ago as 2006. It also has hopes for further orders now that production is seemingly back on track.

The problems with new construction suggest reliance will continue to be placed on life-extensions and refurbishments of Soviet-era ships. A number of these are underway or planned, most notably of the *Kirov* class battlecruiser *Admiral Nakhimov*. However, this is becoming an increasingly difficult and expensive task and the overall availability of older ships is seemingly falling. A major withdrawal over the past year was the final Project 1134B 'Kara' class cruiser, *Kerch*, which has been laid up after yet another major fire to impact a Russian warship under maintenance in November 2014.

Notes:

1. The cost of the year-long Operation 'Mare Nostrum' was reported as around €114m (c.US$130m), of which the EU contributed less than €2m. In addition, Italy was left with the problem of determining how to deal with the more than 150,000 refugees it had rescued in the face of refusal by other EU countries to accept a share of these migrants.

2. This certainly appears to have been the United Kingdom government position, as reported by Alan Travis in 'UK axes support for Mediterranean migrant rescue operation', *The Guardian* – 27 October 2014 (London: Guardian News & Media Ltd, 2014). The article referred to a Parliamentary written answer by the responsible British foreign minister, Baroness Anelay of St John's, on 15 October 2015, which stated, 'We do not support planned search and rescue operations in the Mediterranean. We believe that they create an unintended "pull factor", encouraging more migrants to attempt the dangerous sea crossing and thereby leading to more tragic and unnecessary deaths.'

3. A summary of the problems the new EU operation faces was set out by Tom Kington in 'Politics Delays EU Anti-Human Trafficking Ops', *Defense News* – 27 June 2015 (Springfield VA: Gannett Government Media, 2015).

4. A good source of news on the progress of the 'Barracuda' class submarine programme, as well as on *Marine Nationale* news stories more generally, is the online *Mer et Marine* news site at: http://www.meretmarine.com/fr

5. Detailed information on the progress of the new Italian warship building programme has been regularly provided in a series of reports by Luca Peruzzi in *Jane's Navy International* (Coulsdon: IHS Jane's).

6. For further details of this incident, see *Seaforth World Naval Review 2013* (Barnsley: Seaforth Publishing, 2012), p.54.

7. Amongst many reports on the Royal Navy's manning crisis was Michael Powell's 'Defence cuts farce: Navy spent £10 million on engineers' redundancy payments … now it's splashing £2.5 million trying to get them back', *Mail on Sunday* – 28 June 2015 (London: Associated Newspapers Ltd, 2015).

8. The story was reported by Steve Bush under the heading '*Talent* Damage Occurred in Late 2014' in *Warship World* – July/August 2015 (Liskeard: Maritime Books, 2015).

9. Readers are directed to Devrim Yaylali's informative *Bosphorus Naval News* blog at http://turkishnavy.net/ for ongoing news of Turkish Navy developments.

10. For more details of this little-known programme, see Burak Ege Bedkil's 'Aselsan System to Arm Croatian Patrol Boats', *Defense News* – 9 April 2015 (Springfield VA: Gannett Government Media, 2015).

11. Further information on the contract and the particulars of the class were provided by Victor Barreira in 'Portugal to buy two more OPVs', *Jane's Defence Weekly* – 10 June 2015 (Coulsdon: IHS Jane's, 2015).

12. A summary of Sweden's defence policy can be found on the Swedish Government's website at: http://www.government.se/globalassets/government/dokument/forsvarsdepartementet/sweden_defence_policy_2016_to_2020. A good overview of Saab's new A-26 submarine design was provided by Christopher P. Cavas in 'Sweden's Sub-Building Capability Resurfaces, *Defense News* – 9 May 2015 (Springfield VA: Gannett Government Media, 2015) whilst Richard Scott reported on the demise of Sweden's planned new logistics support ships in 'Sweden to run on existing logistics support vessels', *Jane's Navy International* – June 2015 (Coulsdon: IHS Jane's, 2015). An interesting question relating to the A26 programme concerns Sweden's ability to construct the new submarines given a considerable gap in production at Kockums' Malmö facility. There have been suggestions that at least partial assembly abroad may be contemplated as part of a deal to produce the design in alliance with a foreign partner.

13. The shaky foundations on which Russian military modernisation is built were highlighted in Lidia Kelly's article, 'Finance minister warns Russia can't afford military spending plan' in a Reuters news agency report dated 7 October 2015 and currently accessible at: http://www.reuters.com/article/2014/10/07/us-russia-economy-spending-defence-idUSKCN0HW1H420141007

14. Users with a good knowledge of Russian (or an appropriate language translation programme) are directed to the excellent http://flot.com/ website for an ongoing source of Russian Navy news.

Author:
Richard Beedall

2.4A Fleet Review

ROYAL NAVY A Thin Blue Line

The United Kingdom elected the Conservative Party to government on 7 May 2015, replacing a previous Conservative-Liberal Democrat coalition. One of the new government's first tasks will be to finalise the 2015 Strategic Defence and Security Review (SDSR 2015). Whilst SDSR 2015 will nominally cover the period until 2020, in practice it will take decisions which will fundamentally affect the Royal Navy until the middle of this century.[1] SDSR 2015 will also greatly determine the United

Kingdom's influence in an increasingly turbulent world, and its credibility as a major military power and valued ally.

SDSR 2015 is a badly-needed successor to the last SDSR, published in October 2010 (SDSR 2010). This was a hasty and poorly thought-through document – the Chairman of the House of Commons Defence Committee, James Arbuthnot, stating in January 2014 that it was 'governed by the overriding strategic objective of reducing the UK's budget

deficit. We have found it difficult to divine any other genuinely strategic vision.' SDSR 2010, combined with subsequent cuts in spending, reduced the British defence budget by about 10 per cent in real terms. The Royal Navy was particularly badly affected, as described in *Seaforth World Naval Review 2012*.[2]

The first and by far the most important decision for SDSR 2015 is how much the United Kingdom (UK) is willing to spend on defence. The 2015/16 defence budget is c. £35bn (c.US$52.5bn) – expected to just meet the 2 per cent of national GDP mandated by NATO as a member's minimum level of defence expenditure.[3] During the election campaign, the Conservative Party's manifesto and Prime Minister David Cameron failed to commit to the NATO target beyond the current year or even to rule out further cuts in defence expenditure. Indeed, on 4 June 2015, it was announced that the defence budget would fall by a further £500m in the current financial year.

In the medium term, a defence budget that is essentially static in real terms seems to be the most likely outcome, and that is assumed in this article. Equipment spending is however planned to increase by 1 per cent a year in real terms (this was repeatedly confirmed by the last government), primarily to support renewal of the UK's nuclear deterrent. In practice, this will inevitably result in reductions elsewhere.

BACKGROUND TO SDSR 2015

The Royal Navy is entering the decision-making part of SDSR 2015 in a much stronger position than it was in 2010. A *UK National Strategy for Maritime Security* was published in May 2014; this established five objectives for the Royal Navy but left resourcing them to SDSR 2015:[4]

■ To promote a secure international maritime area

The helicopter carrier *Ocean* steaming alongside the last remaining *Invincible* class carrier, *Illustrious*, on 22 July 2014 – prior to the latter's final return to her home port of Portsmouth for decommissioning. *Illustrious* had acted as a helicopter carrier following SDSR 2010's decision to 'gap' a strike carrier capability; one of a number of controversial decisions in a hasty and poorly thought-through review. *(Crown Copyright 2014)*

The Royal Navy Type 23 frigate *Kent* pictured leading the Type 42 destroyer *Dauntless* into Portsmouth Harbour on 15 May 2015. Both were returning from lengthy overseas deployments. The Royal Navy was badly impacted by SDSR 2010 but should be in a much stronger position for the forthcoming SDSR 2015. *(Conrad Waters)*

where international maritime laws are upheld.

- To help other nations develop their own maritime security.
- To protect the UK and the Overseas Territories, their citizens and economies by supporting the safety and security of ports and offshore installations, and passenger and cargo vessels.
- To assure the security of vital maritime trade and energy transportation routes.
- To protect the resources and population of the UK and the Overseas Territories from illegal and dangerous activity.

World events also favour the Royal Navy, for example:

- The decision made in 2010 to gap the UK's aircraft carrier capability proved to be a major mistake; the UK's lack of an aircraft carrier has repeatedly restricted the government's military options in a crisis, including Libya in 2011, Syria in 2013 and Iraq (Islamic State) in 2014–15.
- The UK has been greatly embarrassed by increased Russian naval activity around British waters, including suspected submarine activity off

Scotland in December 2014 and January 2015 that led the UK to request the support of maritime patrol aircraft from France, America and Canada.[5]
- The Royal Navy has repeatedly demonstrated its unique ability to quickly respond to natural and man-made disasters, e.g. the Philippines typhoon in 2014 and the Mediterranean refugee boat crisis in 2015.

BASES

For the foreseeable future, the Royal Navy will continue to operate from three main naval bases –

An aerial view of the North Yard of Devonport Dockyard in February 2015. Although all three of the Royal Navy's remaining naval bases in the United Kingdom are likely to remain open for the foreseeable future, the huge Devonport facility is under-utilised, as evident from the few ships in this picture. The southern area of the site is no longer in active use and will be released for commercial use. *(Crown Copyright 2015)*

The Royal Navy maintains a substantial force in the Arabian Gulf and Indian Ocean as part of Operation 'Kipion' and has recently opened a new headquarters and support facility in Bahrain to replace previous *ad hoc* arrangements. This photo shows the line-up on 19 August 2012: the Type 45 destroyer *Diamond*, the 'Bay' class afloat forward support ship *Cardigan Bay* and minehunters *Ramsey*, *Quorn* and *Shoreham*. The regional commitment is a significant strain on the Royal Navy's depleted surface flotilla. *(Crown Copyright 2012)*

Her Majesty's Naval Bases (HMNBs) – in the United Kingdom. These are HMNB Clyde in Scotland, HMNB Devonport near Plymouth and HMNB Portsmouth. These bases cost about £300m (US$450m) a year to run – most spent via contracts awarded to Babcock Marine and BAE Systems in 2014.

The huge Devonport facility is slowly being run down and it will cease to host any operational submarines by 2020. These will then be solely based at HMNB Clyde. The South Yard of Devonport is no longer used by the Royal Navy and discussions are underway to release it for commercial use. Portsmouth is currently undergoing a £250m (US$375m) upgrade to prepare it as home port for the new *Queen Elizabeth* class aircraft carriers.

The Royal Navy's most substantial overseas facility is the brand-new £6m headquarters and forward support facility for the UK Maritime Component Command in Bahrain. This accommodates eighty Royal Navy personnel and replaces previous *ad hoc* arrangements that relied upon the generosity and co-operation of the Bahraini and United States Navies.

The Royal Navy also maintains a presence in Gibraltar and the Falkland Islands, and small naval parties at several other locations around the world, including Singapore and Diego Garcia.

PERSONNEL

On 1 March 2015, the Royal Navy had 22,730 trained personnel (down from 27,960 on 1 March 2010), plus 7,040 Royal Marines. Personnel shortages mean that in some specialisations the unexpected loss of even one officer or senior rating can affect operations. It is also difficult to resource new activities; for example, when eight personnel were needed to support the deployment of a newly-acquired Scan Eagle unmanned aerial vehicle (UAV), five were civilian contractors. Another problem is that frequent long deployments and career uncertainty has made it difficult to retain trained and experienced personnel. Eleven per cent of Royal Navy engineering ratings voluntarily left the service in 2014.

In order to help alleviate manpower shortages, the Royal Navy is making maximum use of secondments from other countries; for example US Coast Guard enlisted personnel are joining Type 23 frigates for up to three years.

General Sir Nicholas Houghton, the Chief of the Defence Staff, said in a speech on 18 December 2013, 'Unattended, our current course leads to a strategically incoherent force structure – exquisite equipment, but insufficient resources to man that equipment or train … I would identify the Royal Navy as being perilously close to its critical mass in manpower terms.'

SURFACE FLOTILLA

The Royal Navy is struggling to meet too many tasks with too few ships.[6] Examples of over-stretch are:

- The Royal Navy is unable to provide sufficient escorts and helicopters for its Response Force Task Group (RFTG). During the RFTG's Cougar 2014 deployment a German frigate, *Schleswig-Holstein*, was the primary escort.
- In the first half of 2015 one the Royal Navy's offshore patrol vessels (OPVs), *Severn,* was deployed to the West Indies – a role traditionally performed by a frigate or destroyer. This then left only two OPVs to police the UK's 300,000 square nautical mile exclusive economic zone (EEZ). By comparison the Republic of Ireland has eight OPVs for an EEZ half the area.

The lack of frigates and destroyers is a particularly serious problem; the nineteen available are working 'back to back' six or seven month deployments when not in refit or working-up. This is not sustainable, and the Royal Navy is trying to move to one nine-month deployment in every three years.

The Ministry of Defence's (MOD) Equipment Plan proposes to spend £18.2bn (c. US$27bn) on new and existing surface warships over the ten years to 2024. Key items are as follows.

***Queen Elizabeth* Class:** The Royal Navy's flagship project is the design and construction of the two new 65,000-ton aircraft carriers, *Queen Elizabeth* and *Prince of Wales*, at an expected total cost of £6.5bn (c. US$10bn).[7] SDSR 2010 stated that '[a] Queen Elizabeth Class (QEC) carrier, operating as part of a Response Force Task Group will be a key basing option for the projection of air and amphibious power in support of national influence and future complex or simple non-enduring intervention operations'. This capability is termed Carrier Enabled Power Projection (CEPP).

After SDSR 2010, one of the new carriers was

potentially available for sale. However, the high price tag and aircraft operating limitations imposed by their 'ski-jump' flight deck configuration would have been a deterrent to potential buyers. In any event, on 5 September 2014 at the 2014 NATO Summit in Wales, Prime Minister David Cameron confirmed that both would enter Royal Navy service. However, the navy lacks the personnel, aircraft, escorts and support ships needed to operate two carrier task groups. Barring some very improbable decisions in SDSR 2015, it seems that one QEC will be kept at high readiness (i.e. operational) whilst the second is held at extended readiness (i.e. reserve) or in refit, the two ships alternating status roughly every four years.

Queen Elizabeth was formally named on 4 July 2014 and floated out of the dry dock in which she had been assembled a fortnight later. Final fitting out is well underway and her crew – some of whom have trained on US and French aircraft carriers – started to join in April 2015. Assuming no serious problems emerge she is expected to begin sea trials by early 2017, commission at Portsmouth during the summer, and enter service (albeit with a limited

helicopter-only capability) in December of that year. Her sister-ship, *Prince of Wales*, is also under construction, lagging *Queen Elizabeth* by about thirty months.

From December 2020 a small standing Carrier Air Group (CAG) should be available – consisting of a squadron of nine (potentially later twelve) F-35B Lightning II fighters and a squadron of nine Merlin HM2 helicopters, the latter including four configured with Crowsnest airborne early warning and control equipment. This CAG utilises only half the capacity of a QEC and at least one more squadron of Lightning II's could be embarked if available. However, the Royal Air Force (RAF) considers that it will be difficult to assign even one Lightning II squadron regularly to carrier operations and the commitment will have to be restricted to occasional training periods and major exercises. Presumably SDSR 2015 will make the final decision on priorities.

SDSR 2015 is also expected to confirm and fund plans to operate the QEC in a secondary role as a helicopter assault ship (LHA), modifications required include:

After being officially named on 4 July 2014, the hull of *Queen Elizabeth* finally touched water on 17 July 2014. Tugs then moved her from No. 1 Dry Dock to K/J berth for fitting out prior to sea trials that are planned to commence by early 2017. *(Aircraft Carrier Alliance)*

- Expanding the accommodation available for an Embarked Military Force (EMF) from 250 to at least 750 personnel.
- Reconfiguring the flight deck to provide ten rather than six spots for simultaneous Merlin HC4 helicopter operations.
- Providing suitable spaces and facilities for the EMF, including stores, ammunition and vehicles.
- Converting the boat embarkation area at the stern of the QEC to support landing craft and Mexifloat operations.
- The possible provision of davit-mounted landing craft.

An indicative all-helicopter Tailored Air Group (TAG) for LHA operations has been defined as three Chinook, twelve Merlin HC4, eight Apache and six Wildcat helicopters. An intermediate TAG with at least six Lightning IIs is also being studied, resulting in a ship very similar in capability to the US Navy's latest LHA-type amphibious assault ship, *America*.

Type 45 Destroyers: The last of six Type 45 destroyers was only completed in 2013.[8] However, four are benefiting from the installation of Harpoon surface-to-surface missiles taken from decommissioned Type 22 frigates and all have been fitted with Phalanx close-in weapons systems (CIWS). Studies in to the use of the Type 45s in an anti-ballistic missile defence role are also quietly continuing.

Type 23 Frigates: The Type 23 Frigate Sustainability Programme is particularly extensive as the oldest ship is already at the end of her originally planned service life. Major upgrades are therefore required to keep the class viable until replaced by the Type 26 frigate. New equipment that they are receiving during a series of refits includes a replacement surveillance radar system (Type 997, Artisan) and new Sea Ceptor short-range air-defence missiles from the Common Anti-air Modular Missile (CAMM) family in lieu of their original Sea Wolf missiles.

Type 26 Global Combat Ship: The Type 26 class of frigate, often called the Global Combat Ship (GCS) for marketing purposes, will replace the Type 23 frigates. The Type 26 has had a difficult birth but, after a decade of studies, a £127m design contract was awarded to BAE Ships Systems (now BAE Systems Maritime – Naval Ships) on 25 March 2010.

The RN wants a capable and high-endurance vessel that can perform a wide range of tasks independently (from patrol duties to intelligence-gathering), or protect a maritime task group. BAE Systems has struggled to meet these requirements within tight affordability constraints – a maximum 'sail-away' cost was set by the MOD at an early stage and rigorously adhered to. This number has never been publicly revealed but £300m–£400m seems a reasonable estimate. During 2014 it appeared that an agreement might not be possible and that the hulls could even be built abroad. However it was announced in February 2015 that the project would proceed to the Demonstration Phase, and that contracts worth £859m were being placed with BAE Systems and other suppliers to complete the detailed design and provide long-lead items such as gas turbines and gearboxes for the first three ships.

With a displacement of over 6,000 tons, a length of 148.5m (487ft) and a beam of 20m, the Type 26 is much larger than the 4,900-ton Type 23, and only slightly smaller than the Type 45 destroyers. The core crew will be just 118, but accommodation will be provided for another seventy-two, such as Royal Marines or mission specialists. Propulsion will be based on a single Rolls-Royce MT-30 gas turbine and four diesel generators in an unambitious combined diesel electric or gas turbine (CODOG) configuration. Maximum speed will be a relatively modest 26 knots.

Two versions will be built using a common, acoustically-quiet hull – an anti-submarine warfare (ASW) variant and a general-purpose (GP) variant. The only significant difference expected is that the eight ASW vessels will be fitted with Sonar 2087 – a towed-array sonar system taken from decommissioned Type 23 frigates. In order to keep costs down, an unusually large amount of equipment will be transferred from the Type 23s, including their radars, Sea Ceptor air-defence system and 30mm Mk 44 light guns. Forty-eight Sea Ceptor canisters will be carried in two twenty-four cell silos, a significant improvement on the number of Sea Wolf missiles originally carried by the Type 23s. Two Phalanx CIWS will also be fitted. It is not planned

The Type 23 frigate *Iron Duke* pictured in October 2013. She was the first of the class to have the new Type 997 Artisan surveillance radar installed, replacing the old Type 996 system on top of the foremast. Further enhancements, most notably installation of the CAMM-based Sea Ceptor surface-to-air missile system, will keep the class viable until the new Type 26 frigates enter service. (*Conrad Waters*)

to reuse the Type 23's 4.5in Mk 8 main gun; instead the Type 26 will get a new medium-calibre gun, almost certainly the 5in Mk 45 Mod 4 manufactured by BAE Systems in the United States. This will be able to use long-range guided ammunition developed for the US Navy.

An interesting feature of the Type 26 is a connected hangar and 'flexible mission bay'. The former can accommodate one Merlin or two Wildcat helicopters, whilst the latter will normally be used to carry up to four 12m boats, manned or unmanned surface and subsurface vehicles, and specialised mission containers. One area can overflow into the other to provide extra space, for example when carrying UAVs in addition to a helicopter flight. The flight deck itself is large enough to operate a Chinook helicopter.

Another key feature is the provision in the design of a flexible strike silo able to accommodate sixteen missile cells (or twenty-four according to one official document dated October 2014) using the American Mk 41 vertical launch system. This will be able to carry a wide range of missiles – including the Tomahawk land-attack missile. It is not expected that the ships will be completed with the cells, but the silo offers an impressive upgrade path. Notable apparent omissions from the design are anti-submarine torpedo tubes and surface-to-surface missiles such as Harpoon.

Current plans appear to be to order a batch of three ASW vessels in 2016 and further batches of five ASW and five GP vessels at later dates – making sure all the ship are ordered will be a major concern for the Royal Navy. It is expected that all vessels will be assembled at BAE Systems' shipyards on the Clyde. Following abandonment of previous plans for a 'frigate factory' centred on a new £200m modern dock hall to be built at the Scotstoun shipyard, initial construction will now take place at Govan before transfer to Scotstoun for final fitting out and testing, in similar fashion to the Type 45 destroyers. Over £100m will still be spent on upgrading the two yards. Steel on the lead ship should be cut in 2016 and she will enter service in 2022 – a year's delay since 2010. The construction rate of the Type 26 is uncertain; the Royal Navy wants one a year whilst the UK Treasury has proposed one every two years. One every eighteen months is a possible compromise, meaning that some Type 23 frigates will have to serve an excessive 35+ years.

Two computer-generated images of the new Type 26 design, both released in the second half of 2013. In spite of efforts to limit size and cost, the new ships will only be slightly smaller than the Type 45 destroyers. Orders for long-lead items for the first three ships were placed in February 2015 and full production contracts will be placed within the next twelve months. *(BAE Systems)*

THE ROYAL NAVY'S NEW OFFSHORE PATROL VESSELS

Key specifications
Displacement: 2,000 tonnes
Length: 90 metres
Maximum speed: 24 knots
Range: Over 5,000 nautical miles
Endurance: 35 days
Accommodation: 60
Crew size: 34

16 tonne crane
CMS-1 combat system
Enhanced flight deck capable of operating Merlin helicopters
Shared Infrastructure operating system
Two Pacific 24 RIBs
Small calibre machine guns
Medical facilities
30mm main gun
Large stores

de&s

BAE SYSTEMS
INSPIRED WORK

In a somewhat unexpected decision, orders have been placed for three Batch 2 'River' class offshore patrol vessels, which will be named *Forth*, *Medway* and *Trent*. The three ships are based on the *Amazonas* class originally ordered by Trinidad and Tobago but subsequently purchased by Brazil. The first will enter service in 2017. *(BAE Systems)*

Attempts gain an early export win with the GCS have so far come to nothing, with Brazil and Turkey among those believed to have declined overtures. Australia remains a sales target.

Batch 2 'River' Class: On 6 November 2013 it was slightly unexpectedly announced that an order would be placed with BAE Systems for three new OPVs. Their stated mission is 'counter-terrorism, counter-piracy and anti-smuggling operations'. As such it seems likely that the new ships will be additions rather than replacements to existing OPVs, and that they will be used in roles that otherwise would require a frigate or destroyer.

The contract for the OPVs is expensive at a fixed price of £348m including spares and support – about double the price of an export sale. However, this figure probably includes compensation to BAE Systems for cancellation of a fifteen-year Terms of Business agreement signed with the MOD in 2009 and its replacement by a Maritime Composite Option (whose terms have not been published), as well as a subsidy to allow BAE Systems to retain essential manufacturing skills pending Type 26 orders.

Mine Countermeasures and Hydrographic Capability: Mine Countermeasures and Hydrographic Capability (MHC) is another project with a long history. It finally advanced when SDSR 2010 announced plans to replace the existing Mine Countermeasures Vessels (MCMV) of the 'Hunt' and *Sandown* class ships, with a new design 'which will also have the flexibility to be used for other roles such as hydrography or offshore patrol'. Due to funding constraints, progress has still been slow, and the patrol requirements were dropped in 2013, when the Batch 2 'River' class was approved.

Current thinking focusses on a conventional (i.e.

Iridium
Extended Range
Reach Back Data Centres
Seagoing Host Platform
USV
Portable Operations Centre
Mission Management System
Towed Sonar
ROV
Delayed Disposal System
UUVs

KEY
RF Comms
AComms
Iridium Comms
Fixed line connectivity
Primary System Boundary

© Thales

A schematic illustrating the different components of the Maritime Mine Counter Measures (MMCM) system being developed for the Royal Navy in conjunction with France's *Marine Nationale*. *(Thales)*

steel-hulled) 2,000–2,500-ton ship that – in the MCM role – will deploy a flotilla of remotely-controlled systems, including:

- Unmanned surface vehicles (USV) with remotely-operated mine neutralisation systems.
- Autonomous underwater vehicles (AUVs) for reconnaissance and mine hunting.
- Towed synthetic aperture sonar (T-SAS).

Development of these systems – known collectively as the Maritime Mine Counter Measures (MMCM) programme – is being shared with France and a joint contract for development of prototypes for evaluation by both the Royal Navy and *Marine Nationale* was awarded to Thales in March 2015. If trials are successful, production systems will initially be deployed on the 'Hunt' class in Royal Navy service, pending completion of the new MHC vessels.

Under current plans, the first MHC will enter service about 2028, by which time the oldest 'Hunt' will have served for forty-seven years! This has necessitated a major life extension programme for the 'Hunts', *Chiddingfold* being the first vessel to re-enter service in 2012 after replacement of her engines and machinery, replacement of obsolescent equipment and many other upgrades. The *Sandown*s are also receiving substantial enhancements during their own refits.

SUBMARINE SERVICE

In recent years, the size of the submarine service has stabilised at four nuclear-powered ballistic missile submarines (SSBNs) and seven nuclear-powered attack submarines (SSNs).

The biggest single line item in the MOD's Equipment Plan is the £40bn (c.US$60bn) it expects to spend on new and existing submarines by 2024.

An image of the strategic missile submarine *Vanguard* in the Clyde in 2010; the destroyer *Dragon* is in the background. Orders for four replacement boats are expected in 2017. *(Crown Copyright 2010)*

'Successor' Submarines: Design work on a new class of SSBNs has been proceeding at an increasing pace since preliminary approval for the programme (termed 'Initial Gate') was given in 2011. The new submarines will carry the American-made Trident II D5 ballistic missile, and replace the four strong *Vanguard* class.

It is estimated that the new submarines will cost between £12.9bn and £16.4bn (c. US$19bn to US$25bn) in 2013/14 numbers, depending upon whether three or four are built. A decision on the number is expected in early 2016 ('Main Gate'), but the Royal Navy's advice after operating such submarines for nearly fifty years is that four are required. A continuous-at-sea deterrent can theoretically be maintained with three submarines, but this leaves no margin for breakdowns or accidents. As a commitment to build four 'Successor' submarines was included in the Conservative Party's 2015 manifesto, it would seem likely that this is the number that will be confirmed at Main Gate.

By Main Gate, £4.2bn will have been spent on the project, including orders worth £588m for long lead items for the first submarine, such as PWR3 components, main shaft bearing and pressure plates. It is expected that the first submarine will be formally ordered in 2017, will be completed in 2026, and undertake her first patrol in 2028. Additional boats will follow at three-year intervals. All the submarines will be built by BAE Systems at its Barrow-in-Furness submarine yard – which is receiving a £300m upgrade in preparation.

'Successor' will have twelve missile tubes (reduced from sixteen in the *Vanguard* class), and only eight will normally be operational. The missile compartment is being jointly developed with the USA; manufacture of the first missile tube for the first Successor began in November 2014 and they will be delivered to the UK as quad-packs from 2018. The submarines will have a new PWR3 nuclear reactor, which will be able to operate for thirty years without refuelling.

Astute Class Submarines: This class of SSN has a troubled history but two boats (*Astute* and *Ambush*) are now in operational service, and a third (*Artful*) should be commissioned by early 2016. A further three boats are in various stages of construction and long-lead items have been ordered for another. The seventh and last of class (*Ajax*) should enter service in March 2024, at cost of £1.67bn (c. US$2.5bn). As additional *Astute*s enter service, existing *Trafalgar* class boats will be decommissioned, concluding with *Triumph* in 2022 (after thirty years of service).

AMPHIBIOUS WARFARE

Royal Marines: SDSR 2015 will probably see the British Army resuming its fight to absorb the Royal Marines and in particular 3 Commando Brigade, but it would be a major surprise if they were successful. The last few years have also seen proposed reductions in the Brigade's organic artillery and engineer's formations largely fended off, but the lack of attached armoured vehicles (barring the BvS10 Viking Mk 2 all-terrain support vehicle) remains a notable deficiency. The Royal Marines have been disappointed in regards to relatively low-cost requests such as new Force Protection Craft and Fast Landing Craft – neither of which now seems likely to be acquired before 2020.

A particularly overstretched Royal Marines formation is 43 Commando Fleet Protection Group. Primarily responsible with ensuring the security of

The nuclear-powered attack submarine *Artful* undergoing harbour diving trials in the second half of 2014. The third boat of the *Astute* class, she will be commissioned by 2016. A further four submarines are under construction or on order. *(BAE Systems)*

Britain's nuclear weapons, in December 2013 it had responsibility for providing force protection teams to deploying Royal Fleet Auxiliary service ships and minor warships added to its duties.

Amphibious Shipping: The RN's ability to conduct amphibious operations has declined since a brief renaissance in the early years of this century. The current requirement, established by SDSR 2010, is the ability to land from the sea a Royal Marines Commando Group (i.e. a reinforced battalion) of up to 1,800 men.

The landing platform dock (LPD) *Bulwark* is currently in active service and acting as fleet flagship, but her sister-ship *Albion* has been reduced to extended readiness (reserve). The ships will rotate roles in 2017. With the decommissioning of *Illustrious* in 2014, *Ocean* is the only helicopter carrier and assault ship (LPH) left in Royal Navy service. She is expected to decommission by 2018, as she would otherwise need an expensive life-extension refit. Equally importantly, her crew is needed to help man the new aircraft carriers. SDSR 2010 halted early planning for two new large multi-

Table 2.4A.1: STRENGTH OF THE ROYAL NAVY

TYPE	CLASS	NUMBER IN SERVICE (UNDER CONSTRUCTION)		
		1 JULY 2010	1 JULY 2015	1 JULY 2020 - PLANNED
Submarines				
Submarine – SSBN	'SUCCESSOR'	–	–	(2)
Submarine – SSBN	VANGUARD	4	4	4
Submarine – SSN	ASTUTE	(4)	2 + (4)	4 + (3)
Submarine – SSN	TRAFALGAR	6	4	2
Submarine – SSN	SWIFTSURE	1	0	0
Aircraft Carriers				
Strike Carrier – CV	QUEEN ELIZABETH	(1)	(2)	2[2]
Support Carrier – CVS	INVINCIBLE	2[1]	0	0
Amphibious Ships				
Helicopter Carrier – LPH	OCEAN	1	1	0
Landing Platform Dock – LPD	ALBION	2	2[2]	2[2]
Landing Ship Dock – LSD(A)	LARGS BAY	4	3	3
Principal Surface Escorts				
Destroyer – DDG	DARING (Type 45)	2 + (4)	6	6
Destroyer – DDG	SHEFFIELD/MANCHESTER (Type 42)	5	0	0
Frigate – FFG	'GCS' (Type 26)	0	0	(3)
Frigate – FFG	NORFOLK (Type 23)	13	13	13
Frigate – FFG	CORNWALL (Type 22)	4	0	0
Minor War Vessels				
Patrol Vessel – OPV	FORTH ('River'-B2)	0	(2)	3
Patrol Vessel – OPV	TYNE/CLYDE ('River'/Mod. 'River')	4	4	4
Minehunter – MCMV	SANDOWN	8	7	7
Minehunter – MCMV	BRECON ('Hunt')	8	8	8
Afloat Support Ships				
Tanker - AOR	TIDESPRING ('Tide')	0	(2)	4
Tanker - AOR	WAVE KNIGHT ('Knight')	2	2	2
Tanker - AOR	APPLELEAF ('Leaf')	2	1	0
Tanker – AOR	GREEN ROVER ('Rover')	2	2	0
Replenishment Ship – AOR	FORT VICTORIA ('Fort')	2	1	1
Replenishment Ship – AFS	FORT ROSALIE ('Fort')	2	2	2
Casualty Receiving Ship – APCR	ARGUS	1	1	1
Forward Repair Ship – ARH	DILIGENCE	1	1	1

CONSTRUCTION (2015-2030)

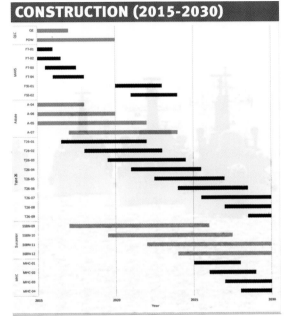

The table shows actual and planned strength of the Royal Navy between 2010 & 2020; the diagram shows the actual and likely construction programme from 2015 to 2030.

Notes – Table:

1 In 2010, the roles of the two *Invincible* class ships were being rotated with that of *Ocean* so as to keep one support carrier and one helicopter carrier in service.

2 One ship held at extended readiness.

3 Other ships in service throughout this period include the three hydrographic ships of the *Scott* and *Echo* classes; the survey launch *Gleaner* and the eighteen inshore patrol vessels of the *Archer* and *Scimitar* classes. In addition, the ice patrol ship *Protector* was commissioned in June 2011 to replace the former *Endurance*.

Notes – Diagram

1 MARS is the Military Afloat Reach and Sustainability programme, with FT referencing the four 'Tide' class Fleet Tankers and FSS the proposed Fleet Solid Support ships.

2 MHC is the Mine Countermeasures and Hydrographic Capability project.

purpose amphibious ships (LHDs) similar to the Spanish *Juan Carlos I* design. Instead the QEC class will be given a secondary amphibious assault ship role, as already described.

The Royal Fleet Auxiliary (RFA) service used to operate four 'Bay' class landing ships, but this was reduced to three by SDSR 2010. These are in much demand, but often for non-amphibious duties such as the afloat forward support base in Bahrain. Finally, four 'Point' class sealift ships are operated by Foreland Shipping on behalf of the MOD. A further two ships were sold in 2011.

ROYAL FLEET AUXILIARY SERVICE

The primary role of the RFA is the afloat support of Royal Navy warships. The service has received no new tankers or replenishment ships since *Wave Ruler* in 2003. However, in March 2015, *Tidespring*, the first of four new 37,000 tons 'Tide' class tankers, was launched by Daewoo Shipbuilding and Marine Engineering in South Korea. She should be delivered in October 2015 and arrive in the UK in December for installation of replenishment and military equipment by A&P Group at its Falmouth yard, prior to entry in to service in 2016. Three sister-ships will follow by 2018.

It is hoped that SDSR 2015 will approve plans to build two new Fleet Solid Support (FSS) ships. These will be equipped with a new high-capacity Replenishment at Sea (RAS) system, and will be optimised to support the QEC. It is tentatively planned to place an order for the ships about 2020, for completion in 2024–5. Two other RFA veterans, *Argus* and *Diligence*, are both now expected to remain in service until the middle of the next decade.

FLEET AIR ARM

The Fleet Air Arm (FAA) is in the midst of one of its most dramatic periods of change since the Second World War. Highlights include:

■ 736 Naval Air Squadron (NAS) was commissioned in June 2013 with seventeen BAE Systems Hawk T1 jet trainers. A key role of the squadron

The Royal Navy's largest warship, *Ocean* (L12), arriving at Gibraltar on 21 September 2014 at the start of the RFTG's Cougar 14 deployment. The timing was a convenient response to recent incidents during which Spanish finishing boats illegally entered Gibraltarian waters. Note the Type 997 Artisan radar on the main mast, installed during a £65m major refit that was completed earlier in the year. She is likely to decommission in 2018, not least because her crew will be needed to help man the new aircraft carriers. *(Moshi Anahory)*

is to maintain a basic level of fixed-wing competency within the RN and FAA.

- The Wildcat HMA2 multi-role helicopter reached operational service in January 2015. The Royal Navy will receive twenty-eight, with 825 NAS acting as both the training and interim front-line squadron, providing flights to ships as required. It will be replaced in the latter role by 815 NAS in 2016.
- 847 NAS, part of the Commando Helicopter Force, has re-equipped with four Wildcat AH1 battlefield utility helicopters.
- 846 NAS commissioned with ex-Royal Air Force (RAF) Merlin HC3 transport helicopters in September 2014 and 845 NAS will follow in the second half of 2015. Seven helicopters will be upgraded to an interim HC3(I) maritime configuration by March 2016 and, ultimately, twenty-five to a fully marinised HC4 configuration.
- The Merlin HM2 anti-submarine helicopter entered service in May 2014. Deliveries of thirty aircraft upgraded from the MH1 standard should be complete by early 2016. These will equip 814 and 820 NAS (assigned to carrier operations), 829 NAS (provides helicopter flights for Type 23 ASW frigates) and 824 NAS as the training unit.

In March 2014 MBDA was awarded a £319m contract for Sea Venom (also known as FASGW Heavy) missiles for use against vessels and land targets, replacing the Sea Skua. This was followed in June 2014 by a £306m contract with Thales Group for the Martlet Lightweight Multirole Missile (FASGW Light) for use against targets such as small boats and fast attack craft. Both missiles systems are due to enter service in 2020, arming the Wildcat HMA2.

May 2015 saw Lockheed Martin selected as the prime contractor for the Crowsnest surveillance and control programme, and it is expected to receive a c. £470m manufacturing contract in 2016. Ten systems will be purchased, typically equipping eight Merlin HM2s. In 2013 the Crowsnest in-service date was advanced to October 2018 and the withdrawal from service of the Sea King ASaC7s oper-

The Type 23 frigate *Lancaster* returning from deployment in December 2013. In March 2015 she became the first Royal Navy warship to deploy with the new Wildcat HMA2 helicopter when one of the rotorcraft from 825 NAS embarked for a nine-month Atlantic patrol. *(Crown Copyright 2013)*

ated by 849 NAS simultaneously delayed from 2016 in order to avoid a capability gap. With the introduction of Crowsnest, the RN will not have enough Merlin HM2s to meet all operational needs and it is strongly advocating the take-up of an option to convert the eight viable Merlin HM1 airframes not already subject to upgrade to the HM2 standard.

Lightning II: The great hope of the FAA is the Lockheed-Martin F-35B 'fast jet', developed in the United States as the short take off and vertical landing variant of the 'Lightning II' Joint Strike Fighter. By the end of 2015, the UK will have four Lightning IIs, three operated by 17(R) Squadron – a joint RAF and FAA manned unit. Fourteen more are on order or are planned as part of an initial commitment reported as being for forty-eight aircraft and will equip the first front-line unit, 617 Squadron RAF. This is due to form in 2017 and start carrier trials on *Queen Elizabeth* in 2018. SDSR 2015 may confirm how many Lightning IIs the UK will ultimately purchase; this will inevitably be constrained given their hefty price tag.

809 NAS will commission with a small number of aircraft as the Lightning II Operational Conversion Unit at a date still to be announced. It is hoped that 809 NAS will become a second front-line squadron early in the next decade.

Maritime Patrol Aircraft: The United Kingdom has badly missed the Nimrod MR2 maritime patrol aircraft (MPA) which was withdrawn from service in March 2010, and whose replacement (Nimrod MRA4) was cancelled a few months later by SDSR 2010. It will be a major surprise if SDSR 2015 does not approve the purchase of a small number of new MPAs, almost certainly the Boeing P-8 Poseidon, although several other manufacturers are advocating their solutions – the Japanese Kawasaki P-1 being an interesting long-shot.

FINAL COMMENTS

The Royal Navy is unlikely to be as badly affected by SDSR 2015 as it was by SDSR 2010 but the 'Successor' submarine project will be a huge drain on the equipment budget for the next fifteen years. Just

Nine upgraded Merlin HM2 helicopters embarked on *Illustrious* for Exercise 'Deep Blue', an anti-submarine warfare exercise that also involved Type 23 frigates and a British and Dutch submarine. Several are shown here on her flight deck on 4 June 2014. This was virtually *Illustrious*' last operational mission before decommissioning. *(Crown Copyright 2014)*

A computer-generated image of a Merlin HC4 helicopter. The upgraded transport helicopters, transferred from the RAF, will provide the core of the Royal Navy's amphibious helicopter capability in the medium term. *(AgustaWestland)*

a tiny proportion of that expenditure would hugely benefit other parts of the naval service.

The Royal Navy is attempting to reconstruct a balanced fleet, the centrepiece of which will be a CEPP task group containing a QEC. Unfortunately – without more resources – providing the required personnel, aircraft, escorts and support ships will undermine the RN's other activities. Further, it is hard to justify the regular use of a £3bn capital ship in the helicopter assault ship role – a purpose-built ship could do this better for a fraction of the cost.

The French Navy has long used lightly-armed warships with the size and appearance – but not the equipment or manpower – of a small frigate for second-line duties. It will be interesting to see how the Royal Navy operates the Batch 2 'Rivers' – will they become just premature replacements for the older 'Rivers', or will they become so useful that a Type 26 Global Combat Ship might be sacrificed in order to build more?

Finally, after three waves of redundancies since SDSR 2010, the biggest single problem faced by the Royal Navy is a desperate shortage of trained personnel. This is affecting morale, retention and operational capabilities. Even a small uplift in approved strength would have a disproportionate benefit.

A computer graphic of an air group operating from *Queen Elizabeth*. Providing the resources to deploy an effective and well-balanced QEC-based task group could severely impact other naval and aviation activities. *(Aircraft Carrier Alliance)*

Notes:

1. The Royal Navy comprises four fighting arms (Surface Flotilla, Submarine Service, Royal Marines and Fleet Air Arm), plus the Royal Fleet Auxiliary and Maritime Reserve forces.

2. See the author's 'Defence Review Reshapes the Royal Navy', *Seaforth World Naval Review 2012* (Barnsley: Seaforth Publishing, 2011), pp.97–107. A further update was provided in *Seaforth World Naval Review 2014*.

3. The Royal United Services Institute (RUSI) has published many informative articles on UK defence spending and SDSR 2015, the essential starter being *The Financial Context for the 2015 SDSR*. These publications are available online at www.rusi.org

4. The *UK National Strategy for Maritime Security* (London: Ministry of Defence, 2014) can be found online at: www.gov.uk/government/publications/national-strategy-for-maritime-security. Reference should also be made to *British Maritime Doctrine: Joint Doctrine Publication 0-10* (Shrivenham: MOD Development, Concepts & Doctrine Centre, 2011), an official publication that 'defines both the purpose of British maritime power and the way in which it

can be applied in pursuit of the national interest.' It provides important background to this article, and can be found at www.gov.uk/government/uploads/system/uploads/attachment_data/file/33699/20110816JDP0_10_BMD.pdf

5. The UK's request for help to track a suspected Russian submarine off the west coast of Scotland was reported around the world. The American magazine *Aviation Week & Space Technology* (www.aviationweek.com) provided particularly detailed coverage.

6. *Joint Concept Note 1/12: Future 'Black Swan' Class Sloop-of-War: A Group System* (Shrivenham: MOD Development, Concepts & Doctrine Centre, 2012) suggests an interesting solution to the Royal Navy's lack of hulls in the water. This is currently available at: www.gov.uk/government/uploads/system/uploads/attachment_data/file/33686/20120503JCN112_Black_SwanU.pdf

7. The Aircraft Carrier Alliance website at www.aircraftcarrieralliance.co.uk is a primary source of information on the Royal Navy's new QEC carriers. However, from the end of 2014 it significantly reduced the amount of detail in the publications that it puts in the

public domain.

8. Since that time, the Royal Navy has had no destroyers or frigates under construction.

9. Although some have a substantial element of public relations 'spin', essential sources of official information on the Royal Navy are:

- The UK Ministry of Defence at: www.gov.uk/government/organisations/ministry-of-defence
- The website of the Royal Navy at: www.royalnavy.mod.uk
- The official newspaper of the Royal Navy, *Navy News*, at: www.navynews.co.uk
- The UK National Audit Office's annual Ministry of Defence: Major Projects Report, found at: www.nao.org.uk
- The House of Commons Defence Select Committee, whose reports can be found at: www.parliament.uk/business/committees/committees-archive/defence-committee
- The House of Commons Library, which regularly publishes briefing papers and research on defence matters. The library can be found on-line at: www.parliament.uk

Author:
Conrad Waters

3.1 SIGNIFICANT SHIPS

HOLLAND CLASS OPVs

The 'Rolls-Royce' of Offshore Patrol Vessels

A significant trend amongst naval construction programmes in recent years has been the growing popularity of the purpose-built offshore patrol vessel (OPV). The current United Nations Convention on the Law of the Sea III (UNCLOS III) has significantly increased the extent of the sea areas many navies have to patrol. Equally, the previous practice of cascading obsolescent front-line warships for secondary constabulary duties has become less attractive when pressures to reduce manning and support costs are taken into consideration.[1] Amongst many navies bringing new OPVs into service is the Royal Netherlands Navy, which commissioned its four *Holland* class ships between 2012 and 2013. Positioned towards the top end of recent designs in terms of size and – particularly – sophistication, the new vessels are starting to prove themselves on operational tasking. The fourth and final member of the class, *Groningen*, is scheduled to deploy to the Horn of Africa in the second half of 2015, marking the class's debut in international stabilisation missions.

Left and right: The *Holland* class OPV *Groningen* seen departing Portsmouth, UK on 24 November 2014. A sophisticated ship, she combines the armament and crew size of a traditional patrol vessel with the size and electronic outfit of a frigate. Sensors and communications equipment are concentrated in the distinctive, pyramid-shaped integrated mast. *(Conrad Waters)*

CLASS ORIGINS

The *Holland* class traces its origins to a fundamental reshaping of the Royal Netherlands Navy in the post-Cold War era. A previous fleet structure focused on large numbers of surface escorts and mine-countermeasures vessels was steadily cut back. By the early years of the new Millennium, the planned force of major surface vessels had shrunk to a core of four of the new *De Zeven Provinciën* 'LCF' type air-defence escorts, supplemented by six of the

original eight *Karel Doorman* 'M' class frigates. However, there was still debate as to whether this mix was appropriate for the navy's likely tasks, particularly given the costs associated with deploying heavily armed and crewed frigates on constabulary and stabilisation missions. A further examination of fleet structure was therefore undertaken under the *Marinestudie* 2005 (Naval Study 2005).

The results of the study were published in October 2005. Taking into account the decreasing magnitude of classic sea control and sea denial tasks, the navy decided to dispose of a further four 'M'

class frigates. The resultant savings were to be used to enhance the navy's capability to support missions in littoral waters – ultimately resulting, *inter alia*, in the acquisition of the joint support ship *Karel Doorman* – and to invest in replacement ships better suited for naval operations at the lower end of the spectrum of violence. The new patrol vessels were considered to be particularly suitable for law enforcement and maritime safety operations in the Dutch Exclusive Economic Zone (EEZ) in the North Sea, as well as for similar missions around the Caribbean waters of the Kingdom of the

Netherlands.[2] A one-for-one replacement of the further 'M' class frigates slated for withdrawal was envisaged, resulting in a requirement for four new ships.

The specifications of the new warships were drawn up by a project team within the Dutch Defence Materiel Organisation (DMO) on the basis of naval staff requirements. Support was provided by industry, most notably Damen Schelde Naval Shipbuilding (DSNS) and Thales Nederland.[3] Relevant areas of the public sector, such as TNO, the Netherlands Organisation for Applied Scientific Research, also played a part. Much of the political support for the new project derived from a wish to support the Dutch shipbuilding and wider marine technology sectors. As such, maximising local industrial benefit was inevitably a key consideration. According to Rob Zuiddam, the programme manager, the particular requirements of the new class resulted in an entirely new design drawing little from previous Dutch warships. Beyond the core requirement of developing a ship optimised for low-intensity operations, a key design imperative was to reduce through life costs by minimising crewing requirements. A core crew size of fifty – around a hundred less than in the 'M' class frigates – was eventually achieved. This required particularly careful attention to the man-machine interface.

CONSTRUCTION AND DELIVERY

The final design of the new patrol ships was completed by the end of 2007, with the necessary report to the Dutch Parliament allowing contracts to proceed being submitted in November of that year.[4] DSNS subsequently announced that they had received a construction contract for the four ships on 20 December 2007. Of the four, the first pair was to be assembled at the company's Vlissingen facility and the second two at the sister Damen group facility at Galati in Romania. It appears that cost considerations were a key factor behind the decision to complete part of the contract outside of the Netherlands, the switch to Galati being made as one of a series of trade-offs made to keep the programme close to the original budget. The split construction arrangement also helped to facilitate project completion within a relatively tight timescale.

An outline of construction progress is set out in Table 3.1.1. Fabrication of the first ship, *Holland*, commenced approximately a year after contract signature on 8 December 2008. She was launched in

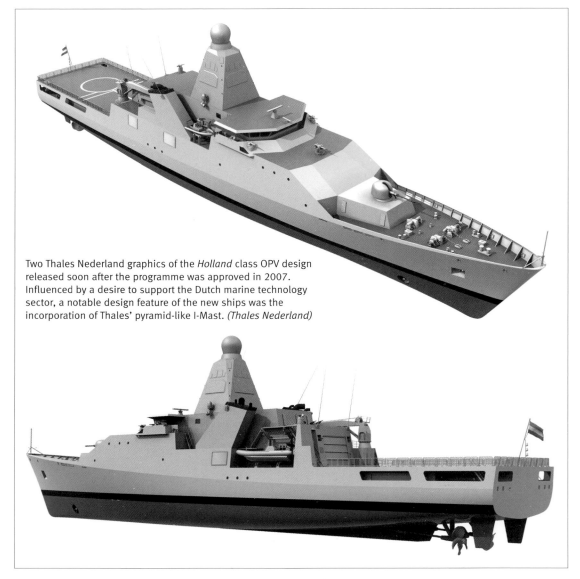

Two Thales Nederland graphics of the *Holland* class OPV design released soon after the programme was approved in 2007. Influenced by a desire to support the Dutch marine technology sector, a notable design feature of the new ships was the incorporation of Thales' pyramid-like I-Mast. *(Thales Nederland)*

Table 3.1.1: HOLLAND CLASS LIST

NAME	BUILDING YARD	YARD NO	LAID DOWN	LAUNCHED	DELIVERED	I-MAST INSTALLED[1]	COMMISSIONED
Holland (P840)	DSNS Vlissingen	408	8 December 2008	2 February 2010	12 May 2011	November 2011	6 July 2012
Zeeland (P841)	DSNS Vlissingen	409	21 September 2009	20 November 2010	20 October 2011	January 2013	23 August 2013
Friesland (P842)	Damen Galati[2]	410	26 November 2009	4 November 2010	11 April 2012	August 2014	22 January 2013
Groningen (P843)	Damen Galati[2]	411	9 April 2010	21 April 2011	16 January 2013	April 2013	29 November 2013

Notes:

1. Refers to completion of installation process.

2. Final pre-delivery work and installation of I-Mast at Damen Schelde Naval Shipbuilding (DSNS) Vlissingen.

February 2010 and delivered to the DMO in May 2011. A notable feature of the new design was the incorporation of the Thales integrated-mast (I-Mast) concept. Under this arrangement, the *Holland* class's principal sensors and communications equipment are incorporated in a separately manufactured mast structure which is then integrated with the rest of each ship as a single unit. One consequence of this decision was that the ships were delivered before their I-Masts had been installed, subsequently returning to the shipyard for the relatively straightforward integration process. The ships then completed the trials process before formal commissioning. *Holland* herself had her I-Mast installed in the course of November 2011, finally being commissioned into Royal Netherlands Navy service on 6 July 2012.

The other class members followed a roughly similar completion schedule to *Holland*, with the Romanian-built *Groningen* the last to commission on 29 November 2013. However, in a variation from the normal pattern, *Friesland* commissioned before her I-Mast was delivered so that she could be used operationally. She subsequently had the mast installed during August 2014, therefore being the last of the quartet to be physically completed. Although austerity-related defence cuts temporarily put two of the class on the 'for sale' list in 2011, the proposal was quickly abandoned and it is now clear that all four will be operated.

Two images of the second *Holland* class OPV *Zeeland* taken off Den Helder in November 2011. *Zeeland* had been delivered by shipyard DSNS a month previously but was not fitted with her separately manufactured I-Mast until over a year later. One of the class members, *Friesland*, actually commissioned before her mast was installed.
(Leo van Ginderen)

OVERALL DESIGN

With a full load displacement of 3,750 tons, the *Holland* class ships are heavier than the 'M' type frigates they have replaced. To an extent, this is a consequence of the application of largely civilian construction standards – including the use of heavier-grade steels – to the fabrication process. Nevertheless, with an overall length exceeding 108m, the ships are large compared with other contemporary European designs. This is a reflection of the need to traverse the Atlantic on a regular basis to fulfil the Caribbean patrol mission – the class are often referred to as ocean-going rather than offshore patrol vessels – and also of an intention that they be fully capable of global deployment on stabilisation missions. The ship's size also facilitates helicopter and boat operations in high Sea States. Similarly, it has been possible to position the bridge and accommodation areas relatively far back from the bow to assist operational effectiveness in adverse weather conditions.

The ships are built to Det Norske Veritas classification standards with improved survivability features.[5] The latter are intended to protect against asymmetrical threats whilst operating in littoral waters, such as an attack by pirates or terrorists armed with rocket-propelled grenades. The survivability features include blast-resistant bulkheads, the use of physical armour and armoured glass, and the provision of a gas-tight citadel for most of the length of the ship. Survivability is further enhanced by a degree of duplication/redundancy, including physical separation of the main diesels from the auxiliary electrical propulsion plant. Conversely – beyond the use of a new, low-visibility light blue-grey colour scheme – there is little of the focus on stealth features seen in contemporary warships. Similarly, the design included no provision for shock resistance and there is only one damage control zone.

The class's general arrangement incorporates a total of ten decks from 'A' deck at the top of the I-Mast down to 'K' deck (there is no 'I' deck). Of these, 'A', 'B' and 'C' decks solely comprise the upper levels of the pyramid-like mast. 'D' deck comprises the base of the mast and the roof of the bridge. The co-located bridge and combat information centre are located on 'E' deck, with the commanding officer's cabin and other accommodation and service compartments on the deck below. The four remaining decks run the length of the ship. Of these, 'H' deck is regarded as the principal deck and the lowest with access along the length of the ship. The two lower decks feature bulkheads that are unpierced by passageways as part of measures to preserve watertight integrity. In general terms, all but the lowest of these four full-length decks is arranged so as to incorporate storage or magazine spaces forward; accommodation and living areas amidships; and flight deck, hangar, machinery spaces and further storage areas aft. There are elevators forward and aft to facilitate the transfer of stores and munitions to the appropriate storage areas.

A picture of first of class *Holland* being fitted with her Thales integrated mast in November 2011. The image shows the large size of the ship compared with other contemporary European offshore patrol vessel designs. The ships have an overall length of 108m and incorporate a total of ten decks (including four in the I-Mast). *(Thales Nederland)*

PROPULSION AND PLATFORM MANAGEMENT

The *Holland* class is propelled by a combined diesel or electric propulsion system. Two MAN 12V 28/33 diesels each linked to a Renk gearbox provide the main propulsion through twin shafts fitted with controllable-pitch propellers. Secondary propulsion is provided through a power take-in (PTI) arrangement under which two ABB electrical motors fed from the ship's electrical system are connected to the gearboxes. The arrangement allows the ship's smaller and more economical diesel generators to provide electric propulsion for low-speed loitering in a patrol area, with the main diesel engines being used for faster – but more fuel-thirsty – transits. Whilst maximum endurance is quoted as being 5,000 miles at 15 knots, the arrangement allows higher figures to be achieved in practice. Similarly, the top design speed was around 20 knots but 22 knots has been achieved on trials.

The ships also benefit from the incorporation of a bow thruster to improve low-speed manoeuvrability and therefore reduce dependency on tug assistance whilst berthing. The facility provides a useful capability when conducting stabilisation missions in the littoral, when port facilities might not be fully functioning.

The platform management function is carried out by an integrated platform management system (IPMS) supplied by Dutch company Imtech Marine. Providing propulsion control, fire detection and other damage control monitoring functions, it has been designed to help the minimal manning levels that were a key design objective and permits an unmanned engine room. Although the IPMS can be managed via a traditional machinery control room and through a secondary position in the combat information centre, an innovative messaging system using personal digital assistants (PDAs) connected via the ship's wireless area network allows crew members to carry out other tasks without losing control of the system.

Imtech Marine was also responsible for supplying the *Holland* class's bridge management system. Encompassing all navigation, meteorological and associated requirements, the automated bridge is capable of one-person operation. In practice, the Royal Netherlands Navy typically operates the ships with two crew members on duty.

COMBAT MANAGEMENT
The *Holland* class's combat information centre or

Holland in December 2011 during a final series of trials after her I-Mast had been installed. These extended to a period off the east coast of the United States in mid-2012 before she commissioned on 6 July of that year. The combined diesel or diesel-electric propulsion system has allowed up to 22 knots to be achieved on trials. *(Thales Nederland)*

The linked combat information centre or CIC (foreground) and bridge (background) on *Groningen*. The linked arrangement improves situational awareness and is particularly well-suited for littoral operations. However, the CIC can be closed off by shutters should the situation require. Apparent in this view are the two main rows of operator consoles for the combat management system and the four large screens that can be used to display a panoramic view provided by the Gatekeeper surveillance system. *(Conrad Waters)*

'operations room' is situated immediately behind the bridge. It is visually linked to it by a series of glass windows which can be shuttered as the situation requires. This effective combination of bridge and operations room, providing seamless connectivity between 'driving' and 'fighting' the ship, is particularly useful in improving overall situational awareness. It has been seen in other warships designed with a particular focus on littoral warfare, including the US Navy's *Independence* (LCS-2) class.

The combat information centre comprises two main rows of operator consoles, supplemented by a third row providing space for the platform management function and a weapon-specific station for the ship's remotely-controlled 30mm gun. The two remotely-operated machine guns are also operated from weapon-specific consoles, these being located in the second row. Each of the multi-function operator workstations typically has access to three screens. The combat management system (CMS) utilises Thales Nederland-supplied hardware operating SEWACO (sensor weapon and command system) software developed by CAMS/Force Vision, the Dutch Ministry of Defence's own internal software house. The basic SEWACO software platform is common across the Royal Netherlands Navy fleet.

This simplifies operator training and overall force-integration.

There are four large flat-panel TV screens at the front of the combat information centre. These are connected to the Gatekeeper electro-optical surveillance system in the I-Mast and can be used to provide a 360-degree panoramic view of the ship's surrounds.

SENSORS

One of the most significant – and visually prominent – features of the *Holland* class is their use of the Thales Nederland I-Mast. This is a discrete,

Table 3.1.2.

HOLLAND CLASS PRINCIPAL PARTICULARS

Building Information (First of Class):

Laid Down:	8 December 2008
Launched:	2 February 2010
Delivered:	12 May 2011
Commissioned:	6 July 2012
Builders:	Damen Schelde Naval Shipbuilding (DSNS), Vlissingen

Dimensions:

Displacement:	3,750 tons full load displacement.
Overall Hull Dimensions:	108.4m x 16.0m x 4.6m. Waterline length is 102.40m.

Equipment:

Armament:	1 x 76mm Oto Melara Compact. 1 x 30mm Oto Melara Marlin. 2 x 12.7mm Oto Melara Hitrole machine guns.
Aircraft:	Flight deck and hangar for 1 x NH-90 helicopter.
Principal Sensors:	Thales IM-400 integrated mast, incorporating SMILE (Sea Master 400) volume-search radar, SEASTAR (Sea Watcher 100) surface-search radar and Gatekeeper IR/TV surveillance system. Navigation radars.
Combat System:	SEWACO. Integrated communications system in IM-400 mast. NATO Links 16 and 22 supported.
Countermeasures:	Electronic Support Measures (ESM) integrated in IM-400 mast.
Other:	2 x RHIBs are carried, one davit launched and one launched via a stern slipway, plus 1 x fast rescue boat. 1 x 10-ton crane.

Propulsion Systems:

Machinery:	CODOE. 2 x MAN 12V28/33 diesels each rated at 5.5MW. 2 x ABB electric motors each rated at 400kW. 2 shafts. 1 x ABB bow thruster rated at 550kW.
Speed:	Maximum speed is 21.5 knots. Range is 5,000 nautical miles at 15 knots in Sea State 3 conditions.

Other Details:

Complement:	Core crew is c. 50. Accommodation is provided for a total of c. 90 personnel
Class:	Four *Holland* class vessels have been constructed. *Holland* (P840) and *Zeeland* (P841) were built by DSNS at Vlissingen; *Friesland* (P842) and *Groningen* (P843) were built at Damen's yard in Galati, Romania, with final outfitting completed at Vlissingen.

pyramid-like structure that incorporates all major radars, other surveillance sensors and communications equipment within a single housing. The mast structure itself is a fully airtight module that forms part of the ship's citadel, protecting sensitive electronic equipment from the elements. The various sensors are largely housed in the external, load-bearing steel walls, with a shielded duct or 'spine' routing cabling and cooling systems through the centre of the mast to serve individual systems. The inside of the mast is hollow to facilitate system maintenance from a series of internal decks at different sensor levels. Thales claims the I-Mast

offers a number of advantages over traditional sensor layouts. These include the avoidance of interference between different sensors, more efficient and economic manufacture and installation, as well as greatly eased maintenance.

The I-Mast on the *Holland* class ships is the IM-400 variant. This incorporates:

SMILE volume surveillance radar: Also known as 'Sea Master 400' in its export version, this is a non-rotating, active phased array with four separate faces. Operating in the S band (NATO E/F bands), it generates multiple beams by means of computer

software to perform medium-range air- and surface-search functions.[6] Manufacturer's published data suggests it is effective out to 250km (c. 135 nautical miles) against aerial targets and to 70km (c. 40 nautical miles) against surface objects. It is also used to provide approach guidance for the ship's helicopter and to carry out the fire-control function for the main 76mm Oto Melara Compact gun.

SEASTAR surface-search radar: Known as 'Sea Watcher 100' for export purposes, SEASTAR is optimised for surface search out to around 40km (c. 20 nautical miles). Another four-faced, active phased array, SEASTAR operates in the X band (NATO I/J

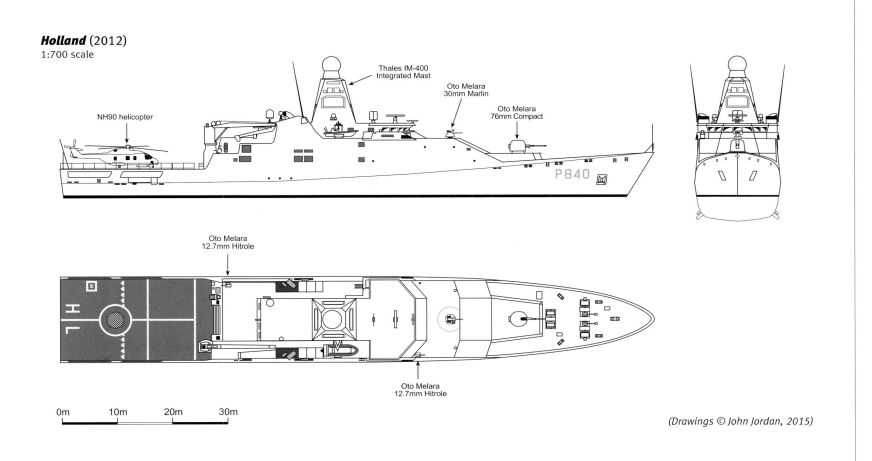

Holland (2012)
1:700 scale

NH90 helicopter

Thales IM-400 Integrated Mast

Oto Melara 30mm Marlin

Oto Melara 76mm Compact

P840

Oto Melara 12.7mm Hitrole

Oto Melara 12.7mm Hitrole

0m 10m 20m 30m

(Drawings © John Jordan, 2015)

band) and is particularly well-suited to detecting and tracking small surface targets, including floating mines, swimmers and small boats. Consequently, it is ideal for identifying the type of asymmetric threats the class is most likely to face when operating on a stabilisation mission in the littoral.

Gatekeeper electro-optical surveillance system: This produces TV and infra-red images to provide panoramic surveillance at shorter ranges. It operates through four sensor heads fitted to the corners of the I-Mast, with each head comprising three IR and three colour TV cameras. The resultant images can

be integrated within the overall CMS picture or displayed on the screens in the combat information centre.

Non-Rotating IFF: The identification friend or foe antenna comprises a non-rotating cylindrical array fitted at the top of the I-Mast, immediately beneath the satellite dome. It is designed to operate with standard IFF interrogator/transponder systems and it is optimised to work in conjunction with the primary radar.

ICAS Integrated Communications Antenna System: This system integrates the antennae needed for the many VHF/UHF and wideband communications services used in the class into a single antenna suite. Key components include flat panel receiving antenna arrays and flat panel transmit arrays fitted to each of the mast's four sides, as well as internal distribution and combination units. There is also a SHF satellite communications antenna in the spherical dome at the masthead and UHF satellite communications antennae at a lower level. The system is fitted to provide NATO Link 16 and Link 22 communications channels, as well as communications electronic support measures (C-ESM).

The ships carry a number of supplementary sensors and communications devices, most notably the ships' navigation radars, in addition to the systems located in the integrated mast,

All in all, the I-Mast provides a sophisticated surveillance and communications capability that would not look out of place in a modern frigate. Whilst optimised towards the class's primary patrol function in low-threat areas, its systems could, for example, provide a useful supplement to the tools available to a task group commander if a *Holland* class ship was integrated into a wider operation.

WEAPONS SYSTEMS

In contrast to their comprehensive surveillance and communications suite, the *Holland* class ships are only fitted with a modest range of weapons systems, proportionate to their primary constabulary mission.

The main armament is the popular 76mm/62 calibre Oto Melara Compact gun. Located forward of the bridge in 'A' position, its configuration in the *Holland* class is optimised for use against surface targets (including shore bombardment) at medium ranges. It is supplemented by a Marlin (modular

A graphic of the Thales IM-400 integrated mast. A satellite communication antenna is located at the head of the mast with a cylindrical IFF array immediately below. Four rectangular panels for the SEASTAR surface-search radar are located high up in the pyramid, with flat receiving and transmitting panels for the communications system immediately below. The largest panels towards the middle of the mast are for the SMILE volume-search and surveillance radar. Sensor heads for the Gatekeeper surveillance system are fitted to the corners of the mast at the bottom of this level. There are additional satellite communications antennae located port and starboard at the mast's base.

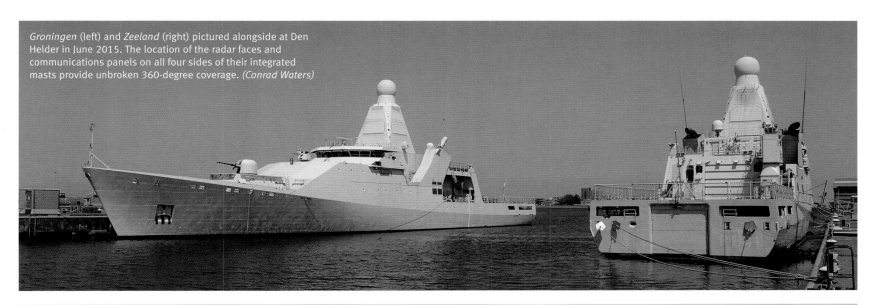

Groningen (left) and *Zeeland* (right) pictured alongside at Den Helder in June 2015. The location of the radar faces and communications panels on all four sides of their integrated masts provide unbroken 360-degree coverage. *(Conrad Waters)*

Friesland pictured off Portsmouth, United Kingdom, in November 2014. The I-Mast is located in a visually dominant position high in the centre of the ship. Also apparent is the lack of significant offensive armament. *(Conrad Waters)*

An aerial view of *Groningen* in November 2014. The image provides a good impression of the class's light armament, confined to a 76mm medium-calibre gun in 'A' position, a lighter 30mm mount in 'B' position and automated machine guns at diagonally opposite ends of the superstructure (the starboard mount, to the side of the bridge, being invisible in this view). *(Derek Fox)*

advanced remotely-controlled lightweight naval) weapon station supplied by the same company and fitted with a 30mm cannon. Located in 'B' position, it has a dual-role capability but is particularly effective in the simultaneous engagement of multiple surface targets, such as a swarm of inshore fast attack craft. A further layer of defence is provided by two 12.7mm Hitrole mounts, which are also of Oto Melara origin. Remotely operated from a dedicated console in the combat information centre like the larger Marlin, these are positioned to give near 360-degree coverage at shorter ranges. Other defensive options are the use of manually-operated 7.62mm machine guns and non-lethal water cannon.

Given its primary constabulary mission, the class's main weapons system is arguably its pair of rigid hulled inflatable boats (RHIBs). One of these is carried on traditional davits to the port side of the hangar. The other is housed in and launched from an internal slipway located underneath the rear of the flight deck at the stern. The slipway system contains no rollers or other moving parts and allows launch and recovery operations in conditions up to Sea State 5. A smaller fast rescue boat is positioned on the starboard side.

The incorporation of a flight deck with a helicopter traversing system and of a hangar into the design significantly increases its operational flexibility. The Royal Netherlands Navy was the first country to receive the NFH frigate variant of the NH-90 helicopter and, despite initial teething troubles, is steadily bringing the type into operational service in its frigates and patrol vessels. The NFH helicopter is equipped with radar and infra-red sensors that have the potential to significantly increase the ship's surveillance capabilities in a range of conditions up to its 800km maximum range. It can also be used to transport limited numbers of

Given the *Holland* class's constabulary role, it is arguable that their rigid hulled inflatable boats constitute their principal weapons system. A stern ramp located underneath the flight deck allows one of these to be launched in a wide range of weather conditions. The image shows the slipway's gate on *Zeeland*. *(Conrad Waters)*

An internal view of the ramp on *Groningen*. The slipway system has no rollers or other moving parts. *(Conrad Waters)*

personnel or in a casualty evacuation role. The NFH helicopter variant is also equipped with sonar and torpedoes for its primary anti-submarine mission onboard the navy's frigates and could therefore, presumably, conduct a similar mission from the *Holland* class if the circumstances required. The *Holland* class's flight deck is also large and strong enough to handle a range of other helicopters up to Sea King-equivalent size.

There has been some criticism of the class's inability to defend itself should one of the ships unexpectedly find itself in a higher-threat environment. Some regard the lack of provision for a close-in weapons system (CIWS) as a particular vulnerability. The extent of internal space needed to accommodate the Royal Netherlands Navy's favoured Goalkeeper CIWS would preclude it being retrofitted to class members. However, an alternative system such as the increasingly popular RAM might be a possibility for installation should the criticism be heeded. In the meantime, consideration is being given to increasing the anti-air capabilities of the existing weapons fit.

OTHER KEY DESIGN FEATURES

The *Holland* class's combination of a relatively large size with a small complement makes for a spacious ship with high standards of crew accommodation and other facilities. The majority of the crew are housed in spacious two berth cabins, with only junior ratings provided with four- or six-berth accommodation. Sufficient berths are provided for a core crew of fifty sailors plus up to an additional forty specialists. For example, these could accommodate a helicopter operating detachment and/or a strengthened medical team.

In a departure from previous practice, dining facilities are concentrated in a single area shared by all ranks. However, separate recreational spaces are provided for officers, petty officers and ratings. The galley also incorporates a number of innovations to reduce demands on catering staff compared with more heavily-manned ships, most notably the use of a system to steam-cook pre-frozen bread in place of the traditional bakery.

The ships' medical facilities include a treatment room and a two-bed sickbay located near the hangar

The *Holland* class are able to embark and support one of the NFH 'frigate' variants of the NH-90 helicopter. The type has experienced significant teething troubles in Royal Netherlands Navy service but it is starting to embark operationally on the class. *(Royal Netherlands Air Force)*

A dramatic view of *Groningen* in April 2015 taken whilst operating in European waters. The class are intended to carry out a 'presence' mission in Netherlands' territorial waters in both the North Sea and the Caribbean, as well as supporting international stabilisation missions. Sufficient berths are provided for forty additional specialists over the core crew of fifty to support such activities. *(Royal Netherlands Navy)*

Zeeland and *Groningen* pictured with locally-deployed navy and coast guard vessels in the Dutch Caribbean during 2014. All four ships have completed at least one deployment to the area as local West Indies Guardship; a permanent Royal Netherlands Navy commitment. *(Royal Netherlands Navy)*

Groningen and *Zeeland* pictured sailing together in 2014 whilst handing over the West Indies Guardship role. The class are superbly equipped for the constabulary role they were designed to fulfil. *(Royal Netherlands Navy)*

on 'G' deck. Provision for disaster relief operations also extends to the ability to house as many as 100 evacuees in temporary accommodation in a large storage area beneath the hangar. Overall storage space is sufficient to support operations of twenty-one days in duration, with a margin of up to three additional days.

A significant feature of the storage system is the ability to ship two standard-size 20ft containers in dedicated spaces positioned below the flight deck on 'H' and 'J' decks. These can be pre-equipped with mission-specific equipment to assist the needs of a particular deployment. A 10-ton deck crane is located on the starboard side immediately aft of the hangar to facilitate stores handling. Again, this is of particular value when port facilities might not be fully functioning.

OPERATIONAL SERVICE

The first member of the *Holland* class has only been in commission for three years, whilst it is less than a

year since *Friesland* was physically completed. However, the new patrol ships are already starting to earn their keep. Home-ported at the Royal Netherlands Navy's principal base at Den Helder in North Holland, the ships completed lengthy work-up periods specifically tailored for the class – including training attachments with the British Royal Navy's FOST organisation at Devonport – after formal commissioning. They have subsequently taken part in a number of NATO exercises, as well as meeting local tasking requirements. All four ships have now also completed deployments to the Caribbean as West Indies Guardship, tasked with external defence, international counter-drugs operations (in co-operation with the United States and other countries) and the provision of assistance to local government, including the Dutch Caribbean Coast Guard. Each Caribbean tasking is typically four months long in duration. These deployments have therefore proved the class's ability to undertake lengthy operations away from their home base. The

icing on the cake has been several narcotics interceptions, as well as conclusion of a number of successful search and rescue missions.

A more challenging test is set to commence in August 2015, when *Groningen* is scheduled to depart to the Middle East for an anti-piracy mission off the coast of Somalia. The deployment is scheduled to last for four months and will mark the first time the class has been involved in an international stabilisation mission. It takes place against the backdrop of continued Al-Shabaab terrorist activity in the East African country and the ongoing civil war in neighbouring Yemen. Preparations for the deployment have already led to steps to enlarge accommodation – for example, by increasing the number of bunks in some cabins from four to six berths – to squeeze in the hundred or so personnel who will participate in the mission. A NFH helicopter detachment, an enhanced marine boarding team, an intelligence unit and a surgery team are amongst those being added to the core crew. In the words of *Groningen*'s commanding officer, Commander Walter Hansen, 'We are fully booked.'

Operational experience is starting to provide some lessons that will assist the future management of the class over its planned 25-year service life. For example, the lean manning principles applied to the design necessarily mean that there is a greater requirement for shore-based maintenance and logistics support; some maintenance regimes have already been changed to pass the burden from ship-based personnel to the shore support function. Similarly, the small size of the crew means that everybody is essential. As such, manning gaps that might be tolerable in the navy's frigates can have more significant consequences on one of the patrol ships. This has to be taken into account by the navy's human resource function.

CONCLUSION

The *Holland* class oceanic patrol vessels have been built to a unique design concept that offers an equally unique set of capabilities. The ships are superbly well-equipped to carry out their intended role of providing maritime security and safety in scenarios where the level of threat is positioned towards the lower end of the spectrum of violence. The comprehensive range of electronic equipment integrated within the Thales I-Mast provides them with the ability to carry out effective surveillance over a wide area and communicate a clear tactical

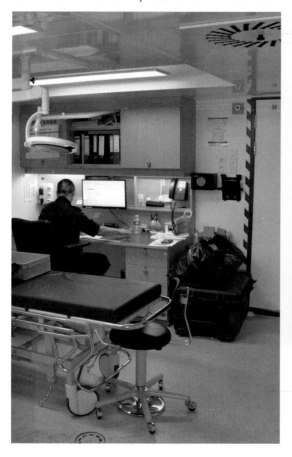
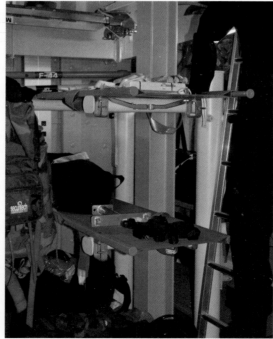

Groningen will deploy to the Horn of Africa in August 2015 on anti-piracy duties. The ship has a medical treatment room (left) and small hospital ward but additional medics will be embarked to support the mission. There is space in the storage area located under the flight deck to house refugees/detainees; the right image shows emergency bunks provided for this purpose. *(Conrad Waters)*

picture to allied units. Whilst the class's armament is no more extensive than that fitted to a more traditionally-designed patrol vessel, it is fully proportionate to their intended role. Turning again to the words of Commander Hansen, 'It's a great concept and it works. You couldn't have built a better ship for its intended role.'

Providing this capability has not been cheap. Programme capital costs when the project was finally approved in 2007 were calculated at €467.8m (c. US$675m) at then current prices. Of this €240m or around half was accounted for by the contract with DSNS to build the ships. The costs of the I-Mast; of government-furnished equipment such as the armament, as well as of development, trials and training outlays, accounted for the balance. However, in contrast to other naval programmes elsewhere in the world, these costs have been well controlled. As confirmed by project manager, Jeroen Waalewijn, at DSNS, the class was delivered to time and to budget. It should also be noted that running costs – estimated at €5.3m p.a. when the programme was authorised – are substantially lower than those for a front-line warship and broadly comparable with figures published with respect to other patrol ship programmes.[7]

The most significant criticism of the new ships has been their inability to flex from their designated role to operate in a higher-threat environment. Their lack of a broad weapons-fit would leave them reliant on other ships in a task group for effective defence from a credible air or naval opponent and their small crews would inevitably struggle to conduct damage control in the event of a major hit. This criticism has found particular support in the British Royal Navy, which has consistently used the argument that its surface escorts are able to switch rapidly between operations in low- and high-threat environments to counter proponents of a force structure encompassing more numerous, less-sophisticated ships.[8]

Ultimately, the argument comes down to the nature of the tasks that a navy is required to perform. As a result of the 2005 Naval Study, the Netherlands took a clear decision to optimise part of their fleet for low-intensity constabulary operations. An important supplementary consideration at the time was a desire to support the domestic maritime sector. The subsequent realisation of these objectives has produced an innovative and capable vessel showcasing a high level of sophisticated equipment produced by local industry and which is set to excel in performing its allocated missions. The design has also attracted significant international interest, for example forming the basis of Bollinger Shipyard's bid for the US Coast Guard's new offshore patrol cutter. All in all, the Defence Materiel Organisation, the Royal Netherlands Navy and DSNS have brilliantly achieved the objectives set for the design. The *Holland* class truly represents the Rolls-Royce of current OPVs.

Notes:

1. The UNCLOS III regime, concluded in 1982 but not taking effect until 1994, formally accepted a developing EEZ concept that gained popularity from the middle of the twentieth century onwards. This UN convention also provides for more limited rights in respect of a country's continental shelf, which can extend national interests up to 350 nautical miles from its coastline. An overview of the convention's impact on European warship designs is contained in the editor's 'Modern European Offshore Patrol Vessels' in *Warship 2013* edited by John Jordan (London: Anova Books, 2013), pp.78–93.

2. The Kingdom of the Netherlands retains significant colonial-era territories in the Caribbean which were once united in the now dissolved autonomous country of the Netherlands Antilles. Aruba left the grouping in 1986 and the union between the remaining five islands was dissolved in 2010. Aruba, Curaçao and Sint Maarten are now constituent countries of the Kingdom of the Netherlands, whilst Bonaire, Sint Eustatius and Saba are special municipalities of the Netherlands alone.

3. Defence procurement in the Netherlands was undergoing significant reorganisation whilst the *Holland* class specifications were being drawn up, merging separate procurement for each of the three services into a more integrated structure. Similarly, what was then Schelde Naval Shipbuilding (otherwise known as Royal Schelde) was becoming more closely associated with the Damen Shipyards Group that acquired it in 2000, changing its name to Damen Schelde Naval Shipbuilding (DSNS) in October 2008.

4. It is an indication of the pressure on the Dutch defence budget that the four 'M' class frigates the patrol vessels were intended to replace had already been sold before the new ships were authorised.

5. More specifically, the *Holland* class have been designed and constructed to Det Norske Veritas classification 1A1 Naval Support (fire, evac) EO RP NAUT-Navy HELDK-SHF CRANE NV. Det Norske Veritas merged with the German Germaischer Lloyd in 2013 and is now DNV GL.

6. It is beyond this chapter's scope to explain the workings of modern phased arrays and the software-controlled scanning technology they commonly use. A detailed description of this subject is found in Norman Friedman's 'Technological Review: Naval Multifunction Radars', *Seaforth World Naval Review 2011* (Barnsley: Seaforth Publishing, 2010), pp.154–62.

7. Comparison of warship construction programme costs is a notoriously difficult exercise given varying methods of cost allocation and the need to take into account the effects of inflation. However, the *Holland* class look reasonable value at a unit cost of c. €120m compared with the follow-on order for two similar but less capable *buques de acción maritima* (BAM) vessels placed by the Spanish Ministry of Defence with Navantia at a unit cost of €166.7m in mid-2014. Estimated *Holland* class running costs – of which €2.5m related to crew costs and €2.8m to logistical support and maintenance – are even more difficult to compare with those for other ships.

8. An interesting insight into the British Royal Navy's possible objections to the *Holland* class concept was set out in 'Neither a Frigate, nor an OPV be …' posted to the *Thin Pinstriped Line* blog on 18 March 2012 at http://thinpinstripedline.blogspot.co.uk/2012/03/neither-frigate-nor-opv-be.html

9. This chapter has drawn heavily on contemporary government and industry brochures, as well as other press releases, to support its preparation. The additional sources listed below provided more structured information:

– Tim Fish, 'Cruising Ahead: Briefing – Offshore Patrol Vessels' *Jane's Defence Weekly – 17 March 2010* (Coulsdon: IHS Jane's, 2010), pp.22–7.
– Hartmut Manseck, 'Ship Special: the "Holland" Class', *Naval Forces – Issue III, 2011* (Bonn: Mönch Publishing Group, 2011), pp.75–80.
– Richard Scott, 'Big is beautiful for RNLN's new Patrol Ship sentinels,' *Jane's Navy International – June 2008* (Coulsdon: IHS Jane's, 2008), pp.16–24.

The author would also like to thank the considerable help and assistance provided by the following Dutch industry, Ministry of Defence and naval personnel in arranging and supporting his visit to the offshore patrol ship *Groningen* on 12 June 2015:

Commander W A (Walter) Hansen EMSD, Commanding Officer of HNLMS *Groningen*.
Jeroen Waalewijn, MSc, Project Manager PS, Damen Schelde Naval Shipbuilding.
R (Rob) Zuiddam, MSc, Programme Manager, Defence Materiel Organisation.

Author:
Scott Truver

3.2 SIGNIFICANT SHIPS

THE US NAVY'S LPD-17 CLASS

'Snake Bit' No More!

'Keep building those damn ships!' naval analyst Norman Polmar exhorted in the August 2009 US Naval Institute *Proceedings*.[1] 'Those damn ships' were the *San Antonio* (LPD-17) class amphibious landing transport dock ships, and – more specifically – the eleventh ship in the class, which had come into then-Secretary of Defense Robert M. Gates' cross-hairs. Gates was intent on delaying the ship if not outright curtailing the programme at ten units – '… a mistake…' in Mr Polmar's assessment – despite a Department of Defense-approved programme of record that called for twelve LPD-17s.

Ultimately, the US Navy and Marine Corps will get all twelve LPD-17 class ships set out in the original plan. More importantly, perhaps, the LPD-17 class's basic hull design and arrangements have become the baseline, of sorts, for the next-generation LX(R) amphibious ship programme. But that gets ahead of what is, frankly, an amazing 'bad-news/good-news' story.

The current amphibious transport dock type is descended from the Second World War dock landing ship designs that made amphibious assaults from the sea possible, the US Naval Institute's *Ships and Aircraft of the US Fleet* attests.[2] Some seventy years later, the *San Antonio* class has been designed and optimised for maximum operational flexibility to satisfy Marine Air-Ground Task Force lift requirements in support of 21st-century expeditionary warfare operations.

All but one of the ships in the LPD-17 class are named after cities in the United States. The bow section of *New York* (LPD-21) contains seven and a

Left and right: The amphibious transport dock ship *San Antonio* (LPD-17) and the amphibious dock landing ship *Carter Hall* (LSD-50) sail in formation in the Atlantic Ocean during early 2013. Although having a troubled birth, the LPD-17 class is increasingly proving itself and it is planned that a variant will ultimately replace the *Harper's Ferry* class of which *Carter Hall* forms a part. *(US Navy)*

half tons of steel salvaged from the debris of the World Trade Center after the '9/11' terrorist attack. Two other ships in the class – *Arlington* (LPD-24) and *Somerset* (LPD-25) – honour locations in Virginia and Pennsylvania also associated with the 2001 terrorist hijackings. The 'odd ship out' is *John P Murtha* (LPD-26), named after a former US marine and long-term member of the US House of Representatives in a controversial decision announced by the Secretary of the Navy Ray Mabus in April 2010, two months after Murtha's death. In 2005, Murtha had accused US Marines of 'killing innocent people' in a firefight in Haditha, Iraq, thus souring relations with some of his 'band of brothers'.[3]

More significant controversies engulfed the *San Antonio* programme almost from its genesis, at times making it appear that the programme was 'snake-bit' – an American idiom for being cursed, extremely unlucky or destined to fail. What seemed like a never-ending litany of design, engineering, integration and construction problems and embarrassments, beginning with LPD-17 herself and continuing with several 'follow-on' ships, caused Admiral John C Harvey, then-Commander, Fleet Forces Command, in October 2010 to lament, 'Every time we think we get to a point where we think that the problem is solved, we find some deeper one.'[4] Even 'Mother Nature' seemed intent on creating challenges for LPD-17 (and other US Navy ships under construction). In late August 2005, Hurricane Katrina slammed into the Gulf Coast, causing more than US$1bn-worth of damage at what was then Northrop Grumman's Ingalls (Pascagoula, Mississippi) and Avondale and Gulfport (New Orleans, Louisiana) facilities, closing the yards for about two months, disrupting the skilled workforce, and substantially increasing the cost of eleven navy ships (including LPD-17 through to LPD-24).

This string of bad luck continued, perhaps best epitomised by the 20 March 2009 collision of the second-of-class, *New Orleans* (LPD-18), with the attack submarine *Hartford* (SSN-768) in the Strait of Hormuz. Although a navy investigation found that *Hartford* was solely to blame for the accident, *New Orleans'* crew had to be wondering, like the Blues singer, Ray Charles, 'If it wasn't for bad luck, we'd have no luck at all.'

Dealing with significant and expensive problems in the first ships in the class did, however, enable forward-fit 'get-well' efforts and changes that were incorporated into later ships of the class. This significantly eased their transition to the Fleet. The renaissance of the overall LPD-17 programme has been so profound that the Board of Inspection and Survey (INSURV) *Somerset* acceptance trials in September 2013 went without a hitch – receiving zero 'Starred Cards'. This is something no other major US Navy warship has achieved in recent memory. According to US Navy Captain Darren Plath, LPD-17 Class Program manager for Program Executive Office, Ships (PMS317), '*Somerset* benefitted from the efforts of a "strike team" that responded to all issues and developed a class build plan first implemented with the USS *San Diego* (LPD-22). The plan combines lessons learned during construction of earlier ships, emphasizing pre-outfitting and resulting in increased first-time quality and higher completion level at launch.'[5]

'The LPD-17 strike team was critical to getting systemic problems addressed, such as lube oil cleanliness,' Allison Stiller, Deputy Assistant Secretary of the Navy, Ships, underscored.[6] 'The collective government and industry team provided the much-needed discipline for getting ships with high levels of quality. It was needed at the time and did help to get the later ships on the right course.' So much so that in mid-2015 *John P Murtha* was beating all cost, schedule and performance goals, Captain Plath added.

The transformation has been so dramatic that the US Congress in 2014 all-but ignored the President's shipbuilding requests and approved long-lead

An early artist's impression of an LPD-17 amphibious transport dock operating alongside other constituents of an amphibious ready group as part of a shore assault. The US Navy initially hoped for as many as twenty-seven LPD-type amphibious transport docks but it has been fortunate to receive authorisation for twelve of the class in the post-Cold War environment. *(US Navy)*

Table 3.2.1: SAN ANTONIO (LPD 17) CLASS

HULL NUMBER	NAME	FY FUNDED	BUILDER	LAID DOWN	LAUNCHED	COMMISSIONED	STATUS MID-2015
LPD-17	USS *San Antonio*	1996	Avondale, New Orleans, LA[1]	9 Dec 2000	12 Jul 2003	14 Jan 2006	AA-Norfolk
LPD-18	USS *New Orleans*	1999	Avondale, New Orleans, LA	14 Oct 2002	11 Dec 2004	10 Mar 2007	PA-San Diego
LPD-19	USS *Mesa Verde*	2000	Ingalls Shipbuilding, Pascagoula, MS	25 Feb 2003	20 Nov 2004	15 Dec 2007	AA-Norfolk
LPD-20	USS *Green Bay*	2000	Avondale, New Orleans, LA	26 Aug 2003	11 Aug 2006	24 Jan 2009	PA-Sasebo
LPD-21	USS *New York*	2003	Avondale, New Orleans, LA	30 Aug 2004	20 Dec 2007	7 Nov 2009	AA-Mayport
LPD-22	USS *San Diego*	2004	Ingalls Shipbuilding, Pascagoula, MS	23 May 2007	7 May 2010	19 May 2012	PA-San Diego
LPD-23	USS *Anchorage*	2005	Avondale, New Orleans, LA	24 Sep 2007	12 Feb 2011	4 May 2013	PA-San Diego
LPD-24	USS *Arlington*	2006	Ingalls Shipbuilding, Pascagoula, MS	26 May 2008	23 Nov 2010	8 Feb 2013	AA-Norfolk
LPD-25	USS *Somerset*	2008	Avondale, New Orleans, LA	11 Dec 2009	14 Apr 2012	1 Mar 2014	PA- San Diego
LPD-26	PCU *John P Murtha*	2009	Ingalls Shipbuilding, Pascagoula, MS	6 Jun 2012	30 Oct 2014	(FY 2016)	Building
LPD-27	PCU *Portland*	2012	Ingalls Shipbuilding, Pascagoula, MS	2 Aug 2013	–	(FY 2017)	Building
LPD-28	[Un-named]	2016	Ingalls Shipbuilding, Pascagoula, MS	–	–	(FY 2022)	Authorised

Notes:
1. Transferred to Ingalls Shipbuilding, Pascagoula MS in October 2004 for completion.
PCU – Pre-Commissioning Unit; AA – Active Atlantic Fleet; PA – Active Pacific Fleet; LA – Louisiana; MS – Mississippi
Sources: Polmar, *Ships and Aircraft of the U.S. Fleet*; Navy Fact File Amphibious Transport Dock (http://www.navy.mil/navydata/fact_display.asp?cid=4200&tid=600&ct=4); LPD 17 Program Office (PMS 317) June 2015.

funding for the twelfth ship in the class, with full funding being provided in FY2015 and FY2016. In addition to help meet daunting force structure requirements, LPD-28 will serve as a 'bridge' to the next-generation amphibious warship LX(R) programme, now dubbed the LPD-17 'derivative' or 'variant', according to US Navy Commander Brent Cotton, Future Amphibious Ships Section Head (N953) in the office of the Chief of Naval Operations.[7] Also, the in-service members of the *San Antonio* class have already supported several critical operations and become key focal points in the evolution of operational-tactical innovations and concept development. The 2012 deployment of *New York* and *Arlington*'s performance in the international Bold Alligator 2014 at-sea exercise, for example, have underscored the design's operational flexibility and command-and-control prowess.[8]

Getting here from there, however, was at times excruciating.

PROGRAMME OVERVIEW

Based on post-Cold War strategic and operational concepts, the US Navy initially identified the need for as many as twenty-seven LPD-type amphibious transport ships to meet mid-1990s' force structure requirements for fifty-nine amphibious warships, with a core of fifteen large-deck/air-capable amphibious assault ships (LHA/LHDs). This force

structure would be necessary to provide amphibious lift for a MEF (Marine Expeditionary Force, some 40,000 marines and sailors) plus a MEB (Marine Expeditionary Brigade, about 16,000 marines and sailors) in the assault echelon of an amphibious assault. That '1 MEF + 1 MEB' goal soon went over the side, primarily as a result of constrained shipbuilding budgets, not changing geopolitical realities. Fifty-nine amphibious warships simply could not be attained, much less sustained, in America's 'Fall-of-the-Berlin-Wall/Peace-Dividend' environment.

Fast-forward to mid-2015, and much is unchanged. 'There is a requirement for over fifty ships on a day-to-day basis, that's what … the combatant commanders are asking for,' General Joseph F Dunford, Jr., then-USMC Commandant, noted at the AFCEA/USNI WEST 2015 Conference.[9] 'We've got an objective of thirty-eight—that's the requirement within the Department of the Navy. We've got a fiscally constrained objective of about thirty-three. We've got an inventory right now of thirty-one … which equates to significant readiness challenges.' A 33-ship force would include fifteen amphibious ships for each MEB, with another three ships in overhaul at any given time. Thus, the twelve-ship LPD-17 programme is vitally important for meeting combatant-commander demands.

'The original acquisition strategy for the LPD-17

program was an upfront winner-take-all competition for the entire twelve ship class,' Ms. Stiller noted. On 17 December 1996 the navy awarded the initial contract to the 'Avondale Alliance' consortium led by Avondale Industries. In addition to the shipyard, the Alliance included General Dynamics' Bath Iron Works, Hughes Aircraft, Loral, Sperry Marine, CAE, AT&T and Intergraph Corporation. The US$641.3m contract was for the design, construction and support of the lead ship, with an option covering two additional ships that, if exercised, would have totalled US$1.5bn for the three. Project start was delayed until 7 April 1997, when the then-General Accounting Office denied the protest by the losing Ingalls Shipbuilding team, which had included Newport News Shipbuilding, National Steel and Shipbuilding Company and Lockheed Martin.

Avondale was to build LPD-17 and, if the navy exercised the two options, Avondale would also construct the second while Bath would construct the third of the class. For both yards, Raytheon was responsible for total ship integration, Hughes Aircraft would integrate the ships' electronic and weapons systems and Intergraph was to provide the first-time-ever total-ship three-dimensional CAD/CAM design tool. If the navy awarded contracts to the Alliance to build all twelve projected ships, the original plan was that Avondale

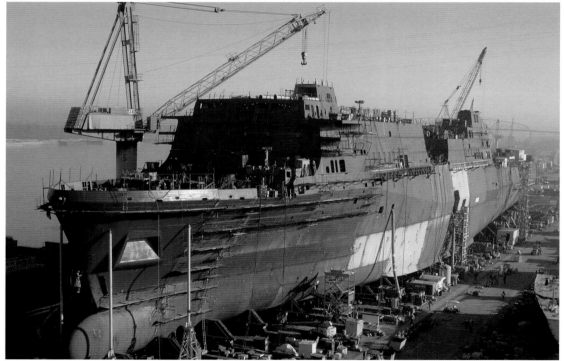

Pictures of the first LPD-17 class vessel *San Antonio* under construction at the Avondale yard in New Orleans during August 2002 and February 2003. A consortium headed by Avondale had won the contract to build the class in December 1996. However, the use of a concurrent design, engineering and construction approach, as well as an immature design tool and high labour turnover, meant the ship was heavily delayed by the time these images were taken. *(US Navy)*

would construct eight ships and Bath would construct four.

'The initial contract was for the detail design and construction of the lead ship and priced options for two ships,' Ms. Stiller confirmed. 'The plan was to buy them at roughly two per year after the lead and first follow ship. The following ships would have the same design and use a common LPD-17 class build plan. As the navy's shipbuilding plan changed over time,' she continued, 'the acquisition strategy also changed. At one point, the plan was to only buy nine ships in total. So, factors such as quantity, stability in the design, impacts of Hurricane Katrina, and other issues made the procurement under a multi-year procurement vehicle impractical.'

The keel for the lead ship was laid on 9 December 2000. Launched on 12 July 2003, *San Antonio* was delivered to the US Navy in 2005 and commissioned on 14 January 2006 at Ingleside Naval Station, Texas. The original schedule had commissioning planned for the second half of 2002, but that was delayed by poor performance at Avondale. For example, to meet tight schedule deadlines, the yard started work on the ship when only about 70 per cent of the design had been completed – an example of the concurrent design, engineering and construction approach which was then in vogue – which, coupled with problems using the 3-D design/manufacturing software, rippled changes throughout the ship, running up costs and moving milestones to the right. 'A key issue was that the design tool was immature and the design products were immature. Starting construction before the design was fully mature has been problematic in numerous lead ships,' Ms. Stiller explained.

The LPD-17 class programme was the first US Navy shipbuilding effort intended to minimise military specifications and standards and allow contractors to take advantage of cost-reducing commercial-off-the-shelf technologies and non-developmental items. A contemporary US Navy press release called *San Antonio* and its follow-on ships 'models of the Navy's ongoing efforts in acquisition reform'.

The programme office also espoused a 'design for ownership' philosophy, i.e., a concurrent-engineering approach that integrated US Navy and US Marine Corps 'customers' – operators, maintainers and trainers – into the design process. The intent was to ensure that operational realities were considered throughout the total ship design, integra-

Who's in Charge? The Shipyard 'Score Card'.

The construction of the LPD-17 class has taken place against a backdrop of change and consolidation amongst the shipyards involved in the programme. The entity currently responsible for building the ships is the Ingalls Shipbuilding division of Huntington Ingalls Industries (HII) but there have been several changes throughout the programme's life.

The original contract for LPD-17 construction was signed with Avondale Industries Inc. in 1996. The company traced its origins to the foundation of Avondale Marine Ways in 1938. Its current Avondale shipyard is some twenty miles upstream of New Orleans, Louisiana on the Mississippi River. There were also significant facilities in Gulfport, Mississippi, where the LPD-17 class's composite masts were fabricated. The company was acquired by Litton Industries in 1999, becoming part of Litton's shipbuilding activities. Litton had previously, in 1961, purchased the Pascagoula, Mississippi, yard of Ingalls Shipbuilding Corporation on the Gulf Coast. Ironically, Ingalls had headed the losing team battling for the LPD-17 project.

In 2001, the aerospace and defence giant Northrop Grumman bought Litton Industries and the former Avondale and Ingalls facilities ultimately became the Avondale and Pascagoula operations of Northrop Grumman Ship Systems (NGSS). This was a key factor in a number of the LPD-17 class being built at Pascagoula. Northrop Grumman also acquired Newport News Shipbuilding around the same time and the two businesses were subsequently merged to become Northrop Grumman Ship Building in January 2008.

Further change occurred in 2011 when Northrop Grumman decided to spin off its shipbuilding entities into a new listed group known as Huntington Ingalls Industries. The group has steadily focused US Navy shipbuilding on the core yards of its separate Newport News and Ingalls Shipbuilding divisions. The Gulfport and Avondale shipbuilding facilities were shut down in 2014, with Somerset (LPD-25) being the last US Navy ship to depart the Avondale yard.

Two images of Arlington (LPD-24) under construction at Ingalls Shipbuilding in Pascagoula, Mississippi during 2010. One of the ships innovative composite AEM/S masts can be seen being craned into position. By this time, many of the problems that had afflicted class construction were being brought under control. Whilst Ingalls was part of the losing consortium for the original LPD-17 contract, its subsequent acquisition of Avondale meant that half of the class were eventually constructed at the Pascagoula yard. (Huntington Ingalls Industries)

tion, construction, test and life cycle support processes. The objectives were to improve combat readiness, enhance quality of life, and reduce total ownership costs, but this also resulted in numerous changes (exacerbated by the separate 3-D design challenges) that drove cost overruns, lengthened schedules and produced poor material quality.

As cost, schedule and quality problems increased at Avondale, the navy decided to have the unfinished *San Antonio* towed in October 2004 from the New Orleans shipyard to Northrop Grumman Ingalls Division at Pascagoula for completion. The ship was unable to move under her own power, despite having been launched fifteen months earlier. Subsequently, fate was to intervene. 'We took delivery and moved aboard three days before Hurricane Katrina made landfall in August 2005, closing the yards,' retired US Navy Captain Jonathan Padfield, the *San Antonio*'s first commanding officer, recalled.[10] '*San Antonio* became a base for regional relief efforts that included generating electrical power and providing accommo-dations for some shipyard workers, the National Guard, Navy diving and salvage personnel, and government officials.'

Delivered around three years after the original plan and substantially over budget, *San Antonio* was not fully complete on commissioning. Over a million hours of construction work remained to be done on the ship – around 9 per cent of the total hours required for the build – equating to total addi-tional costs of more than US$100m. In July 2007, the US Government Accountability Office stated

Table 3.2.2.

SAN ANTONIO (LPD-17) PRINCIPAL PARTICULARS

Building Information:	
Keel Laid:	9 December 2000
Launched:	12 July 2003
Commissioned:	14 January 2006
Builders:	Avondale Industries at its yard in New Orleans LA; transferred to the Pascagoula, MS yard of Ingalls Shipbuilding for completion.

Dimensions:	
Displacement:	24,900 tons full load displacement.
Overall Hull Dimensions:	208.5m x 31.9m x 7.0m. Length between perpendiculars is 202.5m

Weapons Systems:	
Aircraft:	Flight deck for 2 x MV-22 Osprey tilt rotors or equivalent or up to 4 x AH-1 Super Cobra-sized helicopters.
	Hangar for 1 x MV-22 Osprey tilt rotor or 2 smaller helicopters.
Missiles:	2 x RAM Mk 49 launchers for RIM-116 rolling airframe missiles. Space reserved for 2 x Mk 41 VLS modules for ESSM.
Guns:	2 x Mk 46 Mod 2 gun weapon systems with 30mm Bushmaster II cannon; heavy machine guns.
Countermeasures:	SLQ-32B (V)2 electronic warfare suite. Mk 53 decoy launching systems. SLQ-25 Nixie towed decoy.
Principal Sensors:	1 x SPS-48E air search radar, 1 x SPQ-9B target-designation/fire-control radar. Navigation radar.
Combat System:	Ship Self Defense System (SSDS) Mk2. Cooperative Engagement Capability (CEC). Integrated communications include AADS and NATO Links.

Propulsion Systems:	
Machinery:	Diesel. 4 x Colt Pielstick 2.5 STC diesels each rated at 7.8MW provide a total of 41,600hp through two shafts.
Speed:	Designed maximum speed is of 25 knots. Sustained speed is 22 knots. Range is 10,600 nautical miles at 20 knots.

Other Details:	
Complement:	Crew is c. 375, including 28 officers.
Military Lift:	Can accommodate up to 700 troops plus a further 100 in surge conditions. Significant vehicle and cargo-carrying capacity.
	Space in well deck for 2 x LCAC or 1 x LCU.
Hospital:	2 x medical and 2 x dental operating rooms; 24 beds.
Class:	A total of 9 ships were in commission as of mid-2015, with two further units under construction and a final ship pending authorisation.

that more than US\$1.75bn had been invested in constructing LPD-17.[11]

RE-ORGANISATION AND RECOVERY

Indeed, almost from the beginning the programme had been plagued by cost overruns and construction delays. By 2002, the programme had run afoul of the Nunn-McCurdy amendment to the 1982 Defense Authorization Act. This requires the termination of weapons programmes whose total costs have grown by more than 25 per cent above original

estimates, unless the Defense Secretary certifies to the US Congress that the programmes are critical to national security or that the cost growth can be attributed to specific changes in the programmes.

Thus, cost, schedule and performance issues were clearly growing concerns in the early 2000s, causing a two-year hiatus in procurement during FY2001 and FY2002. Effectively dealing with these issues needed an unprecedented change of course. This happened on 12 June 2002, when the navy reached an agreement with Northrop Grumman and General

Dynamics (GD) to swap the workload on their destroyer and amphibious transport dock orders to concentrate LPD production at the former's facilities and therefore help minimise risks that might otherwise threaten even more cost-growth and schedule-slip across the entire programme.

The extraordinary 'Memorandum of Understanding Concerning the Reallocation of LPD-17 and DDG-51 Ship Construction Workload' consolidated Flight IIA *Arleigh Burke* construction at GD's Bath Iron Works, with Northrop Grumman's

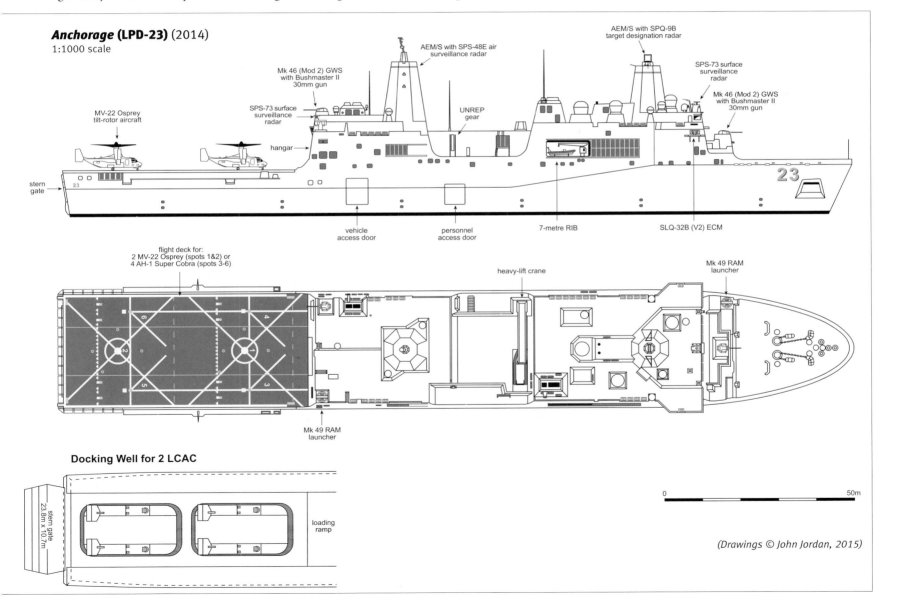

Anchorage (**LPD-23**) (2014)
1:1000 scale

Docking Well for 2 LCAC

(*Drawings © John Jordan, 2015*)

Avondale and Ingalls shipyards focused on getting the LPD-17 class delivered to the navy. The plan essentially called for the four LPD-17s originally planned to be built by Bath Iron Works to be exchanged for four DDG-51s scheduled for construction at Northrop Grumman's Ingalls shipyard. In July 2001, Bath Iron Works had already started work on the third member of the LPD-17 class, *Masa Verde* (LPD-19), but responsibility for her construction was transferred to Northrop Grumman, which laid her keel at their Ingalls yard in February 2003.

With the revised class build plan in place, the threat to the programme was alleviated and orders flowed steadily throughout the middle of the decade.

Nevertheless, programme costs continued to grow, combining with increasing budgetary constraints and a less-than-stellar debut by the first ships of the class to threaten the early curtailment that so excited Mr Polmar.[12] Ultimately, the class's growing utility in service – as well as a desire to maintain continuity in shipyard production – won the day. In May 2014, the US House Armed Services Committee authorised US$813m towards the construction of the twelfth *San Antonio* class ship; a move completed by the allocation of further funds to complete the ship in FY2015 and FY2016. In effect, a coalition of ship-builders, other suppliers and retired senior US officers – the Amphibious Warship Industrial Base Coalition – had persuaded the US Congress to pay

for LPD-28, a ship that the Pentagon had not requested. This has also had the benefit of increasing the planned front-line amphibious force from thirty-three to thirty-four ships.

As of mid-2015, LPD-17 through to LPD-25 have been delivered to the US Navy. The final pre-commissioning units, *John P Murtha*, *Portland* (LPD-27) and the yet-to-be-named LPD-28, are scheduled for delivery in FY2016, FY2017 and FY2022, respectively.

LPD-17 CLASS CHARACTERISTICS

The *San Antonio* class amphibious transport docks are the world's largest LPD-type ships; more than one-third larger in full-load displacement than the

The LPD-17 class amphibious assault ship *Arlington* (LPD-24) sails in company with her sister *Anchorage* (LPD-23) in October 2012. *Arlington* had not been accepted by the US Navy at this time and she still flies the Ingalls Shipbuilding house flag. The image vividly illustrates the size and sophistication of the class: they are the world's largest LPD-type ships. With the delivery of *Somerset* (LPD-25) in 2014, three ships remain to be delivered. This includes the as-yet unnamed LPD-28 due for final authorisation in the FY2016 budget. *(Huntington Ingalls Industries)*

US Navy's *Austin* (LPD-4)-class ships commissioned between 1965 and 1971. Compared to the LPD-4 ships, the LPD-17 design can carry more troops, helicopters and vehicles.

Overview: The LPD-17 amphibious transport docks are the functional replacements for forty-one obsolescent or decommissioned ships (eleven older amphibious transport docks, five dock landing ships, twenty tank landing ships and five amphibious cargo ships/transports). They transport and land marines, their equipment and supplies by means of embarked Landing Craft Air Cushion (LCAC) hovercraft, conventional landing craft, and other amphibious assault vehicles via their well deck, augmented by helicopters or MV-22 Osprey vertical-take-off-and landing (VTOL) aircraft from a large flight deck. Unmanned aerial vehicles can also be deployed. The ships support amphibious assault, special operations or expeditionary warfare missions and serve as secondary aviation platforms for amphibious ready groups.

The LPD-17 design has sufficient capacity to accommodate 700 marines in addition to the ship's company, and this can be increased by a further hundred in surge conditions. There is something in excess of 20,000 square feet of capacity for vehicles on three vehicle decks, as well as sufficient space to carry 34,000 cubic feet of cargo. The flight deck can

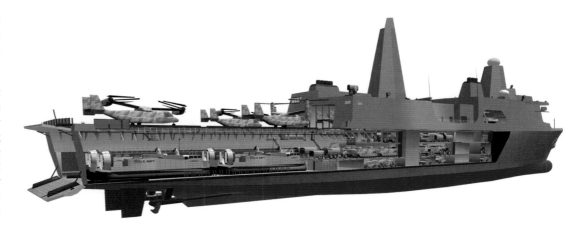

A cutaway image dating from 2006 showing the general layout of the LPD-17 class's helicopter, well and vehicle decks. The ships are primarily designed to transport and land marines and their equipment by means of embarked landing craft, augmented by helicopters and VTOL aircraft. *(US Navy)*

support two MV-22-sized aircraft simultaneously in normal operations or up to four smaller helicopters, whilst the hangar is sufficiently large for one MV-22. The well deck is specifically designed to house two LCACs but other landing craft and vehicles can also be operated.

Advanced features include the composite-material enclosed mast/sensor (AEM/S) system for reduced signature/sensor maintenance; other stealth enhancements; state-of-the-art C4ISR (command,

control, communications, computers, intelligence, surveillance and reconnaissance) and self-defence systems; a shipboard-wide area network linking shipboard systems with embarked US Marine Corps platforms; and significant quality-of-life improvements.

'The more space you have, the less cramped and the better the quality-of-life deployed,' Chief Warrant Officer Darren R Flint, the Marine Corps combat cargo officer aboard *Arlington*, noted to

US Marine Corps amphibious assault vehicles being guided onto the vehicle stowage area from the well deck of the amphibious transport dock ship *San Antonio* (LPD-17) during exercises in 2009. The system of ramps used to move vehicles to the three vehicle decks is apparent. The well deck is large enough to accommodate two hovercraft-like LCACs or one traditional landing craft. *(US Marine Corps)*

Sailors assigned to the amphibious transport dock ship *Anchorage* (LPD-23) wipe down the skin of the ship's AEM/S communications mast commissioning ceremony on 4 May 2013. The composite masts serve to reduce the ship's radar cross section whilst protecting sensitive electronic equipment from the elements. *(US Navy)*

An image illustrating the general concept behind the AEM/S system installed on the LPD-17 type ships. This image shows the assembly of the aft mast, with a SPS-48E search radar installed within the composite housing. *(US Navy)*

Defense Media Network during a March 2014 interview. 'We have multiple gyms compared to the old LPD 4-class, which had no dedicated gym space. There also is an on-board marksmanship trainer – a computer-based "weapon" firing range for everything from an M9 pistol up to a .50-cal machine gun. And we can bring a lot more medical capability aboard, both corpsmen and equipment.' Medical facilities include two surgical operating theatres and a 24-bed hospital ward. There is the ability to receive contaminated casualties through a specially-designed triage centre off the flight deck.

Structure, Propulsion and Networks: Each LPD-17 class ship is constructed from 210 separate units utilising modular construction techniques. The hull and structure are largely comprised of steel and survivability features include blast, fragmentation and shock protection measures, as well as a four-zone collective protective system. Extensive use is made of fire insulation, along with mist firefighting and smoke-ejection systems. As with most modern front-line warships, considerable attention has been paid to reducing radar, infra-red and acoustic signatures.

Perhaps the most striking features are the two AEM/S structures fore and aft. The larger of the two, the aft mast, is a 93ft (28.3m)-high hexagonal structure 35ft (10.6m) in diameter; both are constructed of a multi-layer frequency-selective composite material. It permits the ship's own sensor frequencies to pass through with very low loss while reflecting other frequencies. The tapered hexagonal shape of the AEM/S reduces radar cross section, and enclosing the antennas provides improved performance and greatly reduces maintenance cost.

By way of contrast, the diesel propulsion system is more conventional. Comprising four Colt Pielstick 2.5 STC diesels driving two shafts, it provides a top speed of 25 knots. Caterpillar diesel generators provide electrical power to 'hotel' services. In common with modern design philosophy, maximum use is made of automated systems and networks to keep crew size as small as possible.

The Shipboard Wide Area Network (SWAN) is the 'central nervous system' of the LPD-17 design.[13] Although SWAN development and integration experienced problems in earlier ships, the network ultimately brought unprecedented integration of shipboard electronic systems, using advanced, affordable hardware and software technology. SWAN uses a state-of-the-market, highly redundant and modular network-computing environment that can grow and adapt as technology evolves. SWAN is one of the few in-service networks that integrate combat systems, navigation, C4I, email and administrative data with ship, magnetic signature and engineering control system signals. 'It is not too much of an exaggeration to say that the commanding officer can fight his ship from numerous displays throughout the ship,' Commander Cotton said.

However, the Navy has proposed swapping out the SWAN for the new, fleet-wide CANES (Consolidated Afloat Networks and Enterprise Services) system in the LPD-28, as well as possibly incorporating CANES into the next-gen LX(R).[14]

Command Systems, Weapons and Sensors: Command and control functions in the LPD-17 class are based on the Ship Self-Defense System (SSDS), a centralised, automated command-and-control system designed for non-Aegis equipped warships such as carriers and amphibious ships. It is primarily focused on providing defence against air attack, particularly from anti-ship missiles, by providing better integration of weapons and sensors. SSDS Mk 2 Mod 2 installed in the LPD-17 ships also provides strike group interoperability by means of Cooperative Engagement Capability (CEC) and Tactical Data Information Link-Joint (TADIL-J).

The ship is armed with two Mk 49 21-cell Rolling Airframe Missile (RAM) launchers firing the RIM-116A Rolling Airframe Missile. The combination forms the RAM Mk 31 Guided Missile Weapon System (GMWS), a high rate-of-fire, low-cost system designed to engage anti-ship missiles and aircraft. RIM-116A is a 5in (127mm) diameter surface-to-air missile with passive dual-mode radio frequency/infrared (RF/IR) guidance and an active-optical proximity and contact fuse. Once the ship's sensors have identified a particular threat, it requires minimal shipboard control, being autonomous after launch. Effective against a wide spectrum of existing threats, the RAM Block 1 IR (RIM-116B) upgrade incorporates IR all-the-way-homing to improve performance against evolving missile technologies. A further upgrade – RAM Block 2 – will provide increased kinematic capability against highly manoeuvring threats and improved RF detection against low probability of intercept threats. This latest iteration of the missile achieved initial operating capability in May 2015.

Space and weight are also reserved for a future installation of the Evolved Sea Sparrow Missile (ESSM) in a modified Mk 41 vertical-launching system (VLS). This would provide sixteen launch cells for up to sixty-four ESSMs in quad packs (although some cells could potentially be used to house Tomahawk land-attack cruise missiles) forward of the superstructure. A kinematic upgrade to the RIM-7P missile, the ESSM is the next-generation Sea Sparrow Missile that serves as a primary self-defence weapon on aircraft carriers and large-deck amphibious warships and provides layered-defence for cruisers and destroyers.

Close-in defence against surface attack is in the hands of two Mk 46 Mod 2 gun systems; two-axis stabilised 30mm guns that can fire up to 200 rounds per minute. The Mk 46 system uses a forward-looking infrared sensor, a low-light television camera, and laser range finder with a closed-loop tracking system to optimise accuracy against small, high-speed surface targets. The gun itself is a 30mm Bushmaster II that was also intended for use with the cancelled US Marine Corps Expeditionary Fighting Vehicle.

Principal radar systems are located in the AEM/S structures. Long range search and surveillance is provided by the 'E' variant of the venerable AN/SPS-48 system, which was first introduced in the 1960s. It is supplemented by a SPQ-9B search and target-indication radar, an X-Band (NATO I-Band), pulse Doppler, frequency agile, rotating radar that was designed specifically for the littoral environment. It has a very high clutter improvement factor supporting a very low false track rate in the littoral. The radar scans out to the horizon and performs simultaneous and automatic air and surface target detection and tracking of low flying anti-ship missiles, surface threats, and low/slow flying aircraft, UAVs and helicopters. It enables track detection at ranges that allow combat systems to engage subsonic or supersonic sea-skimming missiles at the outer edge of a ship's engagement envelope. It also retains the surface search and gunfire control capabilities provided by previous versions of the SPQ-9. Additional modifications are in developmental testing to add a periscope-detection and discrimination capability to the radar's surface-search capability.

Communications equipment is also primarily located in the AEM/S structures, supplemented by various satellite domes. The principal electronic warfare system is the ubiquitous SLQ-32 suite, whose antennae are located to port and starboard under the bridge. Mk 53 decoy launchers provide a

The Mk 46 Mod 1 weapon system undertaking a live-fire qualification exercise aboard the amphibious transport dock ship *New Orleans* (LPD-18) in 2012. The Mk 46 Mod 1 weapon system is a remotely-operated naval gun system using a 30mm high-velocity cannon and second-generation thermal day-night sight for close-in ship protection. The ship's forward Mk 49 RAM launcher can be seen to the left of the Mk 46 mount. *(US Navy)*

physical countermeasures capability. Also fitted is the SLQ-25A Nixie, a towed acoustic and non-acoustic persistent countermeasure system that is used for defence against torpedoes.

QUALITY CONCERNS

Woe be unto the programme manager of a 'first-in-class' warship! For example, the strident chorus of criticism facing the first ships of the US Navy's new Littoral Combat Ship (LCS) programme underscored the shipbuilding fact-of-life that virtually all new-warship classes experience considerable 'birthing pains'. Indeed, the first six frigates acquired by the fledging US Navy in 1797 were delivered late and over-budget.[15] And so it was for *San Antonio*.

LPD-17 was unable to deploy for more than two years after the Navy took control of the ship.[16] *San Antonio*'s problems began on the computer-assisted 'drawing board,' with the 3-D computer design programme initially unable to design the entire ship. Then, during construction, the shipyard suffered annual labour attrition rates of 35 per cent, which affected schedule and cost. However, sub-quality workmanship at Avondale seemed to be a sub-text to everything else wrong with the ship construction process.

This led then-Secretary of the Navy Donald Winter in a 22 June 2007 letter to excoriate Northrop Grumman Ship Systems for substandard work and questioned the future of additional US Navy ship programmes with the company. 'By taking delivery of incomplete ships with serious quality problems, the Fleet has suffered unacceptable delays in obtaining deployable assets,' Winter wrote to Ronald Sugar, Northrop Grumman's chief executive officer. Two years after accepting the *San*

An image of *San Antonio* (LPD-17) transiting the Suez Canal in September 2008 during her maiden deployment. Many of the problems stored up during the class's troubled design and build history came home to roost in the course of this mission, resulting in years of remedial action. *(US Navy)*

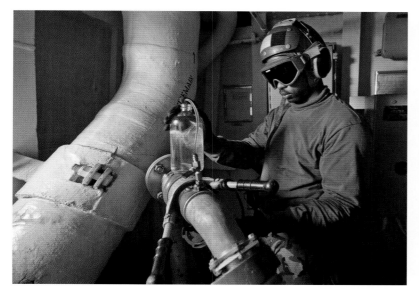

Checks on fuel and lubricating oil being carried out on *San Antonio* (LPD-17) during the course of a 2013 deployment. Contamination of fuel supplies and lubricating oil due to cracked and leaking pipes was a significant source of many of LPD-17's early teething problems. *(US Navy)*

Antonio, he noted, 'the Navy still does not have a mission-capable LPD ship'.

Ronald O'Rourke's Congressional Research Service report outlines more than forty pages of cost, schedule and performance shortfalls across the LPD-17 programme.[17] Indeed, some estimates place the number of flaws in *San Antonio* alone in the thousands. Two are discussed here, but the important aspect is what the navy and Northrop Grumman/Ingalls did to solve the problems.

During *San Antonio*'s initial deployment, in October 2008 the crew discovered leaks in the pipes that deliver lubricating oil to the ship's four diesel engines, a potential fire hazard that required an unplanned 'availability' period in a Bahraini shipyard. A 'strike team' of some forty engineers, pipefitters and welders flew to Bahrain from the United States – already on the pier as the ship pulled in – to make costly fixes, some of which required replacing whole sections of pipe to enable LPD-17 to complete its deployment. The next summer and autumn, however, inspections found more than 1,000 additional feet of piping that had to be replaced and the ship's four diesel engines were out of commission and needed to be re-inspected after metal shavings were found in the engine's main reduction gears, a result of improperly welded piping.

It turned out that the thickness of many welds was insufficient; they met commercial but not military specifications. The inspections also determined that there were too few hangers that held the pipes in place, with too much space between individual hangers that led to excessive vibration of the pipes and caused the welds to fail. The welds would not have failed were there enough hangers spaced more closely together. Changes were consequently made to the ship's design for both the back-fit into completed vessels and forward-fit into later LPD-17 ships. All US Navy ships under construction at Northrop Grumman were also re-inspected for weld problems, and all pipe welders were de-certified and required to go through retraining, as were the navy's Supervisor of Shipbuilding (SUPSHIP) personnel.

In early 2010, Christopher Cavas of *Navy Times* reported that engineers searching for the cause of vibrations in the drive train discovered that imperfections in the way the LPD-17's engines and main reduction gears were installed threatened to wreck the ship. 'The foundation bolts were not properly aligned or tightened. The main reduction gear was not properly installed and checked out,' Admiral John Harvey remarked. 'There was vibration of the entire diesel engine, which was reflected through the crankshaft, down to the couplings with the reduction gear, to the shaft.' That the engines could be installed improperly is 'incomprehensible,' he said.

'A, that it would pass an internal quality check that way, and then B, that it would pass through the navy's quality control that way ... I think we were so focused on getting that ship into service that we rolled over a lot of issues.'

An Avondale inspector discovered the problem, which could lead engine mountings to shear under sudden shock, or loosen enough over time to set up damaging vibrations in the ship's propulsion systems. Fitted bolts that did not meet the tolerances for engine mountings were replaced, and the Navy and its shipbuilder also checked the 520 applicable bolts on every other Avondale-built LPD. Similar problems were discovered in *Mesa Verde*, but the bolts on the fourth ship, *Green Bay*, were much better, and only about four bolts needed replacement on *New York*. Ingalls-built ships from the Pascagoula yard were unaffected.

In May 2011, after some two years in dockyard hands and after ten days of sea trials, the navy declared the ship's power plants ready for service. A final hiccup occurred in July, when navy inspectors determined that the engines' intercoolers were mechanically deficient after the ship failed to gain full power. The additional repairs were completed, and on 3 August 2011 the navy declared that all problems with the ship's engines had been corrected including 'foreign material exclusion plugs left in the drain piping system, use of incorrect material and

The then Pre-Commissioning Unit (PCU) *New York* (LPD-21) enters New York harbour on 2 November 2009 prior to her commissioning on the 7th of that month. The ship has seven and a half tons of steel salvaged from the World Trade Center towers forged into her bow. Although the ship also suffered from some initial construction issues, the problems evident in the first members of the class steadily diminished as later units of the class were delivered. *(US Navy)*

ADM HARVEY MEMO.

Team,

Earlier this month [February 2011], USS NEW YORK (LPD 21) successfully completed her Final Contract Trial (FCT) and received the highest scores to date of any ship in her class. Successfully completing the FCT on her first attempt was a significant milestone for this ship and I believe it's a sign we're making good progress resolving many of the big issues with the SAN ANTONIO class we've seen in the past. In light of NEW YORK's success, I thought this would be a good time to give you an update on SAN ANTONIO (LPD 17) and some of the specific actions we've taken to get this very capable ship back into the Fleet.

As you'll recall, I ordered a JAGMAN [Judge Advocate General] investigation on SAN ANTONIO in November 2009 after she suffered multiple engineering casualties. The investigation found that failures in the acquisition process, maintenance, training, and execution of shipboard programs all contributed to the engineering casualties. These failures also pointed to larger process problems within our Navy and the shipbuilder. In a rush to get SAN ANTONIO's operational capabilities to the Fleet, we overlooked a lot of very critical issues and accepted a ship that was only 90% complete and ultimately did not meet the standards of quality our Sailors and Marines need and expect of a U.S. Navy ship.

It has taken a steady and concentrated approach to get this ship back on track, but I believe we're now on the right path. Of the 32 actions recommended in the JAGMAN investigation, 20 are complete and the final 12 are in progress. Work will be completed on SAN ANTONIO in April followed by three weeks of *rigorous* sea trials where she will be fully tested for *everything* she is supposed to do.

I believe we've learned a lot over the past two years. We brought in the right talent and our actions are having the desired effects––we're now seeing a big difference between how SAN ANTONIO was originally delivered to the Navy and what we now have with NEW YORK.

The SAN ANTONIO class represents our Navy's strong and enduring commitment to expeditionary operations. Our Sailors and Marines love this ship and all the capabilities she brings to the fight. While there is still much work to be done I believe we are back in the channel and headed fair.

All the best, JCHjr

Posted by ADM J.C. Harvey, Jr USN
28 February 2011

1. This message was posted to the US Fleet Forces Command Blog. An archived copy can be found at http://usfleetforces.blogspot.com/2011/02/uss-san-antonio-lpd-17-update.html.

improper installation and sealing of gaskets'. The lessons learned were critical to improvements in follow-on LPD ships.[18]

'As happens with all ships on a learning curve,' Ms Stiller noted, 'performance improves with each subsequent ship. Part of the success on LPD-25 and LPD-26 is the stability in the design and the adoption of a class build plan by the shipyard that was not possible earlier due to the impacts of Hurricane Katrina. Many of the early LPDs had modules outsourced and the same modules weren't always outsourced. HII recognized this and corrected it for later LPDs such that all modules were built by the shipbuilder for LPD-25, LPD-26 and LPD-27. In addition to requiring outsourcing, Hurricane Katrina had a dramatic impact on the shipyard's workforce, with long-lasting effects on the program.'

VARIANTS AND DERIVATIVES

'Think of the baseline LPD-17 as a "truck",' Norman Polmar remarked.[19] 'There is flexibility, space and weight to do what the navy did with the *Spruance* (DD-963), *Kidd* (DDG-993) and *Ticonderoga* (CG-47) warships – three separate classes using virtually the same hull, machinery and electrical systems. Coupled with the LPDs being in production until 2022, well-up on the learning curve in 2015, this experience argues for their continued construction for other roles, missions and tasks.'

Two MV-22B Osprey tilt rotor aircraft lifting off from *New York* (LPD-21) in March 2015 whilst the ship was operating in the Middle East. By this time, the success of the LPD-17 had become well-established. *(US Navy)*

Flagship: One variant that Mr Polmar identified would deliver flagship capabilities. The US Navy's two major flagships – *Blue Ridge* (LCC-19) of the Seventh Fleet and *Mount Whitney* (LCC-20) of the Sixth Fleet – are more than forty years old. The ships should be replaced in the near future. In addition, the US Africa Command and Southern Command would benefit from a dedicated flagship. The LPD-17 design could be modified to provide permanent C4ISR facilities as well as office spaces in the docking well. Aviation capabilities would be retained.

Combat Support: Another concept would serve in an LCS support role. The navy plans to build some fifty-two LCS small surface warships in several variants: about thirty-two of the *Freedom* (LCS-1) and *Independence* (LCS-2) designs, and another twenty of, possibly, two 'small, lethal frigate' designs derived from the LCS-type. In the past, various amphibious

ships have been modified to serve as forward-area support ships for mine countermeasures craft and other 'small boys', as well as for Special Forces operations. Also, spare LCS mission modules could be stowed in the support ship and changed-out in forward areas. In this role, the LCS support ship could also be a forward-area command/flagship and, if linked to other new ships such as the Afloat Forward Staging Base (AFSB) and the Joint High-Speed Vessel (JHSV), could be the focal point of 'mini' amphibious ready groups.[20]

Mr Polmar also noted that Vice Admiral Thomas Rowden, Commander, Naval Surface Forces, has called for increased 'distributed lethality' throughout the surface force.[21] In addition to possibly modifying the twelve baseline LPD-17s with VLS systems for the ESSM and perhaps even land-attack missiles, he outlined two variants that could support what Admiral Rowden described as 'Hunter-Killer Surface Action Groups'.

Fire-support: The US Navy has continually short-changed the US Marine Corps with respect to fire-support ships. The largest gun in the fleet today is the 5in (127mm)/62-calibre weapon. Just over 100 barrels are in active destroyers and cruisers. The three *Zumwalt* (DDG-1000) class ships will provide a total of six 155mm Advanced Gun Systems (AGS), which have a range of about eighty miles. The LPD-17 design could be modified to provide two 155mm AGS in place of the docking well, while retaining some troop-lift capability. As an alternative to the AGS, an electromagnetic railgun could be fitted. This would be able to launch precision-kinetic warheads to ranges of 400 miles.

Ballistic missile defence (BMD): Mr Polmar also pointed to HII/Ingalls' BMD concept based on the LPD-17 to complement the Aegis BMD cruisers and destroyers.[22] The LPD/BMD variant incorporates topside an Aegis-type S-band phased-array radar, greater than 21ft (6.4m) on each side. These are nearly twice the 12.5ft (3.8m) diameter and three times the area of the SPY-1 radars installed in Aegis cruisers and destroyers, and would deliver greater range and resolution. Aft, the design includes eighteen, sixteen-cell VLS launchers, for a total of 288 missile cells – a very favourable number compared to the 122 cells in Aegis cruisers and the ninety or ninety-eight in the destroyers. The VLS would be able to launch a variety of weapons, including SM-2, SM-3 and SM-6 Standard missiles, Tomahawk cruise missiles and anti-submarine rockets. Forward of the superstructure, HII placed a large railgun mount. The concept features 57mm guns similar to those installed on both the LCS variants and the US Coast Guard's National Security Cutters, as compared with the 30mm mounts fitted to existing LPD-17s.

The one thing in common among all these good ideas, however, is that they are nowhere to be found in the US Navy's shipbuilding plan or any approved programme of record. Instead, what does look likely to happen is for a derivative of the LPD-17 to replace the *Whidbey Island/Harper's Ferry* LSD-

The amphibious transport dock *San Diego* (LPD-22) in the course of conducting an underway recovery test for NASA's Orion crew module in February 2014. The inherent flexibility of the LPD-17 design makes them readily adaptable to a wide variety of roles such as flagships, combat support or even ballistic missile defence. *(US Navy)*

41/LSD-49 dock landing ships as they start to retire. The FY2016 US Navy long-range ship-building plan outlines an efficient procurement profile for the lead LX(R) to be acquired in FY2020 – at a projected cost of US$1.8bn – and serial production of the remaining ten to begin in FY2022. The final LX(R) would enter service in 2038.[23]

The design of the ship – whether to start from a clean sheet of paper or use an existing ship for modification to an LX(R) configuration – was resolved on 14 October 2014, when US Navy Secretary Ray Mabus signed a decision memorandum designating a ship using the LPD-17 hull form as the preferred alternative. His decision was based on the results of the analysis of alternatives (AoA) that the Navy conducted in 2013–14. The AoA assessed the baseline LPD-17 design (which Mr O'Rourke speculates was included primarily as a reference design for helping the navy to evaluate other LX(R) design concepts, as the navy apparently considered the LPD-17 design to be unaffordable for the LX(R) programme), a modified (reduced capability/ reduced-cost) version of the LPD-17 design

A dramatic image of *Green Bay* (LPD-20) transiting the East China Sea in March 2013. The LPD-17 class has come a long way since its inauspicious beginnings and is now being used as the basis for the follow-on LX(R) design. *(US Navy)*

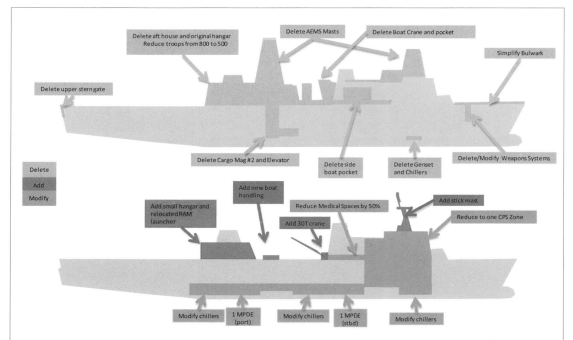

Delete / **Add** / **Modify**

Delete aft house and original hangar Reduce troops from 800 to 500

Delete AEMS Masts

Delete Boat Crane and pocket

Simplify Bulwark

Delete upper stern gate

Delete Cargo Mag #2 and Elevator

Delete side boat pocket

Delete Genset and Chillers

Delete/Modify Weapons Systems

Add new boat handling

Add small hangar and relocated RAM launcher

Reduce Medical Spaces by 50%

Add stick mast

Add 30T crane

Reduce to one CPS Zone

Modify chillers

1 MPDE (port)

Modify chillers

1 MPDE (stbd)

Modify chillers

A HHI graphic showing their initial proposal for modifications to the basic LPD-17 design to form a basis for the follow-on LX(R) programme. In October 2014 US Navy Secretary Ray Maybus accepted the basic thinking behind this LPD-17 Flight IIA proposal for the basis of more detailed LX(R) design work. *(Huntington Ingalls Industries)*

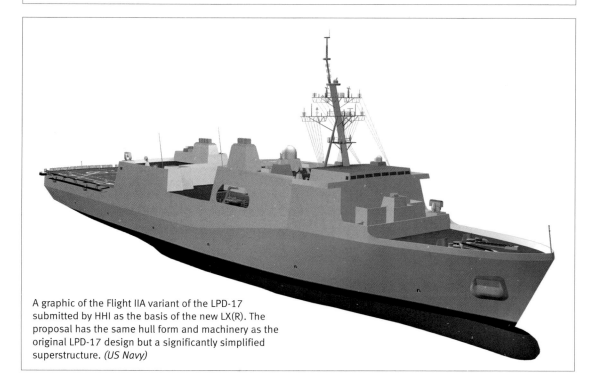

A graphic of the Flight IIA variant of the LPD-17 submitted by HHI as the basis of the new LX(R). The proposal has the same hull form and machinery as the original LPD-17 design but a significantly simplified superstructure. *(US Navy)*

provided by HII, 'clean-sheet' designs and even foreign ship concepts.

'Through a focused and disciplined process that analysed required capabilities and capacities, as well as cost parameters,' Ms Stiller noted, 'the Navy determined that a derivative of the LPD-17 hull form is the preferred alternative to meet the LX(R) operational requirements. By selectively reducing LPD-17 requirements and de-scoping specific spaces and equipment, we can deliver sufficient capability and capacity to meet the LX(R) mission sets using an LPD-17 derivative design with costs that are well understood.'

Secretary Mabus' memorandum called for preliminary design efforts for the LPD-17 derivative/variant to begin 'immediately'. In spite of HHI/Ingalls having been responsible for building all the LPD-17 class, rival firm General Dynamics/ National Steel and Shipbuilding Company (NASSCO) will be competing with them for the programme. In mid-2015, the navy's acquisition strategy called for a combined solicitation comprising separate requests for proposals for contract design support for the LX(R) programme, the detailed design and construction of the LHA-8 amphibious assault ship (to be submitted for authorisation in FY2017), and the detailed design and construction of six Military Sealift Command TAO(X) oilers (the first of which the service wants to procure in FY2016). The navy wants to limit bidding on this combined solicitation to two bidders – HII/Ingalls and GD/NASSCO – on the grounds that these are the only two shipbuilders that have the capability to build LX(R)s, TAO(X)s and LHA-8.

Thus, LX(R) – not to mention LHA-8 and TAO(X) – is sure to be the topic of a future *World Naval Review* 'Significant Ship' chapter!

'SNAKE-BIT' NO MORE!

'You've come a long way, Baby!' a 1960s advertising campaign declared.[24] It might just as well have described the trials and tribulations of the US Navy's *San Antonio* (LPD-17)-class programme. From the depths of utterly visceral frustration with compromised quality, cost overruns and missed schedules in the first ships, to having no 'Starred Cards' and beating cost, schedule and performance goals in the last ships, the programme has indeed come a long way. And, with LX(R) in the wings, it achieves Norman Polmar's exhortation to 'keep building those damn ships!'

Notes:

1. See further Norman Polmar, 'US Navy: Keep Building those Damn Ships', *Proceedings* – August 2009 (Annapolis MD: Naval Institute Press, 2009).

2. This overview of the LPD-17 programme relies heavily on Norman Polmar's, *The US Naval Institute Guide to the Ships and Aircraft of the US Fleet*, 19th edition (Annapolis MD: Naval Institute Press, 2013), pp.82, 176–8 and 187–9; as well as on the various LPD-17 and related issue briefs produced and regularly updated by Ronald O'Rourke of the Congressional Research Service, particularly *Navy LPD-17 Amphibious Ship Procurement: Background, Issues, and Options for Congress RL34476* (Washington DC: Congressional Research Service) and *Navy LX(R) Amphibious Ship Program: Background and Issues for Congress R43543* (Washington DC: Congressional Research Service). Other valuable documents include special studies produced by Eric Labs of the Congressional Budget Office, particularly *An Analysis of the Navy's Amphibious Warfare Ships for Deploying Marines Overseas* (Washington DC: Congressional Budget Office, 2011) and LPD-17 programme and related materials in the *US Navy Program Guide 2015* (Washington DC: Office of the Chief of Naval Operations N80, 2015), pp.86–7. These sources were supplemented by interviews with US Navy programme managers and other experts.

3. Further background to the naming criticism can be found in Phillip Ewing's 'Controversy Flares over Ship Named for Murtha,' *Navy Times* – 28 April 2010 (Springfield VA: Gannett Government Media, 2010).

4. Admiral Harvey's comments were reported by Christopher P Cavas in 'More Engine Woes Found with LPD-17,' *Navy Times* – 1 October 2010 (Springfield VA: Gannett Government Media, 2010). An online version of this article – focused on alignment problems with the ship's drive train can be found at: http://archive.navytimes.com/article/20101001/NEWS/10010319/More-engine-woes-found-LPD-17.

5. Interview with the author, 28 April 2015. Single Starred Deficiencies – the most significant deficiencies applicable to most ship inspections – 'significantly degrade a ship's ability to perform an assigned primary or secondary [Required Operational Capability] or operate and maintain ship systems for which the Navy has assumed responsibility, or which represent general safety, navigational safety, security, firefighting, habitability, or maintainability deficiencies which would prevent the crew from living on board safely' according to INSURV Instruction 4730.1E of 15 April 2005. They require correction or waiver before a ship is delivered.

6. E-mail interview with the author, 18 May 2015.

7. Interview with the author, 6 May 2015. The LX(R) programme was previously referred to as the LSD(X) programme. The navy changed the designation to LX(R) in 2012 to signal that the replacement for the existing LSD-41 *Whidbey Island* and LSD-49 *Harper's Ferry* class ships would be an amphibious ship that would best meet future US Navy and Marine Corps needs and might not necessarily be a LSD dock landing ship type.

8. For details see J R Wilson's 'The LPD 17-Class and the Amphibious Ready Group (ARG)', *Defense Media Network* – 3 April 2014 at http://www.defensemedianetwork.com/stories/the-lpd-17-class-and-the-amphibious-ready-group-arg/ and Sydney J Freedberg Jr.'s 'Bold Alligator Wargame Goes Off-Script, on Purpose,' *Breaking Defense* – 18 November 2014 at http://breakingdefense.com/2014/11/macgyver-at-sea-bold-alligator-wargame-goes-off-script-on-purpose/.

9. General Dunford was quoted by Yasmin Tadjdeh in 'Marine Corps Commandant Dunford: Alternatives for Amphibious Warships Needed,' in the *National Defense Magazine* blog on 13 February 2015, http://www.nationaldefensemagazine.org/blog/Lists/Posts/Post.aspx?ID=1747.

10. Interview with the author, 30 April 2015.

11. This figure was stated by Pail L Frances, Director Acquisition and Sourcing Management Team of the US GAO in *Defense Acquisitions: Realistic Business Cases Needed to Execute Navy Shipbuilding Programs GAO-07-943T* in testimony before the Subcommittee on Seapower and Expeditionary Forces, Committee on Armed Services, House of Representatives on 24 July 2007 (Washington DC: United States Government Accountability Office, 2007).

12. As at the end of 2014, the total cost of the full, twelve-ship LPD-17 programme was estimated at US$20.7bn in 'then year' dollars, equivalent to US$15.3bn re-based to 1996 (the year initial contracts were awarded) according to *Selected Acquisition Report (SAR): LPD-17 San Antonio Class Dock (LPD-17) - 31 December 2014* (Washington DC: Office of the Secretary of Defense, 2015). This compares with a baseline estimate of US$9bn when the programme commenced.

13. Further information on SWAN can currently be found at Raytheon's page on the class at: http://www.raytheon.com/capabilities/products/lpd_17/index.html.

14. For more on CANES, see *Navy Program Guide 2015*, *op. cit.*, pp.104–5. In contrast to the class-specific SWAN, CANES is intended to provide a common network platform across the fleet.

15. Robert D. Holzer, 'Birthing Ships is Never Easy: Give

LCS a Break,' *Breaking Defense*, 7 June 2013, http://breakingdefense.com/2013/06/birthing-ships-is-never-easy-give-lcs-a-break/.

16. 'LPD-17 Reliability Issues Surface Again,' *UTC Defense Industry Daily*, 8 August 2012, http://www.defenseindustrydaily.com/lpd17-reliability-issues-surface-again-03235/.

17. *Navy LPD-17 Amphibious Ship Procurement: Background, Issues, and Options for Congress RL34476, op. cit.*

18. A good overview of *San Antonio*'s early woes – and the process putting them right before the ship's second, successful deployment was provided by Corinne Reilly in 'Shipshape? The *San Antonio*, finally, almost is there', *The Virginia Pilot* – 27 February 2011 (Norfolk VA: Landmark Media Enterprises, 2011).

19. Interview with author, 7 May 2015.

20. Both the *Freedom* (LCS-1) and *Independence* (LCS-2) Littoral Combat Ship variants, as well as the *Lewis B. Puller* (AFSB-3) and *Spearhead* (JHSV-1) types, have been described in detail by the author in previous editions of *Seaforth World Naval Review*.

21. See Vice Admiral Thomas Rowden, Rear Admiral Peter Gumataotao and Rear Admiral Peter Fanta, USN, 'Distributed Lethality,' *US Naval Institute Proceedings* – January 2015 (Annapolis MD: Naval Institute Press, 2015), pp.18–23.

22. See Christopher P Cavas, 'HII Shows Off New BMD Ship Concept at Sea-Air-Defense,' *Defense News*, 8 April 2014, http://intercepts.defensenews.com/2013/04/hii-shows-off-new-bmd-ship-concept-at-sea-air-space/; and Daniel Katz, 'Introducing the Ballistic Missile Defense Ship,' *Aviation Week*, 11 April 2014, http://aviationweek.com/blog/introducing-ballistic-missile-defense-ship.

23. This timetable is based on information in the *Report to Congress on the Annual Long-Range Plan for Construction of Naval Vessels for Fiscal Year 2016* (Washington DC: Office of the Chief of Naval Operations N8, 2015), pp.10, 12–13.

24. The slogan was used to promote the 'Virginia Slims' cigarette brand to its target market of young, professional women. It subsequently gave its name to the 1998 second album released by British big beat musician Fatboy Slim, which contained no fewer than four UK top ten singles.

25. Dr Truver particularly thanks US Navy Commander Thurraya S Kent, ASN RDA PAO, and Mr Matthew J Leonard, NAVSEA PAO, for their assistance with this chapter.

3.3 SIGNIFICANT SHIPS

Author:
Devrim Yaylali

MILGEM CLASS CORVETTES

Turkey's 'National Ship' supports National Industry

TCG *Heybeliada*, the first of the Turkish Navy's new MILGEM or 'Ada' class corvettes, was launched from Istanbul Naval Shipyard on 27 September 2008. It was not an ordinary day in the Turkish naval calendar. September 27th is commemorated as the Turkish Naval Day, marking the victory of the Ottoman Fleet commanded by Barbaros Hayrettin Paşa over the Papal Fleet led by Andrea Doria in the Gulf of Preveza (in today's Greece) in 1538. The victory cemented Ottoman Turkish naval hegemony in the Mediterranean throughout the middle of the sixteenth century. It was therefore a fitting day to launch a ship which is the first warship entirely designed and customised to meet the operational needs, requirements and traditions of the modern Turkish fleet.

DESIGN ORIGINS AND CONSTRUCTION

MILGEM is an acronym of the Turkish words *Milli Gemi* (National Ship). It is used with reference both to the project and the class in general. Subsequent to their commissioning, MILGEM ships have also

been classified as the 'Ada' class by the Turkish Navy.

The history of the MILGEM project goes back to the mid-1990s, when the veteran coastal patrol boats and anti-submarine warfare ships in the fleet were nearing obsolescence. New vessels were therefore needed to conduct anti-submarine warfare and

offshore patrol missions. These new ships had to be inexpensive to produce, maintain and operate.

In 1996 the Turkish Navy declared that it wanted to procure eight corvettes under the MILGEM project. As the name indicated, the greatest possible Turkish contribution was desired from the very

Left & Right: Images of the second Turkish 'MILGEM' or 'Ada' class corvette, *Büyükada*, taken on trials in the summer of 2013. The MILGEM 'national ship' project has created the first warship entirely designed to meet the needs of the modern Turkish fleet. *(Turkish Navy/Devrim Yaylali)*

beginning. After delays due to severe economic crises in the late 1990s, MILGEM was brought into life by the Defence Industry Executive Committee (DIEC) in February 2000. At this stage, acquisition numbers were set at eight plus four optional platforms. Twelve shipyards acquired the Request for Proposal but only two actually submitted proposals. Moreover, both of these were found to be invalid due to deficiencies in the bid bonds supporting their tenders.

As a result, it seemed for a couple of years that the MILGEM project would be put on ice. However, in March 2004 – in an unprecedented move – a dedi-cated design office was created for the MILGEM programme by the Turkish Navy. The MILGEM Project Office (MPO) – which is located at Istanbul Naval Shipyard – was tasked with all design and construction activities regarding the ship. After the MPO started to design the ship, the Under-Secretariat for Defence Industries (the main defence procurement agency in Turkey) started a bidding process in co-operation with the Turkish Navy for various subsystems intended for the ship. In parallel, a series of workshops were organised to arouse the interest of the commercial shipbuilding, machinery and supporting industries. This was necessary in order to obtain the required high level of local contribution.

The keel of the first ship, *Heybeliada*, was laid on 26 July 2005. Construction work on the second ship, *Büyükada*, commenced on 27 September 2008, the same day that *Heybeliada* was launched. Three years later, on 27 September 2011, *Heybeliada* was officially commissioned into the Turkish Navy after successfully completing all her trials and *Büyükada* was launched. *Büyükada* was commissioned into service on 27 September 2013.

Table 3.3.1.

HEYBELIADA PRINCIPAL PARTICULARS

Building Information:

Laid Down:	26 July 2005
Launched:	27 September 2008
Commissioned:	27 September 2011
Builders:	Istanbul Naval Shipyard

Dimensions:

Displacement:	2,300 tons full load displacement.
Overall Hull Dimensions:	99.5m x 14.4m x 3.7m.

Equipment:

Armament:	2 x quad launchers for Boeing Harpoon surface-to-surface missiles.
	1 x 21-cell Mk 49 RAM launcher for RIM-116 surface-to-air missiles.
	1 x 76mm Oto Melara Super Rapid gun. 2 x 12.7mm Aselsan STAMP mountings.
	2 x twin Mk 32 Mod 9 anti-submarine torpedo tubes.
Aircraft:	1 x S-70B Seahawk.
Countermeasures:	ARES-2N ESM system. Ultra Electronics Sea Sentor torpedo defence system. 2 x sextuple chaff launchers.
Principal Sensors:	1 x Thales SMART-S Mk 2 air/surface-search radar. Navigation radar.
	1 x Thales STING-EO Mk 2 fire-control director. 1 x Aselsan ASELFLIR-300D optronic tracker.
	1 x Yakamoz bow-mounted sonar.
Combat System:	Havelsan G-MSYS integrated combat management system including Links 11 and 16.

Propulsion Systems:

Machinery:	CODAG. 2 x MTU 16V595 TE90 diesels each rated at 4.3MW 1 x GE LM-2500 gas turbine rated at 23MW. 2 shafts.
Speed:	Designed speed is 30 knots in full CODAG configuration. Range is 3,500 nautical miles at 15 knots.

Other Details:

Complement:	Normal crew is 85, including 14 officers. There are sufficient berths for up to 120 personnel.
Class:	Two MILGEM or 'Ada' class vessels have been delivered to date: *Heybeliada* (F511) & *Büyükada* (F512). A further vessel, *Burgazada*, has been laid down and a fourth, *Kınalıada,* ordered. An order for four additional ships that will be built to an enlarged design is planned.

In line with the previous sequence, the keel of the third ship in the class, *Burgazada*, was laid on the same day.

PLATFORM AND STEALTH FEATURES

The 'Ada' class corvettes have mono-hull type form. With an overall length of 99.5m and a maximum beam of 14.4m, their full load displacement is some 2,300 tons. The helicopter platform located at the aft end of the ships can support a 10-ton class helicopter and the hangar is big enough to hold one S-70B Seahawk. The seakeeping and stability require-

ments set by the Turkish Navy demanded that the 'Ada' class corvettes remain fully operational in conditions up to Sea State 5, and partially operational in Sea State 6.

Signature reduction was one of the primary design goals of the MILGEM Project Office. The angled design of the class's hull and superstructure is a feature held in common with every modern stealth ship design. The 'Ada' class ships have a meticulously computed and shaped radar cross-section to the extent that a couple of dangerous situations have arisen due to the ships' low signa-

ture. In one instance, a merchant ship got dangerously close to *Heybeliada*, mistakenly thinking she was an agile small boat on the basis of her radar echo. Special care was given to hide everything that might increase the ships' radar echo inside the hull (such as the torpedo tubes) or behind large mesh netting (e.g., the onboard rigid hulled inflatable boats). The Harpoon missiles amidships are also located behind large panels to hide them from enemy radars, as well as protecting them from the elements.

The infra-red (IR) signatures of the 'Ada' class

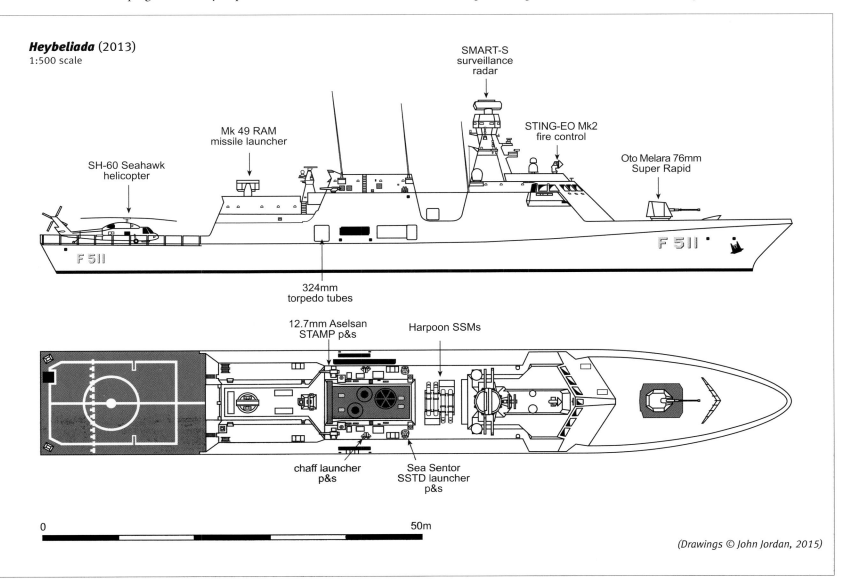

Heybeliada (2013)
1:500 scale

SMART-S surveillance radar

Mk 49 RAM missile launcher

STING-EO Mk2 fire control

SH-60 Seahawk helicopter

Oto Melara 76mm Super Rapid

F 511

F 511

324mm torpedo tubes

12.7mm Aselsan STAMP p&s

Harpoon SSMs

chaff launcher p&s

Sea Sentor SSTD launcher p&s

0   50m

(Drawings © John Jordan, 2015)

A profile view of the lead 'Ada' class corvette, *Heybeliada,* on 18 November 2011, shortly after she had been commissioned. A relatively conservative design incorporates a 76mm main gun in the usual 'A' position, the majority of sensors and electronic equipment clustered around the two masts and the point-defence missile system and helicopter facilities aft. Surface-to-surface missiles are hidden in the gap between the mast and the funnel, whilst fixed torpedo tubes are housed in the superstructure. *(Devrim Yaylali)*

A more detailed view of *Heybeliada*'s superstructure. The main Thales SMART-S Mk2 surveillance is located on top of the mast, with electronic support measures equipment located immediately below. The stub mast aft the funnel supports an electro-optical sensor and the aft navigation radar. Decoy launchers and remote-controlled machine guns can be found on either side of the funnel. *(Devrim Yaylali)*

corvettes are also continuously monitored. Control of IR signature is an important factor in the warmer waters around Turkey. Custom-developed software by Tübitak-Bilgem collects heat information from sensors placed on the ship and creates a real-time IR picture.[1] This information helps the commanding officer to take any necessary actions to reduce the ship's IR signature, either by activation of the wash-down system or by selection of a course which will reduce the heat.

Minimising the class's acoustic signature has also been a significant consideration given the importance of their anti-submarine role. Accordingly, the main components of the propulsion system and other noise generating machinery, such as power generators, are mounted on sound-absorbing rafts. Protection against torpedoes and bottom mines is aided by a degaussing system that decreases the ships' magnetic signature developed by the Marmara Research Centre, Tübitak-MAM.

Apart from their prominent stealth features, the 'Ada' class corvettes have a relatively conservative design. The hull and superstructure are constructed out of steel, whilst both the forward and aft masts, as well as the funnel, have been fabricated out of aluminium. Starting forward, a 76mm gun mounting is located on the forecastle, with the following superstructure blended into the hull. The principal fire-control director is located on top of the bridge. A tall mast with the main surveillance radar at its head marks the end of the forward part of the superstructure, with radomes housing X-band satellite communication antennas placed at both sides of the mast. The gap between the mast and funnel houses the ship's Harpoon surface-to-surface missiles. There is enough space to fit torpedo defence decoy launchers, chaff launchers and remote-controlled machine guns on both sides of the funnel.

Immediately aft, a smaller mast located on top of the hangar supports an electro-optical sensor and the aft navigation radar. A RAM missile launcher for RIM-116 point-defence missiles installed on top of

the hangar's rear portion has a large arc of fire. The areas to the port and starboard of the helicopter hangar are used for underway replenishment.

The davits are located one deck below the decoy launchers on the port side and are positioned inside the ship, so as to reduce the radar echo. They are covered with a metal wire mesh when not in use. An additional rigid-hulled inflatable boat (RHIB) is located at the aft end of the ship, just below the helicopter pad. There is a small staging area with a ramp at the stern of the ship to facilitate launch. When the RHIB is deployed, the stern gate is opened upwards and the ramp lowered to the water to ease its departure and return.

The 'Ada' class corvettes have a standard crew of fourteen officers, forty-seven petty officers and twenty-four ratings, making a total complement of eighty-five. This number includes the eleven-strong aircrew. Berthing on board is designed to accommodate as many as 120 people. Sufficient stores are held

to allow the 'Ada' class to sail for ten days without replenishment.

PROPULSION
The propulsion system of the 'Ada' class corvettes is provided by a combined diesel and gas (CODAG) arrangement. Two Rolls Royce Power Systems MTU 16V595 TE90 diesels each provide 4.3MW of power. A single 23MW GE LM 2500 gas turbine can be coupled through a cross-connecting gearbox. In this configuration, any combination of the main machinery components can propel the ship. A single diesel can propel the ship at its cruise speed of 15 knots, whilst engaging a second increases this to 22.5 knots. The gas turbine alone can provide sufficient power for a speed of 27 knots, whilst a maximum of 30 knots can be achieved in full CODAG configuration. Similar gas turbines and diesels are used in many other ships in the fleet, creating a common logistical base and easing main-

Heybeliada pictured in the Dardanelles in April 2015 at the time of the commemorations marking the First World War Gallipoli landings. The normal mesh covering that hides the portside davits has been removed and one of the ship's RHIBs can be seen. Another RHIB is carried in small staging area below the flight deck and launched from the stern. *(Devrim Yaylali)*

tenance. The ship has two shafts with controllable variable pitch propellers provided by Escher Wyss. Total endurance is some 3,500 nautical miles – or nearly 6,500km – at cruising speed.

WEAPONS SYSTEMS
The main gun of the 'Ada' class is the ubiquitous 76mm/62 cal Oto Melara. Located in 'A' position, the gun is in Super Rapid configuration and has a rate of fire of 120 rounds per minute. It can be used in anti-aircraft and anti-surface roles. The gun's stealth cupola has been designed and constructed in Turkey by ONUK-BG.[2]

Büyükada pictured at speed during trials. The main dual purpose 76mm gun is clearly visible in 'A' postion but the location of the Harpoon missiles forward of the funnel is screened for stealth reasons. (Turkish Navy)

As close-quarters defence weapons, the 'Ada' class corvettes also incorporate two Aselsan-built stabilised machine gun platforms (STAMP). They are located on either side of the funnel and have an almost 180-degree field of fire. The gun platforms are equipped with 12.7mm M2 HB machine guns and have approximately 200 ready-to-use rounds. To the right of the weapon station there is a sensor pod. This sensor suite comprises a daylight TV camera, an 8-12 μm thermal camera and a laser rangefinder. The guns are remotely controlled from the Combat Information Centre (CIC) and can be used against both surface and air targets.

The main weapon system mounted onboard for use against airborne threats is the RAM Mk 31 Guided Missile Weapons System built around the RIM-116 Rolling Airframe Missile (RAM).[3] RAM is a lightweight, fire-and-forget, surface-to-air missile system providing close-in defence against aircraft, helicopters and anti-ship missiles. It encompasses the launcher, below-deck electronics such as the servo control unit and a weapon-control panel in the ship's CIC. There are twenty-one RAM missiles ready to fire in the Mk 49 launcher and additional rounds are carried for reload purposes. The launcher's location on top of the helicopter hangar provides an unrestricted arc of fire to the aft of the ship.

The main surface-to-surface offensive weapon carried onboard the 'Ada' class is the AGM-84 Harpoon anti-ship missile. Up to eight of these large missiles can be carried between the mast and the funnel. The missiles are completely covered by large panels to protect the missiles from the elements and to reduce the comparatively large radar echo produced by the shape of the Harpoon launchers and their supports. Turkey was an early overseas customer for the Harpoon missile system and all major surface ships in the Turkish fleet except the former French A-69 type 'Burak' class corvettes use the weapon.

The ships' main onboard anti-submarine weapons are two Mk 32 Mod 9 torpedo tubes. These are located inside the helicopter hangar, towards its aft end. There are two tubes, one mounted above the other, on a fixed mounting. They are covered by

The 'Ada' is class equipped with the ubiquitous 76mm/62 calibre Oto Melara Super Rapid mounting. Maximum rate of fire is 120 rounds per minute. (Turkish Navy)

hatches which have to be opened prior to a torpedo launch. The positioning of the torpedo tubes has three advantages, viz. (1) it protects the launcher crew from the elements, (2) it reduces the radar echo created by the torpedo tubes and (3) it simplifies handling and reloading of the torpedoes. More specifically, since both the Mk 32 launch system and the Turkish Navy's S-70 B2 helicopter use the same Mk 44 or Mk 46 torpedoes, one storage magazine can easily serve both the torpedo tubes and helicopter.

Probably the most versatile weapon system carried onboard the 'Ada' class corvettes – or on any class of warship – is their naval helicopter. The Turkish Navy currently operates both the older Agusta AB-212 and more recent Sikorsky S-70B Seahawk helicopters. However, the Aircraft-Ship Integrated Secure and Traverse (ASIST) deck-handling system on board of the 'Ada' class is only suitable for the S-70B. Thus only this type of aircraft is deployed on these ships. The helicopter hangar is big enough to accommodate one Seahawk with blades folded and there is enough room for technicians to service the

A picture of *Heybeliada* taken in May 2014 during a test firing of a RIM-116 Rolling Airframe Missile from its Mk 49 launcher. There are twenty-one RAM rounds contained in the launcher and additional missiles are carried as reloads. *(Turkish Navy)*

Close in protection for the 'Ada' class is supplemented by two automated and stabilised STAMP machine-gun mountings produced by local company Aselsan. A sensor pod containing daylight and thermal cameras, as well as a laser rangefinder, is attached to the side of each mount. *(Devrim Yaylali)*

A close-up view of *Büyükada*'s twin fixed Mk 32 torpedo tubes, which are located behind a hatch to each side of the helicopter hangar. *(Devrim Yaylali)*

helicopter whilst inside the hangar. The 'Ada' class are equipped to refuel two helicopters simultaneously: one inside the hanger and the other on the landing platform. The landing deck is strong enough to survive a crash-landing of an S-70B should an accident occur.

Büyükada pictured at sea during November 2014 with a Seahawk S-70B embarked. The deck handling system installed in the class is only suitable for operating helicopters of this type, which can be serviced in the hangar. *(Turkish Navy)*

SENSORS

The Thales SMART-S Mk 2 3D search radar is one of the most prominent features of the 'Ada' class design. Located in the highest possible position on the ship on the top of the mast, the radar has excellent coverage, free from any possible false echoes that might be caused by other sensors and structures. An air- and surface-surveillance and target-designation radar, it operates in the 2,000-4,000 MHz NATO E/F bands (US S band). Published information suggests it can detect surface targets out to around 80km and air targets up to 250km

distant. The radar is popular with the Turkish Navy and has also been retrofitted to four former US Navy FFG-7 type 'Gabya' class frigates (replacing their original SPS-49 radars) and to four MEKO 200 Track II B class frigates (replacing the original AWS-9 radars). In 2010 Thales Nederland and local company Aselsan signed a contract to allow the latter to produce SMART-S Mk 2 radars in Turkey under license.[4]

The main navigation radar is an Aselsan Low Power ECCM Radar (ALPER). ALPER is a low-probability intercept radar system that operates in

A detailed view of the forward sensors on *Heybeliada*. A Thales STING-EO Mk 2 fire-control director is located on top of the bridge, with the same company's SMART-S Mk 2 surveillance radar at the head of the mainmast. The ARES-2N ESM system can be found immediately below the main radar, whilst navigation radars are located to the front of the mast. The twin radomes for satellite communication can also be seen. *(Devrim Yaylali)*

the NATO I/J bands (US Navy X band). Manufacturer's data states it can can detect surface targets in all weather conditions up to 36 nautical miles (c. 65km).

The 'Ada' class corvettes' main underwater sensor is a bow-mounted sonar. The system installed on board *Heybeliada* is the first of its kind to have been made in Turkey. Tübitak and Turkish Naval Research Centre Command (TNRCC) collaborated on the development and construction of the system: Tübitak was responsible for the development and manufacturing of the wet-end, including the transducers, whilst TNRCC focused on the electronics cabinets and onboard equipment. The fibreglass dome was specially made by ONUK-BG. The sonar, known as Yakamoz, is based on the well-known US Navy AN/SQ-56, which is installed in several Turkish warships. Incorporating 280 transducers, Yakamoz operates in medium frequency and has active and passive modes. According to Turkish Navy it can detect targets up to 40km away. As with all the other main sensors, it is integrated into the combat management system.

'Ada' class ships have two main optical sensors. The Thales STING-EO Mk 2 fire-control director located on top of the bridge features a combination of radar and electro-optical sensors. It can be used for surveillance purposes as well as providing fire control for the main 76mm gun. The second optical sensor is located on the small mast just between the funnel and the Mk 49 RAM launcher. As developed for sea platforms, the Aselsan ASELFLIR-300 D has a high-resolution infrared camera, a laser rangefinder/designator, a laser spot tracker and a colour day TV camera. The system can track up to six targets simultaneously and has an excellent view to the aft of the ship. Data

The bridge and forward mast structure on an 'Ada' class corvette, providing a detailed view of the ARES-2N ESM system located immediately below the SMART-S Mk 2 surveillance radar at the top of the mast to give maximum coverage. *(Devrim Yaylali)*

provided by the two sensors can be combined in the CIC to provide an almost 360-degree optical tracking capability.

COMBAT MANAGEMENT SYSTEM

Inevitably, all the weapons systems and sensors aboard *Heybeliada* and her sisters are little better than useless without an effective combat management system (CMS). This is an important element of indigenous content on the class. In 1999, through Turkish Naval Research Centre Command, the Turkish Navy initiated a project to design, develop and integrate a modern CMS utilising national sources and companies. The initial aim was to update the CICs on the 'Gabya' class frigates acquired from the United States. The project is known as GENESIS, an acronym of the Turkish *Gemi Entegre Savas Idare Sistemi* (ship integrated combat management system).

The TNRCC defined the combat system's specifications and subsequently undertook the initial design, system development and integration work needed to create a prototype. After this had been achieved, the project was handed over to local Turkish company Havelsan for industrialisation.[5]

The know-how gained during the installation of GENESIS into the 'Gabya' class frigates was used to develop it further for potential installation into other classes of ship. For example, a derivative of GENESIS will be used in two tank landing ships under construction for the Turkish Navy. Another GENESIS derivative – G-MSYS (GENESIS MILGEM *Savas Yönetim Sistemi*) – has been specially developed by Havelsan for the 'Ada' class ships.

G-MSYS provides a nerve centre that connects all a ship's sensors and weapons. It collects all the data received by the ship's sensors and displays it in the form of standard symbols on operator consoles located in the CIC. It is also used to transmit orders to the weapon and countermeasures systems. As an open architecture design, G-MSYS is sufficiently flexible to be quickly and easily adapted to new sensors or weapons systems that may be acquired in the future. The next batch of 'Ada' class corvettes, *Burgazada* and *Kınalıada*, will incorporate an upgraded version of the CMS called ADVENT (*Ağ Destekli Veri Entegre Savaş Yönetim Sistemi*). The ADVENT CMS will be a first step towards a fully network-centric command and control system.

As commissioned, *Heybeliada* had the NATO Link 11 communications system integrated with G-MSYS. The software house Milsoft has subsequently developed a Multi-Purpose Tactical Data Link Operating System (ÇAVLİS), which has a separate console in the CIC and supports Links 11 and 16 and will support Link 22 in the future. The Link operator console was first introduced in *Büyükada* and subsequently retrofitted in *Heybeliada* in 2013.

PLATFORM MANAGEMENT SYSTEM

While the 'Ada' class's CMS is locally produced, the Dutch company Imtech was selected to provide the integrated platform management system (IPMS) in conjunction with its local partner, Yaltes. They supplied a sophisticated and highly automated monitoring and control system that is linked to virtually every non-combat system on the class. It is supported by forty-five closed-circuit TV cameras, as well as numerous fire detectors and water ingress sensors. The IPMS makes it possible to monitor and operate all vital systems with a minimised crew.

COUNTERMEASURES

The ARES-2N electronic support measures (ESM) system built by the Turkish defence electronics house Aselsan is the main electronic warfare system on board of the 'Ada' class ships. Its antennae are very prominent features on the mast, being located just below the SMART-S Mk2 radar. The eight antennae provide 360-degree coverage, with omnidirectional and individual direction-finding (DF). According to the manufacturer the system has a wide-band intercept capability; detecting, intercepting, classifying and tracking any electromagnetic emissions in the 2-18 GHz operating frequency range. The signals received by ARES-2N are processed to determine their physical characteristics and origin before a software database correlates them with known emitters to aid the system operator in classification and identification.

The 'Ada' class ships are protected against laser-guided weapons by an Aselsan LIAS laser warning system. The system detects, classifies, identifies and gives warning of hostile laser threats targeting the ship. The LIAS system has one processor unit and eight sensor units; six directed towards the sides, one looking forward and one backward. Each sensor unit has a ninety-degree field-of-view in azimuth and ± forty-degree field-of-view in elevation axes. Hostile

A close-up view of the ASELFLIR-300D optical sensor system on *Büyükada*, which is located on a stub mast aft of the funnel. This complements the STING-EO Mk 2 fire-control director and provides near 360-degree optical coverage. *(Devrim Yaylali)*

A stern view of *Heybeliada* in November 2011. She benefits from incorporation of a pressurised citadel to protect against nuclear, biological and chemical attack, as well as a sprinkler-based washdown system. *(Devrim Yaylali)*

laser rangefinders, laser designators and laser beam-guided missiles can be intercepted by the system, which alerts the end user through the ARES-2N ESM system. The 'Ada' class corvettes are the first warships in Turkish inventory to be equipped with LIAS.

The Sea Sentor torpedo defence system provides the main torpedo protection system on board the class. The system detects, classifies and locates incoming torpedoes; provides tactical advice on how to avoid the threat; and decoys them away from the target ship. Sea Sentor is the export version of Ultra Electronics' Sonar 2170 surface ship torpedo defence (SSTD) system, which is also used by the British Royal Navy. The Turkish Navy is the first export customer for this system.

The Sea Sentor system includes one passive towed receiver array and one flexible towed body acoustic countermeasures device. The passive towed receiver listens for enemy torpedoes and gives information about the threat. The towed acoustic countermeasures device can send signals to decoy the torpedo away from the ship. Both the towed array and the towed device are streamed from the stern of the ship by means of a winch. The Turkish Navy specified that the winch should be remotely controlled from the bridge. The other components of Sea Sentor are expendable decoy launchers located to the starboard and port sides of the funnel. Each launcher has eight ready-to-use expendable decoys, which are programmable countermeasures devices. Once launched, a decoy becomes operational within ten seconds, starting to transmit a signal to decoy the incoming torpedo. The 'Ada' class corvettes are the first ships in the Turkish Navy that operate such a comprehensive torpedo protection system. Aselsan has started to produce locally designed decoys and its website advertises a torpedo defence system called Hızır, which will be installed in *Burgazada* and *Kınalıada*. Each 'Ada' class corvette is also fitted with a pair of six-barrelled decoy launcher for chaff and flares, providing 360-degree coverage against incoming anti-ship missiles.

The 'Ada' class are protected against nuclear, biological and chemical (NBC) weapons. The main body of the ship is enclosed in a citadel. The air pressure inside the citadel is higher that the ambient air pressure, thus making it impossible for contaminated air to enter the ship. On the outside there is a washdown system, with dozens of sprinklers located around the ship. This wash down system can be used to wash contaminated material off the outside of the ship. As previously mentioned, it is also frequently used to cool down the ship to reduce its heat signature on the basis of real-time data provided by the infra-red heat measurement software.

DEPLOYMENTS

Both 'Ada' class corvettes have been sent on lengthy deployments by Turkish Navy since first commissioning. These deployments provided the navy with many important lessons about the operation, maintenance and endurance of these ships. Additionally, these deployments should also be seen as part of a marketing effort to promote and present these ships to friendly navies potentially interested in purchasing similar vessels.[6]

From the time of the commissioning of *Heybeliada* in September 2011 until the departure of *Büyükada* for an Indian Ocean deployment in January 2015, both ships had covered four times the length of the equator according to *Büyükada's* commander. That amounts to c. 86,500 nautical miles. The deployment of *Büyükada* will have added around 10,000 more nautical miles to this total.

The first international deployment of *Heybeliada* was as flagship of the now-defunct Black Sea Naval Co-operation Task Group (BlackSeaFor) in April 2013. This was followed by a Mediterranean deployment during June-July 2014, when she visited Egypt, Libya, Morocco, Algeria and Tunisia. She returned home after visiting Albania. However, possibly the most important deployment of *Heybeliada* to date was a circumnavigation of the African continent, also in 2014. The Turkish Navy created a task force for this cruise comprising the 'Gabya' class frigate *Gediz*, the MEKO type frigate *Oruçreis*, *Heybeliada*

Heybeliada at sea in March 2014. She has been subject to extensive deployment since commissioning in 2011 as part of Turkish Navy efforts to learn lessons from their first recent major indigenous design. These deployments have also helped to market Turkey's increasingly sophisticated defence industry. *(Turkish Navy)*

The first two ships of the 'Ada' class, *Heybeliada* and *Büyükada*, pictured in company during August 2013. According to *Büyükada*'s commanding officer, both ships had covered four times the length of the equator un a series of deployments by the start of 2015. *(Turkish Navy)*

and the replenishment tanker *Yarbay Kudret Güngör*. During the 102-day deployment, the ships navigated round the African continent from west to east, making forty port visits in twenty-eight countries and conducting military exercises with their navies. The highlight of this deployment was a series of live missile firings at the Denel Overberg Test Range in South Africa. Meanwhile, the first international deployment of *Büyükada* was between January and April 2015 when she was despatched to the Gulf of Aden, Arabian Sea, and adjacent waters. During this deployment *Büyükada* visited twelve ports in Saudi Arabia, Djibouti, Oman, Pakistan, Kuwait, Bahrain, Qatar and Sudan.

In March 2015, under the leadership of Saudi Arabia, Arab coalition forces started military operations against the Houthi rebels in Yemen. This action, named Operation 'Decisive Storm', worsened the situation of foreigners in Yemen, who were trapped by the fighting between the Yemeni rebels and government forces. At the time, *Büyükada* was in the Gulf of Aden as part of anti-piracy efforts

A February 2015 image of *Büyükada* taken whilst she was deployed to the Indian Ocean and participating in NATO's anti-piracy mission, Operation 'Ocean Shield'. She was involved in rescuing Turkish citizens from Yemen's civil war later in this deployment. *(NATO)*

within NATO's Operation 'Ocean Shield' campaign. She was dispatched to the Yemeni port of Aden on 3 April 2015 to pick fifty-five Turkish citizens, who had requested an emergency evacuation through Turkish Foreign Ministry channels. They were taken by *Büyükada* to Djibouti and then transferred to Turkey on a Turkish Airlines aircraft. The evacuation of non-combatants marked the first true military operation for any 'Ada' class corvette.

THE FUTURE

The Turkish Navy always considered *Heybeliada* as a prototype. Therefore her systems were extensively tested and the ship was sent on the long deployments already mentioned. Many of the lessons learned from the production of *Heybeliada* were incorporated in the second ship, *Büyükada*. She is considered as the production prototype.

When the MILGEM project started, the intention of both the Turkish Navy and the Undersecretariat for Defence Industries was to transfer production of the class to a private shipyard after the completion of the first two ships. Consequently, in 2011, two shipyards – Dearsan and RMK Marine – were invited to tender for the construction of the

follow-on ships, which were also known as MILGEM-S. Since both these yards lacked the necessary know-how and skilled workers to construct complicated warships, the navy decided to start the construction of the third ship of the class, *Burgazada*, in Istanbul Naval Shipyard. Under this arrangement, the winner of the MILGEM-S tender would take part in building this ship and would therefore benefit from on-the-job training for its personnel, who would construct subsequent ships in its own facility.[7]

In January 2013, the Defence Industry Executive Committee announced that RMK Marine, a subsidiary of local conglomerate Koç, had been selected as the main contractor for the MILGEM-S class production contract. If the contract had ever been completed, it is believed it would have cost c.US$ 2.5bn to build the five remaining MILGEM-S class corvettes. However, in August 2013, following a formal complaint by the Sedef Shipyard, the Prime Ministry Inspection Board decided that the tender under which RMK Marine had been selected violated competition rules. As such, the agreement was not in the public's interest and should be cancelled. Subsequently, in September

2013, the Defence Industry Executive Committee announced it had cancelled its previous choice of RMK Marine and decided that both the third and the fourth ships would now be constructed in Istanbul Naval Shipyard. The tender would be re-opened for the remaining four ships.[8]

It is beyond doubt that this intervention had a negative impact on the entire MILGEM programme. The Turkish naval projects road map had envisaged that transfer of MILGEM-S production to the private sector would allow the Under-secretariat for Defence Industries and the Turkish Navy to turn their focus to the planned new larger and more sophisticated TF-100 class frigates. The cancellation of the MILGEM-S tender forced a change of plan. As Turkish bureaucratic and legal regulations require the new tender to have different specifications than the original 'Ada' class, a more complex requirement approaching the TF-100 requirement had been drawn up. The Under-secretariat for Defence Industries is now preparing the paper work for a new tender, which has not yet been opened. The new ships will now be known as MILGEM-G or as 'I' class frigates.

The new design will be c.110m long, with a breadth of 14.4m and a 4m draft. The projected displacement is 2.955 tons or some 900 tons heavier than the original 'Ada' class. The overall hull form and arrangement of the superstructure appears to be similar to the original ships but it is longer and heavier due to an increased weapons load and other detailed design changes. The main gun remains a 76mm mounting in a stealth cupola but there is now a sixteen-cell vertical launch system (VLS) between the gun and the bridge. As the Turkish Navy currently uses the Mk 41 VLS system on many existing ships it is safe to say that the same system will be used in 'I' class frigates. The canisters will be loaded with RIM-162 Evolved Sea Sparrow Missiles (ESSM).

Images suggest the forms of the bridge and mast are almost identical to the existing MILGEMs, with the Smart-S Mk2 radar and ARES-2 ESM suite being retained. Sixteen anti-ship missiles are shown in the area between the main mast and the funnel. This is the twice the usual load of anti-ship missiles carried on existing Turkish warships and indicates that the indigenous 'Atmaca' anti-ship missile will replace the Harpoon system on these ships. Further aft, the MILGEM-G is almost identical to the 'Ada' class. The only major difference is the close-in

Heybeliada pictured at sea during trials in 2010. The Turkish Navy always considered the ship as a prototype and many lessons learned from her construction and trials have been incorporated in other members of the class. *(Turkish Navy)*

weapon system (CIWS). While the existing MILGEMs ship RAM anti-air missiles, the 'I' class frigates will have a Phalanx CIWS. Reasons for this change might include the additional capability provided by the VLS and the high cost of the RAM missile system compared to Phalanx. Remotely-controlled 25mm guns are located on each side of the funnel. The locations of the chaff and torpedo countermeasure launchers have not been changed.

Whilst the above-mentioned external differences between the two generations of MILGEM ships are relatively easy to identify, it is more difficult to assess the major internal changes at this time. Nevertheless, one might safely assume that the combat management system of the second generation of ships will be an improved version of that installed in the first generation. The 'I' class frigates will eventually replace the first four MEKO-200 class frigates, which are nearing the end of their useful lives.

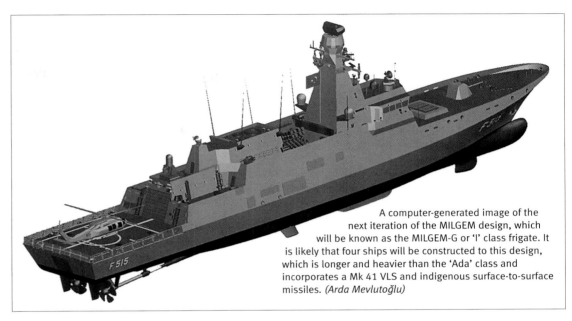

A computer-generated image of the next iteration of the MILGEM design, which will be known as the MILGEM-G or 'I' class frigate. It is likely that four ships will be constructed to this design, which is longer and heavier than the 'Ada' class and incorporates a Mk 41 VLS and indigenous surface-to-surface missiles. (Arda Mevlutoğlu)

CONCLUSION
From the very beginning of the MILGEM project, the Turkish Navy's intention was to achieve the highest possible level of national sovereignty over systems selected for the class. To achieve this goal, a high degree of local contribution by indigenous companies was considered imperative. Indeed, the total level of local content in the 'Ada' class is reported to be around 65 per cent.

The result of this ambition is that the MILGEM project developed from being more than just a straightforward shipbuilding programme, as significant subsystems, equipment and sensors were produced for the first time in Turkey for use in the programme. Examples of these include the Yakamoz hull-mounted sonar – the first ever sonar designed and constructed in Turkey – as well as the ALPER navigation radar. The next-generation MILGEM

ships, which will practically amount to general-purpose frigates, will take this process further. For example, it seems that these ships will be fitted with locally-produced Atmaca anti-ship missiles.

In short, the MILGEM programme is both significant in terms of the recapitalisation of Turkish naval forces and a major step towards the creation of a sovereign maritime military and industrial capability.

Notes:
1. Tübitak-Bilgem is one of a number of research centres that reports to the Scientific and Technological Research Council of Turkey (Tübitak), an autonomous national Turkish agency. Bilgem focuses on informatics and information security.

2. The Turkish Navy claims that the radar cross-section of the cupola designed for the 'Ada' class corvettes is smaller than that of Oto Melara's own stealth cupola.

3. RAM's installation in the 'Ada' class represents the first time the weapon has been used in Turkish naval service.

4. Aselsan, originally founded by the Turkish Army in the 1970s and still majority-owned by the Turkish Armed Forces Foundation, provides defence electronics to the Turkish military. With current turnover approaching US$1bn p.a., the group aims to become one of the world's fifty largest defence companies.

5. Havelsan is the leading C4ISR and mission systems company in Turkey. Originally founded by the Turkish Air Force, it is currently 99.5 per cent owned by the Turkish Armed Forces Foundation.

6. More importantly, perhaps, the deployment also allowed Turkish industry to display the various new systems that have been developed for the navy and which are becoming an increasingly important part of Turkey's drive for naval exports. For example, the GENESIS combat management system has been of considerable interest to the relatively large group of navies that operate second-hand FFG-7 type frigates transferred from the US Navy.

7. Another reason why the Turkish Navy decided to construct Burgazada in the Istanbul Naval Shipyard was to reduce uncertainty with respect to the transfer of work to a private shipbuilder, particularly with respect to financing. When the Turkish Navy constructs a ship, funds for construction are provided directly from state coffers.

However, if a private shipyard constructs a ship, it must secure its own financial resources before reclaiming its costs from the government. It is not a short process for a shipyard to find a financial institution that might be willing to support this arrangement.

8. At the time, there was some mystery surrounding the reasons why Sedef objected to the selection of RMK Marine for the MILGEM-S production contract. Sedef was busily promoting the Juan Carlos class amphibious assault ship designed by Navantia to the Turkish Navy (the design was subsequently selected in December 2013) and had no apparent direct interest in the MILGEM contract. Subsequent reports have suggested that Sedef was put under political pressure to make the complaint due to a desire within parts of the Turkish political establishment to punish the wider Koç group. Koç had been viewed as hostile to the then Turkish Prime Minister (and current President) Erdoğan during the political protests that impacted the country during 2013.

Author:
Guy Toremans

3.4 SIGNIFICANT SHIPS

ROUSSEN CLASS FAST ATTACK CRAFT

Thriving in Adversity

The construction of fast attack craft has seen something of a global downturn in favour of offshore patrol vessels (OPVs) in recent years.[1] However, there are still navies that continue to invest in the renewal of their fast strike capability because this type of platform remains relevant to their specific geographical environment and associated concept of operations. These are frequently navies with archipelagos – strewn with islets and islands, narrow straits, channels and chokepoints – to defend and which, accordingly, seek ships that can exploit this coastal geography. Obviously the Aegean Sea very much falls into this category, explaining why the Hellenic Navy (HN) still places significant emphasis on its fast attack craft force.

The HN's Fast Attack Craft Command (COMHELFAC), one of the subordinate commands of the HN's Fleet Headquarters, is home-ported at the Amfiali Naval Base, opposite the main Salamis Naval Base. It takes great pride in the way its attack craft force has blazed a trail since

the early 1970s. The HN pioneered a number of new technologies. For example, it was a leader in the introduction of the MM38 Exocet surface-to-

surface missile. This was subsequently followed by the introduction of the Norwegian Penguin missile, specifically designed for the littorals, and the instal-

Left and right: Although of declining popularity in recent years, fast attack craft still have a useful role to play in certain geographical environments such as archipelagos. Unsurprisingly, the Hellenic Navy remains a major operator of the type and is currently bringing the British-designed *Roussen* class into service. These images show the first two vessels of the class, *Roussen* and *Daniolos*. (*Hellenic Navy*)

lation of the Vega combat management system onboard its fast attack craft. Over that same period the HN constantly developed and updated its tactics to reflect the capabilities of its fast attack craft fleet.

With the *Roussen* class, the Hellenic Navy has stepped up to another level, achieving better performance in all areas. Bringing the class into service has not been without its travails. Nevertheless, the end product has been well worth the wait. The *Roussen* class units are performing well in front-line service.

CLASS ORIGINS AND CONSTRUCTION

In 1995, the HN identified a need for a new class of fast attack craft to replace its ageing force of 'La Combattante' class vessels. The HN's requirements called for a vessel combining a powerful armament, high-performance sensors, modern command facilities, good endurance, a high degree of combat systems commonality with the *Hydra* (MEKO 200HN) class frigates and the ability to remain operational in conditions up to Sea State 7. The Greek Government stipulated that the new vessels should be built by Elefsis Shipbuilding & Industrial Enterprises,

located in Elefsis Bay near Piraeus. However, given that the yard's previous experience was founded mainly on commercial shipbuilding and ship repair, there was a need to tap into defence expertise from a foreign shipyard. The selected overseas design partner would therefore need to commit to providing a major technology transfer package and other offsets.

In late 1998, a Request for Proposal (RfP) was issued and technical proposals, together with initial commercial and offset terms, were submitted to France's Constructions Mecaniques de Normandie (CMN), Germany's Lürssen Werft, the UK's Vosper

Table 3.4.1.

ROUSSEN CLASS PRINCIPAL PARTICULARS

Building Information:

Laid Down:	1 March 2001
Launched:	13 November 2002
Commissioned:	20 December 2005
Builders:	Elefsis Shipbuilding & Industrial Enterprises at its yard in Elefsis Bay, near Piraeus, Greece.[1]

Dimensions:

Displacement:	670 tons full load displacement.
Overall Hull Dimensions:	61.9m x 9.5m x 2.6m

Equipment:

Armament:	2 x quad launchers for MBDA Exocet MM40 Block 2 surface-to-surface missiles. MM40 Block 3 from fourth unit onwards.
	1 x 21-cell Mk 49 RAM launcher for RIM-116B Block 1 surface-to-air missiles.
	1 x 76mm Oto Melara Super Rapid gun. 2 x 30mm Oto Melara guns. 2 x 7.62mm machine guns.
Countermeasures:	Thales DR 3000 SLW electronic support measures. 2 x Mk 137 Mod 1 sextuple SRBOC decoy launchers.
Principal Sensors:	1 x Thales MW08 3D air/surface-search radar. 1 x Thales SCOUT Mk 2 surface-search radar. Navigation radar.
	1 x Thales STING-EO Mk 2 fire-control director. 1 x Thales MIRADOR electro-optical tracker. 2 x optical TDS.
Combat System:	Thales TACTICOS combat management system. Integrated communications system includes Link 11.

Propulsion Systems:

Machinery:	Diesel. 4 x MTU 16V 595 TE90 diesels each rated at 4.3MW produce 23,000hp through 4 shafts.
Speed:	Designed speed is 34.25 knots; 36 knots has been achieved on trials. Range is 1,800 miles at 12 knots.

Other Details:

Complement:	The core crew is c. 45.
Class:	Four *Roussen* class vessels are currently in service: *Roussen* (P67), *Daniolos* (P68), *Kristallidis* (P69) and *Grigoropoulos* (P70).
	A fifth ship, *Ritsos* (P71) is undergoing final trials and two more, *Karathanasis* (P72) and *Vlahakos* (P73), are under construction.

Notes:

1: The design and technical assistance was provided by Vosper Thornycroft Shipbuilding International, now part of BAE Systems' Maritime – Naval Ships.

Thornycroft Shipbuilding International (now part of BAE Systems) and Haifa-based Israel Shipyards. Of these, only CMN, Lürssen and Vosper Thornycroft elected to bid. In September 1999, following a detailed technical and commercial evaluation, Vosper Thornycroft was selected as preferred bidder. One of the main discriminating factors in favour of the British shipbuilder was the fact that its offer included the transfer to the HN of two 'Hunt' class mine countermeasures vessels being withdrawn from UK Royal Navy service as part of the 1998 Strategic Defence Review.[2] Another key part of the agreement was a long-term commitment by Vosper Thornycroft to the Greek shipyard, comprising the construction of a brand-new covered building berth and office complex, and the delivery of a laser cutter, a unit transporter, welding equipment, a pipe-bending machine and a flat plate seam welder. This made Elefsis one of the most advanced naval shipbuilding facilities in the Mediterranean region. A contract for the construction of an initial three fast attack craft (with options for four additional vessels) was subsequently signed in January 2000.[3]

All ship design activity was undertaken by Vosper Thornycroft in the UK. The entire ship was modelled in 3D using CADDS5 computer-aided design software, after which a full drawing package was given to Elefsis in order to facilitate steel production and manufacturing activities. Vosper Thornycroft established a local subsidiary, VT Hellas SA, to manage day-to-day contract activities in Greece and to provide training to shipyard personnel. A team of twelve people – weapons engineers, materiel procurement coordinators and mechanical, electrical and hull engineers – worked with Elefsis to deliver the programme.

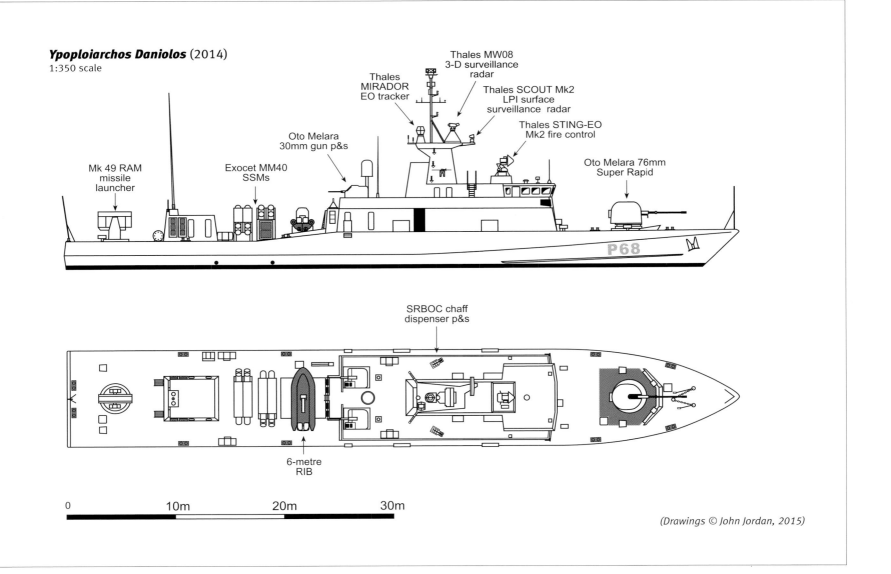

Ypoploiarchos Daniolos (2014)
1:350 scale

Thales MW08 3-D surveillance radar

Thales MIRADOR EO tracker

Thales SCOUT Mk2 LPI surface surveillance radar

Thales STING-EO Mk2 fire control

Oto Melara 30mm gun p&s

Mk 49 RAM missile launcher

Exocet MM40 SSMs

Oto Melara 76mm Super Rapid

P68

SRBOC chaff dispenser p&s

6-metre RIB

0   10m   20m   30m

(Drawings © John Jordan, 2015)

Roussen and *Daniolos,* the first two members of the *Roussen* or 'Super Vita' class to be delivered, pictured on exercises off the Greek coast during 2006, shortly after commissioning. *(BAE Systems)*

The contract became effective on 31 March 2000, covering the firm orders for the initial three ships. Acceptance of the lead vessel was scheduled for November 2003, with the two other units to be handed over at six-monthly intervals thereafter. Options for a further two ships were exercised in August 2003, whilst the final two options were taken up in September 2008. It is understood that the overall value of the total seven-ship programme was over €900m.[4]

The keel of the first-of-class, *Ypoploiarchos Roussen,* was laid on 1 March 2001.[5] Launched on

13 November 2002, she was formally commissioned on 20 December 2005. *Ypoploiarchos Daniolos,* the second unit, joined the fleet on 22 February 2006. The third ship, *Ypoploiarchos Kristallidis,* entered service on 8 May of the same year, completing the initial batch. The fourth unit, *Ypoploiarchos Grigoropoulos,* was launched on 20 December 2005, and commissioned on 1 October 2010. By this time, Greece's financial crisis was well underway and work on the project effectively ground to a halt as money ran out. Equipment from the nearly-complete fifth vessel, *Anthypoploiarchos Ritsos,* launched in October

2006, was used to support the other class members.

In March 2011, BAE Systems (which had by now acquired Vosper Thornycroft's shipbuilding activities) announced that it had terminated its contract with Elefsis, withholding equipment for the completion of the sixth and seventh vessels. This decision resulted from continued non-payment by the shipyard. Although a revised payment schedule had been agreed in mid-2010, Elefsis advised in November 2010 that it could no longer adhere to the terms. In a statement issued at the time, BAE Systems said it had been forced to terminate its agreement because contracted payments (reported to amount to €27m and to have been outstanding for over a year) had not been forthcoming. Elefsis Shipyards filed its own complaint on 3 March 2011, refusing to accept BAE Systems' renunciation. Meanwhile, *Ritsos* was kept alongside pending the reinstatement of the equipment removed by the HN to support the repair and maintenance of the four units already in service. The final two vessels remained in the assembly hall at Elefsis Shipyards.

On 18 December 2014, after more than three years of stalemate, the Greek government, Elefsis Shipyards and BAE Systems concluded an agreement that paved the way for the recommencement of the *Roussen* class construction programme. The accord provided for the handover of *Ritsos* to the Hellenic Navy, as well as the transfer of equipment and materials for the completion of the final two units *Karathanasis* and *Vlahakos* by the Elefsis Shipyards. This settlement also confirmed BAE Systems' exit from the programme, with Elefsis Shipyards having sole responsibility for the completion of both ships from its own financial means. Final sea trials of *Ritsos* commenced in March 2015 and she is likely to be commissioned by the end of 2015. The two final units, *Karathanasis* and *Vlahakos,* are likely to join the fleet by the end of 2016 and 2017 respectively.[6]

OVERALL PLATFORM DESIGN

The *Roussen* class is based on Vosper Thornycroft's 56m-long 'Vita' type (or *Barzan* class) units, which were constructed in Southampton, United Kingdom for the Qatar Emiri Naval Forces (QENF) in the mid-1990s. Perhaps inevitably, the larger Greek variant became known by the proprietary name of 'Super Vita'. At 61.9m in overall length, the *Roussen* class boasts a full load displacement of 660 tons compared with around 400 tons of the earlier class. Classified to Germanischer Lloyd rules, the hull is made of steel and the superstructure is made of aluminium. The whole design incorporates features for reduction of radar cross-section.

Although the *Roussen* class obviously resembles the Qatari Naval Forces' *Barzan* class vessels externally, there are substantial differences in the combat system and, also, in the form of a new and more powerful machinery package. Whilst the round bilge keel hull form remains similar, the superstructure and internal arrangements were redesigned in order to improve seagoing habitability. The above-water

Table 3.4.2: **ROUSSEN CLASS LIST**					
NAME	**PENNANT**	**ORDERED**	**LAID DOWN**	**LAUNCHED**	**COMMISSIONED**
Ypoploiarchos Roussen	P67	January 2000	1 March 2001	13 November 2002	20 December 2005
Ypoploiarchos Daniolos	P68	January 2000	–	8 July 2003	22 February 2006
Ypoploiarchos Kristallidis	P69	January 2000	–	5 April 2004	8 May 2006
Ypoploiarchos Grigoropoulos	P70	August 2003	–	20 December 2005	1 October 2010
Anthypoploiarchos Ritsos	P71	August 2003	–	9 October 2006	[2015]
Karathanasis	P72	September 2008	–	[2015]	[2016]
Vlahakos	P73	September 2008	–	[2016]	[2017]

Notes:
There is a lack of data on the precise progress of the programme and published sources differ on some launch and commissioning dates. This data should therefore only be regarded as being indicative.

hull form was modified by increasing the freeboard amidships and widening the beam at the weather deck by flaring the topsides. These modifications created space for a second accommodation deck and unobstructed external fore-and-aft access along the upper deck of the superstructure.

Whilst not as stealthy as many of today's new ships, the hull and superstructure are inclined at different angles and the sides are broken up. The underwater noise is kept to a minimum by using elastic-mounted engines, and structural acoustic damping. The use of cooling devices, shielding around the engine and hot compartments and the arrangements of the exhaust outlets along the ship's sides just above the waterline, suppress thermal radiation and the IR signature.

In total the ship numbers sixty-eight compartments, incorporating nine water- and gas-tight sections, as well as sixteen fire-detection zones. Structural fire protection includes fire retardant insulating materials. There are two main damage-control centres – one in the engine control room and

The *Roussen* class is a larger derivative of the four 56m 'Vita' vessels of the *Barzan* class built by Vosper Thornycoft for Qatar in the mid-1990s. This picture shows *Al Udeid*, the third member of the earlier class, being prepared for delivery at the company's Portchester facility in Portsmouth Harbour. *(Conrad Waters)*

the other on the bridge – and both are equipped with a machinery control and monitoring system workstation and incident boards. An integrated platform management system (IMPS) monitors and controls the propulsion plant, the generation and distribution of the electrical power, the overall damage-control status and the ship's closure state. It generates an accurate picture of the platform machinery's health for interpretation by ship's staff through a simple and functional user interface. Fully distributed in terms of both data acquisition and user access, it is sub-divided into subsystems encompassing the forward propulsion, aft propulsion and auxiliary machinery/electrical network. An Ethernet dual-redundant local area network links control and data collection units to operator workstations. The system allows operators to identify the platform status quickly at all times and to react to any problems within a very tight timeframe

Damage-control equipment consists of fire-fighting pumps, fire and smoke sensors, a pressurised water/foam fire-extinguishing system, permanent CO_2 gas extinguishing systems (for the forward and aft engine rooms and the emergency generator room), and remotely-activated sprinklers in the engine rooms. Fire detection capabilities are focused on a central controller which monitors and controls all fire detectors, call points, alarms and xenon beacons installed throughout the fire detection zones. There are also CCTV cameras in each

engine room for remote optical surveillance. The fire alarm system automatically governs the ventilating system. Internally, the ship can be over-pressured to maintain the integrity of the nuclear, biological, chemical damage control (NBCD) citadel. A Smiths Detection GID-2A chemical warfare monitoring system is fitted to provide rapid detection and identification of threats from chemical warfare agents. There is also a decontamination station, as well as pre-wetting and sprinkler installations.

PROPULSION

Propulsion is provided by four independent shafts, each fitted with a Bruntons five-bladed fixed-pitch propeller and driven by a 4,320 kW MTU 16V 595 TE90 diesel engine through ZF BW1556/1557S reduction gearing. The class was contracted to have a range of 1,800 nautical miles at 12 knots and deliver a speed of 34.25 knots; a speed of 36 knots has been achieved during sea trials. Machinery is split between two independent engine spaces for the respective inner and outer shaft lines. Two engines are fitted in each engine room. Those in the forward engine room are positioned outboard driving the outboard shafts, whilst those mounted in the aft engine room (AER) are positioned inboard and drive the inboard shafts. G & M Power Plant Ltd supplied the generator set packages, taking responsibility for integrating MTU-supplied diesel prime movers and Newage Stamford alternators as well as

the local control and monitoring systems. Electrical power in the first three vessels is generated by three MTU 6R183 TE52 250 kW prime movers; discontinuation of this line has seen MTU 60 series generators supplied for the fourth and subsequent vessels of the class.

To meet the HN's requirement for good seakeeping performance, the steering system is a variant of VT Marine Products' 900 series, while its US-based subsidiary VT Maritime Dynamics Inc. supplied a 300 Series active fin stabiliser system.[7] This hydraulically-operated and electronically-controlled system provides active roll stabilisation which significantly improves the ships' seaworthiness and consequently their operational effectiveness.

COMBAT MANAGEMENT SYSTEM

One of the HN's key requirements was that the combat system installed in its new fast attack craft had to have commonality with that equipping its four *Hydra* (MEKO 200) class frigates. This drove the choice of the Thales Netherlands TACTICOS combat management system (CMS). This suite fully integrates all sensors, weapons, electronic warfare equipment and associated systems. The suite offers core functionality to support: anti-surface warfare; anti-air warfare; naval gunfire support; electronic warfare; tactical picture compilation/management; and tactical data exchange with

The combat information centre on *Roussen*, showing the dual screen Multifunction Operator Consoles (MOCs) of the combat management system. This comprises two rows of three consoles incoporrating five operator workstations and one command position. *(Guy Toremans)*

other platforms via a Rockwell Collins MDM-2002 Link 11 data terminal set. The combat information centre (CIC) houses six dual-screen Mk 3 Multifunction Operator Consoles (MOCs). There are five operator workstations and one command position, all positioned in the CIC in a double row layout. Only three are needed to work all systems. From ship four onwards, the setting-to-work of the combat management system was undertaken by locally based SSMART, under the oversight and responsibility of Thales Nederland, as part of an offset programme sponsored by the Hellenic Ministry of Defence.

The CMS incorporates automatic threat evaluation weapon assignment and sensor allocation (TEWASA). A Sperry Marine Mk 39 Mod 3A ring laser gyro inertial navigation system provides outputs with respect to position, heading, altitude and velocity data for the ship's fire-control stabilisation and weapons initialisation.

WEAPONS SUITE

In line with their designated primary role as anti-surface combatants operating in the littoral, the *Roussen* class vessels feature a potent anti-surface warfare capability. This is combined with a robust capacity for self-defence.

The principal anti-surface weapon system comprises MBDA-supplied MM40 Block 2 Exocet surface-to-surface guided missiles, which are housed in two quad launchers amidships. The associated ITL 70A launch panel is fitted as a MOC Mk 3 Inter Console Unit in the CIC. Powered by a solid rocket motor, and able to achieve a maximum range of about 70km, the MM40 Block 2 is capable of flying spurious attack axes and executing pseudo-random 'corkscrew' evasive manoeuvres in the terminal phase.

From the fourth vessel onwards, the class is equipped with the enhanced MM40 Block 3 missile, which is compatible with existing launchers and logistic support systems. With a total weight of less than 800kg, the upgraded missile is lighter than the previous version of the weapon but has an increased range due to the use of a turbojet engine as opposed

A detailed view of the Exocet missile launchers on *Daniolos* in 2014, with only four of the potential total of eight missiles shipped. The three oldest ships use the Block 2 variant of the missile but subsequent class members incorporate the longer-ranged Block 3 type. *(Guy Toremans)*

Roussen class vessels are fitted with the ubiquitous 76mm/62 Oto Melara Super Rapid gun on the foredeck for use against both air and surface targets. Interesting, the stealth cupola increasingly used with this mount is not present in the HN's ships. *(Guy Toremans)*

to the solid rocket motor of previous versions. Reported range is in the region of 200km. Other improvements include four air intakes that provide a continuous airflow to the powerplant during high-G manoeuvres, as well as a new mission planning system. This new version accepts GPS guidance system waypoint commands, allowing it to attack naval targets from different angles and providing a limited land-attack capability.

In a typical maritime engagement, the missile is initially directed towards its target by inertial guidance, switching to active radar guidance late in flight to detect and lock-on to its target. A reduced infrared signature and low radar cross-section minimises the prospects of recognition by opposing radar and infra-red seekers, whilst the maintenance of a very low altitude through sea-skimming one to two metres above the surface at a speed of c. Mach 0.9 further complicates the defender's position. A target may not detect the incoming missile until shortly before impact, leaving little time for reaction.

The class also mounts a single 76mm/62 cal. Oto Melara Super Rapid gun on the foredeck. This weapon is capable of intercepting air and surface targets at a distance of 16km, unleashing 6kg shells at 120 rounds per minute. Additionally, two single 30mm Oto Melara mounts, dual-configured for either local or remote control, are fitted on the aft section of the superstructure block. These gyro-stabilised and joystick-controlled guns have a high cyclic rate of fire of 800 rounds per minute and can engage air and surface targets at up to 3km. For close-in defence, a 7.62mm MG3 machine gun is fitted on each bridge wing.

The *Roussen* class's primary air-defence system is a RAM Mk 31 Mod.1 Guided Missile Weapon System (GMWS). Comprising a 21-cell Mk 49 launcher for RIM-116 Rolling Airframe Missiles (RAM) installed

The principal point defence system deployed in the *Roussen* class is a RAM Mk 31 Guided Missile Weapon System. Its Mk 49 launcher is capable of housing up to twenty-one RIM-116 missiles, which are principally intended to provide protection against anti-ship missiles. This image shows a test firing from a US warship. *(Raytheon)*

on the aft deck, it provides point defence against anti-ship missiles and other targets. The Block 1 system configuration features an upgraded IR guidance seeker to introduce an IR-all-the-way guidance capability, enabling the interception of missiles that are not emitting any radar signals.[8] Maximum range exceeds 9km and speed surpasses Mach 2.

For soft-kill defence, Lockheed Martin Sippican has supplied its Automated Launch of Expendables (ALEX) countermeasures suite. This uses two forward-firing 130mm Mk 137 Mod 1 six-barrel SRBOC decoy launchers (one on each bridge wing) configured to fire chaff seduction, infrared seduction and chaff distraction payloads. The system can be operated in an automatic or a semi-automatic mode. Manual override is available at all times. An ALEX ship manoeuvre indicator and a decoy control panel are installed on the bridge, with a master control panel fitted in the CIC.

The ships embark an Arctic 20 type rigid-hulled inflatable boat (RHIB), located amidships, for boarding operations and for use as a general-purpose seaboat.

SENSOR SUITE

As for the CMS, the majority of the sensor suite is manufactured by the Dutch division of Thales Group. The principal above-water surveillance sensor is Thales Nederland's MW08 three-dimensional, all-weather air/surface-search multi-beam radar. Operating in the 4,000-5,000 MHz NATO G-band (US Navy C-band), the radar is capable of performing surveillance, target acquisition and tracking out to an instrumented range of 105km and can track up to 160 air targets and forty surface targets simultaneously. All system functions, including target detection, air-track initiation, target-tracking and built-in test equipment, are automatic. Multistripline antennas, with digital Fast Fourier Transform (FFT) beam formers, Doppler FFT processing and tracking, minimise the effects of clutter and jamming.

The *Roussen* class vessels are also equipped with Thales Nederland's SCOUT Mk 2 low-probability of intercept radar. This short-to-medium range, 2D surface surveillance and tactical navigation radar is an all-weather, solid-state system operating in the 8,000-20,000 I/J-bands (X-band). It is optimised for detecting small targets in very heavy clutter and can track objects from as close as 15m to over 40km. Featuring Frequency Modulation Continuous Wave (FMCW) technology, the radar has extremely low output power and is thus ideal for covert operations in hostile environments where radar silence is required.

The principal fire-control system is a Thales STING-EO Mk 2 fire-control radar located immediately above the bridge. A lightweight dual (I/K) band system with complementary electro-optical sensors, it supports gun fire control, performs kill assessment and can undertake classification and identification of threats. In addition, the system can be used as a surveillance sensor, even under

The *Roussen* class is equipped with a comprehensive range of Thales-supplied electronics. A MW08 3D search radar is positioned on a pyramid-shaped platform towards the forward end of a stubby mast, immediately aft of a shorter-range SCOUT Mk 2 surveillance radar. A secondary Thales MIRADOR tracker is located to the rear. A DR 3000 SLW ESM system can be found atop a pole-like extension to the mast, whilst the main STING EO Mk 2 fire-control director is positioned ahead of the mast, on top of the bridge. *(Guy Toremans)*

radar silence conditions. STING-EO is supplemented by a Thales MIRADOR optronic observation and weapon-control system positioned towards the rear of the mast. Incorporating the latest technological features such as a carbon fibre shell structure and a direct-drive servo system, it combines TV cameras, an IR camera and an eye-safe laser rangefinder for precise fire control against agile air and surface targets.

Passive surveillance and threat warning is provided by Thales Aerospace's DR 3000 SLW electronic support measures (ESM) system. It features a combined, omni-direction finding antenna unit linked to processing and display facilities hosted on a SUN Microsystems Ultra 5 workstation installed in the operations room. An Aeromaritime Mk XII IFF (identification friend or foe) system is integrated with the CMS.

Each vessel is equipped with two optical Target Designation Sights (TDS) on either side of the bridge wings that provide means for optical investigation, target designation and weapon firing. Bearing and elevation data are fed into the CMS system but the TDS can also be used for emergency control of a gun or CIWS system.

The navigation suite includes a Sperry Marine Bridgemaster E (I-band) navigation radar; an MX Marine MX420/8 navigation system; a Raytheon Anshutz autopilot; an L-3 Elec Nautic LAZ4420 dual-frequency echo sounder; an ICS Electronics NAV5 GMDSS Navtex receiver; a Sperry Marine Mk 39 Mod.3A gyrocompass; an AGI electromagnetic speed log; and an AGI solid state meteorological sensor.

COMMUNICATIONS SUITE

Thales Communications UK was the contractor for the integrated communications system (ICS), which provides for the management of all internal and external communication. The system is built around a DCS 2000 distribution switch, a main control station terminal and user terminals fitted ship-wide. The ICS incorporates services such as the broadcast and alarm system, as well as telephony and radio message handling. It interfaces with a supplementary message-handling application based on the ACP127 format. External communications are provided

Left: Two views of *Roussen* taken shortly after delivery. The images show the cluster of radar and electronic sensors clustered around the mast to good effect. *(Hellenic Navy)*

The *Roussen* class provides satisfactory accommodation for a 45-strong crew and is spacious for a relatively small ship, as evidenced by this well-equipped galley. *(Guy Toremans)*

through a comprehensive range of radio receivers in all the main frequencies, supplemented by satellite communications links accessed through a terminal fitted on the aft superstructure. This allows secure voice, fax and high speed data connection for applications such as e-mail and the internet.

Being the 'leaders' of COMHELFAC's Second and First FAC Flotillas respectively, *Roussen* and *Kristallidis* mount a second SATCOM radome immediately forwards of the RAM launcher.

ACCOMMODATION

In spite of its compact design, the *Roussen* class provides satisfactory accommodation for the 45-strong crew. The commanding officer, the executive officer and chief engineer each have a single cabin with an en suite bathroom. Other crew members share four-, six- or eight-bunk cabins. There are three separate dining halls, one for the officers, one for the chief petty officers and one for the petty officers and ratings. The interiors are spacious and very comfortable and all are fitted with entertainment equipment for the crew's leisure time. A well-equipped galley, operating on a self-service principle,

provides meals for the entire crew. There is also a laundry facility. The living areas are concentrated amidships on the lower deck.

There are no dedicated medical facilities on board and, therefore, capacity to deal with major medical incidents is limited. However, at battle stations, special provisions have been made to allow the conversion of the officer's wardroom into a temporary sickbay where trained crew members, equipped with the proper medical equipment, can provide first-aid services.

TASKS AND MISSIONS

The *Roussen* class units are optimised to meet the HN's specific tactical and operational requirements. The potent fast attack craft are capable of conducting a wide variety of missions and tasks in both high-intensity conventional combat and low-intensity conflicts, as well as supporting military operations other than war.[9]

Peacetime responsibilities include 24/7 surveillance operations in Greece's territorial waters and wider exclusive economic zone; fishery protection; combatting maritime terrorism and other illicit

Roussen pictured at speed at sea. The class has been particularly active in NATO's Operation 'Active Endeavour' counter-terrorism mission and has also been a frequent participant in the maritime component of the United Nation's UNIFIL peace-keeping mission in Lebanon. *(Hellenic Navy)*

activities (e.g. counter-drug operations and the prevention of illegal immigration); search and rescue (SAR) missions; the provision of aid during emergencies; social missions (e.g. the transport of medical staff to islands or casualties from the islands); and even participation in ceremonial events.

In times of tension or war, the class will protect Greece's ports and Greek-flagged vessels, participate in combat missions (either alone or as part of a task group). This could encompass attacks on hostile shore installations, the delivery of Special Forces or even the support of offensive mining operations.

Units of the *Roussen* class have already taken part in numerous national exercises, such as Exercise 'Ormi', Exercise 'Parmenion' and Exercise 'Katagis'; multinational exercises such as Exercise 'Niries', Exercise 'Breeze' and Exercise 'Adrion Livex'; and bi-/tri-lateral exercises with units from Cyprus, Egypt, Israel, Italy, Lebanon and the United States. The HN has also been a regular contributor to the UNIFIL (United Nations Interim Force in Lebanon) Maritime Task Force, as well as to NATO's Operation 'Active Endeavour' counter-terrorism mission in the Eastern Mediterranean.

Daniolos became the first of the class to join Operation 'Active Endeavour' when she commenced a fifteen-day patrol at the end of June 2006, being relieved by the first-of-class *Roussen* shortly thereafter. Since then, the HN has regularly deployed a *Roussen* class unit in support of this operation.

CONCLUSIONS

Although classified as a fast attack craft, the *Roussen* class benefits from sufficiently large dimensions and displacement so as to – in combination with its high speed and acceleration – avoid many of the usual operating constraints imposed on smaller fast attack craft when operating in severe weather conditions (conditions worse than Sea State 5). The class therefore has significant potential, as they can continue to make use of their 'state-of-the-art' weapons systems, sensors and command and control whilst sailing in higher Sea States.

Commander Katopodis Panagiotis, commanding

The third and fourth members of the *Roussen* class, *Kristallidis* and *Grigoropoulos*, pictured on a training exercise. *Kristallidis,* seen in the background, is leader of the first FAC Flotilla and ships an additional satellite communications dome forward of the RAM launcher. Although classified as fast attack craft, the ships' command and control facilities, sophisticated weapons systems and good sea-keeping abilities provide much of the potential of larger ships. *(Hellenic Navy)*

officer of *Roussen*, told the *Seaforth World Naval Review*'s correspondent that these fast attack craft are truly 'multi-purpose corvettes'. 'My judgement is that, in all aspects, the ship holds superior performance compared with other known ships of the same size. They are stable in high seas and strong winds, and have superb qualities when it comes to manoeuvrability and ship-handling; especially the ability to manoeuvre the ship in a fine balance thanks to the fin stabilisers and the changeable pitch propellers. The potency of our TACITOS combat system was proved as early as May 2006, when both *Roussen* and *Daniolos* each fired a MM40 Block II missile against the decommissioned destroyer *Nearchos*. The missiles followed their programmed mission profile and scored direct hits. These trials also demonstrated excellent tracking performance from both the Thales MW-08 radar and the STING EO system.'

Being easily adaptable for sea-control operations and having the space to carry extra people and equipment, the *Roussen* class could prove quite useful in European Union or NATO counter-piracy operations. The *Roussen* class units also clearly demonstrate Greece's ability to build and deploy innovative platforms outfitted with appropriate equipment for their intended roles in both the littoral or on the open seas. From the start, both Elefsis and Vosper Thornycroft acknowledged the challenges encountered in undertaking the programme to the satisfaction of the Hellenic Navy. The original staff requirements were described as perhaps the most demanding ever seen. 'We were contracted to deliver a state-of-the-art vessel to a very demanding customer and we had to work hard to ensure that all their requirements were met. The programme certainly carried risks. Obviously we encountered some problems along the way which impacted on the programme schedule. The machinery package threw up issues in build, for example with respect to the mounting and alignment of the main engines. We also had a series of gearbox failures, something traced back to production tolerances with a manufacturer. The major challenge, however, was the integration of all the systems. For instance, it was the first time that RAM had to be integrated into the TACTICOS combat management system', an Elefsis spokesperson stated.

The programme certainly carried risks, although this should, perhaps, not be considered as particularly unusual for a new design of this complexity.

A picture of *Grigoropoulos* taken on a NATO training exercise in October 2014. The class is readily adaptable for sea control operations and has space to carry extra people and equipment. Accordingly, it could be quite useful in European Union and NATO anti-piracy missions. *(NATO)*

Nevertheless, Elefsis Shipyards and VT were obliged to introduce around 1,600 technical amendments during the design and build phase in order to ensure that all technical and operational requirements were met. Ultimately the various challenges were overcome. The yardstick has to be that the first ship was handed over with fewer defects than the final *Sandown* class minehunter built for the Royal Navy' a then Vosper Thornycroft representative remarked.

Notes:

1. The reasons for this are many and varied, including the poor performance of fast attack craft in the 1990–1 Gulf War and the significantly expanded maritime policing requirements resulting from the Exclusive Economic Zone (EEZ) concept.

2. The HN received HMS *Bicester* and HMS *Berkeley* in February 2001. They currently remain in Greek service as *Evropi* and *Callisto*.

3. To be more precise, three contracts were signed, viz. (1) a contract between the Greek MOD and Elefsis; (2) a contract between Elefsis and Vosper Thornycroft Shipbuilding International; and (3) an offsets agreement between Vosper Thornycroft Shipbuilding International and the Greek MOD.

4. Of this total, the value of the programme to BAE Systems and its predecessors was assessed as £449m (c. €650m) in evidence submitted by the company on the value of its exports to the Scottish Affairs Committee in December 2012. A copy of this interesting statement can currently be found at:

http://www.publications.parliament.uk/pa/cm201213/cm select/cmscotaf/139/139we13.htm

5. The class's lead ship is named in honour of Captain Nikolaos Roussen, a distinguished Second World War submarine officer, who was killed whilst suppressing a communist-influenced naval mutiny in 1944.

6. Some local press reports suggest that the commencement of the programme at Elefsis has not gone entirely smoothly. As such, dates for completion of the programme have to be regarded with a degree of caution.

7. These companies were sold to US-based Naiad Dynamics Inc. when VT exited its shipbuilding activities.

8. The original Block 0 RIM-116A missile relied on passive radar homing until the final stages of an engagement, when an infra-red seeker took over for terminal guidance. The Block 1 RIM 116B missile retains this capability.

9. COMHELFAC is tasked with supporting Greece's security and safety-related agencies, not least the Greek Coast Guard.

Author:
David Hobbs

4.1 TECHNOLOGICAL REVIEW

WORLD NAVAL AVIATION

An Overview of Recent Developments

The last year has seen the US Navy take the necessary decisions to maintain strike carrier numbers in spite of ongoing concerns over the affordability of the new *Ford* class carriers. Whilst the previously troubled F-35 programme continues to make progress, past delays to the project threaten the US Navy with a shortage of available aircraft for its carrier wings in the medium term. Elsewhere, both Australia and the United Kingdom are awaiting defence reviews that could have significant consequences for their naval aviation capability. A major decision for the latter is whether to restore the maritime patrol aircraft (MPA) capability that was lost with the decision to scrap the Nimrod MRA 4 programme in 2010. With this decision in mind, this chapter concludes with a review of the 'high end' aircraft currently in service with the major maritime powers.

AIRCRAFT CARRIERS AND THEIR AIR WINGS: US NAVY

The US Navy continues to re-equip the strike carrier air wings and fund the mid-life refuelling and complex overhaul (RCOH) programme for its aircraft carriers. *Abraham Lincoln* (CVN-72) is scheduled to be re-delivered to the Navy in 2016, with *George Washington* (CVN-73) taking her place at the Newport News shipyard after mooted plans to save on the substantial refuelling cost and retire her early were dropped.

Meanwhile *Gerald R Ford* (CVN-78), the first

ship of a new class, is also scheduled to be delivered in March 2016 for the start of her trials programme. However, with an estimated construction cost of US$12.9bn, the US Navy has admitted that it is looking at ways to reduce the cost of the second and third ships of the class, *John F Kennedy* (CVN-79) and *Enterprise* (CVN-80). Indeed, in March 2015, Sean Stackley, the Assistant Secretary of the Navy for Research, Development and Acquisition, told Congress that the Navy is also considering alternative carrier designs for following carriers to enable power-projection capability to be maintained at a more affordable price. So far as the *Ford* class is concerned, Rear Admiral Thomas Moore USN, the programme executive officer for aircraft carriers, told reporters in March 2015 that his office had decided that the expensive dual-band radar originally specified for the class would only be fitted in the first vessel. He also admitted that, with only one ship fitted with the equipment, the Navy may have difficulty keeping the system operable over *Ford*'s projected fifty-year service life. It may therefore be necessary to back-fit a different radar system at an early stage, although Moore said that the Navy would take that decision only when it had to. Northrop Grumman and Raytheon are already working on alternative new air-surveillance radar projects. The system ultimately selected will replace the current radars fitted in aircraft carriers and big-deck amphibious assault ships, starting with the as-yet un-named LHA-8, third ship of the

America class, followed by CVN-79 and CVN-80.

There are continuing concerns about *Ford*'s advanced arrester gear (AAG) system designed and built by General Atomics. Rear Admiral Moore has stated that a design flaw had been found in the 'water twister', a paddle wheel that is designed to absorb 70 per cent of an aircraft's landing energy. General Atomics was instructed to fix the problem and has provided a re-engineered unit which is undergoing jet-sled test at the naval air facility at Lakehurst, New Jersey. A replacement AAG has also already been installed in *Ford*. However, with tests with real aircraft not due to take place at Lakehurst until late in 2015 or early 2016, any further problems could delay the ship's scheduled delivery date. The electromagnetic aircraft launch system (EMALS) that is another new feature of the design also encountered problems that delayed development but, as of mid-2015, two of the four catapults had been installed in *Ford* and work on the other two was close to completion. Testing with dead-loads was due to begin in the summer of 2015 and Moore has indicated he feels confident that EMALS development is unlikely to delay the ship's delivery. That said, development timing remains on the critical path and software improvements are believed to be needed before the ship can launch strike fighters at maximum weight.[1]

Turning to aircraft, Table 4.1.1 sets out planned US Navy aircraft purchases contained in the FY2016 Presidential budget request. The total request for

The aircraft carrier *Abraham Lincoln* (CVN-72) being towed out of one of Newport News Shipbuilding's dry docks and into the James River in November 2014 on completion of the docking portion of her mid-life refuelling and complex overhaul (RCOH). She is due to re-join the US Navy in 2016 once final outfitting and testing is complete. *(Huntington Ingalls Industries)*

FY2016 of 124 aircraft is eleven fewer than that for the aircraft finally authorised in FY2015 and contains only four of the F-35C carrier variant of the Lightning II Joint Strike Fighter. Admiral Jon Greenert, the US Navy's Chief of Naval Operations (CNO), testified to Congress in March 2015 that the delay in bringing the F-35C to operational maturity is having a domino effect on naval strike fighter numbers.

The F-35C was originally intended to enter service in 2012, replacing legacy F/A-18A and C model Hornets. However, its prolonged development has required more F/A-18E/F Super Hornets to be procured to replace the earlier models at the end of their fatigue lives. When legacy Hornets reach 8,000 flight hours they are surveyed and the better airframes taken in hand for a service life extension programme (SLEP) intended to get them to 10,000 hours. No two aircraft require the same amount of work, adding substantial cost to the programme. In addition, the navy estimates that only 150 airframes will be suitable for SLEP. The US Navy wants to fill the gap in the short term by re-equipping further squadrons with Super Hornets that had originally been procured as long-term attrition replacements but this will inevitably increase fatigue life in the F/A-18E/F pool and exacerbate the shortage of fighters in the longer term. Rear Admiral Michael Manazir, the Director of Air Warfare, briefed Congress in April 2015 that Super Hornets may have to operate until 2040 and might therefore have to undergo their own SLEP in due course. Admiral Greenert has stressed that, with F-35C production not due to ramp up to twenty aircraft a year until

Table 4.1.1: US NAVY PLANNED AIRCRAFT PROCUREMENT: FY2015–FY2020

TYPE	MISSION	FY2015[1]	FY2016[2]	FY2017	FY2018	FY2019	FY2020	FYDP 2015–20[3]
Fixed Wing (Carrier Based)								
F-35B Lightning II JSF	Strike Fighter (STOVL)	6	9 (9)	14 (14)	20 (20)	20 (20)	20	83 (69)
F-35C Lightning II JSF	Strike Fighter (CV)	4	4 (2)	4 (6)	8 (10)	10 (16)	12	38 (38)
EA-18G Growler	Electronic Warfare	15	0 (0)	0 (0)	0 (0)	0 (0)	0	0 (15)
E-2D Advanced Hawkeye	Surveillance/Control	5	5 (5)	6 (6)	5 (5)	4 (5)	4	24 (26)
Fixed Wing (Land Based)								
P-8A Poseidon	Maritime Patrol	9	16 (15)	12 (13)	12 (13)	7 (7)	0	47 (57)
C-40A Clipper	Transport	0	0 (1)	0 (0)	0 (0)	0 (0)	0	0 (1)
KC-130J Hercules	Tanker	1	2 (1)	2 (2)	2 (1)	2 (1)	2	10 (6)
Rotary Wing								
AH-1Z/UH-1Y Viper/Venom	Attack/Utility	28	28 (28)	27 (26)	27 (26)	27 (27)	0	109 (135)
VH-92A	Presidential Transport	0	0 (0)	0 (0)	0 (0)	6 (6)	6	12 (6)
CH-53K Super Stallion	Heavy-Lift	0	0 (0)	0 (2)	4 (4)	7 (7)	13	26 (13)
MV-22B Osprey	Transport	19	19 (19)	18 (18)	8 (4)	8 (4)	8	61 (64)
MH-60R Seahawk	Sea Control	29	29 (0)	0 (0)	0 (0)	0 (0)	0	29 (29)
MH-60S Seahawk	Multi-Mission	8	0 (0)	0 (0)	0 (0)	0 (0)	0	0 (8)
Unmanned Aerial Vehicles								
MQ-8C Fire Scout	Reconnaissance	5	2 (0)	2 (0)	2 (0)	2 (0)	2	10 (5)
MQ-4 Triton	Maritime Patrol	0	3 (4)	3 (4)	4 (4)	4 (4)	4	18 (16)
RQ-21A Blackjack	Tactical reconnaissance	6	7 (0)	4 (1)	4 (2)	5 (5)	5	25 (14)
Totals:		135	124 (84)	94 (92)	96 (89)	102 (102)	76	492 (502)

Notes:
1. FY2015 base numbers relate to the authorised procurement programme. This varied quite significantly from the initial Presidential budget request for just 102 aircraft, with nearly half the numerical difference being accounted for by authorisation for an additional fifteen EA-18G Growler electronic warfare aircraft to keep Boeing's production line open for another year.
2. Numbers for 2016 to 2020 relate to base FY2016 budget plans; numbers in brackets reflect purchases for that year previously envisaged in the FY 2015 budget.
3. Future Years Defence Programme; numbers in brackets reflect FYDP for 2015–19 as adjusted for the authorised 2015 programme.

2020, the risk of a significant fighter 'gap' in the mid-2020s needs to be addressed. In May 2015, the US House of Representatives Appropriations Sub Committee reacted to Navy pressure by approving the addition of five F/A-18E/Fs Super Hornets (and seven EA-18G Growler electronic warfare aircraft) to its FY2016 spending bill to keep Boeing's production line open. However, it is not clear at this stage whether this proposal will ultimately be authorised.

Beyond 2030, the US Navy is examining the need for a next-generation strike fighter, the F/A-XX, to replace the Super Hornet and operate alongside the F-35C in its carrier air wings. Ray Mabus, Secretary of the Navy, speaking at the 2015 Sea-Air-Space Exposition, said that 'the F-35 should, and almost certainly will, be the last manned strike fighter that the . . . Navy will ever buy or fly'. This was not quite the line that had been taken by Admiral Greenert in February when he briefed the US Naval Institute

that F/A-XX should have 'interchangeable manned and unmanned options'. In his opinion, stealth capability was hardly worth its high cost and penetration of enemy air defences would be better achieved by suppressing or overwhelming them rather than trying to hide from them. Arguments and the analysis of alternative options will make interesting reading as they evolve.

In the meantime, US Navy enthusiasm for the projected unmanned carrier-launched air surveillance and strike system, UCLASS (provisionally designated the RAQ-25) seems to have diminished in the past year. This possibly reflects a lack of consensus between the Navy, which wants a specialised surveillance capability, and the US Congress, which argues that with surveillance assets such as the P-8A, E-2D, MQ-4C, MQ-8B/C and RQ-21A all either in service or approaching operational maturity, the Navy really needs long-range

strike platforms. The proposed in-service date for the new system has moved out to 2023 and the requirement will have to be balanced against the proposed F/A-XX.

Trials of the Northrop Grumman X-47B unmanned demonstrator programme have, however, continued into 2015. On 15 April 2015, a X-47B, call sign 'Salty Dog 502' successfully linked up with an airborne tanker aircraft, the first time an unmanned combat aircraft had ever done so. No fuel was passed on this occasion but a week later the X-47B successfully took on 4,000lb of fuel. Whilst this marked the end of the type's funded demonstration programme, the US Senate's Armed Service Committee has proposed additions to the FY2016 Defence Appropriations Bill that would allow them to continue flying in order to mature technologies that will be of benefit to a strike-oriented UCLASS. Two follow-on unmanned combat aircraft would also be procured as a step towards its aim of developing UCLASS into a long-range, penetrating strike system. The Navy still diverges from this view: Captain B V Duarte USN, the UCLASS project manager, briefed the US Naval Institute in early 2015 that the X-47 differs too much from the airframe that the Navy envisages to justify the expense of keeping it flying. However, Ray Mabus obviously believes that unmanned systems are becoming the 'new normal'. To reinforce his view he has created a new US Navy under-secretary post with specific responsibility for unmanned systems.

Theodore Roosevelt (CVN-71) began a round-the-world deployment in March 2015 with VAW-125, the first E-2D Advanced Hawkeye in an operational carrier air wing (as well as HS-11, the last legacy SH-60F Seahawk) squadron embarked. The EA-18G Growler has now replaced the EA-6B in all ten squadrons attached to carrier air wings and five other units have been re-equipped to support training and expeditionary operations ashore.

The Navy has decided to replace its C-2A Greyhound carrier on-board delivery (COD) aircraft with a modified version of the MV-22 Osprey tilt-rotor aircraft. A memorandum of understanding outlining the Navy's requirements and the level of support to be provided by the US Marine Corps has been agreed. Modifications include an extended range fuel system, high-frequency radio and a public address system to enable the crew to communicate with seated passengers. The Navy requires a range of 1,150 nautical miles without air-to-air refuelling under the environmental conditions commonly found in the Pacific theatre of operations. The present range fully loaded is 428 nautical miles but aircraft have flown over considerably greater distances with aerial refuelling. US Marine Corps Reserve pilots trained to fly the MV-22 are to join the first deployments in 2020 and, subsequently, the marines will train Navy air and ground crews to operate the type. The C-2A is expected to be phased out in the mid-2020s.

OTHER AIRCRAFT CARRIER OPERATORS

An agreement was announced during a visit to India by President Obama in January 2015 that the US Navy would co-operate with the Indian Navy on the development of aircraft carrier technology. India has recently accelerated design work on its planned second indigenous carrier, a project referred to as

The US Navy's X-47B unmanned demonstrator, call sign 'Salty Dog 502', receiving fuel from a tanker aircraft on 22 April 2015 whilst operating in the Atlantic Test Ranges over Chesapeake Bay. The test marked the first time an unmanned aircraft has refuelled in flight and also marked the end of the X-47B's funded demonstration programme. The course of the follow-on U CLASS carrier-launched air surveillance and strike system remains unclear. *(US Navy)*

An image of India's first indigenous aircraft carrier, *Vikrant*, being undocked from Cochin Shipyard in June 2015 after completion of underwater work. The inset is a computer-generated image of the completed ship at sea. *(Indian Navy)*

IAC-II, following the decision to withdraw *Viraat* (the former Royal Navy *Hermes*) from service after the international fleet review scheduled to be held in Vizag during February 2016.[2] Construction of the first indigenous carrier, the 40,000-ton INS *Vikrant* II, is already five years late and reportedly several US$ billions over budget so a working group established under the bilateral agreement with the United States is seen as a considerable boost for IAC-II. The Indian Navy has provisionally named the projected carrier *Vishnal* and envisages a nuclear-powered ship of c. 65,000 tons with electromagnetic catapults and advanced arrester gear. This clearly makes her a considerably more complicated ship to build than

the short take-off barrier-assisted recovery (STOBAR) configured *Vikrant*. The Indian Navy hopes that, with US Navy help, *Vishnal* could be in service by 2033. In April 2015 Frank Kendall, the US Department of Defence Chief of Procurement, announced that the United States would indeed be willing to sell aircraft carrier related technologies to India, including EMALS. Although it has not been explicitly stated, India's turn to the United States reflects both the US Navy's world lead in carrier technology and, perhaps also, considerable disappointment with the late delivery of the refurbished Russian carrier *Vikramaditya* and her poor reliability in service.

The French aircraft carrier, *Charles de Gaulle*, undertook two months of strike operations against the Islamic State in Iraq and Syria in the first half of 2015, during which her air wing of Rafale and Super Etendard-Mod. strike fighters, supported by E-2C Hawkeyes, flew an average of ten to fifteen sorties a day. Strike missions and surveillance flights were closely co-ordinated with US carrier aircraft from *Carl Vinson* (CVN-70) and *Theodore Roosevelt*. After her strike operations, the French carrier task force moved to the area of the Arabian Sea off Goa for exercises with the Indian Navy.

China continued to develop its carrier capability during 2015. There were unconfirmed reports that

Liaoning carried out exercises in Bohai Bay in April 2015 with a significant number of J-15 Flying Shark fighters embarked to increase their pilots' familiarity with carrier operations. The J-15 could reach limited operational status in 2016, with more embarked periods planned. These will also include Z-8YJ Black Cat airborne early warning and control (AEW&C) aircraft to bring the People's Liberation Army Naval Air Force's (PLANAF's) first embarked air wing closer to maturity. Derivatives of the French Super Frelon anti-submarine helicopter are already in service and available for operations. There have been frequent reports that the PLAN intends to construct a class of nuclear-powered strike carriers but no details have yet emerged and their design and construction would be a formidable task that will take a significant length of time to implement. Meanwhile, the Russian Navy continues to operate a single carrier, *Admiral Kuznetsov*, but she is able to do little more than maintain the 'state of the art'. The unit assigned to her, the 279th Independent Carrier-Based Fighter Air Regiment, only gets a trickle of new pilots every year and the majority fly barely enough hours annually to retain operational currency.

The British Royal Navy still has more than five years to wait for the restoration of an operational carrier strike capability but significant progress towards this aim has been made. *Queen Elizabeth* was named by Her Majesty The Queen on 4 July 2014. She was floated out later in the month and her sister-ship, *Prince of Wales,* is making rapid progress in the vacated dry dock. Diesel fuel was pumped into *Queen Elizabeth* in mid-2015 so that her own systems could be powered-up prior to structural completion in 2016. After that, the ship has an extensive trials programme planned that will include three periods of fixed-wing trials, all of them in United States waters to use facilities that do not exist in the United Kingdom. The first is due in late 2018, with 17 Squadron, the British trials unit, embarked. The third will culminate in late 2020 with an operational readiness inspection for 617 Squadron which is to be manned, like 17 Squadron, with alternate Royal Navy and Royal Air Force

An overhead view of the French carrier *Charles de Gaulle*. She undertook a further deployment to the Middle East in the first half of 2015 with an air wing of Rafale M and Super Etendard-Mod. Jets and E-2C Hawkeye early warning aircraft embarked. The Super Etendards are expected to be withdrawn from French service during 2016.
(Alex Paringaux via Dassault Aviation)

Above: The new British aircraft carrier *Queen Elizabeth* being towed to her fitting-out birth following float-out from her building dock at Babcock's Rosyth facility on 17 July 2014. Work on her sister, *Prince of Wales*, is already making good progress in the vacated dock. It is anticipated that *Queen Elizabeth* will be able to deploy an operational squadron of F-35B jets by late 2020, albeit this is unlikely to comprise more than nine aircraft. *(Crown Copyright 2014)*

Right: A computer-generated image of a Merlin HM 2 helicopter fitted with Thales' Searchwater radar. A modified version of the radar and associated Cerberus mission system currently used in the Sea King ASaC 7 helicopter has been selected to provide the heart of the new airborne surveillance system destined for the new British carriers under the Crowsnest project. *(Thales UK)*

(RAF) commanding officers. The operational squadron is unlikely, at least initially, to deploy more than nine aircraft at any one time.

An ongoing AEW&C capability for the new carriers is being assured by the decision that the Sea King ASaC 7s of 849 Naval Air Squadron (NAS) are to run on until the end of 2018, two years after all other Sea Kings are withdrawn from service at the end of March 2016. Further clarity with respect to the replacement 'Crowsnest' project to fit Merlin HM 2 helicopters with role-change equipment suited to the airborne surveillance and control mission was provided in an announcement on 22 May 2015 that Thales had been selected as the chosen bidder to provide the radar and mission system at the heart of the capability. Their solution will essentially be an upgrade of the Searchwater radar and Cerberus mission system fitted to the existing Sea Kings. There is more uncertainty as to how a limited number of modernised Merlin airframes – and associated aircrew – will be able to cover airborne surveillance, anti-submarine and surface warfare roles concurrently.[3]

F-35 LIGHTNING II PROGRESS

2015 will see VMFA-121, the 'Green Knights', based at Marine Corps Air Station (MCAS) Yuma reach initial operational capability. Their aircraft have Block 2B software, which does not include the capacity to use external weapons stations and gives only limited use of internal weapons, surveillance and combat manoeuvring capability. This is deemed good enough to give the US Marines a close-air support capability in the short term. A second squadron, VMFAT-501, the 'Warlords', at MCAS Beaufort trains both USMC and British pilots and ground crews. Block 3F software, which is still in development, is to be the version used by all US Navy and British F-35s from 2019 and by all previous versions after that as they are upgraded. It will allow greater combat capability than 2B, including the use of a wider range of external and internal weapons and the full transfer of imagery and data. The US Navy has formed a training unit for the F-35C, VFA-101, the 'Grim Reapers', but is not expecting to achieve initial operational capability until late 2018 or early 2019.

The F-35 is completely reliant on the autonomous logistics information system (ALIS) for the management of flight operations; planned and un-planned maintenance; aircraft diagnostics and

Initial at-sea trials of the F-35C carrier variant of the Lockheed Martin Lightning II Joint Strike Fighter took place aboard *Nimitz* (CVN-68) off the Californian Coast in November 2014. The US Navy formed a training unit, VFA-101, for the F35-C type in 2012 but initial operational capability is only expected in the 2018/19 timeframe. *(Lockheed Martin)*

repair; supply chain management; both pilot and technical training and qualification; and individual aircraft documentation. Development of this system has been far from trouble-free. Data is transferred by Wi-Fi between aircraft and laptop computers known as portable maintenance aids (PMAs), which form part of the ship and squadron operating kit. This also includes standard operating unit servers, paperless manuals, maintenance, low-observable management and mission planning software. Data from the server is sent to a central location in each F-35 user country known as the central point of entry (CPE). In 2016 the American CPE is at Eglin Air Force Base and, eventually, the British CPE will be at the Joint Forces Base at Marham. Core data is passed to the Global Sustainment System (GSS) run by Lockheed Martin at Fort Worth to provide maintenance data for the whole fleet. However, individual user nations cannot interrogate each other's data.

Before a sortie, mission planning data is worked out on PMAs and downloaded into aircraft mission systems. These, in turn, provide weapon load and fuel state data to the maintenance teams. ALIS calls up routine aircraft inspections and is constantly updated with information from the CPE to ensure that all operational information is maintained at the latest, uniform standard. Faulty aircraft send a coded message to the PMA together with 'troubleshooting' information, a video of the appropriate procedure to fix the problem and order any necessary components 'just in time' for use. ALIS also checks that the technician doing the work has the appropriate qualification. Information about every fault is passed to the GSS to be added to the total understanding of aircraft systems and their support. ALIS can be used for short periods without connection to the CPE but will not receive updated information. This may limit operations at remote sites.

Problems have stemmed from the fact that ALIS has never worked as anticipated. Early in 2015, US Department of Defence officials described it as a 'dysfunctional automated system that needs to undergo considerable evolution before it can be considered reliable'. Sean Stackley, Assistant Secretary of the Navy for Research, Development and Acquisition, told the House Armed Services Committee in April 2015 that the operations and sustainment plan for the F-35 had to be evolved and improved in order 'to do better than what US lawmakers had been hearing from maintainers on the flight line'. His comments followed a visit by Congressmen to Eglin Air Force Base, where personnel had complained of an 80 per cent failure rate by ALIS that required innovative 'work-round' solutions to allow the aircraft to fly. The supposedly portable system was too bulky for deployment to the *Wasp* (LHD-1) for F-35B trials and a 'lightweight' improvement is being produced as a matter of urgency. On a more positive note, deck landing trials with the F-35C went well at the end of 2014, confirming that the revised hook design and the aircraft's innovative integrated direct lift control on final approach to the deck are very successful.

BIG-DECK AMPHIBIOUS SHIPS AND THEIR AIRCRAFT

The British *Queen Elizabeth* class ships have evolved into big-deck, multi-purpose vessels with amphibious as well as strike capability. The US Navy's new *America* class LHA type amphibious assault ships have similar 'cross-over' capabilities but enjoy much better accommodation for marines and their equipment in addition to their ability to embark a significant number of F-35Bs. *America* (LHA-6) carried out an extensive first-of-class trials programme in 2015, which Captain Chris Mercer USN, amphibious programme manager at the Naval Sea Systems Command, described as going very well across the board. Overall, only about half the normal quantity of defects was encountered. After a post-trial shake-down she will carry out operational preparations centred on US Marine Corps evaluations of how best to make use of her enhanced aviation facilities since, unlike previous amphibious assault ships, she has no well deck and is intended to operate from further off shore. She is expected to take part in the 2016 RIMPAC international exercise with an air wing of AV-8B Harriers and MV-22 Ospreys. Her sister-ship, *Tripoli* (LHA-7), is 25 per

cent complete and due for delivery in 2018 with modifications made to her flight deck during build to enable her to operate F-35B Lightnings from the outset. These will be back-fitted to *America* during an early refit. A third, as yet un-named ship of the class, LHA-8, is projected and will differ in re-introducing a well deck to allow surface as well as airborne assault operations. She will also have an improved command, control and communications outfit. After more than a decade since her last deployment and a period spent as a test platform for F-35B deck operating trials, *Wasp* joined an amphibious ready group in 2015 after her combat systems had been upgraded with the latest fleet standard ship self-defence system (SSDS). In May 2015 she carried out the first operational trials for any F-35 variant when six F-35Bs from VMFA-121 and VMFAT-501 embarked for an exercise off the eastern coast of the United States. These evaluated the full spectrum of F-35B effectiveness, including maintenance and logistical supply chain support at sea during operations by day and night.

The US Marine Corps has heralded the F-35B's initial entry into operational service by outlining its

new concept of operations or 'conops' for the type. This will involve using mobile forward arming and refuelling points known as M-Farps to support small groups of F-35Bs, which would return to USN or allied amphibious carriers for routine maintenance. Interestingly, the new scheme was explained by Lieutenant General John Davis USMC, the Deputy Commandant for Aviation, at a conference in London and *Queen Elizabeth* was mentioned specifically in this context. The new conops is intended to address concerns that an amphibious force operating within 150 nautical miles of a hostile coast would be vulnerable to attack by lethal and elusive ground-mobile missile systems and easily tracked by small, unmanned air vehicles. It would allow the big-deck ships to remain outside anti-access missile range because they would be launching aircraft for movement to M-Farps rather than running a close-air support flying programme. The conventional forward operating bases (FOBs) used previously by the Marines are now considered too big and vulnerable but M-Farps will be smaller and more nimble, moving every 24 to 48 hours, a time-frame believed to be outside the average enemy targeting cycle.

The new US Navy LHA type amphibious assault ship *America* (LHA-6) seen off the coast of San Diego in February 2015. Different from previous US Navy amphibious assault ships in omitting the traditional well deck, she has been undergoing an extensive first-of-class trials programme. *(US Navy)*

The plan resembles the way the RAF planned to operate Harriers in Germany during the last years of the Cold War which hoped to use sites known as war locations or 'warlocs' for dispersed operations. However, the new USMC plan appears to place great emphasis on the new Sikorsky CH-53K King Stallion, an asset not available during the Cold War. It first flew in 2015 and is due to enter operational service in 2019 with three times the external load-lifting capacity of the CH-53E that it will replace; it is designed to carry a 27,000lb load over a mission radius of 110 nautical miles, making it the essential asset for M-Farp mobility. Neither the CH-53K nor the MV-22, some of which the Marines plan to use as in-flight-refuelling tankers, are stealthy, however, and the operation of these types together with F-35Bs in the vicinity of M-Farps would seem to make the latter's very expensive stealth characteristics pointless. M-Farp operations would also need to be defended against attack by Special Forces or even insurgents armed with man-portable missile systems. A perimeter would therefore need to be held by marine infantry who would have to be moved with the aviation support element, increasing the transfer's size and complexity.[4] M-Farps, if they are adopted, must be far more vulnerable than an LHA positioned 150 miles off the coast behind a layered system of defence. The ship also can generate a much higher sortie rate besides simplifying maintenance and battle-damage repair opportunities. It will be interesting to see if British plans for the Joint Lightning Force follow the USMC concept.

In the meantime, the US Marine Corps will enter 2016 with six AV-8B Harrier squadrons and a training unit. It expects the type to remain in service well into the 2020s. Conversely, the CH-46E Sea Knight, affectionately known as the 'Phrog', reached the end of its fifty-year active duty career in 2015, however. Appropriately the last unit to transition to the MV-22 Osprey was Marine Medium Helicopter Training Squadron MMHT-164, the 'Knight Riders', at Camp Pendleton, California which had also been the first to operate the 'Phrog'.

France halted the sale of two *Mistral* class amphibious helicopter carriers to Russia in late 2014 as part of an embargo put in place after the latter's

In May 2015, six F-35B STOVL variants of the Lightning II Joint Strike Fighter embarked on *Wasp* (LHD-1) off the eastern coast of the United States for the first operational trials of the type. British Royal Navy and Royal Air Force personnel were reported to have participated in the two-week long series of tests. The US Marine Corps were anticipated to reach initial operating capability with the type later in 2015. *(US Navy)*

A US Marine Corps AV-8B Harrier lands on the amphibious assault ship *Boxer* (LHD-4) in March 2015. The US Marine Corps will enter 2016 with six Harrier squadrons and a training unit, with the type expected to serve well into the 2020s. *(US Navy)*

annexation of the Crimean peninsula and continuing support for rebels in Ukraine. A group of sailors had been in France learning to operate the first, *Vladivostok*, but they returned to Russia in December 2014. The second, *Sevastopol*, carried out her initial sea trials with a civilian crew in March 2015. In April 2015 the Russian news agency TASS reported that France had announced its intention to retain the two ships and sell them to a third party of its choosing. Russia had already paid US$811m for the ships and France has reportedly offered $1.2bn in compensation for its termination of the deal. There are several potential customers for the two 21,000-ton ships. Meanwhile, in Russia, Kamov carried out the delayed first flight of the Ka-52K 'Katran' (Dogfish) attack helicopter, intended to operate from these ships, in March 2015. They have folding rotors and stub wings and, among many weapons options, they are capable of being fitted with Kh-35 anti-ship missiles. Now that the helicopter carriers will no longer be delivered, it is believed that Russian Naval Aviation intends to deploy them to a newly-formed shore-based attack helicopter squadron at Elizovo on the Kamchatka peninsula, where they will come under

The modified *Mistral* type amphibious assault ships *Vladivostok* and *Sevastopol* built in France for Russia are now both complete and have undertaken sea trials. However, it is unlikely Russia will ever take delivery of the ships. *(Bruno Huriet)*

The Royal Australian Navy has been steadily working up its new amphibious assault ship, *Canberra*, to full operational capability. This dramatic image shows night flying trials with a MRH90 helicopter whilst the ship was sailing off the coast of Queensland. *(Royal Australian Navy)*

the command of the Russian Pacific Fleet.

As is the case for the United Kingdom, Australia is due to carry out a Defence Review in the latter part of 2015. It has been studying the option of buying a small number of F-35Bs for embarked operations in addition to the F-35As already planned for the Royal Australian Air Force (RAAF). Arguments to date have been finely balanced but those in favour of the scheme make the valid point that resistance to any future Australian amphibious operation will make viable, 'on hand' air support essential. Whatever the outcome of the debate, *Canberra* – the first of the Royal Australian Navy's (RAN's) new class of LHD-type amphibious assault

ships – will be fully operational by 2016 and capable of embarking a tailored air wing made up from RAN SH-60R Seahawks, RAN and Army multi-role helicopters, and Army Tiger attack helicopters. She would also, in theory, be able to operate US Marine Corps F-35Bs in a coalition operation and her potential use may be included in the USMC conops in future. *Adelaide*, her sister-ship, will soon be carrying out trials before joining the fleet before the end of 2016.

Turning to the United Kingdom, 846 NAS returned to Royal Naval Air Station (RNAS) Yeovilton in March 2015 with six Merlin HC3 helicopters, having previously re-commissioned at RAF

Benson in 2014. Later in the year a Flight of 845 NAS will re-form with Merlins from the disbanded 28 Squadron RAF and follow 846 NAS to Yeovilton, ending the operational service of the Merlin HC3 with the RAF. The remainder of 845 NAS will continue to operate a residual force of eleven Sea King HC4s to provide the embarked capability that the Merlin HC3 lacks until 31 March 2016, when the type will be withdrawn from service. In early 2015 AgustaWestland began work to convert seven Merlin HC3s to HC3 (interim) standard for delivery in November 2015. The work will allow them to be cleared for embarked operation and includes the installation of a power-folding main rotor system taken from surplus Merlin HM1 airframes in storage, and an undercarriage modified to allow safe deck operations and lashing points. These will become operational from March 2016. Eventually, the plan is to convert the whole fleet of twenty-five Merlin HC3, HC3A and H 3(i) to an upgraded H4 standard with power-folding main rotors, a folding tail pylon and a 'glass' cockpit similar to those fitted in the Merlin HM2. The work will be carried out in two phases, with nine aircraft in the first phase and the remaining sixteen in the second. Operational capability with the full force will not, however, be achieved until March 2022 so a fully-capable Royal Navy commando helicopter force is still a long way off. The re-equipped force will comprise three squadrons; 847 NAS with six Wildcat AH1s, and 845 and 846 NAS with ten Merlins each. Five additional Merlins will be held as attrition reserves and to replace aircraft that require deep maintenance. 845 NAS is to be capable of deploying three 'go-anywhere' flights whilst 846 NAS will contain the operational conversion flight, a specialised maritime counter-terrorist flight, and a third 'go-anywhere' flight to back up 845 NAS if required.

SEA CONTROL HELICOPTERS

The US Navy frigate *Gary* (FFG-51) returned home to San Diego in April 2015 after a seven-month deployment. She was the last west-coast based frigate in service and had embarked the last active-duty SH-60B Seahawk detachment. A 'sundown' ceremony at NAS North Island marked the legacy type's formal retirement from service in May. Production of the replacement MH-60R model for US Navy service is being continued for a further year after an ill-judged attempt to terminate a multi-year purchase early was abandoned but FY2016 appropriations are likely be the last for the type.

Turning to the future, the US Navy carried out deck landing trials with a development MQ-8C Fire Scout unmanned helicopter on the Flight IIA *Arleigh Burke* class destroyer *Jason Dunham* (DDG-109) in December 2014. A total of twenty-two landings and take-offs was carried out, all of them successfully, taking the type a stage nearer operational capability. This is expected in 2016, after which the 'C' will begin to replace the earlier 'B' model in deployed flights. Both have the same avionics but the 'C' is based on the larger Bell Jet

Ranger airframe and will, therefore, have superior endurance and load-carrying capabilities. Meanwhile, the first composite detachment of manned and unmanned rotary aircraft was deployed to the western Pacific in *Fort Worth* (LCS-3) in early 2015. Comprising a MH-60R Seahawk and a MQ-8B Fire Scout, the unit was fully operational but tasked additionally with evaluating the best way of using the two aircraft systems to enhance the ship's effectiveness. The detachment had four pilots, all trained to fly both the MH-60R and the MQ-8B, the latter from a console in the ship's combat information centre. Examples of the detachment's capability include the use of the MQ-8B to locate a surface target and then illuminate it with its laser designator for AGM-114 Hellfire missiles launched by the MH-60R. For long-term surface surveillance or shadowing missions, the MQ-8B is more effective than the MH-60R because single pilots can operate a watch routine at the control console for considerable periods. Conversely, the manned helicopter has proved more effective in dynamic combat situations but needs two pilots and crew fatigue can become a factor more quickly.

The new 27,000-ton Japanese helicopter carrier *Izumo* continues to attract attention. Comparable in size to the Italian *Cavour* and larger than the former Spanish *Principe de Asturias* and British *Invincible* class, she could potentially be modified to operate F-35B strike fighters. However, the Japanese Government has announced no intention of doing so, despite Prime Minister Shinzo Abe's policy of loosening the constraints on Japan's pacifist post-war constitution. Her anticipated air wing comprises seven SH-60K Seahawks and seven MCM-101 mine-countermeasure helicopters but analysts at the US Naval Institute calculate that she has the capacity to operate up to twenty-seven aircraft, including MV-22s and F-35Bs. In addition to the air wing she has accommodation for 400 troops or personnel for use in humanitarian relief missions. A sister-ship, as yet unnamed, is under construction for completion in 2017.

The New Zealand Defence Force formally accepted its first two Kaman SH-2G(I) helicopters from Kaman Aerospace in March 2015 Eight aircraft have been procured to replace the SH-2G versions formerly in service. They are the aircraft originally built for, but subsequently rejected by, the RAN and have been brought to a viable operational standard by Kaman. The Royal New Zealand Navy

Deck landing trials of the enhanced MQ-8C variant of the Fire Scout unmanned helicopter were carried out on the destroyer *Jason Dunham* (DDG-109) in December 2014. The MQ-8C retains the same avionics installed in the earlier MQ-8B but has superior endurance and load-carrying abilities. (*Northrop Grumman*)

Chief of Navy, Rear Admiral Jack Steer, said at the handover that the aircraft marked a significant milestone for New Zealand's maritime capability. All eight are to be in service by 2016, operated jointly by naval pilots and observers with air force engineers as part of 6 Squadron based at Royal New Zealand Air Force Whenuapai.

By 2016, the new AgustaWestland AW159 Wildcat HMA2 will equip two front-line squadrons shore-based at RNAS Yeovilton. 702 and 700W NAS were both absorbed into a re-commissioned 825 NAS in August 2014 and the new unit is responsible for Wildcat training and operational development. It will also deploy the first four operational flights. 815 NAS has begun to convert aircrew and maintainers from the Lynx to the Wildcat and will take over the parenting of deployed flights from 2016. Delays in procuring new missiles for use on the Wildcat, known as the future air-to-surface missiles (heavy) and (light), has meant that a small number of Lynx HMA8 helicopters will be retained by 815 NAS, together with their Sea Skua missiles, until March 2017. There will then be a gap in surface-ship helicopter strike capability until the new missiles become available at some time after 2020. Deliveries of AW159s to South Korea are also underway, with both the Philippines and Vietnam also reportedly interested in the type.

The Royal Navy continues to deploy a small number of ScanEagle UAV detachments in the Gulf. They are provided by Boeing under a 'contractor owned and operated' deal and deployed by 700X NAS, which provides an RN safety officer trained to 'fly' the air vehicle from a console in the operations room. They provide real-time reconnaissance from frigates and auxiliaries out to 50 nautical miles or for up to twelve hours airborne. In mid-2015, consideration was also being given to operating them in the Mediterranean to search for migrant boats making the perilous passage from Africa to Europe. AgustaWestland had a contract from the United Kingdom Ministry of Defence in 2015 to evaluate future unmanned or optionally-manned helicopters to supplement the Wildcat and Merlin HM2 in Royal Navy service.

The RAN formed 725 NAS, its first MH-60R Seahawk unit, at NAS Jacksonville in Florida to convert aircrew and maintainers onto the new type alongside their US Navy counterparts prior to the arrival of the first MH-60Rs in Australia late in 2014. First of class trials subsequently took place on

The Royal New Zealand Navy has been taking delivery of upgraded Kaman SH-2G(I) Seasprite helicopters throughout 2015 to replace its earlier variant of the type. Three had been delivered by early March 2015, with a further five due by September. All eight were expected to be operational by 2016. *(Royal New Zealand Navy)*

A Wildcat helicopter from 825 Naval Air Squadron pictured flying over the English Channel in September 2014. The squadron is temporarily responsible for deploying operational flights until 815 NAS assumes this responsibility in 2016. The new helicopter made its first operational deployment when it embarked on the Type 23 frigate *Lancaster* for a nine-month Atlantic patrol in March 2015. *(Crown Copyright 2014)*

Perth early in 2015. 725 NAS was subsequently formally commissioned on 12 June 2015 at its long term base at RANAS Nowra, where it will continue the training task and support the first two operational flights. 816 NAS, which operates the legacy S-70B-2 version of the Seahawk, began conversion in 2015 and will take over the operational task of parenting MH-60R flights from 2016. The RAN's new 'Romeos' are identical to the USN standard on delivery but several improvements are planned during their first deep maintenance periods, some of which have also been adopted for incorporation in USN aircraft in due course. The Seahawk continues to pick up other export customers, being selected for the Indian Navy's multi-role helicopter requirement in December 2014 and approved for sale to Saudi Arabia.

Production of the NFH variant of the NH90 helicopter continues, with past reliability and corrosion issues being steadily overcome. The Royal Netherlands Navy resumed deliveries at the end of 2014 after reaching agreement with the manufac-

turers on remedial action following the discovery of undue corrosion on two helicopters that had been deployed at sea.

MARITIME PATROL AIRCRAFT: A DETAILED REVIEW

Alone among the major and medium naval powers, the United Kingdom had no maritime patrol aircraft in service after the withdrawal of the Nimrod MR 2 and the cancellation of the much-delayed Nimrod MRA 4 in the 2010 Strategic Defence & Security Review (SDSR). It is widely believed that this shortcoming will be addressed in the 2015 SDSR but whether this will happen – and, if so, the aircraft selected – will not be known until the end of 2015. The one certainty is that the United Kingdom cannot afford the risk and cost of a unique, national project like the Nimrod MRA 4. If it does decide to restore the capability it must procure an operational system 'off the shelf' from a source with which it can share training and support.

In the meantime, the following 'high end'

maritime patrol aircraft are in service around the world.

P-3C Orion: The P-3 Orion has been in service with the US Navy since 1962 and exported to eighteen countries. Arguably the United Kingdom should have bought into the project a long time ago like the Commonwealth air forces of Australia, Canada and New Zealand. Over 700 P-3s were manufactured, with around 550 going to the US Navy, which constantly upgraded the type from the original P-3A to the current P-3C update 4. The aircraft remaining in US Navy service are equipped with AN/APY-10 radar with inverse synthetic aperture radar (ISAR) and synthetic aperture radar (SAR) modes to provide imaging, detection, classification and identification of ships and overland surveillance. Other equipment includes ultra highresolution infra-red and optical imaging cameras; passive, active and multi-static sonobuoys; and electronic support measures. Sonobuoys are carried in launch tubes aft of the wing and there is a bomb-bay

Table 4.1.2: REPRESENTATIVE MARITIME PATROL AIRCRAFT

AIRCRAFT[1]	P-3C ORION	P-8A POSEIDON	BREGUET ATLANTIQUE 2	IL-38 'MAY'	TU-142M 'BEAR'	KAWASAKI P-1
Manufacturer	Lockheed Martin	Boeing	SECBAT/Dassault	Ilyushin	Tupolev	Kawasaki
Country	United States	United States	France[2]	Russia	Russia	Japan
Length	35.6m	39.5m	31.7m	40.2m	49.5m	38.0m
Wingspan	30.4m	37.6m	37.5m	37.4m	51.1m	35.4m
Max Take-off Weight	63,000kg	86,000kg	46,000kg	66,000kg	188,000kg	80,000kg
Engines[3]	4 x Allison T-56 A14 TP	2 x CFM56-7B TF	2 x RR Tyne Mk21 TP	4 x Ivchencko AI 20M TP	4 x Kuznetsov NK-12M TP	4 x IHI F7 TF
	3,700 Kw each	120 kN thrust each	4,500 Kw each	3,200 Kw each	11,000 Kw each	60 kN thrust each
Maximum Speed	410 knots (750km/h)	490 knots (900km/h)	350 knots (650km/h)	350 knots (650km/h)	500 knots (925km/h)	540 knots (1000km/h)
Max Altitude	28,000ft (8,500m)	41,000ft (12,500m)	30,000 ft (9,100m)	36,000ft (11,000m)	44,000ft (13,500m)	44,000ft (13,500m)
Range	3 hours on station	4 hours on station	4 hours on station	4,000nm maximum	7,000nm maximum	4,300nm maximum
	1,350nm from base	1,200nm from base	1,500nm from base			
Endurance	16 hours	10.5 hours	18 hours	13 hours	17 hours	10 hours
Weapons	Total 9,000kg	Total 9,000kg	Total 3,600kg	Total 9,000kg	Total 20,000kg	Total 9,000kg
	AGM-65 Maverick	AGM-65 Maverick	AM39 Exocet	Freefall bombs	AS-17 Krypton	AGM-56 Maverick
	AGM-84D Harpoon	AGM-84D Harpoon	GBU-12 LGB	Torpedoes	Torpedoes	AGM-84D Harpoon
	AGM-84K SLAM ER	AGM-84K SLAM ER	MU-90 torpedoes	Depth charges & mines	2 x 23mm canon	ASM-IC
	Mk 54 torpedoes	Mk 54 torpedoes	Depth charges & mines		Depth charges & mines	Torpedoes
	Depth charges & mines	Depth charges & mines				Depth charges & mines
Crew	11	9	12	8	10	13

Notes:

1. Data has been compiled from manufacturers' documentation and other publicly available information. Due to considerable variations in published information, data should be regarded as indicative only.

2. Original Atlantic produced by a multi-national consortium.

3. TF = turbofan; TP = turboprop.

forward of the wing capable of carrying up to 3,636kg of weapons including depth charges, Mk 54 torpedoes, mines and other weapons. A further total of 5,454kg can be carried on six underwing hard-points including AGM-65 Maverick, AGM-84D Harpoon and AGM-84K SLAM-ER air-to-surface missiles. There are currently twelve US Navy P-3C units that have yet to complete the conversion to the new P-8A Poseidon.[5]

P-8A Poseidon: As its P-3C fleet began to run out of fatigue life early in the twenty-first century, the US Navy set in train a project to produce a replacement, multi-mission aircraft. The winning submission, selected in 2004, was the Boeing P-8A Poseidon. It is based on the 737 series 800 airframe and series 900 wings, giving large scale economies through airframes and engine commonality with these civil types. The US Navy programme of record calls for the production of 117 aircraft and initial operational capability was achieved on target in 2013. As of mid-2015, four squadrons – VP-5 'Mad Foxes', VP-8 'Tigers', VP-16 'War Eagles' and VP-45 'Pelicans' – had been re-equipped with the new aircraft, to be followed later in the year by VP-26 'Tridents'.[6] Aircraft were produced in low-rate initial batches until 2014 when a contract was signed for the first full-production batch with eight aircraft for the US Navy and four for Australia. The P-8A has the same sensors as the P-3C with the addition of a CAE advanced, integrated magnetic anomaly detector (MAD), an AN/ALQ-213(V) electronic warfare management system and a BAE Systems countermeasure dispenser. They are accessed through an integrated, open-architecture system with 'glass' screens at every crew station, including those of the pilots, which are compatible with the installation of future upgrades. To conserve fuel the P-8A patrols at high altitude and, to facilitate this, a new range of sonobuoys and weapons have been developed that can be dropped from the new operational altitudes. These include the high-altitude anti-submarine warfare weapon capability (HAAWC), a variant of the Mark 54 torpedo fitted with precision wing kits. This leveraged proven technologies already designed for weapons such as the joint direct attack munition and small-diameter bomb to reduce development risk and cut cost for the Navy. HAAWC offers a number of advantages including the ability to be released at considerably greater range from a target than a low-level drop allowing

A Norwegian P-3N Orion pictured making a landing approach in March 2015. The P-3 Orion has been in service since 1962 and was exported to eighteen countries. Although steadily being replaced by the P-8A Poseidon, the P-3C variant currently remains the most numerous US Navy MPA. *(Nis P Skipnes / Norwegian Armed Forces)*

Boeing's P-8A Poseidon production line. The fact the type is derived from a civil aircraft, as well as the significant quantities of the aircraft ordered by the US Navy, offers other customers the possibility of economies of scale. Australia and India have already placed orders. *(Boeing)*

The unmanned Northrop Grumman MQ-4C Triton is intended to complement the US Navy's P-8A Poseidon fleet in service by using a succession of aircraft to fly designated orbits to monitor very large areas of ocean. This September 2014 photograph shows the type on its first transit flight from Northrop Grumman's factory in Palmdale California to the NAS at Patuxent River.in Maryland, where it will undergo further testing. *(US Navy)*

A French Breguet Atlantique 2 maritime patrol aircraft at Sola airbase in Norway on 5 May 2015 whilst participating in NATO's anti-submarine warfare exercise 'Dynamic Mongoose'. Although the basic airframe traces its origins to the 1960s, the type has been progressively modernised and continues to give France's Marine Nationale a credible MPA capability. *(NATO)*

the aircraft to remain outside the threat zone of short-range anti-aircraft missile systems.

The P-8A has already earned export success with the first of eight P-8Is being delivered to the Indian Navy at INAS Rajali in 2013 in addition to the initial RAAF order. The P-8I incorporates sensors, command, control and communications systems designed in India but the RAAF aircraft will closely resemble the US Navy specification. If the United Kingdom does decide to restore a maritime patrol aircraft capability in the 2015 SDSR, the most logical choice given the close relationship between the UK and the United States with respect to carrier-borne aviation would be a buy of P-8A aircraft, perhaps starting with a leasing arrangement for an initial four before purchasing a larger batch outright. Given the British Government's determination to operate the F-35B Lightning Force as a joint organ-isation, it would also be logical to operate P-8As as a joint force to capitalise on the skills of the Royal Navy as well as those of the RAF, which formerly operated the Nimrods.

MQ-4C Triton: The unmanned MQ-4C is intended to complement the P-8A in service in a mission described as broad area maritime surveil-lance (BAMS). This involves a succession of aircraft maintaining designated orbits over large areas of ocean and transmitting real-time intelligence, surveillance and reconnaissance (ISR) data to a command centre in the United States and to task forces at sea. The first air vehicle flew in 2013 and VUP-19 Squadron, the 'Big Red', has been formed at NAS Jacksonville to participate in development and bring the new system into operational service from 2017. A second unit, VUP-11, formed at NAS Whidbey Island in 2015. Both units will deploy detachments to FOBS from where the air vehicles will be launched for transit to their orbits; flying autonomous flight paths and descending from high altitude when necessary to identify surface contacts positively. Control whilst on task is to be exercised from a remote command centre in the United States which can, if necessary, re-task the aircraft. The US Navy plans to procure sixty-eight Tritons. A batch will also be ordered by Australia, which intends to operate a P-8A/MQ-4C partnership like the US Navy. The Indian Navy has also shown interest in procuring the type.

Individual MQ-4Cs are designed for a 51,000-hour fatigue life and, with no human limitations, are capable of spending 80 per cent of their time airborne. They carry no weapons but sensors include a multi-function active-sensor electronically-steered array radar, an electro-optical/infrared sensor, automatic identification system (AIS) receiver and a AN/ZLQ-1 electronic support measure package. This uses a 'library' of known specific emitters to identify and track radar contacts of interest. The payload also includes communications relay equipment and Link 16 to facilitate secure communications links between surface ships. The MTS-B multispectral targeting system carries out automatic target tracking and gives high-resolution imagery at multiple field-of-views and full motion video outputs. The air vehicle is controlled (but not flown) on task by a team of four at the command centre comprising a mission commander, vehicle operator and two sensor operators. Detachments will operate from forward bases where a launch and recovery element (LRE) will control ground support equipment and co-ordinate landing and take-off operations. Co-located with the LRE will be a mission control element (MCE), for mission planning, image processing and communications monitoring. Should the new United Kingdom Government decide to restore a maritime patrol capability in its 2015 SDSR it will be interesting to see if it elects to follow the US Navy and Australian lead and procure the MQ-4C. Its cost-effective operation offers many advantages not least in the remote waters of the South Atlantic where the United Kingdom maintains considerable interest in the defence of the Falkland Islands.

Breguet Atlantique 2: Developed from 1958 in response to a NATO Requirement for a long-range maritime patrol aircraft, the Atlantique was constructed by a multi-national consortium and the first flew in 1961. An early version entered service with the French *Aeronavale* in 1965 and the type achieved limited export success, with aircraft sold to the German, Italian, Netherlands and Pakistan naval air arms. It evolved progressively through ATL1 and ATL2 standards and twenty-two of the latter (out of twenty-eight delivered) remain in service with the *Aeronavale*. It has a crew of twelve with seven tactical stations. Sensors include a Thales Iguane multi-mode radar which incorporates track-while-scan and IFF capabilities. A forward-looking infrared sensor under the nose allows search, detection and tracking of surface contacts out to 100 nautical miles and

A Russian Il-20M 'Coot' electronic intelligence aircraft pictured in 2015. The Il-38 'May' maritime patrol aircraft, which is used by the Russian Navy for reconnaissance work in the littorals, has a common airframe, with both types being derived from the 1950s Ilyushin Il-18 turboprop airliner. *(Crown Copyright 2014)*

camera systems provide a vertical and oblique photography capability. An MAD is fitted in the tail and the DSAX 1 Sadang acoustic data processing system can monitor up to sixty-four sonobuoy channels simultaneously. The aircraft has an ARAR 13A ESM suite which automatically detects, tracks and identifies radar signals using its own signature library. Weapons can be carried in an internal bombbay or on underwing hardpoints and can include a mix of up to two AM 39 Exocet air-to-surface missiles or eight MU-90 torpedoes, GBU-12 laser-guided bombs, depth charges and mines. The aircraft are operated by two units, Flotilles 21F and 23F. Fifteen aircraft are undergoing an upgrade programme to further improve their mission systems and avionics.

Ilyushin Il-38 'May': The Il-38, given the NATO reporting name 'May', is a derivative of the Ilyushin Il-18 airliner designed for maritime patrol duties. About sixty-five were constructed for the Soviet Navy from 1967 and a limited number remain in service with Russian Naval Aviation. The type was remarkable for the distinct forward shift of the wing

structure compared with the Il-18, a design feature exacerbated by a lengthened after fuselage. This was probably done to reduce the amount of metal near the aft-mounted magnetic anomaly sensor as there was no other obvious reason to shift the aircraft's centre of gravity. The only export customer was the Indian Navy, which operates five aircraft with 315 Squadron at INAS Dabolim. The original sensor outfit included a Berkut STS search radar NATO coded as 'Wet-Eye', an acoustic analysis unit to monitor RGB-56 and -64 sonobuoys and an APM-73 MAD unit in the tail. Several aircraft have undergone a modernisation to Il-38N standard under the Sea Dragon project with the installation of the Novella system, which includes a new search radar able to track surface contacts out to around 170 nautical miles. More aircraft are likely to be upgraded as funds become available since there is no immediate plan to produce a replacement. Both versions are capable of carrying a combined total of up to 9,000kg of weapons in bomb bays forward and aft of the wing. These include torpedoes, depth charges, mines and free-fall bombs. There are no under-wing hardpoints for air-to-surface missiles.

The Russian Navy uses the Tu-142M (see below) for longer-ranging patrols and the Il-38 for littoral patrol work. In 2015 Il-38s served with the Russian Northern Fleet at the 7050th Air Base at Severomorsk-1 airfield and with the Pacific Fleet with the 7060th and 7062nd Air Bases at Yelizovo and Nikolayevka airfields, as well as with a training unit that forms part of the 859th Naval Aviation Training Centre at Yesk airfield on the Azov Sea coast. The Indian Navy may replace its Il-38s with a further buy of P-8Is or, conceivably, with MQ-4Cs modified with Indian sensors.

Tupolev Tu-142M 'Bear': Russian Naval Aviation also operates the Tupolev Tu-114M, which has the NATO reporting name 'Bear F', as a very long-range patrol aircraft. It was derived from the Tu-95 bomber and, like it, is unusual in having swept wings but turboprop engines. It first flew in 1968 and entered service with the Soviet Naval Air Arm in 1972; an estimated total of 225 aircraft were

produced at a steady rate of about one per month until the type went out of production in 1988. Again, the Indian Navy was the only export customer and operated eight until they were replaced by the P-8I. Sensors include the same 'Wet-Eye' search radar as the Il-38 and similar MAD, sonobuoy and ESM systems. Some aircraft have been modified to Tu-142J standard with electronic intelligence (ELINT) equipment and enhanced communications including VLF radios to contact submerged strategic nuclear-powered ballistic missile submarines. The 'M' version can relay data to other platforms via a satellite link; a necessary feature to pass on time-sensitive target information given its endurance of seventeen hours (which can be increased by in-flight refuelling). The Tu-142 was originally designed with a defensive armament of two GSh-23 cannon in a tail mounting and some aircraft still have this feature. However, principal weapons, up to a combined weight of 20,000kg, include up to eight AS-17 Krypton anti-shipping

cruise missiles on pylons under the wings, supplemented by anti-submarine torpedoes and depth charges in an internal bomb bay. In 2015 Russian Naval Aviation operated Tu-142Ms with the Northern Fleet as part of the 7050th Air Base in the Severomorsk complex at Kipelovo airfield and with the Pacific Fleet with the 7062nd Air Base at Nikolayevka complex at Kamennyy airfield.

Kawasaki P-1: The Kawasaki P-1 was developed for the Japanese Maritime Self Defence Force to replace its ageing fleet of P-3C Orions. It has many advanced features including a fly-by-light control system which uses fibre optics to transfer flight commands at high speed and is highly resistant to electromagnetic interference. Sensors include a Toshiba HPS-106 active electronically-scanned array radar, MAD, an electro-optical/infrared detection system and an acoustic analysis unit to monitor active and passive sonobuoys. A new open-architecture tactical mission system has been designed specifically for the aircraft by Shinko Electrics with coloured displays for every crew station. The new type has an internal bomb bay and eight external hardpoints for AGM-65 Maverick, AGM-84D Harpoon and ASM-1C air-to-surface missiles, RX-5, Type 97 and Mark 46 torpedoes, depth charges and mines. The first aircraft flew in 2007 and the type is now in operational service with Fleet Air Wing 4 of the JMSDF at Atsugi. It is gradually replacing the P-3C fleet and began patrol activity in 2015. A recent statement by a JMSDF official said that the Service plans to procure seventy P-1s with eight production examples delivered as of 2015. Interestingly, following a United Kingdom Government initiative intended to improve Anglo-Japanese trade in 2014, the Japanese offered to sell P-1s to Britain at a competitive price; it has, therefore, to be considered as a possible contender should the 2015 SDSR decide to restore an MPA capability. Initial talks reportedly took place at the 2014 Farnborough Air Show. Logically the P-1 might seem to be less attractive than the P-8A which capitalises on the close relationship with the US Navy. However, it might just appeal to a cash-strapped United Kingdom Government as part of a wider trade deal and consequently cannot be ruled out of the equation.

A Russian Tupolev Tu-95MS 'Bear H' strategic bomber pictured from an intercepting RAF aircraft in October 2010. The aircraft shares the same airframe as the TU-142M 'Bear F', which provides long-range maritime patrol for Russian Naval Aviation. *(Crown Copyright 2015)*

In addition to the maritime patrol aircraft described above, many nations operate lighter aircraft capable

Japan's Kawasaki P-1 maritime patrol aircraft has now entered series production to replace the Japan Maritime Self Defence Force's P-3C Orions. It represents an interesting alternative to the US Navy's P-8A Poseidon and is an outside contender for any requirement for a renewed British MPA capability that emerges from the 2015 SDSR. *(JMSDF)*

of surveillance and surface search in a littoral environment in support of coast guard-type activities. Typical among them is the Indian Coast Guard, which operates Dornier Do-228 twin turboprop aircraft fitted with MEL Super Marec search radar and a Micronair pollution detection system together with the ability to spray dispersal agent over a designated sea surface. Other avionics include weather radar, an elctro-optic/infrared turret-mounted camera, a Spectrolab SX-16P searchlight, a Sextant inertial navigation system and both vertical and oblique cameras. The aircraft have two Allied Signal TPE331-5-252D engines rated at 578 KW and have a maximum speed of 255 knots and a range of 1,320 nautical miles. Optional armament includes gun pods, rockets or short-range air-to-surface missiles and role-change equipment includes an Indian-

The Boeing P-8A Poseidon and Kawasaki P-1 maritime patrol aircraft pictured side by side at Naval Air Facility Atsugi in Japan. Compared with the militarised Boeing, the Japanese aircraft is a purpose-built design and is considered by some to have the greater capability of the two aircraft. However, this also makes it a more expensive proposition. *(US Navy)*

designed ESM package which can be fitted to about a third of the fleet if necessary. In 2015 one aircraft was fitted with an Israeli Aircraft Industries' EL 2022A-V3 radar and the Indian Navy intends to fit this throughout the fleet in due course. The radar forms part of a new operational package known as the airborne multi-mission optronic stabilised payload which includes a low-light charge coupled device (CCD) camera, an infrared camera and a laser rangefinder developed by Hindustan Aeronautics. With a maximum take-off weight of only 5,700kg the D0-228 represents an affordable and effective patrol aircraft that complements the capabilities of larger types.

Some countries have acquired far more sophisticated aircraft that more nearly match the larger MPAs in capability. For example, in April 2015, the Japanese Coast Guard announced that it had selected the Dassault Falcon 2000 maritime surveillance aircraft to enhance its operational fleet. This is a type that more closely resembles the big MPAs, with a range of 4,000 nautical miles and a purpose-designed mission system that will enable it to undertake maritime surveillance, piracy control, drug interdiction, fishery patrol, law enforcement, search and rescue, intelligence and reconnaissance missions. Dassault claim that the type offers the best combination of size, payload, speed, range, acquisition and operating costs on the market. If they are right, this might possibly be another type that could

A Dassault image of their Falcon 2000MSA maritime surveillance aircraft. Closer to the larger MPAs in capability than some of the less sophisticated alternatives, the type was selected by the Japan Coast Guard in April 2015 to enhance their aircraft fleet. *(Dassault Aviation – All Rights Reserved)*

appeal to a United Kingdom Government seeking a tentative return to MPA capability without the expense of a major acquisition programme. Similar aircraft that could be considered in this category include the Airbus Military C295 and CN-235 MPAs; Brazilian Embraer's EMB145MP/ASW; the Franco-Italian ATR 72 ASW, and the Swedish SAAB 2000 MPA variant.

Notes:

1. A more detailed overview of the *Ford* class design, as well as that of *America* (LHA-6), *Queen Elizabeth* and of India's *Vikrant*, is contained in the editor's 'Modern Aircraft Carriers' in *Warship 2015*, ed. John Jordan (London: Bloomsbury Publishing Plc, 2015), pp.127–41.

2. The Indian Navy had reluctantly decided that it would not be cost-effective to give the veteran *Viraat* another refit to keep her in service until the new *Vikrant* is commissioned. A lack of serviceable Sea Harriers following a high attrition rate was probably an important contributor to this decision.

3. A credible carrier strike force requires more than just the purchase of ships and aircraft; it requires trained and experienced personnel who are ready to deploy at short notice and at distance to operate in all weathers, by day or night. Experience with joint operations has shown a lack of commitment by the RAF and a need to train pilots before they can embark. It takes eighteen months before an embarked pilot is competent to undertake sorties by day and night in all weathers and a joint partner that insists shore-based operations take greater priority is unlikely to facilitate this. Protagonists of joint operations have been quick to point out that the RAF's 1 Squadron embarked in *Hermes* during the South Atlantic War of 1982. However, they may not appreciate that the unit was not ready to embark until after the ship deployed, relied on the deep experience of the ship's air staff and its squadrons to show them how to operate in an unfamiliar environment, and was then only capable of operations by day.

4. The concept seems to envisage an amphibious assault against sophisticated opposition that is not covered by at least one strike carrier and its air wing but it is difficult to imagine the circumstances in which this would happen.

5. Readers with an interest in finding more detail about the P-3 Orion's capabilities and history are recommended to access the website of the P-3 Orion Research Group The Netherlands at http://www.p3orion.nl/index.html

6. In addition, VP-30, the 'Pro's Nest', operates both the P-3C and P-8A in its training role as the navy's MPA fleet replacement squadron.

7. This chapter has been compiled from a wide range of periodicals, of which *Air International, Flight, Jane's Defence Weekly, Warship World* and *The Navy* (the journal of the Navy League of Australia) provide particularly good sources of further reading. Reference should also be made to the following publications, as well as to the websites of relevant aircraft manufacturers and navies:

– Gunter Endres and Michael J Gething, *Jane's Aircraft Recognition Guide – Fifth Edition* (London: Collins-Jane's, 2007).
– Norman Friedman, *The Naval Institute Guide to World Naval Weapon Systems – Fifth Edition* (Annapolis, MD: Naval Institute Press, 2006).
– *Jane's Fighting Ships* – Various Editions (Coulsdon, Surrey: IHS Jane's).

Author:
Norman Friedman

4.2 TECHNOLOGICAL REVIEW
ELECTRONIC WARFARE AT SEA

Electronic warfare (EW) is the flipside of the radar coin: it uses radar against itself, both to understand a situation and to evade or confuse detection and targeting. Typically there are Electronic Support Measures (ESM) systems, which receive and try to make sense of the pulses, often coupled to Electronic Counter Measures (ECM), which seek to confuse the enemy's radar. For some time the United States government has supplanted these names with Electronic Support (ES) and Electronic Attack (EA) designations.[1]

SOME BASIC CONCEPTS

Imagine a battle fought out with anti-ship missiles. First the target must be located, most likely by means of a long-range radar; then it must be identified. There is very little point in wasting missiles on non-targets. A few surface radars have a chance of identifying a target (using inverse synthetic aperture processing), but anyone firing missiles wants to stay beyond the horizon. How does the attacker know what is out there? His best chance is to use whatever

Right: The threat and the countermeasure. An Exocet MM40 surface-to-surface missile being launched from the French FREMM type frigate *Aquitaine* in May 2015. Immediately behind the missile is the shielded housing for a JASS (jamming antenna sub system) which forms part of the NETTUNO-4100 ECM radar jamming system installed in the ship. Designed to confuse incoming missiles, it is major component of the frigate's electronic warfare defences. *(MBDA/Michel Hans)*

the potential targets emit to identify them. Measures intended to frustrate effective attempts at identification are sometimes called 'confusion'.

Confusion can therefore be described as an anti-targeting measure. For example, during the Cold War the Soviet Navy relied heavily on air-launched anti-ship missiles. It was concerned to direct its missiles at the appropriate targets – the aircraft carriers – within what might be complex formations. It therefore applied considerable effort to make sure that missiles were locked onto the right ships. For its part the US Navy planned to use airborne jammers (EA-6B Prowlers) to confuse the targeting radars on board the Soviet missile bombers. The Royal Navy deployed powerful anti-targeting (deception) jammers on board some of its surface ships, for example to ruin targeting by 'Bear D' (Tu-95RTs) radar reconnaissance aircraft.

Although a few missiles, such as the Norwegian NSM, rely on the target's infrared emissions, most anti-ship missiles rely on their own radars to take them to their targets. In a few cases, they add a target-identification function based on whatever the target is emitting. The defence can hope to confuse incoming missiles in various ways – i.e., through electronic warfare. It can also, of course, try to shoot them down. None of these ideas is new, but the rapid evolution of digital electronics is changing the way they fit together. Measures intended to lead a missile away from a real target are sometimes called 'distraction'. For example, imagine a missile locked onto a ship. As it approaches, the ship lures the missile onto a decoy such as a chaff cloud while it turns away. This is distraction in action.

There has always been a question as to whether active confusion or distraction measures may themselves identify a target to an attacker. Many missiles have home-on-jam operating modes, so that a jammer may sometimes act as a beacon rather than as protection.

HISTORY

Both ESM and ECM were born during the Second World War. For example, beginning in 1941 the British Royal Navy deployed ESM systems to find German coastal radars. It also developed an ECM system to jam them. When the British battleship *Duke of York* engaged the German *Scharnhorst* on 26 December 1943, she jammed the German ship's fire-control radar (*Scharnhorst* later hit the mainmast of the British battleship, knocking out the jammer – certainly unintentionally – but that did not do her much good). The force which attacked Normandy had large numbers of radar jammers of various sorts, plus jammers intended to interfere with the guidance links of German anti-ship missiles. U-boats had ESM sets to detect Allied airborne radars, but they did not keep up with Allied changes of frequency. In the Pacific, the Japanese had grossly inferior radar but they did field ESM receivers. By 1944 receivers on board their aircraft had forced United States

Electronic Counter Measures (ECM) systems seek to confuse radar-guided enemy missiles. Various equipment is used to achieve this effect. This picture shows an EA-6B Prowler attached to the 'Garudas' of Electronic Attack Squadron (VAQ) 134 opening its wings before launching from the aircraft carrier *George H W Bush* (CVN-77) in August 2014 during the type's last operational deployment on a US carrier. The US Navy intended to use Prowlers as airborne jammers to confuse targeting radars on board Soviet missile-carrying bombers during the Cold War. *(US Navy)*

submariners to stop using their air-warning radars (SD), because Japanese aircraft could detect them before they got to within detection range of the radars. By the end of the war, US Navy ships had numerous jammers on board.

ESM and ECM have been constant themes in naval warfare ever since. They are linked with electronic reconnaissance (a form of ESM) which concentrates on collecting the signals of enemy or potentially hostile radars in the most covert way possible; many 'Western' submarines had elaborate ESM installations during the Cold War, and electronic reconnaissance is sometimes considered the most important current submarine mission.

DETECTION

The main divide in ESM design for many years was the type of antenna and receiver the system used. Generally the narrower the beam or the narrower the frequency range of the receiver, the greater the sensitivity and therefore the greater the range. However, the beam may not be pointed at the enemy radar, and the receiver may not be set at the right frequency. To find signals, they both must scan, and their chance of finding a target on any one scan may be small. The alternative is 'wide open' antennae and broad-band receivers. The wide-open antenna is far less sensitive, but it picks up all signals which are strong enough to be distinguished from the surrounding noise. A wide-band receiver similarly picks up signals over a broad frequency range, but it

Right: The Royal Navy Type 23 frigate *Somerset* shows the directional arrays of her UAF ESM system in a 2009 photograph. Electronic Support Measures (ESM) systems receive and try to make sense of radar pulses but have to find the signals. Each of *Somerset*'s eight antenna groups is a stack of three rounded and approximately semi-cylindrical radomes (top to bottom, 12–18, 2–6, and 6–12 GHz) with a prominent horn below (wire-wrapped, for 500 MHz – 2 GHz). Instantaneous bearing accuracy is three degrees, but the system can use interferometry for fine DF cuts. This was a version of the first British system to use a computer to disentangle (de-interleave) trains of pulses to create a usable picture. The contract was awarded in October 1983 (after a 1982 competition, following the Falklands War) and first production sets were delivered in the autumn of 1989, for installation on board Type 23 frigates. By that time the processor was no longer fast enough: reportedly it was unable to correlate different pulses of pulse-agile radars (at a fixed bearing), carrying each as a separate emitter, hence overloading itself. The Royal Navy continues to use the same set of antennae with much more powerful processing. *(Norman Friedman)*

Thales showed the display of its Vigile 100 system, which is typical of ESM systems, at Euronaval in 2014. The vertical axis is frequency, with higher-frequency at the top because missile seekers use the highest-frequency radars. The horizontal axis is bearing. The associated system tries to identify the emitters; in this case a degree of identification shows in the symbols surrounding the dots indicating emitters. The operator can query the system to obtain further details, such as the pulse rate and pulse width of the emitter. Even the best frequency-agile radars are limited in the range over which they can shift frequency, so this kind of characterisation remains worthwhile. *(Norman Friedman)*

lens antenna which formed multiple beams and kept them open simultaneously. This technique is used in the current SLQ-32, which has had mixed reviews.

JAMMING

Very broadly, jamming means overwhelming a radar with noise, so that it cannot see real targets. Radars are often credited with burn-through ranges against particular jammers – the ranges at which pulses reflected off targets are strong enough to be distinguished against the background of jamming noise. Radars can also be designed to evade such noise by changing frequency to channels which are not being jammed, the jammer retuning as the radar retunes. Deception means creating false pulses, preferably stronger than the ones reflected by real targets. To do that, the attacker has to detect the enemy's radar pulses and then rapidly produce false pulses the radar is likely to receive. An important factor in successful jamming is that radar antennae typically

may not distinguish between different frequencies (wide-open instantaneous frequency measurement solves much of this problem). In the 1950s, the US Navy was interested in detecting enemy aircraft at long range over the open sea. To do that it employed narrow-beam antennae spun at high speed, backed by narrow-band receivers. The contemporary Royal

Navy expected to operate in narrower waters; it wanted to pick up pop-up targets. Its Cold War systems were wide-open. When the Soviets deployed anti-ship missiles, the US Navy counter, ULQ-6, employed a wide-open receiving system associated with a trainable jammer. Eventually the US Navy tried for a compromise, in the form of a microwave

A 2010 view of the French 'Horizon' class frigate *Forbin* showing the arrangement of her electronic warfare system. The radome atop the forward mast is for the ship's EMPAR multifunction radar. Below is a housing for the ESM arrays, with lower-frequency arrays contained within the lower ring and above a ground plane. A housing on the hangar carries the JASS element of Elettronica's NETTUNO-4100 jammer, which uses electronic scanning to point its beam. It can simultaneously produce several jamming signals pointed in different directions, using both noise and deception techniques, and exploiting its DRFM (see p.181). The system is electronically roll-stabilised. The ship has another jammer forwards, the combination offering cross-eye capability (see p.182). A decoy launcher can be seen at the foot of the mast. *(Conrad Waters)*

receive signals from directions other than the ones in which they are pointed, albeit at much weaker strength. The radar perceives signals it receives through these 'back lobes' and 'side lobes' as though they came from the direction in which it is pointed. No radar antenna, even a fixed phased array, can avoid this problem.

Like ESM, jamming may employ a broad-band or a narrow-band technique. Narrow-band jamming concentrates on the known (measured) frequency of the enemy radar, and it must periodically check to see whether the enemy has switched frequency. A broad-band (barrage) jammer covers a wider band, but with less power over the particular band the enemy is using. Early jammers could not easily be retuned, but after the Second World War the French firm of TSF (now Thales) developed a broad-band electronically-tuned jamming tube, the carcinotron, and tuning has not been a problem for decades. How quickly an ECM system can tell that the target radar has retuned may be a different proposition.

STEALTH

Stealth figures in electronic warfare in two distinct ways. One is the obvious: a stealthy ship or aircraft grossly reduces the signals an attacking radar picks up. Anything it emits may swamp whatever the attacking radar receives. Any decoy it fires has a good chance of being seen more clearly than the ship or aircraft. Really complete stealth eliminates the attack problem altogether, but it seems to be impossible to achieve; there is always a trick which defeats stealth to some extent. For example, stealthy design is usually effective over a limited, even if wide, frequency range. Low-frequency radars are often advertised as anti-stealth measures (but those advertising may have limited access to real stealth aircraft, for example). Anything which forces a stealthy aircraft or missile to emit of course compromises its stealth to some extent.

That brings us to the second form of stealth; the attempt to make radar signals themselves difficult to detect. For many decades radar designers have known that the probability of a radar detecting a target depends not on the strength of individual pulses but rather on the average amount of radar energy poured onto the target. That may be an average of very powerful pulses at a fixed frequency, well-spaced so that target range can be calculated, or it may be some other combination of pulse frequency and spacing – for example, the energy can

be spread over a frequency range. This perception was initially used to design longer-range radars which could overcome electrical breakdown (due to excessive pulse power), but it also led to the development of stealthy radars. The key is that an ECM receiver must distinguish real signals from noise. To do that it applies a threshold – a minimum power, based on the surrounding noise – to decide whether what it sees is or is not a real signal. If the radar signal is spread over a wide frequency range, the signal at any one frequency (or a narrow frequency band) may fall below the threshold, but the radar receiver may still know enough to reassemble the signal into something usable. The best-known example of this method is the Dutch (Thales Nederland) Scout low probability of intercept surface-search radar. The technique does have limits, for example in the face of fast targets whose reflections are Doppler-shifted in frequency, but it is nonetheless effective.

What can ESM designers do? They can produce

wideband receivers and they can lower their noise threshold, using computer techniques to distinguish patterns representing real signals. The wideband receiver picks up enough of the distributed signal to see that a real signal is present. Since no one has yet abandoned ESM altogether, it seems clear that this technique works, at least to some extent. Systems advertised as capable of dealing with 'complex' signals are designed in this way. Thus far no one is indicating just how complex the signals a system can handle may be.

THE PLACE OF ELECTRONIC WARFARE

The status of ESM and ECM has varied up and down in line with belief in their efficacy. For example, in the early 1960s the US Navy had little interest in electronic warfare, much preferring hard kill as the solution to the Soviet anti-ship missile threat. Hard kill had and still has the considerable attraction that the user can tell whether it has

A detailed view of the forward superstructure of the Greek *Roussen* fast attack craft *Daniolos*. The small array on the forward extension to the mast is a Thales Nederland Scout Mk 2 surface-surveillance radar which uses low energy output spread over a broad frequency range – frequency modulated continuous wave (FMCW) energy – to limit the risk of detection from hostile electronic support measures equipment. The Thales Sting Mk 2 fire-control director mounted below it on the bridge has the capacity to be used solely in electro-optical mode to further reduce the risk of detection. *(Guy Toremans)*

worked: the missile falls out of the sky. With ECM the situation is more complex, because there is no way to be sure that the missile has been deflected. It may have sufficient onboard intelligence to track the target and to distinguish it from decoys of various kinds, turning away and then back. It may simply turn back if it misses a target and does not detonate; some versions of Harpoon and Exocet have had that capacity for years. It is entirely possible for the jammer to celebrate success as the missile hits.

However, the high cost of major hard-kill systems encouraged some in the US Navy to look elsewhere. They pointed out that missile defence systems could support only a limited number of engagements; what would happen after that? By way of contrast, an effective ECM ('soft kill') system could, in theory, support an infinite number of engagements. It might not be able to fight many of them at a time, but, then again, neither could existing hard-kill missiles. The advertising was irresistible. ESM could identify the incoming missile, and a computer could programme the ship's ECM to deal with that particular threat.

There was one problem. The US Navy had no information about most Soviet missiles, apart from a few satellite photos. By around 1968 it had acquired a few 'Styx' missiles (SS-N-2s), but it could not even be sure that they represented the whole of the 'Styx' line-up. 'Styx' was known only because it had been widely exported, and because some Soviet clients were willing to sell their weapons and sometimes their expertise. The Soviets had fielded large numbers of much longer-range missiles, which were not exported at all and hence were unknown electronically. Presumably matters improved as the United States fielded electronic reconnaissance satellites over the Soviet Union and its test areas, but no one could be sure of how much was or was not

Left: The relative importance accorded to electronic warfare systems compared with more traditional 'hard kill' methods of defeating missile threats has varied over time, the US Navy historically preferring the latter. Although electronic warfare systems have the advantage of being able to support a theoretically infinite number of engagements, this preference may have had some influence on the selection of the relatively austere SLQ-32 electronic warfare suite in the 1970s (although it has been upgraded over time). This image shows a SLQ-32 antenna on the *Vicksburg* (CG-69), immediately beneath a hard-kill Vulcan Phalanx CIWS and a Nulka decoy launcher. *(Conrad Waters)*

Several navies, including the Royal Navy and the US Navy, employ a floating decoy, Irvin's 'rubber duck'. Its corner reflectors increase its radar cross-section to that of a real ship, and it persists because it floats. A ship carries such decoys in canisters resembling those which hold inflatable rafts. If they can be launched early enough in an engagement, they can confuse a targeting radar. Later they may attract missiles into the sea. These images show the canisters in which the decoys are normally housed on the deck of a US Navy destroyer and the decoy itself. *(US Navy / Dr Raymond Cheung)*

known. A very elaborate ESM/ECM system envisaged about 1968 was dropped in favour of the austere 'Design to Cost' system, SLQ-32. This story raised the question, which remains relevant, of how much an ECM system can do if details of the hostile radar system are not known in advance.

Some important details of Soviet missiles became clear only after the Cold War's end, a sobering fact considering how much effort was expended in discovering details during the 'war'. For example, some long-range missiles were fired in salvos which communicated among themselves to choose the right target in a formation. These were huge missiles; some carried onboard jammers of their own (bouncing their signals off the water) which might well have frustrated defensive systems. How well missile-borne ECM would have worked in practice is, of course, anyone's guess.

ELECTRONIC WARFARE TECHNIQUES

Despite its lack of information, an ESM system may still be able to say that something is coming or is

probing for the ship. It may be able to associate a series of incoming pulses with some sort of threat. The radar watching or locking onto the ship ultimately relies on whatever signals are reflected back. The timing of the reflected signals gives it the range and bearing data it needs. If the pulses can be amplified and sent back with altered timing, the attacking radar may be fooled. If the timing is changed progressively, the incoming missile may be walked off the target and onto a decoy of some sort, such as a chaff cloud or a floating 'rubber duck'. Typically missile designers try to protect their weapons from false signals by creating electronic gates around the target in range and bearing. Anything outside the gates is ignored. The hope of deception is to begin to walk off the missile within its range gates, and then move the gates themselves off the target. Ideally this 'range gate (or bearing gate) pull-off' technique leads the missile onto a decoy of some kind.

The key to such deception is a radio-frequency memory (RFM), which carries a usable image of the incoming pulses. Current countermeasures systems

use digital RFMs (DRFMs), which can not only create confusion in the missile but which, in theory, can provide the missile with multiple false targets, something impossible with an analogue RFM. In theory, range gate pull-off works, using an RFM or DRFM, even if all details of the missile guidance system are unknown. All that is needed is a countermeasures system with a sufficiently broad operating band to encompass whatever signals the missile emits. A key developmental issue is how well a DRFM can mimic a complex radar waveform. Another is how quickly it can respond to a shift in waveform, for example a frequency hop between bursts of pulses.

Missile designers are not fools. What happens if the missile simply ignores most of the pulses it receives? In that case it can defeat range gate pull-off because the deceptive signal it does receive shows a range too far from the range gate it has accepted. Say the radar on the missile shuts down for eight pulses after each pulse it receives. Range gate pull off without knowledge of such a counter-counter-measure assumes that by the eighth pulse it had better be feeding in a range far outside the missile's original range gate; otherwise the missile will not be drawn far enough off its original path. This mechanism was implemented in Soviet 'Styx' missiles in the early 1970s. That was long before digital technology made much subtler counter-countermeasures possible.

There is another problem, too. A missile detonates if it hits a ship. It is most unlikely to detonate as it flies through the cloud of chaff into which a DRFM may have directed it. It may keep going and run out of fuel, or it may emerge from the cloud, notice that it has not exploded and start looking for a new target – some missiles do exactly that. This problem makes physical decoys which lie on the water's surface – 'rubber ducks' – attractive. If they work, they may attract the missile into the water, which will detonate it. However, the missile designer may incorporate an altimeter to keep the missile from doing just that. The altimeter of course offers

Nulka, which is used by both the Royal Australian Navy and the US Navy, attempts to mimic the movement of a ship by using its rocket motor both to keep it aloft and to move it sideways. The image shows the launch of a Nulka round from the US Navy's *Chosin* (CG-65) during RIMPAC 2012. *(US Navy)*

ESM yet another signal to detect. As a kind of radar it too can be jammed and deceived. Any sea-skimming missile must have an altimeter to keep it from crashing into waves.[2]

It may be that because DRFMs make it possible to create multiple false targets, they overcome existing defensive mechanisms. If some of the false targets are stronger than real ones, a missile really may redirect itself, and the computer controlling the ECM device may create much more realistic apparent movement of the false targets than that built into earlier analogue systems.

Ideally, deception drives away an incoming missile. Until the 1970s, missiles typically used scanning dishes to find the direction to a surface target. In effect such a device associates timing in its scanning cycle with direction. Shifting the pulse in timing affects not only the missile's perception of range, but also its perception of direction. Successful jamming causes the missile to turn away.[3]

The missile designers' solution to this problem was to adopt a technique called monopulse. A monopulse receiver compares radar returns in, typically, four slightly-different directions. In that way it measures the direction from which the reflected pulses are coming; it is said to measure the angle of the wave-front. The missile tries to fly in a direction at right angles to the wave-front, which is the direction right into the ship.

It seems unlikely that a single jammer can somehow turn the wave-front the missile sees. However, two separated ones have a better chance. For many years there has been a theoretical counter-technique called cross-eye. The two jammers return signals with slightly different timing (phasing). Presumably DRFMs make this sort of jamming practical. The current leader in cross-eye jammers is the Italian firm, Elettronica, which has supplied such jammers to various European navies.

In any case, the missile turned away by ECM has to be turned towards something that it will mistake for a real target. The most common such false target is a cloud of chaff, strips of aluminium foil which together have the radar cross-section of a ship. Missiles deal with this problem in two ways. One is to try to measure the movement of the new target. Chaff drifts with the wind; ships steam at higher speed in a straight line. Another subtler way is to use two different ship detectors, typically both radar and infrared. If the decoy does not display both signatures, it is false. That is why many decoys combine

chaff and infrared torches. It is far more difficult to fake an infrared signature than a radar signature.[4]

An alternative approach is to place a repeater jammer in a decoy, as in the Australian-US Nulka. Its special feature is that it moves in a ship-like way. The main problem with this type of decoying is that the decoy has only limited onboard power. For a time the US Naval Research Laboratory experimented with an electric model aircraft which drew its power from the launching ship, but it was never fielded.

COMPLICATIONS FROM RADAR ADVANCES

Once the radar-countermeasures struggle was, at least in theory, relatively simple. Most radars were built around tubes which emitted fixed recognisable signals. Libraries of signal characteristics – typically pulse duration and pulse spacing at a given frequency – could be built up, if only the radars' emissions could be detected and identified in peacetime (hence the enormous amount of snooping during the Cold War). The main countermeasure against such snooping was to build a war reserve mode into a radar, in the form of a separate, differently-tuned power tube. The war reserve mode could be tested under cover and never used where it could be detected by a snooper. In 1991, during the run-up to the Gulf War, Western electronic intelligence aircraft feinted towards Iraq in order to force the Iraqis to turn on their radars in war reserve mode; the data they collected then went into the Coalition's electronic warfare systems. The main Cold War exception to fixed radar emissions was a spin-tuned magnetron made by Philips, a multinational electronics company based in Sweden, the United Kingdom and the Netherlands.

Fixed radar characteristics were key. During the decades after the Second World War, radars proliferated. In the 1950s a listener might hear hundreds of pulses per second. Then that became thousands, then tens and hundreds of thousands. The listener has to disentangle that mess into files representing, he hopes, particular radars (in modern systems, computer files). Then he can identify the radars as a basis for action of some sort. Before disentanglement, all the listener knows is when a particular pulse is received, its frequency and duration, and (more or less) the direction from which it has come. In theory the file gives the spacing of the pulses and also the rate at which the emitting radar scans, both of which may be valuable clues to the radar's identity. As the number of pulses exploded, electronic surveillance systems evolved from earphones (to measure pulse rates) to computer disentanglement, and from libraries an operator could consult to data bases which would automatically suggest what a given signal represented.

Even then there were significant problems. Radar countermeasures receivers do not measure direction as precisely as radars. Usually they employ four or six or eight wide-open receivers. In modern systems, each receiver incorporates an instantaneous frequency measurement (IFM) device. The system compares the strength of the signal received at a particular time to decide its direction. These systems find it difficult to distinguish signals from directions near each other, or arriving at nearly the same time. The published specifications of electronic warfare receivers generally indicate how many pulses per second the receiver can handle.

Beginning in the 1970s, some radars used a different kind of transmitter with brutal implications for electronic warfare. Instead of a power tube such as a magnetron, they used computers to create radar waveforms, amplified by a travelling wave tube for transmission. The radar's computer could rapidly change its waveform and, to an extent, the frequency at which it operated. The most startling application of this idea was to airborne radars. The US F-14 Tomcat seems to have been the first example. Its radar system was designated AWG-9 because it combined a radar with a waveform-creating computer and a track-keeping computer. The waveform-creating computer made it possible for the same radar to have multiple functions, such as air-to-air combat and air-to-surface attack. The more different functions, the more difficult it was for an electronic warfare operator to distinguish one radar from another with a similar function – a radar designer will, after all, choose his waveform to fit his radar's function. This was more than academic. In 1987 an Iraqi plane using a French anti-ship radar attacked the *Stark* (FFG-31) with Exocet missiles. Her countermeasures operator thought what he was seeing was an Iranian F-14 operating in anti-ship mode.

It took a massive aircraft to lift the AWG-9 radar, but by the late 1970s the onward march of digital technology had shrunk computer-controlled radars dramatically. The US Navy's Hornet is designated the F/A-18 because its radar can operate in, among other things, air-to-air and surface attack modes. A pair of F/A-18s showed what that meant during the

An image of the US Navy frigate *Stark* (FFG-31) on fire – and listing as a result of damage-control measures – after being hit by two Iraqi Exocet missiles in the Persian Gulf in May 1987. Due to advances in radar technology, her countermeasures operator was not able to accurately identify the nature of the attack. *(US Navy)*

First Gulf War in 1991. They were on a bombing mission when Iraqi MiGs jumped them. They flipped their radars to air-to-air mode, shot down the Iraqis, then finished the bombing mission using the same radars. No previous radar could have been switched in that way.

For electronic warfare, the implication of digital radar control is that it is no longer possible to be sure that a given signal represents a particular type of radar. Not only do radars have multiple operating modes, but once a radar has been bought its new owner may change its programming, if he is sophisticated enough. Some radars, which may seem to have limited capabilities, can easily be modified into threats. For example, about three decades ago the US Navy's electronic warfare training organisation showed that by modifying the receiver of a standard airline weather radar they could produce an effective anti-ship targeting radar. No one receiving that radar's pulses could have guessed as much; the radar would have seemed to be on board an airliner.

If much of the point of ESM is to clarify an operational situation, can anything be done? There is a

possible way out. Individual radars can be fingerprinted. Their physical structure – antenna and waveguides, for example – imposes subtle but measurable effects on radar antennae. They make Specific Emitter Identification (SEI) possible. At the least, it should be possible to know that the same radar produces a series of pulses, even if they vary radically in frequency and other attributes. The larger promise of SEI is that it may be possible to know what each emitter is. The narrower version of SEI suggests that there really is a way of disentangling the mass of pulses ESM systems now receive.

The most ambitious application of SEI appears to be the current Joint Strike Fighter (JSF, or F-35). The fighter is provided with broadband receivers distributed over its body. What they receive is converted rapidly into digital signals so that they can be disentangled in a computer. In theory, the result provides the pilot with an unprecedented level of awareness of the environment around him, as indicated by radar pulses he picks up. Given the modern technology of computer radar control, that suggests that the system is intended to exploit SEI.

The rub is that to exploit SEI fully, to know not only that pulse 88532 is associated with pulse 87431 and pulse 90537, but also that all three have been produced by an X-23 anti-aircraft missile guidance radar (with serial number 33746, rather than say 33748), someone must have listened to that particular radar – indeed, to all radars of interest in a particular area. Data on these radars' peculiarities (SEI) must be assembled into a usable database on board the plane. Since the only important radars are those in a potentially hostile area, it is not clear that such data are generally available.

FUTURE DEVELOPMENTS

Where are we now? The electronic world is dominated by Moore's Law: computing power doubles every eighteen months, if not sooner. Moore's Law is why the F/A-18 could accommodate a computer-driven radar with greater flexibility than that in the much larger F-14 about a decade earlier. In the radar world the other great development is active arrays. The radars of the past interposed a power tube, such as a magnetron or klystron or travelling wave tube, between a signal generator and an antenna. One tube meant one radar beam, however it was scanned. In a passive phased array, a computer adjusts the phasing of the different parts of the antenna, but there is still only one beam sweeping across the sky.

In an active array, each element is a small radar emitter and receiver, computer-controlled and provided with power and a waveform. The array can emit all the time, dramatically increasing the sheer load of pulses any EW system must analyse. The main limit on its performance is the speed (remember Moore's Law) with which it can translate back and forth between the signals it sends and receives and their digital equivalents, which its computer processes. The processes of transmission and reception, which are intimately linked in a conventional radar, are no longer directly connected. There is no basic reason why radar and ECM functions should not be fulfilled by the same system. At the very least, that could offer much larger antennae for ESM reception and for ECM transmission. Whether that happens depends on questions such as how broad-band antenna elements really are.

Missile and radar designers have raised the bar for effective ECM, but the manufacturers consistently claim that they are keeping up with such progress. That all navies continue to buy ECM systems makes that claim quite credible. However, it seems less and

An image of the F-35A conventional takeoff and landing (CTOL) variant of the Lightning II Joint Strike Fighter. Its advanced sensor package, which includes Specific Emitter Identification technology designed to pick up radar pulses in the surrounding environment through broadband receivers distributed over its body, is designed to gather and distribute more information than any fighter in history. *(Lockheed Martin)*

less likely that anyone can credibly say that ECM should replace hard-kill as a defensive measure. It is extremely attractive but its success is too difficult to test with any certainty. The question is increasingly how to integrate ECM with hard-kill measures. One possibility is to rely on ECM up to some critical range, then switch to hard-kill if it has not succeeded. In that case hard kill has to become much more effective; that may explain current United States' interest in short-range lasers. A key problem is that jammers may affect the radars which control hard-kill systems.

Notes:

1. Note that this chapter concentrates on radar electronic support and countermeasures and not communications electronic support/countermeasures (C-ESM/C-ECM), which are a related but different subject area. All of the author's views are his own, and should not necessarily be associated with the US Navy or with any other agency with which he has worked.

2. Such altimeters raise an interesting question. There is often a shallow waveguide-like layer above the sea. The downward-facing altimeter signal will probably hit waves, some of which will reflect it forward, possibly in such a way that the layer above the sea carries its signal beyond the horizon to a target ship. The missile may be programmed not to turn on its attack radar until the last moment, when it is expected to cross the ship's horizon (some Soviet

missiles were designed that way) but the altimeter cannot be turned off as long as the missile is flying at low altitude.

3. The logic of early infrared-guided missiles, such as most versions of Sidewinder, is analogous; their sensor lies behind a spinning disc with an off-centre hole in it. That is why many countermeasures against such missiles are flashing heat sources. Imaging infrared is broadly analogous to monopulse radar, hence is much more difficult to defeat.

4. The problem is the relationship between the total energy of the infrared decoy and its temperature. A ship is relatively cool but emits considerable energy. To emit as much energy, a torch must be quite hot. It emits at different wavelengths. Some decoys employ balloons with torches inside, to mimic an extended heat source.

Author:
Conrad Waters

4.3 TECHNOLOGICAL REVIEW

RNPCS

The Royal Navy's new working uniform

The majority of analysis on the balance of global naval power focuses on warships and on the capabilities of their weapons systems and sensors. Much less attention is paid to the sailors that serve this equipment in spite of numerous lessons from history demonstrating that it is the quality of the man – and, increasingly, the woman – in uniform that often determines the result of combat.[1] Inevitably, an important contributor to the overall ease and efficiency with which the sailor is able to perform his/her allotted task is the practicality and quality of his/her working clothing or uniform. Equally, effective uniform design is becoming an increasingly important recruitment and public relations tool in this brand-conscious age.

Having overseen a wholesale revision of British Army combat dress to take account of the harsh experience of the prolonged stabilisation mission in Afghanistan, the United Kingdom's Ministry of Defence (MOD) has recently turned its attention to revamping the Royal Navy's standard 'working' uniform. The resulting Royal Navy Personal Clothing System (RNPCS) represents the first major design change to the Navy's combat uniform since the end of the Second World War. Taking full account of the needs of both practicality and corporate branding, it is already attracting attention from overseas fleets.

HISTORICAL BACKGROUND

Regulations relating to the appropriate uniform for Royal Navy officers were first issued in the middle of the eighteenth century. However, more than a hundred years were to elapse before the Admiralty established standardised clothing for ratings. Over time, various types of uniform or 'dress' were devised for ceremonial, 'at sea' and general duties, sometimes incorporating sub-categories such as the white uniforms issued for use in the Tropics.[2] An impor-

A crew member from the Type 45 destroyer *Diamond* pictured in the new Royal Navy Personal Clothing System (RNPCS) whilst operating a CMS-1 console in the ship's operations room. It is the quality of the man – and increasingly the woman – in uniform that often determines the results of naval missions. *(Crown Copyright 2015)*

tant development took place in 1943, when – as a result of wartime experience – the Admiralty decided to seek tenders for a new uniform broadly similar to army 'battledress' for crew working or in action at sea. It took time for the resultant Action Working Dress (AWD) or No. 8s to be trialled and formally approved. As such, it was not until 1950 that wholesale issue of the new uniform commenced.

In overall terms, the familiar blue shirt and

trousers of the AWD have stood the test of time. This is possibly best evidenced by the fact that it was to be some seventy years before wholesale redesign was implemented. However, post-Second World War combat experience – particularly the incidence of burn injuries after bomb and missile strikes on ships during the Falklands War – did result in changes to materials to enhance the uniform's flame-retardant properties in the mid-1980s. This

Left: Royal Navy sailors aboard the 'Hunt' class mine countermeasures vessel *Chiddingfold* conducting a sonar search whilst observed by Royal Australian Navy counterparts during the International Mine Countermeasures Exercise (IMCMEX) held in the Gulf of Oman November 2014. Both Royal Navy crew members are wearing fire-retardant Improved Action Working Dress (IAWD), although the shorts are a concession to local climatic conditions. IAWD is a practical but somewhat old-fashioned uniform with origins dating back to the Second World War. *(US Navy)*

enhanced working uniform became known as Improved Action Working Dress (IAWD) or as No. 4s in the navy's current uniform numbering system.

THE DRIVE FOR CHANGE

Meanwhile, the pace of change was much more rapid in the British Army, where combat experience during Operation 'Herrick' in Afghanistan had resulted in significant revisions to combat uniform design. The Combat Soldier 95 (CS95) clothing system had already brought the concept of layered clothing into widespread army use. However, changed requirements driven largely by the widespread use of body armour resulted in the decision to design a new 'skin-out' clothing system that was fully integrated with armour and other kit. Developed under Project PECOC (Personal Equipment & Common Operational Clothing), the resultant PCS (Personal Clothing System) was rolled out from 2011 onwards after extensive trials. Widely acclaimed on introduction, calls soon began to arise for the issue of a blue, navy version.

This desire for change was shared within the Royal Navy's own logistics branch and by senior naval officers, not least because of the potential public relations benefits of a modernised uniform. Following approval from the Naval Service Clothing Committee, a statement of requirement was forwarded to the Defence Clothing Team at the MOD's Defence Equipment & Support (DE&S) organisation, who commenced work on the new project during the winter of 2011/12.[3] The overall approach was to use the Army's PCS as the basis for

Left: RAF Regiment soldiers await recovery by a RAF Merlin helicopter following a forward patrol in Afghanistan. Combat experience in Afghanistan resulted in a complete redesign of the British Army's working uniform. The resultant British Army Personal Clothing System (PCS) formed the basis for the new RNPCS. *(Crown Copyright 2012)*

Amongst ships trialling the prototype of RNPCS were the new Type 45 destroyer *Daring* and the ice patrol ship *Protector*. The aim was to gain maximum feedback from sailors working in different operational and climatic conditions. *(Conrad Waters)*

design work, combining this with the fire-retardant treatment used in IAWD. Revisions were then made to take account of shipboard conditions resulting, for example, in a need to redesign pockets to prevent snagging in confined areas. Corporate branding issues such as the use of the RN logo and the revised placement of rank insignia were also considered. The MOD's current supplier of combat uniforms was fully involved in these discussions, being tasked with creating a prototype version for use in a series of trials at sea to test the revisions in practice.

TRIALS AND INTRODUCTION

The trials programme commenced in 2012. Five ships were selected to test the prototype uniform in a range of climates and operating environments, viz.

■ The Type 45 destroyer *Daring*.
■ The Type 23 frigate *Westminster*.
■ The 'River' class offshore patrol vessel *Tyne*.
■ The ice patrol vessel *Protector*.
■ The nuclear-powered attack submarine *Talent*.

Extensive feedback on the new combat outfit was sought both from individual crew members (submitted by means of answers to a five-page questionnaire) and on a unit basis and was almost invariably positive. The comfort of the new clothing in extreme climatic conditions was particularly praised. However, there was inevitably also some negative

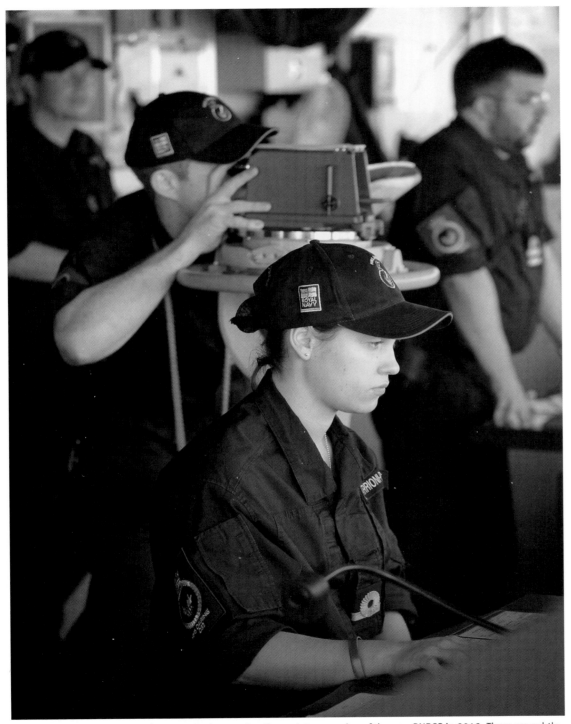

Crew members of the Type 45 destroyer *Daring* wearing the prototype version of the new RNPCS in 2012. There are subtle differences between the prototype and final versions; for example Royal Navy branding is far more prominent on the latter. The much commented-on baseball cap is clearly in evidence. *(Crown Copyright 2012)*

criticism amongst the feedback that was used to improve the final design. For example, there were still problems with snagging hazards (resulting in a redesign of pockets). In addition, the use of Velcro to attach items such as name labels tended to produce a somewhat dog-eared image over time and therefore gave rise to a presentational issue. Although creating something of a backlash from die-hard traditionalists, the introduction of a baseball cap in place of the long-established woollen beret was particularly popular amongst crew serving in hot climates such as the Persian Gulf.[4] A reduction in sailor complaints that the standard-issue headwear was 'melting my head' was particularly noticeable!

The overall success of the trials, coupled with senior-level support for the proposed change up to and including the then Second Sea Lord, Vice Admiral Sir David Steel, resulted in a decision to proceed with the new uniform in spite of the impact of financial austerity on overall resources. This did, however, slow the pace of implementation. As such, it was not until March 2015 that sailors in the Type 23 frigate *Lancaster* became the first to deploy with the final version of the uniform when they departed Portsmouth on a nine-month Atlantic patrol. A press release at the time stated that 22,000 sets of the new uniform would initially be issued to operational and seagoing ships. Other units must wait longer, as it will not be until 2017 that the changeover to the new look is finally complete.

THE NEW UNIFORM

The new RNPCS is in an overall dark blue colour compared with the contrasting dark blue trousers and lighter-blue shirt of IAWD. In line with the Army clothing it is derived from, it is a layered system with a cotton T-shirt, a micro-fleece and a cotton jacket-style working shirt allowing the uniform to be readily adapted to different climatic conditions. For example, the fleece can be used to create a thermal layer between the T-shirt and jacket to improve comfort when sailing in colder climates such as the South Atlantic. Trousers, a belt and an optional baseball cap complete the standard clothing issue. The trousers are lighter in weight than the previous version and incorporate slanted pockets for ease of access, as well as side adjustment and smaller belt loops to reduce the risk of snagging. Although the fire-retardant qualities of the clothing material are little changed from those found in IAWD, detailed design changes such as the ability to fasten the working shirt at the neck to form a high collar provide more protection from flash fires.

As well as looking more modern – 'It is time for individuals in the navy to change the way they are presented. We have always been professional, but we did look a bit out of date' in the words of Vice Admiral Steel – RNPCS has also allowed the incorporation of additional Royal Navy branding to promote the service's corporate image. This is focused on the jacket-style shirt and includes a large White Ensign badge on the left shoulder as well as a switch in the positioning of rank badges to the middle of the chest rather than the traditional position on the shoulders. Royal Navy branding is carried on the top right pocket and the sailor's surname on the top left pocket. Trade badges continue to be worn on the right shoulder. Additional branding is applied to the baseball cap.

Production of RNPCS is sourced from Northern Ireland-based Cooneen Defence Ltd, part of the broader Cooneen Group. The company has a medium-term contract to supply all the MOD's combat clothing requirements and RNPCS is produced as part of this overarching agreement. A standard issue of RNPCS comprises:

- One baseball cap.
- Four T-shirts.
- One micro-fleece.
- Two working shirts (jackets).
- Three pairs of trousers.
- One belt.

Total cost amounts to £72 (c. US$110 at current exchange rates), which is slightly cheaper than the standard issue of IAWD it replaces. This seems to be very good value for the taxpayer, particularly when considering the retail cost of equivalent outdoor wear.

REACTIONS

The positive reception to RNPCS suggests the MOD's project to modernise the Royal Navy's working uniform has been timely. The service's reaction can probably best be summed up by the words of *Lancaster*'s commanding officer, Commander Peter Laughton, before the ship's maiden deployment with sailors wearing the new kit. He was quoted as saying, 'We are extremely proud and genuinely delighted to be the first ship to wear the Royal Navy's new uniform. It is a really practical, smart and modern uniform, and the extra branding allows us to

ROYAL NAVY ACTION WORKING DRESS THEN AND NOW

Dark blue woollen beret

Dark blue woollen beret. Optional RN baseball cap at sea for visor protection against strong sunlight. Central rank badge.

Navy cotton shirt. Jacket style and flame resistant. Enhanced pockets and map and compass compatible. Can fasten at neck for high collar and long sleeve protection for initial fire-fighting protection

Rank worn on shoulder epaulette

Navy Thermal fleece. Second layer protection to be worn below the shirt in colder climates.

Navy cotton T-shirt. First step in 'layering system'

Blue cotton tradition cut shirt with Flame Resistant properties. Name above left breast pocket white tape (hand written)

White ensign badge

Trade badge (Specification) as appropriate on right shoulder

Rank worn in middle of chest on single epaulette

Navy cotton RN stable belt. Chrome fittings including waist adjustment and clasp.

Trade badge (Specification) as appropriate on right shoulder

ROYAL NAVY   RICHARDSON

RN branding on the top right of pocket and surname on the top left of breast pocket.

Dark blue trousers with flame retardant properties

Lighter weight Navy flame resistant trousers with slanted pockets. Re-enforced crotch area, side adjustment and reduced sized belt loops to avoid snagging.

THEN NOW

navy**graphics** 15/267

A Royal Navy infographic highlighting the key changes between the old IAWD and the new RNPCS. *(Crown Copyright 2015)*

Images showing (left) a crew member wearing RNPCS in the Type 45 destroyer *Diamond* and (right) crew members onboard the Type 23 frigate *Lancaster* wearing old (IAWD) and new (RNPCS) variants of the Royal Navy's working uniform. The new, overall dark blue RNPCS, with Royal Navy branding focused on the jacket-style shirt, has been positively received and is attracting interest from other fleets. *(Crown Copyright 2015)*

US Navy sailors wearing the predominantly blue digital print patterned Type 1 variant of the Navy Working Uniform (NWU) pictured during a firing practice with a M-240B machine gun on the carrier *Ronald Reagan* (CVN-76). The so-called 'Aquaflage' or 'Blueberries' has not been universally popular with US Navy personnel, who have questioned the value of camouflaged clothing aboard ship. *(US Navy)*

much better represent our service.' Equally, the roll-out of RNPCS resulted in considerable positive comment in the usually cynical British press.

There has already been interest in the new uniform amongst foreign services, with Malta, Portugal and the United States amongst a number of navies seeking briefings on the project. The US Navy itself has also introduced new working clothing in recent years, with its current Navy Working Uniform (NWU) being rolled out from December 2008 after a redesign effort that began in 2003. Based on the US Marine Corps' Combat Utility Uniform, the shipboard Type 1 variant uses a predominantly blue, multi-colour digital print pattern and has been influenced by the same considerations of practicality and comfort as the RNPCS.[5] However, reaction to the US Navy's so-called 'Aquaflage' or 'Blueberries' has not been universally positive. Criticism has included questions over the relevance of adopting a camouflage pattern for use aboard ship or on a base, as well as concerns over the uniform's potential flammability.[6]

THE FUTURE

Having overseen RNPCS's successful introduction, those responsible for developing the new uniform are determined not to rest on their laurels. As one member of the project team told *Seaforth World*

Naval Review, 'It has taken us the best part of seventy years to get here. We don't now want to sit back and wait even ten years for further improvement. We will take note of the feedback we get on the new uniform and improve it to make the best it can possibly be.'

Some areas for further enhancement have already been identified. One area for future examination is the possibility of making a change from the current navy blue to a different basic colour given that shade's propensity towards fading. Developments in materials technology will also be considered. The current version of RNPCS was essentially created by sliding tried-and-tested materials into a new design but the existing cotton-based fabric used for much of the uniform has vulnerabilities, for example, in terms of shrinkage. New materials might offer better water resistance or faster drying qualities. Work is also being carried out in conjunction with the Institute of Naval Medicine into the benefits of materials with improved thermal properties that would provide better resistance to temperature extremes.

In the meantime, however, both the Royal Navy's Logistics Branch and the DE&S Clothing Team can be justifiably satisfied with a job well done in providing today's sailors with a practical and up-to-date working uniform. Turning again to the words of Vice Admiral Steel, 'This is a modern uniform which suits a modern navy'.

Royal Navy crew members wearing the new RNPCS on the bridge of *Diamond*. RNPCS is intended to be a modern uniform for a modern navy. *(Crown Copyright 2015)*

Notes:

1. It is also worth noting that personnel costs account for a material proportion of the overall through-life costs of a modern warship.

2. There are currently five main Royal Navy uniforms, viz.

- Ceremonial Uniform (No. 1 Dress). A uniform worn on formal occasions, accompanied by decorations, medals and other appropriate accessories. Blue and white versions, the latter used, for example, in tropical regions.
- Evening Uniform (No. 2 Dress). Formal evening dress worn at naval and appropriate civilian functions. Blue and white versions.
- General Duty Rig (No. 3 Dress). Normal 'day-to-day' uniform for use ashore and, as directed, at sea. Blue and white versions.
- Action Working Dress (No. 4 Dress). Functional, protective clothing for use at sea and in naval bases. This is now being replaced by RNPCS.
- Occupational Clothing (No 5. Dress). A collective category for all specialist working uniforms such as firefighters and nurses who require unique clothing to carry out their duties.

3. The Naval Service Clothing Committee (NSCC) ensures that Royal Navy clothing policy is delivered through a structured process that takes account of funding and supply issues. It currently comprises sixteen representatives drawn from various navy branches that can take account of operational, medical, ceremonial, corporate identity and human resource requirements.

4. The introduction of baseball caps and Velcro was given particularly prominent coverage in media stories about the trials programme, which tended to focus on crew experience of the new uniform on *Daring*. For example, see Tom Whitehead's 'New Royal Navy uniforms to involve baseball caps and Velcro', *The Telegraph* – 18 March 2012 (London: Telegraph Media Group Ltd, 2012).

5. Replacing seven different working uniforms, the US Navy's NWU was designed for durability, safety, comfort and ease of cleaning. It has several elements of similarity with RNPCS, including the adoption of a layered approach to allow use in different climates.

6. There have been many comments about the great camouflage the new US Navy uniform provides if a sailor

falls overboard and needs to be spotted and recovered! Perhaps more seriously, there have also been reports that the uniforms' 50/50 cotton-nylon mix is extremely flammable, potentially melting in a fire. For example, see Cristina Silva's 'Navy: Working Uniforms Extremely Flammable', *Stars and Stripes* – 16 December 2012 (Washington, DC: US Department of Defense, 2012). The article states that the US Navy removed its requirement for all uniforms to be flame-resistant in 1996, instead providing flame-retardant clothing in a 'case of need' basis.

7. The editor would like to acknowledge with thanks the considerable help provided by the following MOD personnel in the production of this chapter:

- Samantha Chapman, Royal Navy Operational Newsdesk, RN Media & Communications.
- Emma Hallett, Press & Public Relations Officer, Defence Equipment & Support.
- Adrian Randall, R & D Manager, Defence Clothing Team, Defence Equipment & Support.
- Gary Rickman, Lead for Commodities, RN Logistics Branch.

Contributors

Richard Beedall: Born in England, Richard is an IT Consultant with a long-standing interest in the Royal Navy and naval affairs in general. He served for fourteen years in the Royal Naval Reserve as a rating and officer, working with the US Navy and local naval forces in the Middle East and around the world. In 1999 he founded *Navy Matters,* one of the earliest naval websites on the Royal Navy. He has contributed to *Seaforth World Naval Review* since the initial 2010 edition, and has written extensively on naval developments for many other organisations and publications, including *AMI International, Naval Forces, Defence Management* and *Warships IFR*. He currently lives in Ireland with his wife and daughters.

David Hobbs: Commander David Hobbs MBE RN (retired) is an author and naval historian with an international reputation. He has written eighteen books, the latest of which is *The British Carrier Strike Fleet after 1945*, and has contributed to many more. He writes for several journals and magazines and in 2005 won the award for the Aerospace Journalist of the Year, Best Defence Submission, in Paris. He also won the essay prize awarded by the Navy League of Australia in 2008. He lectures on naval subjects worldwide, including on cruise ships, and has been on radio and television in several countries. He served in the Royal Navy for thirty-three years and retired with the rank of Commander. He is qualified as both a fixed and rotary wing pilot and his log book contains 2,300 hours with over 800 carrier deck landings, 150 of which were at night. For eight years he was the Curator of the Fleet Air Arm Museum at Yeovilton.

Mrityunjoy Mazumdar: Mr Mazumdar has been writing on naval matters since 1999. His words and pictures have appeared in many naval and aircraft publications including *Jane's Defence Weekly, Jane's Navy International, Naval Forces, Ships of the World,* the USNI's *Proceedings* and *Warship Technology* published by the Royal Institute of Naval Architects. He is also a regular contributor to the major naval annuals such as *Combat Fleets of the World, Flotes des Combat, Jane's Fighting Ships, Seaforth World Naval Review* and *Weyers Flotten Taschenbuch*. Mr Mazumdar lives in Vallejo, California with his wife.

Norman Friedman: Norman Friedman is one of the best-known naval analysts and historians in the US and the author of over forty books. He has written on broad issues of modern military interest, including an award-winning history of the Cold War, whilst in the field of warship development his greatest sustained achievement is probably an eight-volume series on the design of different US warship types. A specialist in the intersection of technology and national strategy, his acclaimed *Network Centric-Warfare* was published in 2009 by the US Naval Institute Press. The holder of a PhD in theoretical physics from Columbia, Dr Friedman is a regular guest commentator on television and lectures widely on professional defence issues. He is a resident of New York.

Guy Toremans: Guy Toremans is a Belgian-based maritime freelance correspondent and a member of the Association of Belgian & Foreign Journalists, an association accredited by NATO and the UN. His reports, ship profiles and interviews are published in the English language naval magazines *Jane's Navy International, Naval Forces* and *Warships IFR*, as well as in the French *Marines & Forces Navales* and the Japanese *J-Ships*. Since 1990, he has regularly embarked on NATO, Asian, South African and Pacific-based warships, including aircraft carriers, destroyers, frigates, mine-countermeasures vessels and support ships.

Scott Truver: Dr Scott C Truver is Director, Team Blue, at Gryphon Technologies LC, specialising in national and homeland security, and naval and maritime strategies, programmes and operations.

Since 1972 Dr Truver has participated in numerous studies and assessments – most notably supporting the inter-agency task force drafting the US *National Strategy for Maritime Security* (2005) – and has also written extensively for US and foreign publications. He has lectured at the US Naval Academy, Naval War College and Naval Postgraduate School, among other venues. His further qualifications include a Doctor of Philosophy degree in Marine Policy Studies and a MA in Political Science/ International Relations from the University of Delaware.

Conrad Waters: A lawyer by training but a banker by profession, Conrad Waters was educated at Liverpool University prior to being called to the bar at Gray's Inn in 1989. His interest in maritime affairs was first stimulated by a long-family history of officers in merchant navy service and he has been writing articles on historical and current naval affairs for over thirty years. This included six years producing the 'World Navies in Review' chapter of the influential annual *Warship* before assuming responsibility for *Seaforth World Naval Review* as founding editor. Now taking a break from his career in the City, Conrad is married to Susan and has three children: Emma, Alexander and Imogen. He lives in Haslemere, Surrey.

Devrim Yaylali: Cem Devrim Yaylali was born in Paris and raised in Istanbul, where he currently lives. He has a degree in economics from the University of Istanbul. His interest in naval issues began by taking photos of warships visiting Istanbul. His first photos were published in *Jane's Fighting Ships* in 1991. Since then his photos and articles have been published in various naval publications both Turkish and foreign such as *Combat Fleets of the World* and *Warships IFR*. He is the author of the blog: www.turkishnavy.org. He is married with one son.

Jacket images:
Front, main: *San Diego* (*US Navy*), **top, left to right:** *Anzac & Arunta* (*Royal Australian Navy*), *Saif* (*Royal Australian Navy*), F-35C (*Lockheed Martin*), *Queen Elizabeth* (*Aircraft Carrier Alliance*).

Back, main: *Vicksburg & Theodore Roosevelt* (*US Navy*) ; **insets:** *Holland* (*Thales Nederland*); *Success & Büyükada* (*Royal Australian Navy*);.